PRODUCT LIFE CYCLE UNTANGLED

The Art and Science of Building Products

DINKER CHARAK

notionpress.com

INDIA · SINGAPORE · MALAYSIA

ISBN 979-8-89415-218-9

Contents

Who Should Read This Book?

Whether you're already knee-deep in managing products, unexpectedly landed in a product-focused role, running your own show, or eyeing a shift into this realm, this book is your go-to guide!

Let's check how this book can be a game-changer for you:

- Aspiring Product Managers: If you're passionate about building a career mastering the Product Life Cycle, this book is your go-to reference. It dives deep into the essentials, introducing you to key principles, methodologies, and best practices that will get you packed and ready for an adventurous journey.

- Newcomers to Product Management: If you've recently stepped into the world of Product Management and are hungry for deeper insights, this book is a treasure trove. It helps you navigate the challenges and intricacies of the role, particularly in larger organizations. You'll uncover relevant strategies for product development, road mapping, prioritization, and stakeholder management.

- "Accidental" Product Managers: Sometimes, fate lands you in a product-focused role unexpectedly. If you find yourself in this position and strive to shine, this book is your ally. It equips you with the skills needed to thrive, even if becoming a Product Manager wasn't in your original plan. You'll learn how to lead product teams, gather customer insights, and make data-driven decisions that propel product success.

- Career Changers: Maybe you're currently rocking it as a Business Analyst, Developer, QA Engineer, or Project Manager, but are contemplating a switch to the product side. This book is tailor-made for you! It will help you grasp the unique aspects of the Product Life Cycle and provide practical advice for making a smooth transition. You'll discover how to leverage your existing skills and experiences to shine in your new role.

Whether you're setting sail on your Product Life Cycle journey or the tide has turned midway, let this book be your compass, guiding you toward excellence in managing products.

Preface

"Can you recommend a book?," is the most comment question I hear from startup founders, software professionals aspiring to transition into Product Management, current Product Managers in enterprises, and those seeking to enhance their Product Management skills

While there are many excellent books discussing topics such as innovation, problem-solving through product development, and achieving product-market fit, I noticed a gap. Existing books tend to cater to specific audiences, focusing either on startup environments or enterprise product life cycles. However, my experience has shown me that many Product Managers span multiple audience segments throughout their careers.

This realization led me to write the book I felt was missing.

One of the most challenging aspects was creating the Table of Contents. It may be surprising, but it took me about six months to finalize it. The complexity arose from the need to cover the wide-ranging aspects of product management, including various product types, customer segments, organizational structures, and role expectations.

Once the Table of Contents was set, I began writing each chapter, which took nearly two years. The result was an 800-page book. However, recognizing that few people read such lengthy books nowadays, I decided to split it into two volumes.

The first volume, titled Product Management Untangled, published by Notion Press (ISBN 13: 979-8892336161), focuses on Product Management. The second volume, which covers the product life cycle, is the book you are reading now.

My goal is not to prescribe a single path for Product Managers working in specific organizational types or developing products for particular segments. Instead, I aim to present a breadth of options for each stage of product development. I trust that each Product Manager will find value in knowing their choices and choosing what best suits their specific product and situation.

The book brings to its readers 71 scenarios showcasing how a concept can be implemented. The book also shares 13 canvases and 22 illustrations to highlight real-life examples, 35 tables, and 80 figures to make it easy to read and learn from.

The MsgMsg App used in many scenarios is a fictitious one. So are the organizations Timingila Delish, Timingila Media, Timingila Auto, Timingila Sports, and Timingila Solutions.

All figures are available under the Creative Commons Attribution-ShareAlike 4.0 International License at www.dinker.in/plcu.

Access all figures from the book

https://bit.ly/plcu-site

1

Understanding the Product Life Cycle

The process from generating ideas to retiring a product involves several stages, each requiring specific strategies and decisions. Understanding these phases is crucial for Product Managers to effectively develop, maintain, and eventually discontinue a product in the market.

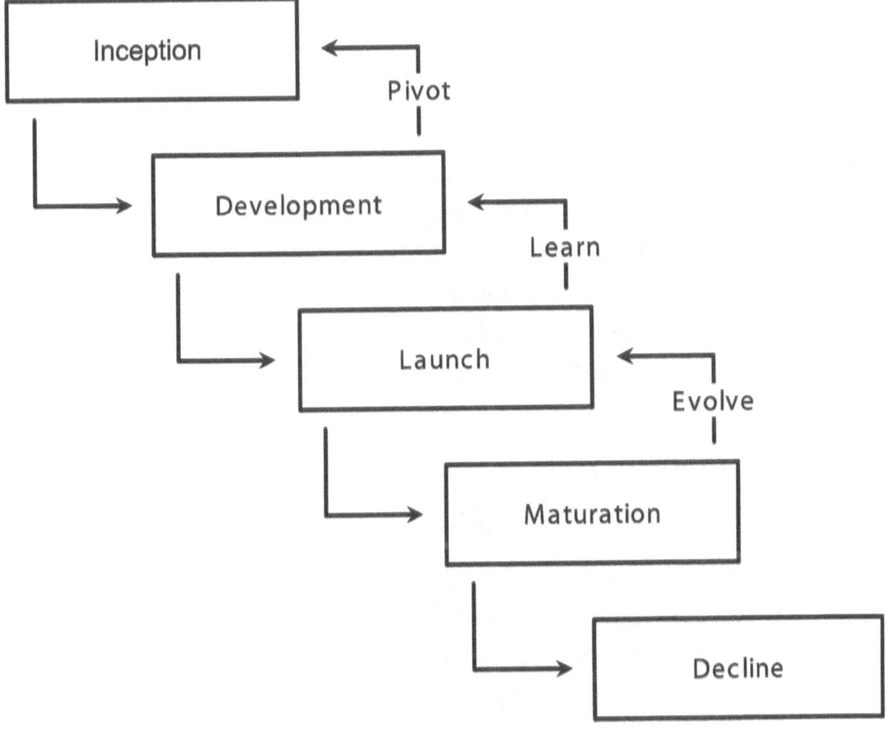

Fig 1: Product Life Cycle

Stage 1: Inception

Identifying, Researching, and Conceptualizing

The inception of a product revolves around **identifying opportunities and pain points** in the market. Some of the key components of this stage are as follows.

Through meticulous **market research**, Product Managers assess the viability of potential solutions. They perform **product ecosystem mapping** to ensure that the proposed product seamlessly integrates into the existing market landscape. Simultaneously, they conduct **competition analysis** and **market segmentation** to present a clear picture of the target audience and potential adversaries in the domain.

At this stage, they also work toward alignment with **regulations and compliance** to avoid legal pitfalls during and after product development. During these preliminary stages, **hypothesis** development, conducting **experiments**, and developing a **Minimum Viable Product (MVP)** to gauge product viability, are paramount. The cycle then nudges towards **business modeling, product definition**, and **branding**, laying a robust foundation for the subsequent phases.

Stage 2: Development

Designing, Building, and Validating

In the development phase, **product design** and **architecture** become focal points. These elements, underpinned by cohesive **product metrics** and a future-focused **product roadmap**, dictate the usability and scalability of the product. Here, Product Managers harmonize technology and user experience, ensuring the final product is not only functional but also user-centric.

Before hitting the market, preparing for the **product-market fit** discovery is imperative. This can be attained through **product analytics** and **optimization**, enabling the tailoring of the product to meet market demands effectively.

Stage 3: Launch

Unveiling, Marketing, and Supporting

With a refined product in hand, the attention shifts towards **go-to-market** strategies and an impactful **product launch. Digital advertising** is a potent tool for Product Managers, creating visibility and attracting the target demographic. After the launch, Product Managers delve into **product analytics** to dissect user engagement and scrutinize performance & outcome metrics.

Product re-engagement strategies, along with comprehensive **product support**, enhance user satisfaction and loyalty. **Governing user data** judiciously safeguards user privacy and fortifies the product's credibility in the market.

Stage 4: Maturation and Evolution

Enhancing, Adapting, and Transforming

As the product settles into the market, it enters a phase of maturation. **Product evolution** is pivotal to perpetuating its relevance amidst evolving market dynamics and emerging technologies. **Legacy modernization** and **digital transformation** become crucial, enhancing the product's features and maintaining its competitive edge.

In this stage, Product Managers must balance introducing innovative features and maintaining the core functionality that users have come to depend upon. Continuous **product optimization** is pivotal to fine-tuning features and ensuring sustained alignment with user expectations and market trends.

Stage 5: Decline and Retirement

Sustaining and Withdrawing

Eventually, the product may enter the **"lights on" maintenance mode**, where the focus shifts towards sustaining operations with minimal investment. The product's journey culminates in **product retirement**, involving thorough planning to ensure a smooth transition for users and the organization.

In reflection, the product life cycle model is a journey from conceptualization to retirement, through a structured pathway. By understanding and adeptly maneuvering through each stage, this model not only facilitates the successful navigation of the product through the market but also constructs a legacy that informs future initiatives.

2

Identifying Opportunities

New product ideas can originate from anywhere. By integrating various methodologies and approaches for new product idea generation, organizations can create a rich pipeline of potential products that are both innovative and attuned to future market needs.

Here's a list of typical sources and methods that companies and entrepreneurs use to generate and identify new product concepts.

Customer Feedback	Market Research	Competitive Analysis	Internal Brainstorming
Innovation Labs/Teams	Trade Shows & Conferences	University Research & Collaboration	Customer Journey Mapping
	Observational Research	Technological Advances	
	Regulatory Changes	Cultural Shifts	
	Open Innovation & Crowdsourcing	Mergers & Acquisitions	
	Greenfield Thinking	Blue-Sky Thinking	
Futurecasting	Cross-Industry Inspiration	Design Thinking	Frugal Innovation
Reverse Innovation	Biomimicry	Technology Convergence	Ethnographic Studies

Fig 2: Identifying New Product Opportunities

1. **Customer Feedback:** Listening to customers is a primary source for new product ideas. This could be gathered from surveys, focus groups, online reviews, and direct interactions.

2. **Market Research:** Through market research, companies can identify gaps in the market, changing trends, and evolving consumer needs.

3. **Competitive Analysis:** By observing what competitors are doing, organizations can identify what's missing in their product lineup or how they can innovate beyond what's currently offered in the market.

4. **Internal Brainstorming:** Teams, including those in R&D, marketing, sales, and product development, often engage in brainstorming sessions to generate new ideas. This is typically done by taking team members out of their usual environments and immersing them in creative workshops that can lead to fresh ideas.

5. **Innovation Labs/Teams:** Many large companies have dedicated innovation teams or labs where they experiment with new concepts and technologies.

6. **Trade Shows & Conferences:** These events are great for gauging market trends, discovering emerging technologies, and interacting with potential partners or customers.

7. **University Research & Collaboration:** Collaborating with academic institutions or tapping into their research can provide insights into cutting-edge technologies and innovations.

8. **Customer Journey Mapping:** By mapping out the customer's experience with a product or service, companies can identify pain points and areas for innovation.

9. **Observational Research:** Sometimes, simply observing how people use products or interact with services in their natural environment can lead to valuable insights.

> **Illustration 1:** The Post-it Note Story
>
> In the 1960s, Art Fry, a scientist at 3M, was frustrated by constantly losing the bookmarks in his choir notes.[1] As an observational researcher by nature, he noticed colleagues using scraps of paper to mark pages, only to have them fall out later. This simple observation sparked an idea: what if there was a reusable adhesive that wouldn't damage paper?
>
> Through further observation, Fry noticed how his colleagues instinctively stuck these adhesive squares on other surfaces, not just paper. This led him to the aha moment: these little squares weren't just bookmarks, they were multipurpose reminders and notes!
>
> Despite initial skepticism from 3M executives, Fry championed his invention through clever demonstration. He placed notes on executives' doors and desks, subtly showing their utility in everyday work. His observational research on how people interacted with his creation proved invaluable, eventually convincing the company to launch the product in 1980.
>
> Today, Post-it Notes are a global phenomenon, a testament to the power of observational research. From a choir singer's simple frustration to a billion-dollar business, this anecdote perfectly illustrates how observing everyday interactions can lead to groundbreaking products.

10. **Technological Advances:** As technology evolves, new possibilities for products and enhancements emerge. For instance, the growth of AI, AR/VR, and IoT has led to a plethora of new product ideas.

11. **Regulatory Changes:** Sometimes, changes in laws or regulations can create opportunities for new products or services. For instance, stricter environmental regulations might drive the need for greener products.

12. **Cultural Shifts:** As societal values and norms evolve, so do the types of products that resonate with people. The rise of health and wellness awareness has led to a myriad of new health-related products and services.

13. **Open Innovation & Crowdsourcing:** Some companies use open innovation platforms or contests to gather ideas from the general public or specific communities.

14. **Mergers & Acquisitions:** Acquiring or merging with another organization can bring in new product ideas or enhance existing ones.

15. **Greenfield Thinking:** This is the process of starting from scratch, with no constraints from existing products, systems, or processes. It offers a "blank canvas" to imagine what could be possible without being held back by current realities.

16. **Blue-Sky Thinking:** Similar to greenfield thinking, blue-sky thinking involves brainstorming, out-of-the-box and creative ideas without being bogged down by practicality or current feasibility.

17. **Futurecasting:** Also known as "future thinking" or "foresight," this method involves envisioning potential futures and scenarios. By predicting what the world might look like in 5, 10, or even 50 years, organizations can develop products and services that cater to those anticipated needs.

18. **Cross-Industry Inspiration:** Looking at developments and innovations in adjacent and unrelated industries can inspire new product ideas. For instance, how might innovations in the gaming industry influence healthcare or education?

Illustration 2: The Story of the Roomba Vacuum Cleaner

In the early 1990s, Helen Greiner and Colin Angle[2] were MIT graduate students working on a project to build robots for the National Aeronautics and Space Administration (NASA). Their robots were designed to explore the surface of Mars, but Greiner and Angle realized that the same technology could be used to create robots for more mundane tasks, such as cleaning floors.

Based on their observations, Greiner and Angle decided to develop a robot vacuum cleaner. They named their product the Roomba, and it was first introduced to the market in 2002.

---

19. **Design Thinking:** A user-centered approach to problem-solving that involves empathy, ideation, and prototyping. It's a method of creating solutions with the end-user in mind, which can often lead to innovative product concepts.

20. **Frugal Innovation:** Sometimes called "Jugaad" (a term from India meaning a temporary but innovative fix), this is the art of overcoming challenges with limited resources, leading to simple, effective, and affordable solutions. This is a useful method as long as it is understood that output should be used to validate the concept & generate interest and not as a replacement for a scalable & reliable product.

21. **Reverse Innovation:** Developing products in emerging markets first, and then bringing them to developed markets. This challenges the traditional flow of innovation and can result in novel solutions.

22. **Biomimicry:** Drawing inspiration from nature to design products and solve human problems. By observing the ways plants, animals, and natural systems have evolved solutions, designers can innovate new products.

Illustration 3: Slime Mold and Tokyo Rail System

Slime mold is a fascinating single-celled organism that exhibits remarkable intelligence despite lacking a brain. This organism grows in the form of a greenish-yellow network of veins, which serves as a tubular system for efficiently transferring nutrients throughout its structure.

One intriguing experiment involving slime mold was conducted using oat flakes arranged in the pattern of Japanese cities around Tokyo.[3] Despite its lack of neurons or any form of central nervous system, the slime mold managed to construct a network of nutrient-channeling tubes that strikingly resembled the layout of the Japanese rail system. This astonishing behavior highlights the organism's ability to solve complex problems and adapt to its environment without any form of cognitive ability.

Building on this discovery, researchers have delved deeper into understanding how slime molds construct their networks[4]. They created a computer model that simulates this process, aiming to validate its accuracy by comparing it with real-life experiments conducted on agar plates where slime molds were fed with oatmeal.

To assess the efficiency of the networks created by their model, the researchers used three key metrics: cost, mean travel time, and vulnerability. Cost is determined by the overall length of all segments, while mean travel time represents the average distance between any two points. Vulnerability measures the average increase in travel time caused by the removal of a segment.

Remarkably, the results of their model closely mirrored those observed in living slime molds, with a deviation of less than four percent.

The computer model based on biomimicry can now be used to study decentralized network construction, which has potential applications in various fields, including transportation and infrastructure planning.

Biomimicry has also been used to find the shortest path in a maze.[5]

- **Technology Convergence:** As different technologies mature, they can be combined in new ways, leading to innovative products. For instance, the convergence of AI, sensors, and smartphones led to smart home devices.

- **Ethnographic Studies:** Spending time with people in their environment to deeply understand their lifestyles, needs, and challenges, which can then inspire product innovations.

1. Idea Canvas

Whatever the source of an idea, effective communication is essential to bring it to life.

Merely expressing it as a casual one-liner does the idea a disservice. Such an approach might work in in-person conversations. However this is not scalable.

An even greater injustice to an idea is subjecting it to a one-dimensional analysis. Overlooking its various facets gives rise to underdeveloped concepts that struggle to earn credibility.

The gravest mistake, however, is presenting an idea without sufficient clarity. When inadequately articulated, those unfamiliar with its context may find it inscrutable.

Enter the Idea Canvas—a tool designed to solve the above problems and more. The Idea Canvas isn't just a tool—it's a catalyst for innovation. It encourages comprehensive contemplation of an idea, ensuring its fullest development and expression.

1.1 Using the Canvas

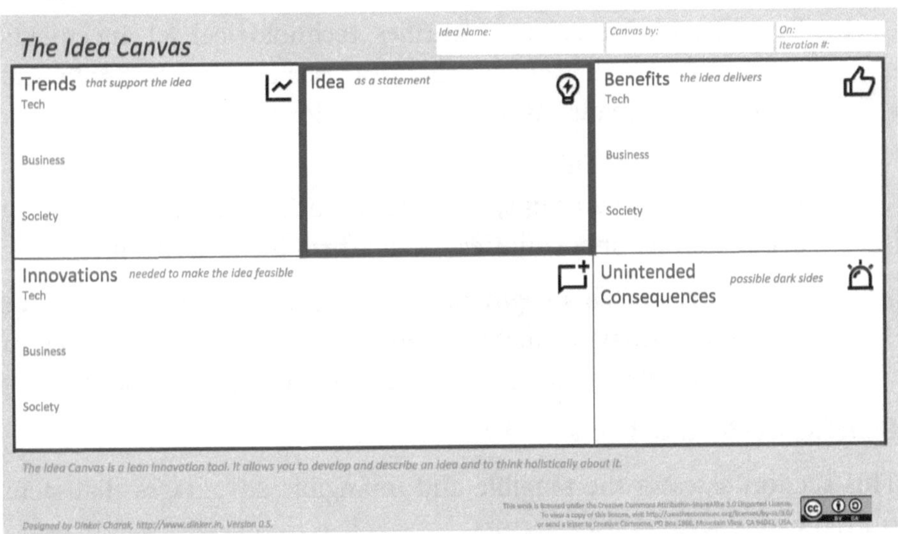

Fig 3: The Idea Canvas

The recommended sequence is:

1. Idea as a statement

2. Trends that support the idea

3. Benefits the idea delivers

4. Innovations needed to make the idea feasible

5. Unintended Consequences

1.2 Detailed Overview

The Idea Canvas provides a structured approach to ideating and developing a one-liner of an idea. Here's a breakdown of its sections:

Idea as a Statement

This captures the essence of the idea succinctly. It is the primary description, usually the first articulation of the thought. This is what we'll build on.

Trends Supporting the Idea:

This section delves into the various trends across multiple spheres that validate and support the idea's relevance and timeliness.

1. Tech Trend: Here, one identifies technological advancements or movements that bolster the idea. Has a recent technological development made this idea more viable or pressing?

2. Business Trend: This spotlights the shifts in the business realm—be it emerging startups, innovative business models, or newly arisen market opportunities—that affirm the idea's significance.

3. Social Trend: This segment pinpoints societal movements or changes in behaviors that resonate with the idea. Has there been a shift in societal norms or values that align with the concept?

Benefits the Idea Delivers

This section assesses the tangible and intangible advantages that stem from the idea across varied sectors.

1. Benefits to Tech: What value does the idea bring to the technological sector? Additionally, how might it specifically advantage the technological teams within the organization?

2. Benefits to Business: In the commercial domain, what promise does the idea hold? Might it herald a groundbreaking business

model? How can it bolster revenues, pare down costs, or streamline operations?

3. Benefits to Society: This ponders on the broader societal implications. How might the idea enhance the lives of individuals or the community at large?

Innovations Needed for Feasibility

The success of some ideas hinges on the emergence of certain innovations. This section explores what needs to be in place for the idea to become a reality.

1. Innovations in Tech: What technological breakthroughs or advancements are imperative for this idea's fruition?

2. Innovations in Business: Are there specific business strategies or models that need to be established or validated for the idea to be executable?

3. Innovations in Society: Beyond technology and business, are there societal shifts required? Might it necessitate new societal acceptances or the breaking down of pre-existing barriers?

Unintended Consequences

Every innovation, especially in technology, may come with unforeseen repercussions. This section mandates a proactive approach, urging thinkers to anticipate and address potential drawbacks or undesired outcomes linked with the idea.

1.3 Example Scenario

> **Scenario 1:** Given that AI-based technology is growing, a founder wants to evaluate an AI-based messaging app. The founder chooses the Idea Canvas.
>
> **Idea as a Statement:** A next-generation AI-powered messaging app, MsgMsg App, is designed to streamline communication with intelligent features, enhancing user experience.

Trends Supporting the Idea:

Tech Trend:

1. Rising integration of AI in everyday applications
2. Growth in natural language processing (NLP) capabilities, allowing for better understanding and prediction of user communication behaviors
3. Faster development using AI tools

Business Trend:

1. Shift towards personalized communication platforms
2. Increase in remote work and reliance on digital communication tools
3. Growing market for AI-driven business solutions

Social Trend:

1. Increasing comfort with and demand for intelligent assistants in daily activities
2. Desire for quicker, more efficient modes of communication

Benefits the Idea Delivers:

Benefits to Tech:

1. Showcases the capabilities of advanced AI in real-world applications
2. Drives innovation in NLP and AI-assisted communication

Benefits to Business:

1. Offers businesses a more efficient tool for internal communication
2. Provides insights into communication patterns, potentially aiding in decision-making processes
3. Reduces communication lags and misunderstandings, promoting productivity

Benefits to Society:

1. Simplifies communication for users, catering to various needs, from professional to personal

2. Fosters global connections by breaking down language barriers with real-time translation features (assuming this feature exists in the MsgMsg App)

Innovations Needed for Feasibility:

Innovations in Tech:

1. Enhanced NLP algorithms for more accurate message predictions and suggestions

2. Secure encryption methods to ensure user privacy in an AI-driven environment

Innovations in Business:

1. Collaborative partnerships with other tech entities to incorporate a wide range of AI functionalities

2. Business models that ensure user trust, especially when handling sensitive communication data

Innovations in Society:

1. Wider acceptance of AI's role in intimate areas of life, such as personal communication

2. Awareness and education regarding the safe use of AI-driven platforms

Unintended Consequences:

1. Potential privacy concerns with AI analyzing user messages

2. Over-reliance on AI predictions could hamper genuine human communication

3. Misinterpretations by AI, leading to communication mishaps

Download Ideas Canvas

https://bit.ly/plcu-idea-canvas

2. Opportunity Assessment

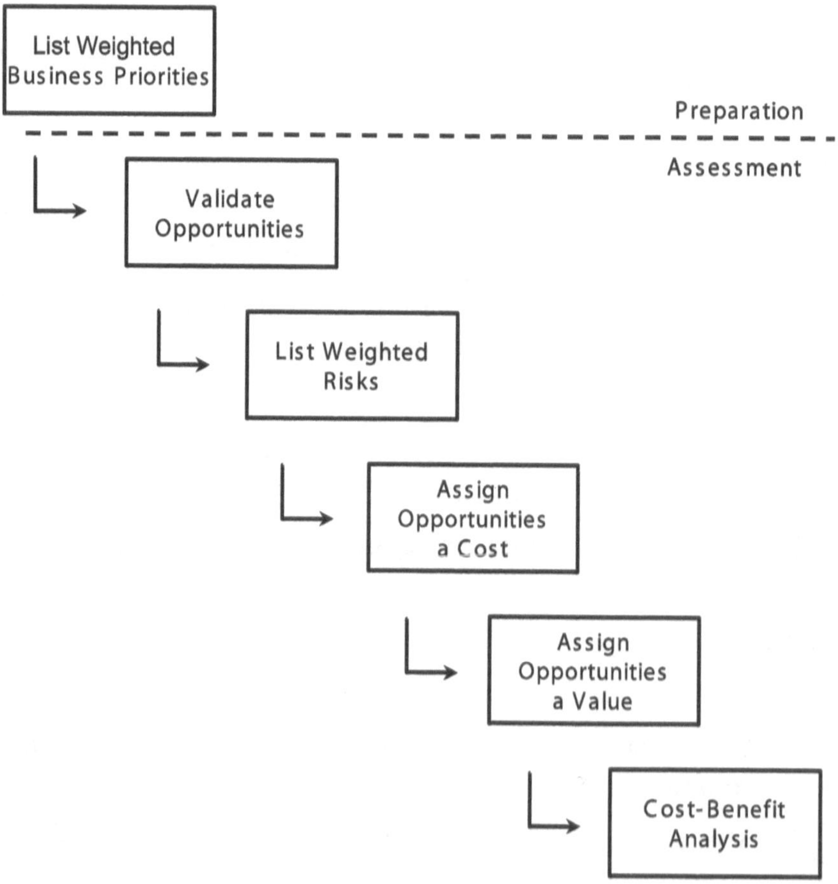

Fig 4: Opportunity Assessment Flow

Product Managers need to constantly identify and evaluate new opportunities. Whether it's to capitalize on new market trends, cater to emerging customer needs, or innovate ahead of competitors, Product Managers constantly find themselves at the crossroads of making decisions about which opportunities to pursue.

At its core, opportunity assessment is about making informed decisions and taking calculated risks.

To effectively evaluate an opportunity, it is crucial to clearly define the goal against which the opportunity will be assessed. This clarity can be achieved by adhering to the following preparatory steps.

2.1 Preparatory Step: List Weighted Business Priorities

Based on your organization's mission and vision, define and understand the primary objectives or goals that drive its operations.

Here's a breakdown of some common priorities, a combination of which an organization may adopt:

1. **Increase revenue:** Boost the total income generated from goods, services, or other business activities

2. **Improve margins:** Enhance the difference between the cost of producing goods/services and the selling price, leading to higher profitability

3. **Reduce cost:** Minimize the expenses incurred during business activities without compromising quality or efficiency

4. **Reduce operational expense:** Decrease the day-to-day costs associated with running the business, such as customer onboarding, introducing new services, and support

5. **Improve customer experience:** Elevate the overall satisfaction and experience of customers when interacting with the organization's products or services

6. **Improve employee experience:** Enhance the satisfaction, motivation, and engagement levels of employees within the organization

7. **Increase revenue funnel:** Expand the number of potential customers or leads entering the sales process, ultimately aiming to boost sales and revenue

8. **Avoid opportunity cost:** Make decisions that ensure the highest possible value is obtained from resources, avoiding losses from missed potential

9. **Build competitive edge:** Develop unique strengths or attributes that set the organization apart from competitors, giving it an advantage in the market

Not all business priorities hold the same significance. Assigning weightage helps in effectively allocating resources and attention where they're most impactful.

Use Critical, High, Medium, and Low

This is a common method to gauge the urgency and importance of each priority when stakeholders share the importance qualitatively.

1. **Critical:** Priorities that are absolutely essential for the business's survival and immediate growth. They demand urgent attention and typically have significant consequences if not addressed.

2. **High:** Important priorities that can drive significant value but might not be as immediately urgent as the critical ones.

3. **Medium:** These are essential for long-term growth and stability but can be addressed after the more urgent priorities.

4. **Low:** These priorities, while valuable, have the least immediate impact on the business's operations or growth.

Avoiding the 'Everything is Critical' Scenario

Some business leaders have a tendency to label every business opportunity as critical. It is important to distinguish between truly critical priorities and those that may not yield a significant return on investment.

The 10-20-30-40 Distribution Model provides a structured approach to prevent stakeholders from categorizing every priority as critical, ensuring that resources are allocated appropriately based on their potential impact.

Here is the method:

1. No more than **10%** of priorities should be labeled as critical, emphasizing their utmost importance

2. Up to **20%** can be labeled as high, ensuring that these significant but not immediately urgent matters get attention

3. Up to **30%** can be considered medium, providing a balance between urgency and long-term strategy

4. The remaining **40%** can be allocated to low-importance priorities, ensuring that even the least pressing issues are still addressed

Scenario 2 (a): After external market research and internal brainstorming, an organization has arrived at a list of opportunities to invest and place a bet on. A Product Manager has been hired as a consultant to review this backlog of opportunities and asked to prioritize these opportunities for the best Return on Investment (ROI).

As a first step, the Product Manager seeks the business priorities from a senior business executive who is sponsoring the initiative.

As a follow-up, the Product Manager arrives at the following weightage for the shared business priorities based on the inputs of the senior business executive and others in the team.

- **Increase revenue:** Critical (Urgently needed to fuel growth and operations)

- **Improve margins:** High (Significant for profitability and sustainable growth)

- **Improve customer experience:** Medium (Important for long-term loyalty and brand reputation)

- **Develop a competitive edge:** Low (A gradual process, important but not immediately pressing)

> By discerning the weightage of each priority, the Product Manager can build a rubric for opportunity assessment that's both balanced and aligned with their overarching goals.
>
> Before proceeding further, the Product Manager confirms the same with the senior business executive.

By establishing weighted business priorities, a structured approach can be adopted to evaluate a set of opportunities. The following steps can be followed for each opportunity to determine its contribution towards achieving the goal, allowing for a comparative analysis among them.

2.2 Assessment Step 1: Validate Opportunities

Now that the opportunities have been identified, it's imperative to determine their viability.

This is where validation comes into play, a step to ensure that the perceived potential aligns with reality.

Methods for Validation:

1. **Market Research:** A systematic gathering of data regarding market conditions, customer preferences, and competitor analysis. This helps in understanding if there's genuine demand for the opportunity in question.

2. **Data-driven Projections:** Leveraging existing data to forecast potential success. This includes analyzing trends, historical data, and other relevant metrics to predict how the market might respond.

3. **Business Modeling:** Creating a theoretical framework or model of how the opportunity will operate within the market. This includes revenue models, operational plans, and growth strategies, giving a blueprint of the potential success path.

4. **MVP (Minimum Viable Product) to Validate Hypothesis:** Develop a basic version of the product or service to test its

reception in the market. It's a cost-effective way to gauge real-world response before a full-fledged launch.

Every validation method has its associated costs. Whether it's the workforce required for market research, the tools and platforms needed for data analysis, or the resources to develop an MVP, understanding these costs upfront ensures the organization can budget appropriately.

Scenario 2 (b): In the process of evaluating the new CRM product opportunity, the Product Manager has identified a method of validation considering the constraints of time and budget.

This method involves validation through Market Research, which includes conducting surveys to gain insights into user needs, preferences and how much would they pay for such a product.

Based on the interest shown by potential users, the Product Manager tags this opportunity as valid.

2.3 Assessment Step 2: List Weighted Risks

Before diving headfirst into addressing any opportunity, understanding potential pitfalls is crucial. Every opportunity has its set of risks. Identifying and understanding these risks ensures that the organization is well-prepared to handle them, should they arise.

Here's a list of the common risks:

1. **Opportunity and organizational mismatch:** When a potential opportunity doesn't align with the organization's mission, values, or capabilities, it can lead to wasted resources or a misdirection of efforts.

2. **Loss of reputation:** Pursuing certain opportunities, especially those that are experimental or unconventional, might not always resonate well with stakeholders, leading to potential harm to the organization's reputation.

3. **Risk to existing products:** Introducing new products or services can sometimes overshadow or even cannibalize existing offerings,

negatively impacting their ROI. *(Note: In some disruptive scenarios, this may not be a risk but an expected outcome.)*

4. **Loss of team's reputation:** If a team consistently pursues opportunities that fail to deliver, their credibility within the organization can diminish, which might affect morale and trust.

5. **InfoSec risk:** Opportunities, especially those that involve new technologies or platforms, might expose the organization to cybersecurity threats or data breaches.

6. **Loss of investment:** Not all opportunities guarantee a return on investment. Some might lead to financial losses if they don't pan out as expected.

Once the potential risks are identified, it's equally important to ascertain their severity or potential impact on the organization. This assessment allows for better resource allocation, preparation, and decision-making.

The 'Critical, High, Medium, Low' weightage and using '10-20-30-40 Bucketing' described above can be used.

Scenario 2 (c): The Product Strategist now examines the first opportunity in the backlog - a new CRM product. While evaluating this product, the Product Manager identified the following risks and assigned weightage to them in discussion with a Subject Matter Expert:

- Opportunity and organizational mismatch: Low Risk (The organization has experience in digital launches)

- Loss of reputation due to product failure: High Risk (The brand's image is closely tied to product success)

- InfoSec risk (potential data breaches): Critical Risk (The digital nature of the product makes security paramount)

- Loss of investment in development and marketing: Low Risk (While significant, the organization has budgeted for such endeavors)

2.4 Assessment Step 3: Assign Cost to each Opportunity

Before committing resources to any opportunity, it is essential to understand the financial implications associated with pursuing it. This step involves assigning costs to opportunities. There are three key aspects to consider when doing so:

Cost of Delivering the First Value to Customer (aka MVP)

Estimating the cost of delivering the first value to the customer, typically represented by the Minimum Viable Product (MVP), requires a high-level analysis of the resources and efforts involved.

This cost includes expenses related to product development, testing, and initial marketing efforts. To estimate this cost, consider the following factors.

1. **Development Costs:** Expenses related to designing, coding, and testing the MVP. It also includes any costs associated with acquiring or licensing necessary technologies or software.

2. **Marketing Costs:** Initial marketing efforts to promote the MVP to potential customers. This includes costs related to advertising, promotional materials, and market research.

3. **Operational Costs:** Costs related to operational activities such as hosting, customer support, and maintenance.

4. **Team Costs:** Salaries and wages of the team members involved in developing and launching the MVP.

Cost of Full Product

Estimating the cost of the full product involves predicting the expenses associated with scaling up the MVP to a fully developed and market-ready product. This estimation should take into account additional development, marketing, and operational costs required. To estimate this cost, consider the following factors.

1. **Scaling Costs:** Expenses related to scaling up the product to meet market demands, including additional development and testing efforts.

2. **Marketing and Sales Costs:** Increased marketing and sales efforts to reach a larger audience and drive sales of the full product.

3. **Operational Expansion Costs:** Costs associated with expanding operational capabilities to support the full product, such as hiring additional staff or investing in infrastructure.

Opportunity Cost

The opportunity cost of not pursuing an opportunity is the absence of the potential value that could have been gained by choosing an alternative opportunity. Estimating this cost involves evaluating the potential benefits that could have been realized if resources were allocated to a different opportunity instead. To estimate this cost, consider the following factors:

1. **Potential Revenue Loss:** Estimate the potential revenue that could have been generated by pursuing an alternative opportunity.

2. **Cost of Delay:** Consider the cost of delaying the pursuit of an alternative opportunity, including any potential impact on market share or competitive advantage.

3. **Strategic Value:** Evaluate the strategic value of the alternative opportunity in comparison to the current opportunity.

2.5 Assessment Step 4: Assign Opportunities a Value

Now that we've assigned each opportunity a cost, it's time to also give it a potential value. Without a clear grasp of the potential benefits, it's challenging to justify investments or prioritize one opportunity over another.

Estimating the value of an opportunity:

1. **Immediate Value vs. Long-Term Value:** It's essential to distinguish between immediate gains and long-term benefits. While some opportunities might offer quick wins, others may provide sustained advantages over time, even if the initial impact seems minimal.

2. **Aligning with Organizational Priorities:** Recall the priorities set in Step 1. For an opportunity to be truly valuable, it should ideally align with or bolster your organizational objectives.

3. **Quantifying the Value:** Where possible, assign numerical values or metrics to gauge the potential benefits. This can be in terms of projected revenue, cost savings, percentage increase in customer retention, or any other relevant measure.

Scenario 2 (d): In the process of evaluating the new CRM product opportunity, the Product Manager has identified the following benefits:

1. **Immediate Value:** A 5% projected increase in sales due to interest shown by existing customers in the proposed CRM during Market Research.

2. **Long-Term Value:** A projected 20% increase in adjacent sales over the next three years due to bundling of the CRM product with existing services.

3. **Aligning with Priorities:**

   a. **Increase Revenue:** Direct alignment with the immediate value of increased sales.

   b. **Improve margins:** Considering the significant expense associated with Product Operations, the envisioned automation is expected to enhance the margin for the new CRM product compared to other products within the organization's portfolio.

> c. **Improve Customer Experience:** Enhanced engagement
> tools in the CRM will benefit customers to understand and
> serve their customers better.
>
> Based on this analysis, the Product Manager tags this opportunity as
> viable.

2.6 Assessment Step 5: Cost-Benefit Analysis

To comprehensively assess the potential of any opportunity, it is crucial
to conduct a holistic evaluation that thoroughly considers the associated
risks, costs, and benefits. Tabulating your findings can serve as a valuable
starting point.

Opportunity	Validity	Risks	Cost	Cost to Benefit Indicator

Table 1: Cost Benefit Analysis Template

Scenario 2 (e): After evaluating the new CRM product opportunity, the Product Manager summarizes the findings.

Opportunity	Risks	Cost	Benefit	Cost to Benefit Indicator
Build a new CRM Product	• Opportunity and organizational mismatch: Low Risk (The organization has experience in digital launches) • Loss of reputation due to product failure: High Risk (The brand's image is closely tied to product success) • InfoSec risk (potential data breaches): Critical Risk (The digital nature of the product makes security paramount) • Loss of investment in development and marketing: Low Risk (While significant, the organization has budgeted for such endeavors)	• Estimated cost of MVP is within specific budget • Opportunity cost of not doing this is medium	• Immediate Value: A 5% projected increase in sales • Long-Term Value: A projected 20% increase in adjacent sales over the next three years • Improved margins: The envisioned automation is expected to enhance the margin for the new CRM product compared to other products within the organization's portfolio • Improve Customer Experience: Enhanced engagement tools in the CRM will benefit customers to understand and serve their customers better	The potential benefits outweigh the cost and risk factors

Table 2: Cost Benefit Analysis

With a detailed analysis based on these four dimensions, decision-makers can have a well-rounded understanding of each opportunity. This ensures that investments are made judiciously, maximizing potential returns while being cognizant of the associated risks and costs.

3

Market Research

Market Research is the practice of gathering, analyzing, and interpreting information about a market, about a product or service to be offered in that market, and about the past, present, and potential customers for the product or service.

For a Product Manager, the primary objectives of market research are to identify opportunities in the market, understand the potential risks, and gather data that can guide product development and marketing strategies. Market research helps Product Managers make well-informed decisions, minimize uncertainties, and reduce the risk of product failures.

Market research can be broadly categorized into two types.

1. **Primary Research:** Collecting data directly from the source. Methods used here include surveys, interviews, focus groups, and observations. For instance, a Product Manager might conduct a survey to understand user preferences or organize focus groups to get feedback on a prototype.

2. **Secondary Research:** Analyzing data that already exists. It can be information gathered from industry reports, business websites, scholarly articles, or any other published data. Product Managers often use secondary research to gain insights into market trends or to analyze competitive products.

1. Sampling

At the heart of Market Research lies sampling. Before we delve into Primary and Secondary Research, let us understand the concept and the importance of Sampling.

Sampling is the process of selecting a subset of individuals from a larger population to represent it in research. Sampling's inherent power is its ability to provide meaningful insights without having to consult the entire population. Here's how.

1. **Representativeness:** Sampling ensures that the selected subset accurately represents the larger population. For Product Managers, this means gathering insights from a diverse range of users or customers to inform product decisions.

2. **Cost-Effectiveness:** Conducting research on a large population can be time-consuming and expensive. Sampling allows Product Managers to gather insights efficiently by focusing on a manageable subset of the population.

3. **Time Efficiency:** Sampling enables Product Managers to gather data quickly and efficiently, allowing them to make timely decisions.

4. **Accuracy and Reliability:** Sampling, when done correctly, can yield results that are highly accurate and reliable. By using statistical techniques, Product Managers can ensure that their sample size is sufficient to draw meaningful conclusions.

5. **Mitigating Bias:** Sampling helps mitigate bias and avoid following HiPPO (Highest Paid Person's Opinion) in research by ensuring that the selected sample is representative of the population. This reduces the risk of drawing inaccurate conclusions based on skewed input data.

1.1 Sampling Methods

While sampling, it's important to choose an approach that aligns with the survey's objectives and ensures the results are representative of the target population. Several common techniques are available:

Simple Random Sampling

Technique: Every individual in the population has an equal chance of being selected.

Example: Imagine a company launching a new smartphone feature. To gather feedback, they select 1,000 users at random from their entire user base to test the feature. Here, every user has an equal chance of being chosen, ensuring that the feedback is unbiased.

Stratified Sampling

Technique: Divide the population into non-overlapping groups or "strata" and then randomly sample from each stratum.

Example: A music streaming service aiming to refine its playlist algorithm might divide its users into groups based on age ranges: 18-24, 25-34, 35-44, and so on. The service then randomly selects users from each age group to ensure feedback from all demographics.

Cluster Sampling

Technique: Divide the population into clusters (often geographically) and then randomly select some clusters. Every individual within a chosen cluster is then sampled.

Example: A retail company launching a new store layout might want to get feedback from customers across various locations. Instead of sampling from every store, they select 5 stores at random and survey all customers from these stores.

Multi-stage Sampling

Technique: Multi-stage sampling is similar to cluster sampling, but instead of including all units from the selected clusters, a sample is taken from within each chosen cluster.

Example: An online grocery platform is looking to understand shopping behaviors across various cities. They first divide their user base into clusters by city. From each city, they then randomly select a few neighborhoods (first stage). From those neighborhoods, they might choose a handful of households to survey (second stage). This way, instead of surveying every user in a city or every household in a neighborhood, they gather insights in stages.

Systematic Sampling

Technique: Choose every *nth individual from the population.*

Example: An e-commerce platform introducing a new checkout process might survey every 50th purchase to gather feedback about the new design and flow.

Convenience Sampling

Technique: Select individuals that are easiest to reach.

Example: A SaaS company at a trade show might gather feedback on its new interface from booth visitors, as they're readily available and willing to provide insights.

Judgment or Purposive Sampling

Technique: Handpick individuals based on specific criteria or knowledge about the population.

Example: An enterprise software company might want feedback on a new admin dashboard. They specifically select familiar IT managers from their client base since they have firsthand experience and can provide detailed insights.

Quota Sampling

Technique: Like stratified sampling, but instead of randomly selecting from each stratum, researchers select based on a fixed number or quota.

Example: A fitness app aiming to introduce new workout routines might decide to collect feedback from 100 users of each fitness level – beginners, intermediates, and experts. They'll continue to gather feedback until they meet their quota for each group.

1.2 Sample Size Calculation

In determining the appropriate sample size for a survey, several factors must be considered to achieve reliable results. The objectives of the study, the desired level of precision, and the diversity within the target population all play crucial roles in this decision-making process.

Statistical tools and formulas, such as Cochran's formula[1], are often employed to calculate the ideal sample size. These tools help ensure that the sample size is sufficient to yield statistically significant results. It is important to note that while larger samples generally provide more accurate results, there is a point of diminishing returns where the additional effort and cost may outweigh the marginal increase in accuracy.

For quick estimations, especially in large populations (exceeding 100,000) seeking a 95% confidence level with a margin of error of ±5%, a rule of thumb suggests a sample size of around 384. This approximation is based on Cochran's formula.

Ultimately, selecting the right sample size is critical for obtaining reliable and actionable insights from surveys, ensuring that the findings accurately represent the broader population. While a larger sample size generally results in more accurate findings, it's important to balance this with practical considerations such as cost and time. Conducting a cost-benefit analysis can help determine the optimal sample size that provides reliable results without unnecessary expenditure of resources.

Scenario 3: A Product Manager is planning for a survey to gather some feedback. Following is the analysis they made to plan for the budget.

Decision on the number of samples for the preliminary survey

The Product Manager carefully determined the necessary sample size for a high-quality survey by calculating it for various confidence levels and estimating the associated costs. The survey costs $2 per person.

Population	Confidence Level	Margin of Error	Ideal Sample Size	Survey Cost
1,00,000	80%	5%	164	$328
1,00,000	85%	5%	207	$414
1,00,000	90%	5%	272	$544
1,00,000	95%	5%	383	$766

Table 4: Cost of Surveying the Population

For a population of 100,000, the calculations showed that to achieve an 85% confidence level with a 5% margin of error, the ideal sample size would be 207, requiring a budget of $414. While a larger sample size would have increased the confidence level, the team decided that surveying 207 individuals was a suitable compromise given their $500 budget constraint.

> Since this survey was intended as a preliminary study, the team recognized that they would conduct a follow-up survey after conducting additional research. This follow-up survey would be more focused and specific, providing more conclusive answers to their questions.

2. Primary Research

Let us start with some common best practices that are applicable across all methods of primary research:

1. **Define Objectives Clearly:** Before beginning, clearly define the purpose and objectives.

2. **Take Comprehensive Notes:** If possible, record the interactions (with consent) to ensure accuracy. Take notes to capture key points and non-verbal cues.

Fig 5: Common Primary Research Methods

3. **Ensure Informed Consent:** Before any interaction, ensure participants understand the purpose of the survey, how their data

will be used, and any potential risks. Obtain written or verbal consent.

4. **Maintain Confidentiality:** Protect the identity of the participants and ensure data is stored securely. If quotes are used in reporting, make sure they're anonymized unless explicit permission is given.

5. **Be Respectful of Time:** Stick to the agreed-upon duration for the interactions unless the participant is willing and able to continue.

Following are common primary research methods Product Managers use.

2.1 Interviews

One-on-one conversations aimed at gathering in-depth qualitative insights.

Example: Developers of a novel graphics editing software conduct interviews with graphic designers to understand their workflow and challenges.

To ensure the quality of the information collected and the integrity of the research process, consider the following best practices.

1. **Choose the Right Interview Type:** Decide between structured (fixed set of questions), semi-structured (guideline of questions with flexibility), or unstructured (open-ended, more like a conversation) based on the research needs.

2. **Script Development:** Prepare a list of questions or topics to cover. This helps in ensuring consistency across multiple interviews.

3. Pilot Testing: Conduct a test interview to refine the questions and approach.

4. **Establish Rapport:** Start by introducing yourself, explaining the purpose of the interview, and ensuring the participant feels comfortable.

5. **Stay Neutral:** Avoid leading questions that might influence the respondent's answer. Maintain a neutral demeanor to avoid inadvertently signaling approval or disapproval.

Illustration 4: Avoid asking leading questions.		
Leading Question	**Flaws**	**Recommended Version**
Do you find it challenging to use our advanced masking feature because of its complexity?	This question suggests that the advanced masking feature is challenging due to its complexity, leading the respondent to agree with the statement.	How do you feel about the complexity of our advanced masking feature? Can you describe any challenges you've faced while using it?
Would you agree that our software's user interface is more intuitive than other graphic design tools?	This question implies that the software's user interface is more intuitive than other tools, prompting the respondent to confirm the statement.	How would you describe your experience with our software's user interface compared to other graphic design tools you've used?
Since our software offers a wide range of filters, do you think it provides more creative possibilities than other tools?	This question presupposes that the software's wide range of filters offers more creative possibilities than other tools, leading the respondent to agree.	How do you utilize the various filters available in our software to enhance your creative process?

Table 3: Avoiding Asking Leading Questions

1. **Practice Active Listening:** Focus on the participant, avoid interrupting, and be open to follow-up questions that might not be on the original script.[A]

2. **Encourage Openness:** Use open-ended questions to allow participants to provide detailed responses. Phrases like "Can you tell me more about that?" can help delve deeper.

3. **Be Adaptable:** While having a script is useful, be flexible in your approach. The conversation might lead to valuable insights not covered in the original plan.

4. **Ask for Clarification:** If unsure about a respondent's answer, ask for clarification to ensure you're capturing their perspective accurately.

5. **Conclude Properly:** At the end of the interview, thank the participants, offer them an opportunity to ask questions, and inform them about the next steps in the research process.

6. **Post-Interview Reflection:** Immediately after the interview, spend a few minutes reflecting on the conversation. Note any immediate insights, surprises, or areas to explore in future interviews.

By following these best practices, researchers can ensure that interviews are conducted professionally and ethically to yield valuable data for the primary research objectives.

2.2 Focus Groups

A small group of people discuss a topic or test a product, while researchers observe and ask questions.

Example: A tech firm invites a group of IT professionals to discuss the usability and features of a new cloud-based storage solution they're developing.

Here are some best practices to consider when conducting focus groups.

1. **Participant Selection:** Choose participants that represent the diversity of the target audience. However, ensure enough homogeneity (similar demographics, experiences, purpose) so participants feel comfortable sharing.

2. **Moderator Skills:** Select a skilled moderator who can facilitate the discussion effectively, ensuring everyone participates and stays

on track. The moderator should be neutral and avoid influencing participants' responses.

3. **Preparation of Discussion Guide:** Prepare a set of open-ended questions or topics to guide the discussion. This should be flexible, allowing for unplanned but relevant discussions.

4. **Logistics and Setting:** Choose a comfortable location free from distractions. Arrange seating in a circle or semicircle to promote open discussion. However, in some scenarios, participants are asked to face the moderator so they are not influenced by others' body language or facial expressions. Ensure all necessary equipment, such as recorders or cameras, are set up and functional.

5. **Set Ground Rules:** At the beginning, establish some basic rules, like one person speaking at a time, respecting others' opinions, and ensuring confidentiality within the group.

6. **Manage Group Dynamics:** To foster participation and engagement among all participants, including those who may be quieter, an ice-breaker game can be used. The moderator can employ various tactics to ensure balanced participation, such as directly asking quieter participants for their opinions. Additionally, all participants can be asked to write their opinions and answers on sticky notes, which can help to level the playing field and prevent dominant individuals from overshadowing others. In instances of disagreements or conflicts, the moderator can tactfully address these situations without shutting down the discussion. This can be achieved by calling a timeout or using a tactic like ELMO (Enough, Let's Move On). Alternatively, questions or issues causing conflicts can be placed in a "parking lot" for later discussion. In more severe cases, unruly participants can be separated to ensure a productive and respectful discussion environment.

7. **Stay Neutral:** Avoid leading questions or showing approval/disapproval, to ensure genuine responses.

8. **Duration:** Typically, focus groups run between 60 to 90 minutes.

9. **Thank Participants:** Recognize the participants' contributions, and if applicable, distribute incentives or compensations.

By adhering to these best practices, researchers can ensure focus groups are both effective and ethical, yielding deep insights that might not emerge from other research methods.

2.3 Observations

Watching and recording the behavior of software users in their natural environment.

Example: A company designing a new e-commerce platform observes online shoppers to understand their navigation patterns and purchase behaviors.

Here are some good practices for conducting observational research:

1. **Choose the Appropriate Observation Method:** Decide between participant observation (where the observer is also a participant in the activity) and non-participant observation (where the observer is a passive watcher). Each has its advantages depending on the research context.

2. **Minimize Observer Effect:** The mere presence of an observer can sometimes alter the behavior of participants. While this isn't always avoidable, being discreet, using unobtrusive methods, or giving participants time to acclimate to the observer's presence can help.

Illustration 5: The "Clever Hans" Phenomenon

In the early 1900s, a horse named Clever Hans[2] gained fame for seemingly performing complex arithmetic and answering questions by tapping his hoof. His owner, Wilhelm von Osten, believed Hans possessed extraordinary intelligence. However, psychologist Oskar Pfungst conducted an experiment where he hid the answer from von Osten, revealing it only to another observer who wasn't interacting

---

> Hans. Remarkably, Hans's accuracy dropped significantly, suggesting he was picking up on subtle cues from von Osten, even unconscious ones, rather than truly understanding the questions.
>
> This became a classic case study in the observer effect, demonstrating how unintentional biases & cues of the observer can influence behavior.

1. **Maintain Objectivity and Neutrality:** Personal biases can cloud judgment. It's vital to approach observations without preconceived notions and to document findings impartially.

2. **Use Structured Instruments When Applicable:** For some observations, it's beneficial to use structured tools like checklists or behavior coding sheets to ensure consistency in what's being observed.

3. **Document Context:** The surrounding environment, time of day, interactions, and other contextual factors can influence behavior. Make sure to document these to provide a comprehensive understanding of the observed behaviors.

4. **Stay Adaptable:** Field situations can change, and unexpected events can occur. Being flexible and adaptable in the approach ensures the Product Manager makes the most of the observational research.

2.4 Usability Testing

Asking users to complete specific tasks with a software product to evaluate its user-friendliness and functionality.

Example: A startup testing its new mobile game asks users to play the first three levels, observing where they encounter difficulties or bugs.

Here are some good practices for conducting usability testing:

1. **Recruit Representative Users:** Participants should closely represent the actual or intended users. This might mean segmenting users by demographics, tech-savviness, or other relevant criteria.

2. **Prepare a Structured Test Plan:** Design specific tasks or scenarios that users need to complete. These tasks should represent typical actions users would perform with the product.

3. **Opt for Realistic Environments:** Whenever possible, conduct tests in environments similar to where users would typically use the product. This helps in understanding real-world challenges.

4. **Moderated vs. Unmoderated Tests:** Decide whether a moderator will be present. Moderated sessions allow for real-time clarifications and probing, while unmoderated sessions can be more scalable and may lead to more natural user behaviors.

5. **Minimize Observer Influence:** If a session is being observed, ensure the presence of observers doesn't influence participants' behaviors. One-way mirrors, remote observation tools, or post-test interviews can help mitigate this.

6. **Encourage Think-Aloud Protocols:** Ask participants to verbalize their thoughts, feelings, and reasons for their actions as they navigate the product. This provides rich insights into their decision-making process.

7. **Capture Both Qualitative and Quantitative Data:** While observing user behavior and collecting feedback is qualitative, also consider capturing quantitative metrics like task completion rates, time taken for each task, and error rates.

8. **Stay Neutral:** Avoid giving hints, leading participants, or providing feedback during the test. This ensures the Product Manager captures genuine user experiences.

9. **Regularly Review and Iterate:** After each round of usability testing, analyze findings, implement changes, and consider re-testing to ensure issues have been resolved.

10. **Involve Stakeholders:** Engage designers, developers, and other stakeholders in the testing process. Their involvement ensures findings are acted upon and incorporated into the product's evolution.

2.5 Ethnographic Research

Ethnographic Research, which finds its roots in anthropology, involves in-depth study and observation of people in their natural environment, typically over extended periods. The aim is to understand cultures, behaviors, rituals, and dynamics from an "insider" perspective. When incorporated into primary research for products or services, ethnography can provide profound insights into user needs, pain points, and contexts of use.

Example: Developers of a health app spend time in gyms and nutrition centers to understand how fitness enthusiasts track their activities and meals.

Here are some good practices for conducting ethnographic research:

1. **Immerse Yourself:** Ethnographic Research requires deep immersion in the setting or community under study. Spend considerable time in the field, observing and engaging with participants.

Illustration 6: "Follow Me Home" program

The "Follow Me Home" program, initiated by Intuit co-founder Scott Cook, is a customer research approach where company representatives observe how customers use their products in real life.

FMH is a way to step into our customers' shoes, in order to understand the full picture of how they run their business with our products.(3)

This method helps understand customers' experiences, challenges, and preferences without any preconceived assumptions. It is useful for any business with a tangible product or service and involves a simple setup with an interviewer and a note-taker. The insights gained are used to improve products and services, emphasizing the importance of direct customer observation.

---

2. **Develop Rapport:** Building trust with participants is crucial. Spend time getting to know them, understand their norms and values, and respect their ways of life.

3. **Use Multiple Data Collection Methods:** Beyond observation, use interviews, participatory methods, visual methods (like photography), and artifact analysis to gather a holistic understanding.

4. **Maintain Reflexivity:** Be continuously aware of your own biases, beliefs, and the influence you might have on the environment. Documenting personal reflections can be invaluable in data analysis.

5. **Adopt an Iterative Approach:** Ethnographic research often evolves as understanding deepens. Be prepared to adjust focus or methods based on emerging insights.

6. **Involve Interdisciplinary Teams:** Given the holistic nature of ethnography, involving experts from various disciplines (like sociology, psychology, or design) can enrich interpretations.

2.6 Surveys

Surveys are structured tools used to gather quantitative and qualitative data from a sample of individuals to infer insights about a larger population. They can be administered through various mediums, including online platforms, phone, or in-person, and are essential for gauging opinions, behaviors, and preferences.

Designing an effective survey requires careful consideration to ensure that the results are accurate, insightful, and actionable. Here are some good practices to follow when creating a survey:

1. **Define Objectives Clearly:** Before you start with the survey, be clear about what you want to achieve. Understanding your goals will guide the types of questions you ask.

2. **Keep it Short:** Respondents are more likely to complete shorter surveys. Aim for a survey length that respects your respondents' time while still gathering the necessary data.

3. **Use Simple and Clear Language:** Avoid jargon or complex words. Ensure that all respondents, regardless of their background or expertise, can understand your questions.

4. **Avoid Leading Questions:** Ensure your questions don't lead respondents to a particular answer. For example, instead of asking, "Don't you think our app is helpful?", you could ask, "How would you rate the usefulness of our app?"

5. **Offer a Range of Response Options:** For multiple-choice questions, provide a comprehensive range of options so respondents can accurately express their opinions.

6. **Include Open-Ended Questions Sparingly:** While they can provide richer insights, open-ended questions take more time to answer and analyze. Use them when you genuinely want detailed feedback.

7. **Randomize Answer Choices:** This reduces the risk of order bias, where respondents might choose the first or last option due to its position rather than its content.

8. **Ensure Anonymity and Confidentiality:** Assure respondents that their responses will be anonymous (if they are) and explain how their data will be used.

9. **Avoid Double-Barreled Questions:** These are questions that touch on more than one issue but allow only one answer. For instance, "How satisfied are you with our product's price and quality?" should be split into two separate questions.

10. **Use a Logical Flow:** Start with general questions and then move to specific ones. It's also helpful to group similar questions together. Airlines use this approach frequently. They begin with questions about the overall experience. Then, they ask specific questions about each stage in the order a passenger experiences their services, starting from booking until picking up the luggage at the destination.

11. **Include a Mix of Question Types:** Depending on the information you want, you can use a mix of multiple choice, Likert scale (a rating scale ranging from "Strongly Disagree" to "Strongly Agree" or similar)[A], ranking, or open-ended questions.

12. **Pre-test Your Survey:** Before sending it out to your entire target group, test the survey with a smaller group to identify any confusing questions or technical issues.

13. **Be Mindful of Demographics:** If demographic data is crucial for your survey, include questions about age, gender, location, etc., but also be aware of privacy concerns.

14. **Include a Progress Indicator:** If your survey is online and has multiple pages, a progress indicator helps respondents know how much of the survey is left, reducing the chances of abandonment.

15. **Thank Respondents:** Always express gratitude to respondents for taking the time to complete your survey. If applicable and ethical, you can also offer incentives.

By adhering to these best practices, you can increase your survey's response rate, ensure the quality of the data collected, and gain meaningful insights from the results.

Response Rate

In survey design, estimating and managing response rates is crucial for obtaining a sufficient number of completed surveys to draw meaningful conclusions. Several factors influence response rates, including the survey medium and the characteristics of the target audience.

For example, email surveys typically have lower response rates compared to in-person surveys. To ensure an adequate response rate, it's important to estimate the expected response rate based on experience or pre-tests.

If, for instance, a 20% response rate is anticipated and 200 completed surveys are required, the survey should be distributed to approximately 1,000 participants.

By carefully managing response rates, Product Managers can maximize the usefulness and reliability of their survey results.

Ethical Considerations

Ensure that your participants are informed about the purpose of the survey, how their data will be used, and that their responses are confidential. Disclose when the data collected will be purged and who will have access to the data in the interim.

3. Secondary Research

Secondary research, also known as desk research, involves the collection and analysis of existing data and resources rather than generating new data. Here are some methods for secondary research.

Fig 6: Common Secondary Research Methods

3.1 Literature Review

Analyze academic and other publications related to the industry of the product.

Example: Reviewing academic articles on usability design principles to enhance the user experience of a new software application.

Here are some popular sites and databases for literature reviews.

1. **ACM Digital Library:** Managed by the Association for Computing Machinery, it offers articles, magazines, and conference proceedings related to computing and information technology.

2. **arXiv:** arXiv is a free service and archive of scholarly articles in fields like physics, mathematics, computer science, biology, finance, statistics, engineering, systems science, and economics. Articles on arXiv are not peer-reviewed by them.

3. **EBSCOhost:** A platform that offers various databases, including Academic Search Premier, Business Source Premier, and more, covering various disciplines.

4. **Google Scholar:** A freely accessible web search engine that indexes the full text or metadata of scholarly literature across an array of publishing formats and disciplines.

5. **IEEE Xplore:** Provides access to technical literature in electrical engineering, computer science, and electronics. It contains IEEE journals, conferences, and standards.

6. **JSTOR:** Provides access to thousands of academic journals, books, and primary sources in various disciplines including arts, humanities, and social sciences.

7. **ProQuest:** Hosts multiple databases with access to dissertations, newspapers, journals, magazines, and other sources.

8. **Scopus:** A comprehensive abstract and citation database covering a broad range of subjects, from science and technology to social sciences.

9. **SpringerLink:** Offers access to millions of scientific documents from journals, books, series, protocols, and reference works.

10. **Taylor & Francis Online:** Provides access to journals, books, and reference works across multiple disciplines.

3.2 Industry and Market Reports

Assess reports by software industry analysts or market research firms.

Example: Consulting a Gartner report on the top CRM software products to understand market leaders and their features.

Here are some popular platforms and publishers for industry and market reports.

1. **BCC Research:** Provides market research reports and industry analysis for major industries, including advanced materials, chemicals, and technology.

2. **Deloitte Insights:** A major consultancy, Deloitte offers research, reports, and insights on various industry sectors.

3. **Euromonitor:** Specializes in global strategic market research, offering detailed data and analysis on industries, economies, and consumers worldwide.

4. **Forrester:** Delivers thorough market research reports about the impact of technology change on businesses and consumers.

5. **Gartner:** A renowned research and advisory company that provides technology-related insights, including magic quadrants, which rank technology providers in various sectors.

6. **IBISWorld:** Offers comprehensive industry research reports that provide key statistics and analysis on market characteristics, operating conditions, current and projected performance, major industry participants, and more.

7. **IDC (International Data Corporation):** Offers global market intelligence, advisory services, and events for the IT, telecommunications, and consumer technology markets.

8. **MarketResearch.com:** An extensive market research platform that hosts reports from top publishers, providing insights on numerous industries and markets.

9. **McKinsey & Company:** As a global management consulting firm, McKinsey regularly publishes insights and reports on various industries.

10. **Mintel:** Provides market analysis reports for a range of sectors, including finance, retail, and consumer products.

11. **Nielsen:** Known for its insights into consumers, Nielsen provides market research related to what people watch and what they buy.

12. **PwC's Research and Insights:** The global consultancy firm PwC provides research and insights on various industries and market trends.

13. **Statista:** A portal for statistics that aggregates data and provides market and consumer insights across various industries.

14. **Technavio:** Produces detailed market research reports across a range of sectors, with a focus on emerging trends and their impact on various industries.

15. **Thoughtworks:** As a global software consulting firm, Thoughtworks regularly publishes insights and TechRadar.[A]

16. **Zensar:** Offers market research and industry analysis services, providing insights and solutions for businesses in various sectors.

3.3 Company Publications

Evaluate annual reports, product whitepapers, or investor relations documents from software companies.

Example: Analyzing Microsoft's annual report to assess the performance and future projections of its Office Suite products reveals their bet on Microsoft 365 Copilot and turning the Office Suite into an AI-first platform[4].

3.4 Government and Institutional Databases

Access data related to software regulations, compliance, or industry standards.

Example: Using the Federal Trade Commission's website (https://www.ftc.gov/media/71318) to understand advertising and privacy guidelines for mobile apps.

3.5 News and Media Outlets

Review tech news sites, blogs, or podcasts.

Example: Reading TechCrunch articles to track the launch and reception of a new software-as-a-service (SaaS) platform.

3.6 Trade Journals and Magazines

Engage with software or tech-focused journals.

Example: Going through Software Development Times (https://sdtimes.com/) to grasp emerging trends in DevOps practices.

3.7 Historical Records

Check past software releases, updates, or version histories.

Example: Using archives.org to analyze the historical contents of a website or using crunchbase.com to study the business history of the competition.

3.8 Competitor Websites and Materials

Review software product details, feature lists, user reviews, and FAQs on competitors' websites.

Example: Analyzing the features listed on Slack's website to understand its offerings compared to other communication tools. Visit similarweb.com to compare web traffic with competing websites.

3.9 User Forums and Communities

Browse online forums or communities where users discuss software products.

Example: Visiting Stack Overflow to understand common issues developers face with a particular programming library.

3.10 Product Review Sites

Consult platforms that aggregate software product reviews.

Example: Reviewing user feedback on G2 Crowd for a cloud storage product to gauge its strengths and weaknesses.

4

Product Ecosystem Mapping

A Product's ecosystem encompasses a complex network of interconnected software, hardware, applications, and services that collaboratively function to support a product's operation. In an enterprise setting especially, numerous products and services heavily rely on interconnected systems for data exchange, communication, and control. These systems range from databases, APIs, third-party software, and cloud services, to internal tools, creating a web of dependencies that is critical for a Product Manager to comprehend to ensure the success of their product within the broader ecosystem.

While it is natural for a Product Manager to concentrate on their assigned product, intense focus on the product when operating within an intricate network of interconnected systems can lead to tunnel vision.

This issue is particularly prevalent in enterprises, where teams are often funded to focus solely on specific aspects of the entire solution. These teams are scrutinized against commitments made at the onset of the funding cycle. As a result, leaders often prioritize meeting these commitments over focusing on the ultimate outcomes delivered to customers.

To combat this challenge, Product Ecosystem Mapping is a valuable step in Product's Life Cycle. It empowers Product Managers to systematically recognize the systems on which their product depends and those that depend on their product. This insight allows the Product Manager and the entire team to identify value tributaries and distributors, ensuring the awareness of dependencies that directly impact end customers. By always considering these dependencies, the team remains cognizant of how their product affects the overall customer experience.

1. Ecosystem Mapping Canvas

Ecosystem Mapping Canvas allows a team to systematically realize which system their product depends on and which system depends on their product. This awareness ensures that these dependencies that affect end customers are always in consideration. The Ecosystem Mapping Canvas also helps teams realize the potential of building a platform rather than a channel.

The Ecosystem Mapping Canvas[1] is a strategic management tool. It allows you to discover an ecosystem around your product to make it a value multiplier.

1.1 Using the Canvas

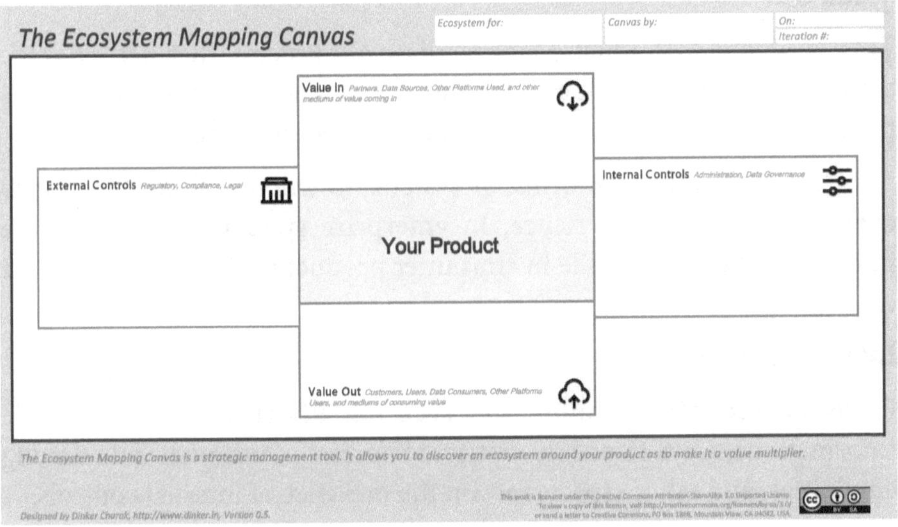

Fig 7: The Ecosystem Mapping Canvas[1]

The components of the Ecosystem Mapping Canvas are:

1. Value In
2. Value Out
3. Internal Controls
4. External Controls

1.2 Detailed Overview

Let us look at the various sections of this canvas.

Value In

This is where a Product Manager lists all systems that act as value tributaries to the product, like data sources, platforms for which the product is a consumer, and systems that hand over customer experience to the product. Along with that, the Product Manager adds the value they bring to the product and the value the product generates for their customers.

In enterprise systems these could be internal applications and in consumer product settings these could be external applications.

Value Out

This is where a Product Manager lists all systems that act as value distributaries of the product. Along with that, the Product Manager adds the value the product creates for them and their customers.

List data sinks, platforms, or systems to whom the product hands over the customer experience. In enterprise systems, these could be internal applications, while in consumer product settings, they could be external applications.

Internal Controls

Focus on security, scanning and securing PII (Personal Identifiable Information), ways to ensure restricted access to customer data among employees, and other aspects rely on the presence of internal controls.

This is the section where a Product Manager lists all systems and processes to ensure that data and personal information are safe while it is in motion or at rest within the product. For example, the service the product uses to tokenize PII data. Another example is an internal admin tool that controls access permissions for team members, operations, or support officers. This tool determines who has access to what information when the product is in production and has real business data. Or, the audit flow the Product Manager may prioritize.

External Controls

Adherence to pertinent regulations is of paramount importance. Alongside generic standards like PCI-DSS, GDPR, or CCPA, it is crucial to prioritize regulations tailored specifically to the product. This section acts as a comprehensive catalog, ensuring that every aspect of the product aligns with regulatory requirements. Other items in this section could be regulatory reports that need to be generated and management of logs for audits.

1.3 Example Scenario

Scenario 4: Given that AI-based technology is growing, the startup building the MsgMsg App wants to understand the ecosystem of such an app. The Product Manager chose to use the Ecosystem Mapping Canvas to run a workshop with the team to understand the app's potential ecosystem.

Here's an Ecosystem Mapping Canvas for the MsgMsg App:

Value In:

1. Data sources:

    a. User messages, the key content

    b. Integration with social media platforms (e.g., Facebook, X) for importing contacts and messages for network effect and virality

2. Platforms for which the app is a consumer:

    a. AI and NLP services for message prediction and real-time translation, that help with a key value prop of the app

    b. Cloud storage services for storing message history and media files, optimizing the cost and scalability

3. Systems that hand over customer experience to the app:

    a. APIs for integrating with other apps and services for seamless communication to increase the number of users

Value Out:

1. Data sinks:

   a. Other messaging apps for cross-platform communication, for network effect and virality

   b. Analytics platforms for user behavior analysis to improve the product

2. Platforms which consume data from the app:

   a. Social media platforms for sharing messages and updates, for network effect and virality

   b. Cloud storage services for sharing media files, to benefit from scale of the app's operations

3. Systems to whom the app hands over the customer experience:

   a. Third-party apps for additional features (e.g., games, productivity tools) integrated within the MsgMsg App, adding value to app's users and providing new user to such apps

Internal Controls:

1. Security measures:

   a. Encryption algorithms for message security

   b. Access controls to ensure only authorized personnel can access user data

2. PII data protection:

   a. Tokenization service for securing personal information while data is at rest

   b. Internal admin tool for managing access permissions and data handling

   c. Regulated access to production access

   d. Auditable and regulated access to cached messages

5. **Customers**: The final piece of the puzzle is the customers, who are the recipients or beneficiaries of the outputs. Understanding customer needs, preferences, and pain points is essential for tailoring the product to its intended audience. In an e-commerce context, customers are the individuals purchasing products through the platform.

2.2 Example Scenarios

Scenario 5: SIPOC for a E-Commerce Platform

The product is an e-commerce platform. Suppliers provide the products and inventory data as inputs. The processes involve order management, inventory tracking, and payment processing. The outputs are shipped orders and order status updates for customers. The end customers are the online shoppers using the platform.

The Product Manager drew the following SIPOC diagram:

Suppliers	Inputs	Processes	Outputs	Customers
Wholesalers, Manufacturers	Products, Inventory Data	Order Management, Inventory Tracking, Payment Processing	Shipped Orders, Order Status Updates	Online Shoppers

Table 5: SIPOC for E-Commerce Platform

Scenario 6: SIPOC for Software Development Project

The process is for a software development project. The suppliers provide APIs and third-party libraries as inputs. The processes consist of coding, testing, and debugging. The outputs are the final software application and any bug reports generated during testing. The customers are the end users who will utilize the software.

The Product Manager drew the following SIPOC diagram:

Suppliers	Inputs	Processes	Outputs	Customers
API Providers, Third-party Libraries	Code, Design Specifications	Coding, Testing, Debugging	Software Application, Bug Reports	End Users

Table 6: SIPOC for Software Delivery

Scenario 7: SIPOC for Content Creation Platform

The product is a content creation platform. Suppliers are content contributors and freelancers who provide written articles and visual content as inputs. The processes involve editing, design, and publishing. The outputs are published articles and visual media. The customers consist of readers and viewers who consume the content.

The Product Manager drew the following SIPOC diagram:

Suppliers	Inputs	Processes	Outputs	Customers
Content Contributors, Freelancers	Written Articles, Visual Content	Editing, Design, Publishing	Published Articles, Visual Media	Readers, Viewers

Table 7: SIPOC for CMS

5

Competition Analysis

Competition Analysis refers to the process of identifying, assessing, and evaluating the products, strategies, strengths, and weaknesses of one's direct and indirect competitors in the marketplace.

Dissecting competitors' offerings and operations helps businesses develop an in-depth understanding of the market dynamics and identify potential gaps or opportunities. For a Product Manager, understanding these nuances can be pivotal in steering the direction of product development, marketing, and strategy.

1. Identifying Competition Landscape

Similar & Competing	Similar & Not Competing
Similar & Different Domain	Inspirational

Fig 8: Identifying Competition Landscape

The competitive landscape is vast and varied, much like a spectrum. Not every competitor poses a direct threat; some might even emerge as potential collaborators or sources of inspiration.

To navigate this complex matrix, Product Managers need to categorize and understand the nuances of the products and companies they're juxtaposed against. This not only allows them to strategically position their products but also enables them to find opportunities for growth, differentiation, and partnership. Here's a deeper dive into the four categories that can help Product Managers decipher their competitive surroundings:

Similar and Competing

These are products that offer nearly identical features and target the same market segment. They pose the most direct form of competition and often compete for the same set of customers.

For such competitors, it's crucial to identify differentiators, whether in terms of product features, pricing, or customer service. Regular benchmarking and staying updated with their offerings can ensure your product remains ahead or at par.

Illustration 7: Apple Watch and Samsung Galaxy Watch

Both the Apple Watch and Samsung Galaxy Watch offer similar features such as fitness tracking, notifications, and app support, targeting the same market segment.

Competitive Strategy: Apple differentiates with its seamless integration with the Apple ecosystem, while Samsung focuses on its compatibility with Android devices and customization options.

Similar and Not Competing

While these products may have overlapping features or functionalities with a product, they serve a different market or segment and don't directly compete with the product.

Collaboration or partnership opportunities might arise here. By understanding the unique aspects they bring to a different market, there could be potential to expand one's product reach or jointly create solutions that cater to a broader audience.

> **Illustration 8**: Apple Watch and Garmin Forerunner
>
> While both the Apple Watch and Garmin Forerunner offer fitness tracking features, they target different markets; Apple Watch is more consumer-focused, while Garmin Forerunner caters to serious athletes.
>
> **Competitive Strategy**: Collaboration opportunities may include joint promotions with fitness apps or cross-brand partnerships to offer specialized fitness packages.

Similar but Different Domains

These products operate in domains but have a feature set or functions that are related. They might address a different problem but use a method or approach that is familiar.

Studying these can provide insights into adjacent markets or inspire innovative ways to tweak a product. There's also potential for cross-domain partnerships or integrations that enhance the value proposition for both products.

> **Illustration 9**: Apple Watch and Tile Tracker
>
> Both products leverage technology for tracking purposes; Apple Watch tracks health and fitness metrics, while Tile Tracker helps users locate lost items.
>
> **Competitive Strategy**: Insights from Tile Tracker's user-friendly tracking interface could inspire Apple Watch to enhance its tracking features for better user experience.

Different but Inspirational

These are products that might not share any direct similarity in terms of features or domain but have elements—be it design, user experience, marketing strategies, or even their business model—that are commendable and inspiring.

Product Managers can benefit from studying products that stand out. By drawing inspiration and learning from leading products, even those outside their direct industry or market, Product Managers can gain valuable insights to enhance their product's offerings and strategies.

Illustration 10: Apple Watch and Tesla Electric Cars

Apple Watch and Tesla Electric Cars are in different industries but share elements such as innovative design, advanced technology, and a focus on user experience.

Competitive Strategy: Apple Watch could draw inspiration from Tesla's direct-to-consumer sales model and emphasis on sustainable technology for its marketing and sales strategies.

In essence, the competitive landscape isn't just about rivalry; it's a rich tapestry of learning, adaptation, and potential collaboration. Recognizing where each player fits allows a Product Manager not only to strategize effectively but also to draw inspiration and find unique avenues of growth and innovation.

Example Scenario

Scenario 8: The Product Manager of the MsgMsg App has been tasked with identifying competitors to analyze. Using the Similar-Different 2x2 matrix for a Comparative Study, the Product Manager arrives at the following:

Similar and Competing: Telegram

Both the MsgMsg App and Telegram are messaging apps designed for quick, efficient communication. They target digitally savvy users and offer a range of features, from text messaging to multimedia sharing. While the MsgMsg App emphasizes its AI-driven features for better communication, Telegram boasts about its speed and security.

Similar and Not Competing: Slack

While both MsgMsg App and Slack are platforms designed for communication, Slack is specifically tailored for professional team communication and collaboration, particularly in a workplace setting. Its features, like channels and integrations with other work tools, distinguish it from more general-purpose messaging apps. There's potential for MsgMsg App to integrate with Slack, offering its AI-driven messaging enhancements to Slack users.

Similar but Different Domains: Duolingo

At its core, Duolingo is a language-learning app. While it doesn't serve as a communication tool like MsgMsg App, the app's AI-driven personalized learning paths, and instant translation quizzes align with MsgMsg App's emphasis on language translation. Insights from Duolingo could inspire MsgMsg App's translation algorithms or even lead to collaborative efforts for users learning new languages.

Different but Inspirational: Spotify

Spotify, a music streaming app, operates in an entirely different domain. However, it is powerful AI algorithms that curate playlists based on user preferences and listening habits could serve as inspiration for MsgMsg App. Just as Spotify understands user music tastes, MsgMsg App could refine its algorithms to understand user communication patterns, enhancing message suggestions and personalization.

2. Comparative Study

A direct comparison is the foundational method every Product Manager should begin with. Below are the criteria for such an evaluation:

1. **Features and Capabilities**: Evaluating the functionalities, usability, and design aspects of competing products

2. **Product Pricing**: Assessing how competitors price their products and the perceived value they offer

3. **Market Position and Brand Strength**: Analyzing market share, brand awareness, and customer loyalty

4. **Sales and Distribution Channels:** Understanding how and where competitors' products are sold

5. **Customer Feedback and Reviews**: Gathering insights from customers' experiences with competing products

6. **Marketing and Promotional Strategies**: Scrutinizing advertising, promotions, and other marketing initiatives

Example Scenario

Scenario 9: The Product Manager of MsgMsg App has been tasked with a comparative study against the popular Messaging app, WhatsApp. Using the basic criteria for a Comparative Study, the Product Manager arrives at the following:

Key Criteria of Competition Analysis	MsgMsg App	WhatsApp
Product Features and Capabilities	- AI-powered real-time message suggestions - Instant language translations - Tailored user experiences based on communication patterns - Designed for enhanced clarity in personal and professional interactions - Predictive, personalized, and productive messaging	- Basic messaging with end-to-end encryption - Voice and video calls - Status updates and group chats - Media sharing capabilities - Lacks AI-driven predictive messaging and tailored experiences

Pricing Structures	- Freemium model: Free basic features with premium features under subscription - Ads on the free version; ad-free for premium	- Completely free for personal use - Costs for business accounts, especially with API integrations
Market Position and Brand Strength	- New entrant with AI-driven features - Potential for niche market capture	- Dominant global player - Strong brand recognition and trust
Sales and Distribution Channels	- Available on major app stores - Direct downloads from the website - Partnerships with device manufacturers for pre-installs	- Available on all major app stores - Pre-installed on many devices due to popularity
Customer Feedback and Reviews	- Monitor initial feedback to improve features - Feedback likely related to AI suggestions and translations	- Generally positive reviews with occasional privacy concerns - Feedback on functionality, usability, and glitches
Marketing and Promotional Strategies	- Differentiate from traditional apps through AI - Campaigns showcasing AI-driven messaging benefits	- Relies on word-of-mouth and reputation - Campaigns emphasizing security and encryption

Table 8: MsgMsg App v/s WhatsApp

3. Competition Analysis Canvas

The Competition Analysis Canvas offers a structured approach to gain insights about competitors, helping businesses carve a niche for themselves in the market. It allows you to systematically analyze competition's products to extract competitive advantages they present.

3.1 Using the Canvas

The various components of the Competition Analysis Canvas help a Product Manager to discover key aspects of the competition's product in a systematic way.

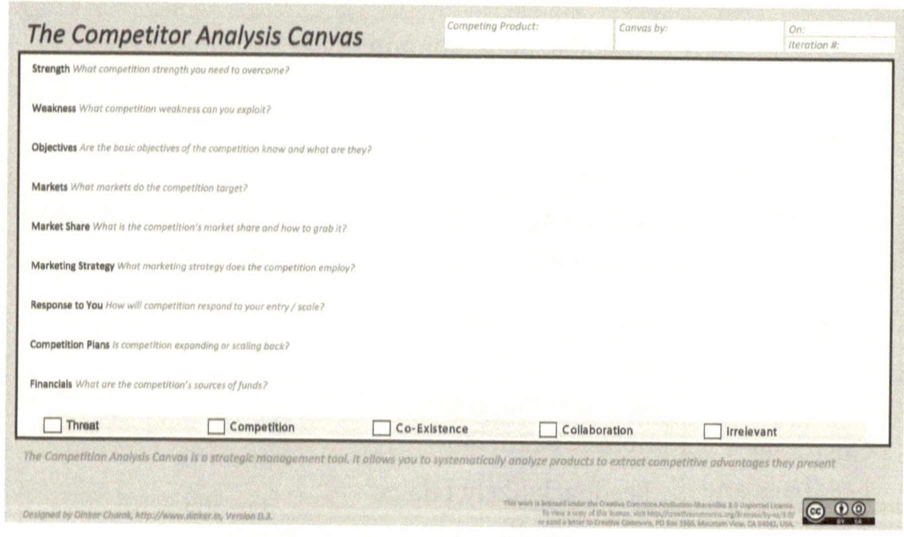

Fig 9: The Competition Analysis Canvas

3.2 Detailed Overview

Let us look at the various sections of this canvas:

Strength

Every competitor has their forte. It could be their brand image, technology, customer service, or any other aspect that makes them stand out. Product Managers must identify these strengths and strategize on how to counteract or surpass them.

Weakness

No competitor is without flaws. Recognizing these weaknesses is crucial, as they present opportunities. Can your product offer what the competition doesn't? Exploiting these gaps can be a game-changer.

Objectives

Understanding a competitor's core objectives offers insight into their long-term vision and strategy. Is their goal to expand internationally? Focus on niche markets? Diversify their product range? By discerning these objectives, one can predict a competitor's moves and align their strategies accordingly.

Markets

Which markets does your competition cater to? Are they focusing on urban consumers, a particular age group, or a specific industry? Knowing where they are making their mark can guide where you might want to pivot or penetrate.

Market Share

Possessing knowledge about a competitor's market share can indicate their influence and reach in the industry. Analyzing how to grab a piece of this share, either by directly competing or finding untapped niches, can steer product strategy.

Marketing Strategy

Is your competitor big on digital ads, influencer collaborations, or grassroots marketing? Deciphering their marketing strategy can hint at their target demographics and their approach to engaging them.

Response to You

The entry or scaling up of a new product will undoubtedly cause ripples. Predicting how competitors might react—be it through aggressive marketing, price cuts, or even partnerships—allows Product Managers to be prepared and better plan the go-to-market (GTM) strategy. (we delve more into GTM in a chapter coming up).

Competition Plans

Is your competitor on an expansion spree or are they retracting and becoming more niche-focused? Insights into their plans can be gleaned from their current moves, public announcements, or financial reports.

Financials

Understanding a competitor's financial health and sources of funding can provide a more comprehensive view of their stability, potential for expansion, or R&D investments.

Classifying the Competition

After thoroughly evaluating the aforementioned sections, the Product Manager can classify the competition into one of the five categories:

1. **Threat**: Competitors that have the potential to significantly impact your market position or growth

2. **Competition**: Direct rivals offering similar products or services targeting similar audiences

3. **Co-Existence**: Businesses that operate in the same space but don't necessarily interfere with each other's operations or customer base

4. **Collaboration**: Competitors that could be potential partners, pooling resources or capabilities for mutual benefit

5. **Irrelevance**: Entities that, despite existing in the same market, don't influence your business strategy or outcomes

The Competition Analysis Canvas is an invaluable tool for Product Managers, facilitating a systematic evaluation of the competitive landscape. By effectively utilizing the canvas, businesses can not only identify their standing in the market but also uncover opportunities for growth, collaboration, and differentiation.

3.3 Example Scenario

Scenario 10: The Product Manager of MsgMsg App has been tasked with a comparative study against the popular Messenger App by Facebook.

Using the Competition Study Canvas, the Product Manager arrives at the following study of the Messenger App:

1. Strength

Vast User Base: Messenger App benefits from Facebook's immense user base, making it one of the most widely used messaging platforms worldwide.

Integration with Facebook: Direct tie-in with Facebook profiles eases user onboarding and facilitates seamless communication.

Feature-Rich: Offers video calls, group chats, stickers, payment options, and more.

2. Weakness

Privacy Concerns: Facebook has faced criticism over user privacy and data handling.

Bloat: Over time, Messenger has incorporated many features, which some users find overwhelming or unnecessary.

3. Objectives

Maintain User Base: Retain and grow the current user base by continuously adding value.

Monetization: Introduce features that contribute to Facebook's revenue, e.g., advertisements, chatbots for businesses, or payment options.

4. Markets

Global Reach: Messenger targets users worldwide with particular strength in regions where Facebook is dominant.

Demographics: While Messenger caters to a broad demographic, younger users are gravitating towards newer platforms.

5. Market Share

With billions of users, Messenger has a significant share in the messaging app market, particularly in regions where WhatsApp (also owned by Facebook) isn't dominant.

6. Marketing Strategy

Cross-Promotion: Leveraging Facebook's platform to promote Messenger.

Feature Highlights: Promotional campaigns to highlight new or unique features.

7. Response to MsgMsg App

Feature Adoption: Messenger could potentially incorporate AI-driven messaging enhancements if they see traction with MsgMsg App.

Promotion: Increase marketing efforts or campaigns emphasizing their strengths against newer entrants like MsgMsg App.

8. Competition Plans

Feature Expansion: Continuous introduction of features to keep users engaged.

Business Integration: Further integration with business tools, e-commerce, or other platforms.

9. Financials

Funded by Facebook: Messenger, being a part of the Facebook ecosystem, benefits from Facebook's substantial financial resources and revenues.

Classification for Messenger App:

Threat: Given Messenger's massive user base and the financial backing of Facebook, it poses a significant threat to MsgMsg App. While the AI-driven features of MsgMsg App offer differentiation, the sheer scale and reach of Messenger make it a formidable competitor.

4. SWOT Analysis

One competition analysis tool at a Product Manager's disposal is the SWOT analysis. This strategic framework—examining strengths, weaknesses, opportunities, and threats provides a structured approach to dissecting a competitor's product, revealing insights that can drive informed decision-making and strategic planning.

SWOT analysis has its origins in strategic planning and business management. It was pioneered by Albert S. Humphrey in the 1960s at the Stanford Research Institute (now SRI International).

Interestingly, the concept of SWOT was influenced by an earlier framework known as SOFT analysis,[1] which focused on what is "satisfactory" in present operations, "opportunities" in future operations, "faults" in present operations, and "threats" to future operations. The SWOT analysis realigned the four criteria as internal (strengths and weaknesses) and external (opportunities and threats).

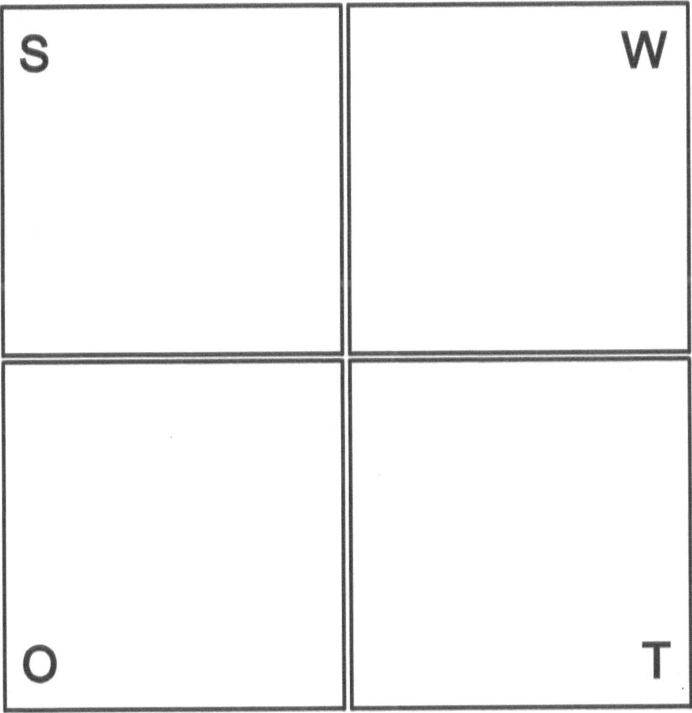

Fig 10: SWOT Template

Strengths

A key objective of SWOT analysis for Product Managers is to identify the strengths of competitors' products, helping them understand what sets these products apart in the market. For example, in the smartphone industry, a Product Manager might analyze a rival's latest flagship device.

Through SWOT analysis, a Product Manager could uncover that the competitor's product has exceptional camera quality, a high-resolution display, and positive brand reputation. Armed with this information, the Product Manager can adjust their product strategy, such as enhancing camera technology or refining marketing messaging to address these competitive strengths.

Weaknesses

For Product Managers, identifying the weaknesses of a competitor's product is crucial, as these shortcomings present opportunities for their product to excel.

For instance, in the smartphone industry, a Product Manager might discover that a rival's device has a shorter battery life and a less user-friendly interface. With this insight, they can emphasize their product's longer battery performance and user-centric interface, leveraging the weaknesses in the competitor's offering to highlight their own product's strengths.

Opportunities

The SWOT analysis also illuminates potential opportunities within competitors' product offerings.

For example, if a software company is analyzing a competitor's project management tool, it might uncover that the tool lacks seamless integration with popular collaboration platforms. This could present an opportunity to develop a feature-rich integration, thereby catering to a demand that the competitor is failing to meet.

Threats

Anticipating threats posed by competitors is crucial for formulating effective strategies.

For example, a fitness tech company evaluating a competitor's wearable device might discover that the competitor's product is gaining traction due to its affordability and sleek design. This realization alerts the company to the potential threat of losing customers who prioritize aesthetics and affordability. Consequently, the company can pivot its marketing to highlight the advanced health-tracking capabilities and premium design of its product.

Example Scenario

Scenario 11: You are the Product Manager at Timingila Media, a Conspiracy Theory Debunking Video Streaming Service. You have been asked to suggest a few strategic moves based on the following SWOT analysis of a competing product.

Analysis of Competitor's Service:

Strengths:

- Expert Credibility: The service is backed by renowned experts and credible sources in various fields, lending credibility to the debunking content.

- Comprehensive Library: A vast collection of well-researched videos addressing a wide range of conspiracy theories.

- User-Friendly Interface: Intuitive navigation and search features make it easy for users to find and access content.

- Educational Value: The service provides an educational platform that promotes critical thinking and evidence-based analysis.

Weaknesses:

- Niche Audience: The service may attract a limited audience segment interested in debunking conspiracy theories, potentially restricting growth.

- Controversial Content: Addressing controversial topics could lead to backlash from conspiracy theorists and misinformation proponents.

- Resource Intensive: Thoroughly researching and debunking each theory requires significant time, effort, and research.

- Potential Biases: There could be perceptions of bias in content production, affecting trust among some users.

Opportunities:

- Educational Partnerships: Collaborate with schools, universities, and educational platforms to promote critical thinking and media literacy.

- Interactive Features: Implement forums or live Q&A sessions with experts to engage users and address their concerns.

- Cross-Platform Integration: Extend content to podcasts, articles, and social media platforms for broader reach and engagement.

- Localized Content: Address conspiracy theories specific to certain regions or cultures, expanding the service's appeal.

Threats:

- Misinformation Proliferation: As conspiracy theories continue to spread online, the debunking service may struggle to keep up.

- Platform Credibility Challenges: Maintaining a reputation for unbiased analysis and credible sources is crucial; any breach could lead to a loss of trust.

- Potential for Legal Threats: Some theories and their proponents may resort to legal action or public campaigns against debunking efforts.

- Competition from Counter-Narratives: Misinformation sources could create their content to counter debunking efforts.

Recommendations

Based on the analysis the Product Manager made the following recommendations:

- Collaborate with schools, universities, and online educational platforms to integrate your debunking content into educational curricula.

- Extend your content beyond video streaming by creating related podcasts, articles, and infographics. By providing information in various formats, you cater to different learning preferences and tap into audiences that may not be as inclined to watch video content.

- Address the threat of misinformation proliferation by ensuring your content is thoroughly researched, well-sourced, and consistently updated.

- Optimize your platform's content for local SEO to capture audiences searching for conspiracy theories specific to their region. Tailored marketing campaigns that address the most prevalent theories in various areas can attract localized attention and boost user engagement.

It should be noted that SWOT analysis can be done on one's own products too.

5. Product Comparison Rubric

The Product Comparison Rubric enables you to juxtapose your product's capabilities against the competition. This rubric provides invaluable guidance, highlighting the most impactful functions, and enabling an optimized prioritization based on assessment results. Designed as a visually intuitive tool, this framework is a boon for Product Managers striving to gauge the standing of their products vis-à-vis the alternatives available in the market. The methodology leans heavily on a metrics-driven rubric approach, ensuring a structured and objective evaluation.

5.1 Implementation Process

1. **List Criterias**: Start by defining the comparison criteria. This includes a list of important capabilities of both the product being considered and its competitors. Make sure to consider these capabilities from the perspectives of both the end user and the organization.

2. **Prioritize Criterias**: Identify the essential criteria that are relevant for making informed decisions. Keep in mind that not all factors may be relevant to the comparison.

3. **Assign Weights**: Attribute importance to each criterion by assigning appropriate weights. This could range from a basic High, Medium, or Low classification to a more granular scale, perhaps from 0 to 5.

4. **Compute Score**: Compute products' score for each criterion. This could either be a binary score, reflecting the presence or absence of a feature, or a graded assessment such as High, Medium, or Low, which factors in the extent of implementation, functionality, or user-friendliness of a given feature.

5.2 Building the Rubric

Assign Value Score

Assign a value to each criterion based on its contribution towards the anticipated outcomes for the product. Commonly, these values are categorized as High, Medium, and Low, which correspond to numerical values of say 5, 3, and 1 respectively.

Criteria	Value	Product	Competitor A	Competitor B
A	High (5)			
B	Medium (3)			
C	Medium (3)			
D	Low (1)			
E	High (5)			

Table 9: Assigning Numeric Score to Value to Facilitate Calculation

Giving Feature a Score

At times, the comparison may hinge on whether a specific feature is present. In such cases, for each product, determine the presence of that feature. If it's implemented, assign a score of 5; if absent, a score of 0 is given.

In other scenarios, the comparison might focus on the usability or richness of a feature (like High Usability, Medium Usability, and Low Usability).

Many times a capability is implemented in its minimum form. Such capability may have low usability as they cover specific use cases or are cumbersome to use. On the other hand, another product team may have spent more time understanding, solutioning, and implementing a capability in a way that solves more problems and is very user-friendly. Such capability would have high usability.

Here, evaluate each product based on the effectiveness of the feature in delivering value to the end user. Typically, values of High, Medium, and Low are assigned with corresponding scores of say 5, 3, and 1.

Criteria	Value	Product	Competitor A	Competitor B
A	High (5)	Implemented (5)	Not Implemented (0)	Implemented (5)
B	Medium (3)	High Usability (5)	Low Usability (1)	Medium Usability (3)

Criteria	Value	Product	Competitor A	Competitor B
C	Medium (3)	Medium Usability (3)	Medium Usability (3)	High Usability (5)
D	Low (1)	Low Usability (1)	High Usability (5)	Low Usability (1)
E	High (5)	Not Implemented (0)	Implemented (5)	Implemented (5)

Table 10: Scoring Product and its Competitors Based on Usability

Generally, the aforementioned methods are employed distinctly. However, there are occasions when they might be combined. This integration doesn't compromise the integrity of the model, as it is adaptable. As long as the assigned scores are consistent and comparable (as demonstrated with scores ranging from 0 to 5 in the examples), the model remains robust.

Finding Product Score

To ascertain a product's score for a particular feature, multiply the criterion value by the weight that reflects its importance. Summing up these weighted values yields an overall score for the product.

Criteria	Value	Product	Competitor A	Competitor B
A	High (5)	5*5	5*0	5*5
B	Medium (3)	3*5	3*1	3*3
C	Medium (3)	3*3	3*3	3*5
D	Low (1)	1*1	1*5	1*1
E	High (5)	5*0	5*5	5*5

Table 11: Multiplying Score and Weightage for Value

Criteria	Value	Product	Competitor A	Competitor B
A	High (5)	25	0	25
B	Medium (3)	15	3	9
C	Medium (3)	9	9	15

Criteria	Value	Product	Competitor A	Competitor B
D	Low (1)	1	5	1
E	High (5)	0	25	25
		50	42	75

Table 12: Arriving at Cumulative Score

Interpreting Cumulative Score

A product with the highest cumulative score is deemed optimal for the intended purpose. Product Managers can then scrutinize this top-scoring product, assimilating best practices embedded within it to refine their product offerings.

5.3 Example Scenario

Scenario 12: The Product Manager of MsgMsg App is tasked with comparing it with WhatsApp and Messenger. The Product Manager used the Product Comparison Rubric and here is the analysis.

Criteria	MsgMsg App	WhatsApp	Facebook's Messenger
Platform	iOS, Android (3)	iOS, Android, Web, Desktop (5)	iOS, Android, Web (5)
USP	AI-driven messaging (5)	End-to-end encryption (3)	Integration with Facebook & Games (3)
Real-time Message Suggestions	Yes (AI-powered) (5)	No (0)	No (0)
Instant Language Translation	Yes (5)	No (requires third-party integration) (0)	Limited (mostly via third-party bots) (0)
Tailored User Experience	Yes (based on communication patterns) (5)	Limited (mostly user settings) (3)	Limited (mostly user settings) (3)
Enhanced Clarity in Communication	Yes (AI suggestions & translations) (5)	No (standard messaging) (0)	No (standard messaging with stickers) (0)
Security/Privacy	Data privacy paramount (5)	End-to-end encryption (5)	Conversations are encrypted (5)
Customer Support	Online tutorials, chat support (3)	FAQ, Email support (3)	FAQ, Email support (3)
AI-Powered Features	Yes (core feature) (5)	No (0)	No (0)
Regulatory & Compliance	Data privacy, international regulations (5)	Data privacy, international regulations (5)	Data privacy, international regulations (5)

Table 13: Product Comparison

After the analysis, the Product Manager readies the rubric for numerical analysis. Here is the numeric analysis and cumulative score:

Criteria	MsgMsg App	WhatsApp	Facebook's Messenger
Platform (3)	3*3	3*5	3*5
USP (4)	4*5	4*3	4*3
Real-time Message Suggestions (5)	5*5	5*0	5*0
Instant Language Translation (5)	5*5	5*0	5*0
Tailored User Experience (5)	5*5	5*3	5*3
Enhanced Clarity in Communication (5)	5*5	5*0	5*0
Security/Privacy (3)	3*5	3*5	3*5
Customer Support (3)	3*3	3*3	3*3
AI-Powered Features (5)	5*5	5*0	5*0
Regulatory & Compliance (3)	3*5	3*5	3*5
	193	81	81

Table 14: Product Comparison Rubric

The Product Manager concludes that with AI and translation features in place, MsgMsg App is well placed ahead of WhatsApp and Messenger for the intended user base.

6

Market Segmentation

Market segmentation is a marketing term that refers to aggregating prospective buyers into groups or segments with common needs and who respond similarly to a marketing action.[1]

Segmentation is essentially the identification of subsets of buyers within a market who share similar needs and demonstrate similar buyer behavior. Segmentation allows a Product Manager to identify the subset that will benefit from their product most, enough to pay what the product is priced at.

Market segmentation also enables the identification of potential opportunities in the market, illuminates unaddressed customer needs, and helps fine-tune both short-term and long-term product strategies.

Let us delve into various ways the market is segmented.

1. Demographic Segmentation

This is perhaps the most common form of market segmentation, where the market is divided into groups based on parameters, such as age, gender, income, occupation, etc.

Example Scenario

Scenario 13: A B2C software company that specializes in personal finance and budgeting apps.

The company wants to launch a new version of its software and employs demographic segmentation to identify the most lucrative customer segments.

Segmentation Variables:

- Age Groups: 18-24, 25-34, 35-44, 45-54, 55+
- Gender: Male, Female, Non-binary

- Income Levels: Low, Middle, High
- Life Stage: Students, Young Professionals, Parents, Retirees

Findings:

- The 18-24 age group, mainly consisting of students and young adults, is interested in budgeting for daily expenses and student loans.

- The 25-34 age group, mostly young professionals and new parents, focuses on saving for short-term goals like vacations and down payments for homes.

- The 45-54 age group, who are generally more established in their careers and may have older children, is interested in investment tracking and retirement planning.

- Among the surveyed, men in the high-income bracket showed interest in investment features, whereas women in the same bracket are more interested in budgeting and expense tracking.

Product Strategy:

Based on the findings, the Product Manager decided to:

- Create a "Student Edition" of the software that offers features like student loan tracking and daily expense budgeting.

- Launch a "Family Edition" geared towards parents in the 25-34 and 35-44 age groups, focusing on features like joint budgeting and short-term savings goals.

- Develop a "Retirement Planning" module targeting the 45-54 age group, featuring investment tracking and retirement calculators.

- Consider gender-specific marketing for high-income brackets, emphasizing investment features for men and budgeting tools for women.

2. Firmographic Segmentation

Similar to demographic segmentation, firmographic focuses on organizations rather than individuals. Criteria for segmentation might include an organization's number of employees, number of customers, number of offices, or annual revenue.

Example Scenario

> **Scenario 14**: A B2B software company that develops Customer Relationship Management (CRM) solutions.
>
> The company wants to expand its market reach and improve its existing product offerings. To do so, it employs firmographic segmentation to identify key customer groups.
>
> **Segmentation Variables:**
>
> - Industry: Technology, Healthcare, Manufacturing, Retail
> - Company Size: Small (1-50 employees), Medium (51-200 employees), Large (200+ employees)
> - Annual Revenue: Less than $1M, $1M-$10M, Over $10M
> - Geographic Location: North America, Europe, Asia-Pacific
>
> **Findings:**
>
> - Small companies in the technology sector, particularly startups, are looking for cost-effective, easy-to-implement solutions.
> - Healthcare organizations, often medium to large, require CRM software with robust compliance features to meet industry regulations.
> - Large manufacturing companies with over $10M in revenue are interested in CRM software that can integrate with their existing enterprise resource planning (ERP) systems.
> - European companies show a preference for CRM solutions that offer multilingual support.

Product Strategy:

Based on these findings, the Product Manager decided to:

- Create a "Startup Edition" of the CRM, focusing on affordability and ease of use, targeting small technology companies.

- Introduce a "Compliance Edition" of the software, incorporating features that help healthcare organizations meet industry-specific regulations.

- Develop an "Enterprise Edition" for large manufacturing companies, focusing on advanced integration capabilities with ERP systems.

- Offer a "Global Edition" with multilingual support to target European and other international markets.

---

3. Geographic Segmentation

This type of segmentation divides the market based on geographical boundaries. This could be region, country, state, or even neighborhood.

Example Scenario

Scenario 15: A B2C software company that develops a weather forecasting application.

The company wants to enhance its user base and has decided to employ geographic segmentation to better understand how location-specific needs affect usage patterns.

Segmentation Variables:

- Regions: North America, Europe, Asia, Africa, South America, Australia

- Climate Zones: Tropical, Dry, Temperate, Cold

- Urban vs Rural: Metropolitan areas, Suburbs, Rural areas

Findings:

- Users in North America and Europe, particularly in temperate and cold zones, show interest in features that forecast snow and winter storms.

- Users in tropical regions like parts of Asia and Africa are more interested in monsoon and hurricane forecasts.

- Metropolitan users are keen on real-time weather updates and air quality forecasts.

- Users in rural areas prioritize agricultural weather forecasts like rainfall and temperature, which impact farming activities.

Product Strategy:

Based on the findings, the Product Manager decided to:

- Develop a "Winter Edition" featuring snow and winter storm forecasts for users in temperate and cold zones.

- Create a "Tropical Edition" focusing on monsoon and hurricane tracking for users in tropical regions.

- Introduce real-time updates and air quality forecasts as features for metropolitan users.

- Include agricultural weather forecasts for rural users, helping them with farming decisions.

---

4. Psychographic Segmentation

This type divides the market based on social class, lifestyle, or personality characteristics. It focuses on the intrinsic traits that your target customer possesses.

Example Scenario

Scenario 16: A FinTech company that offers a mobile app for personal investment.

The app offers various features like stock trading, cryptocurrency investment, and retirement planning. The company decides to use psychographic segmentation to understand its users' attitudes, lifestyles, and behaviors better.

Segmentation Variables:

- Risk Tolerance: Conservative, Moderate, Aggressive
- Financial Goals: Retirement, Wealth Accumulation, Daily Expense Management
- Lifestyle: Tech-savvy, Traditional, Eco-conscious
- Values: Financial Independence, Social Responsibility, Asset Diversification

Findings:

- Users with a conservative risk tolerance are more interested in features like fixed-income investments and retirement planning.
- Tech-savvy users are enthusiastic about cryptocurrency investment and high-tech analytical tools.
- Users who value social responsibility are keen on sustainable investing options.
- Users interested in wealth accumulation exhibit a moderate to aggressive risk tolerance and are attracted to features that offer quick returns, like day trading.

Product Strategy:

Based on these findings, the Product Manager decided to:

- Develop a "Retirement Planning" feature with low-risk investment options to cater to conservative investors.
- Introduce advanced analytics and real-time data features for tech-savvy users interested in trading.
- Create a "Sustainable Investing" portfolio that includes ESG (Environmental, Social, and Governance) compliant options for signatory investors.
- Roll out a "Day Trading" feature with quick buy and sell options aimed at users with wealth accumulation as their primary financial goal.

5. Behavioral Segmentation

This type divides the consumers into groups based on their knowledge, attitude, usage, or response to a product. It could be as simple as separating regular customers from occasional buyers.

Example Scenario

Scenario 17: A company that offers a social media management platform designed to help businesses and individuals schedule posts, track social media engagement, and analyze results.

The company wants to understand its users' behaviors and patterns to refine its product and marketing strategies. To do so, it employs behavioral segmentation.

Segmentation Variables:

- Usage Rate: Heavy users, Moderate users, Occasional users

- User Loyalty: Loyal users, Switchers, New users

- Feature Adoption: Users who utilize all features, Users who use only basic features, Users who use specialized features

- Buying Behavior: One-time purchasers (of premium features), Subscription-based users, Free trial users

Findings:

- Heavy users are mostly businesses that are looking for advanced analytics and reporting features.

- Occasional users are often individual content creators who are primarily interested in basic scheduling capabilities.

- Loyal users value reliability and customer service and are more likely to recommend the product to others.

- Users who opt for one-time purchases prefer to buy specialized features a la carte, rather than commit to a monthly subscription.

Product Strategy:

Based on these findings, the Product Manager decided to:

- Develop an "Enterprise Edition" tailored for heavy users, offering advanced analytics, reporting capabilities, and API integrations.

- Introduce a "Lite Version" focusing on ease-of-use and basic scheduling features, targeting occasional users and individual content creators.

- Roll out a loyalty program with benefits like early access to new features or customer support priority to reward loyal users.

- Offer more flexible pricing options, including a la carte feature purchases, to accommodate users who prefer one-time buying.

---

6. Needs-based Segmentation

This approach segments the market based on the various needs that the product or service satisfies.

Example Scenario

Scenario 18: A company that develops project management software to help organizations streamline workflows, manage tasks, and improve productivity.

Recognizing that different organizations have varying needs, the company decided to use needs-based segmentation to tailor its offerings more precisely.

Segmentation Variables:

- Collaboration Needs: Organizations requiring extensive team collaboration features.

- **Scalability Needs:** Organizations looking for a solution that can grow with them.

- **Customization Needs:** Organizations desiring a high level of customization to adapt the software to their specific workflows.

- **Compliance Needs:** Organizations in highly regulated industries that require stringent data security and compliance features.

Findings:

- Small creative agencies often have high collaboration needs for real-time communication and file-sharing but require less emphasis on scalability.

- Startups with rapid growth trajectories prioritize scalability, so the software can expand along with their team size.

- Manufacturing or logistics companies may have unique workflows and thus a high need for customization features.

- Financial or healthcare organizations often prioritize compliance features due to regulatory requirements.

Product Strategy:

Based on these insights, the Product Manager decided to:

- Create a "Collaboration Suite" offering extensive team communication and file-sharing options.

- Roll out a "Scalable Edition" featuring easy team onboarding and flexible pricing tiers based on company size.

- Develop a "Custom Edition" that allows a higher level of customization in task management and workflow setup.

- Offer a "Compliance Edition" focused on stringent data security protocols and features that help meet industry-specific compliance regulations.

Customer Segmentation

The terms "Market Segmentation" and "Customer Segmentation" are often used interchangeably, but they refer to slightly different processes, each with its specific focus and application.

Customer segmentation is narrower and usually focuses on dividing an organization's existing customer base into specific groups.

This is generally used for optimizing customer service, tailoring marketing efforts, and increasing sales by better understanding who the current customers are. Customer segmentation is used to create a more personalized experience, thereby increasing retention, loyalty, and, ultimately, profitability.

In addition to the factors used in market segmentation, customer segmentation often uses data like purchasing history, customer lifetime value, and customer engagement metrics.

Here are key segmentation types.

1. Value-Based Segmentation

This approach looks at customers based on the economic value they bring to the business. It can consider lifetime value, revenue generated, potential for upsell, etc.

Example Scenario

> **Scenario 19**: A company that offers a B2C video editing software suite, with features ranging from basic video trimming to advanced effects and color grading.
>
> The company wants to maximize its revenues and customer lifetime value by targeting users more effectively. To do so, it decides to employ value-based customer segmentation.

Segmentation Variables:

- High-Value Customers: These are users who have purchased the most expensive subscription plan and regularly invest in additional in-app purchases for advanced features.

- Medium-Value Customers: These users have opted for a mid-tier subscription plan but seldom make additional in-app purchases.

- Low-Value Customers: These users stick with the basic, free version of the software and have not made any in-app purchases.

Findings:

- High-value customers often seek professional-level editing capabilities and usually have needs like 4K editing, color grading, and advanced audio editing.

- Medium-value customers are mostly serious hobbyists who appreciate good editing tools but don't require extremely advanced features.

- Low-value customers are usually beginners, using the software for simple tasks like cutting and joining video clips.

Product Strategy:

Based on these findings, the Product Manager decided to:

- Develop and offer exclusive, advanced features like AI-powered editing tools and plugin support for high-value customers.

- Introduce intermediate features such as basic color correction and audio enhancements for medium-value customers, making these available as in-app purchases.

- Improve the user interface and onboarding tutorials for low-value customers to make the software more accessible to convert them to medium- or high-value customers over time.

2. Benefit Segmentation

This divides customers based on the benefits they seek from the product. For example, some customers of a skincare brand may seek anti-aging benefits while others may seek moisturizing.

Example Scenario

Scenario 20: A software company that offers a comprehensive suite of cloud storage solutions.

This suite includes file storage, sharing capabilities, collaboration tools, and advanced security features. The company wants to understand which specific benefits different customer groups are seeking, so it employs benefit segmentation.

Segmentation Variables:

- Security Seekers: Customers who are primarily interested in secure storage and advanced encryption.

- Collaboration Enthusiasts: Customers who use the service mainly for its collaboration tools, like shared folders and real-time editing.

- Accessibility Fans: Customers whose main requirement is easy accessibility across multiple devices.

- Storage Maximizers: Customers looking for the most storage space at the best price.

Findings:

- Security Seekers are often businesses or individuals with sensitive information.

- Collaboration Enthusiasts are usually project teams, remote workers, or educational institutions.

- Accessibility Fans tend to be individuals who switch between various devices, such as tablets, smartphones, and laptops.

- Storage Maximizers are often digital creatives or data-heavy businesses requiring large storage capacities.

Product Strategy:

Based on these findings, the Product Manager decided to:

- Develop a "Secure Vault" feature specifically designed with multiple layers of encryption, targeted at Security Seekers.

- Enhance real-time editing and commenting features to better cater to Collaboration Enthusiasts.

- Improve cross-platform synchronization and easy file retrieval for Accessibility Fans.

- Offer bulk storage options at discounted rates for Storage Maximizers.

---

3. Life-Cycle Segmentation

Also known as Customer Lifecycle Segmentation, this divides customers based on their current phase in the customer life cycle, such as new, returning, loyal, or at-risk of churning.

Example Scenario

Scenario 21: An e-commerce software platform that provides businesses with tools to create their online stores.

This platform offers various services, from website building and hosting to inventory management and payment processing. The company wants to segment its customers based on their stage in the customer lifecycle to deliver more targeted and relevant offers and services. To do this, it employs Customer Lifecycle Segmentation.

Segmentation Variables:

- New Customers: Those who have recently signed up for the platform but have not yet set up a fully functional online store.

- Engaged Customers: Users who have an active online store and regularly update inventory, make sales, or use premium features.

- At-Risk Customers: Users who have shown a decrease in activity, such as reduced inventory updates or lower usage of the software's features.

- Lapsed Customers: Those who have not used the platform for an extended period and may have moved on to another service.

Findings:

- New Customers often require guidance on setting up their online store and understanding the platform's features.

- Engaged Customers are looking for ways to optimize and scale their operations.

- At-risk customers may be facing issues that are preventing them from fully utilizing the platform, such as usability or pricing concerns.

- Lapsed Customers have already churned and may need strong incentives to return.

Product Strategy:

Based on these findings, the Product Manager decided to:

- Implement a robust onboarding process for New Customers, complete with tutorials and customer support availability.

- Develop advanced analytics tools and integrations with other sales channels to cater to Engaged Customers.

- Identify potential pain points and offer solutions through targeted communications or feature updates to retain At-Risk Customers.

- Conduct exit surveys and offer win-back promotions or feature improvements to re-engage Lapsed Customers.

4. Occasional or Seasonal Segmentation

This involves dividing the market based on occasions or seasons when customers are likely to purchase a product or service, such as holidays, weddings, or back-to-school seasons.

Example Scenario

Scenario 22: An e-commerce platform that provides businesses with a customizable storefront, inventory management, and other essential e-commerce tools.

This platform wants to better target its existing and potential users during different seasons or occasions. To do so, it employs Occasional or Seasonal Segmentation.

Segmentation Variables:

- Holiday Businesses: Businesses that see a surge in sales during major holidays like Christmas, Halloween, or Easter.

- Back-to-School Businesses: Stores that specialize in school supplies or children's clothing.

- Summer Seasonal Stores: Businesses that sell seasonal summer items like swimsuits, outdoor furniture, or BBQ equipment.

- Event-Based Stores: Stores that focus on specific occasions such as weddings, birthdays, or anniversaries.

Findings:

- Holiday Shoppers often need features like bulk inventory management and flash sale capabilities.

- Back-to-School Businesses benefit from promotional tools and inventory bundles (e.g., a "school starter kit").

- Summer Seasonal Stores require inventory turnover features and pre-season promotional tools.

- Event-based stores need gift registry features or event countdowns to entice buyers.

Product Strategy:

Based on these findings, the Product Manager might decide to:

- Implement holiday-themed templates and flash sale features targeted at Holiday Businesses.

- Create bundle promotion features and templates aimed at Back-to-School Businesses.

- Roll out pre-season sale functionalities and quick inventory turnover tools for Summer Seasonal Stores.

- Introduce a gift registry feature or event countdown timers for Event-Based Stores.

8

Regulations and Compliance

Regulation and compliance are related concepts but have distinct meanings.

Regulation refers to a set of rules, laws, or policies established by governing bodies or authorities, such as government agencies, industry regulatory bodies, or international organizations. Regulations are designed to govern specific areas or industries, ensuring standards, safety, fairness, and accountability. They provide guidelines and requirements that organizations must follow to operate within a particular jurisdiction or industry.

Compliance, on the other hand, refers to the act of adhering to the regulations and fulfilling the obligations set forth by the governing bodies. It is the process of ensuring that an organization and its activities, processes, products, and services align with the applicable regulations and legal requirements.

1. Importance of Regulations Awareness

As a Product Manager, it's crucial to be aware of various regulations that impact your product's development, launch, and operation.

1. **Compliance:** Regulations ensure that products meet legal requirements and standards. Non-compliance can result in legal consequences, penalties, damage to the organization's reputation, and loss of customer trust. By being aware of regulations, Product Managers can ensure their products are designed, developed, and operated in accordance with applicable laws.

2. **User Privacy and Security:** Regulations often focus on protecting user privacy, data security, and consumer rights. Product Managers need to understand these regulations to implement appropriate measures for data protection, consent management,

secure transactions, and user rights, enhancing user trust and satisfaction.

3. **Market Access:** Different regions and countries have their own regulations and compliance standards. Understanding these regulations enables Product Managers to assess market opportunities, plan product launches, and ensure their products can enter and operate within specific markets. Many governments require adherence to certain regulations to be used in government programs, which often are a big source of revenue for product organizations.

4. **Risk Mitigation:** Regulations help identify and mitigate potential risks associated with product development and deployment. By being aware of regulations, Product Managers can proactively address risks, avoid legal disputes, and prevent potential harm to users or the organization.

2. Discovery of Relevant Regulations

The discovery of regulations applicable to a product is a subject matter of experts. To find out what regulations may be applicable to their products, Product Managers can follow these steps:

1. **Research and Familiarize:** Product Managers should conduct research to understand the regulatory landscape in the target markets. This includes identifying relevant laws, industry-specific regulations, data protection laws, privacy regulations, and product safety standards.

2. **Consult Legal and Compliance Experts:** Seeking advice from legal and compliance professionals who specialize in the respective domains or regions can provide valuable insights into specific regulations applicable to the product. These experts can help interpret and navigate complex legal requirements.

3. **Industry Associations and Government Websites:** Industry associations and government websites often provide resources, guidelines, and updates on regulations. These sources can be

valuable references for Product Managers to stay informed about current and upcoming regulations.

3. Acting on Regulatory Considerations

Once a Product Manager has identified the applicable regulations, they can incorporate this knowledge into the product backlog in the following ways.

1. **Requirements and Features:** Product Managers can ensure that compliance requirements are reflected as specific product requirements and features in the product backlog. This helps the development team understand and prioritize the necessary work to meet regulatory standards.

2. **Timeline and Planning:** Incorporating regulatory compliance tasks into the product backlog helps in estimating the effort, dependencies, and timelines required to achieve compliance milestones. It ensures that compliance-related activities are appropriately prioritized and scheduled.

3. **Risk Assessment:** The knowledge of regulations can aid Product Managers in identifying potential risks and dependencies associated with compliance. They can work with the development team to mitigate risks, allocate resources, and plan for any necessary product modifications or updates.

4. Common Regulations

Here is a list of common regulations across different domains and regions that are affecting a larger share of products. This list, however, is neither exhaustive nor definitive. Also, this list has been provided for general awareness and descriptions should not be considered accurate or complete.

4.1 Information Technology Act, 2000 (IT Act 2000)

The Information Technology (IT) Act[1] is an important legislation in India that governs various aspects of electronic communication, data protection, and cybercrimes. It was enacted in the year 2000 and has undergone several amendments to keep up with the evolving digital landscape.

Here is a brief overview of the IT Act and some features that can help address its requirements.

1. **Coverage of the IT Act:** The IT Act provides a legal framework for electronic governance and regulates electronic transactions, digital signatures, and cybersecurity. It covers a wide range of areas, including data protection, privacy, hacking, cybercrimes, and penalties for offenses related to information technology.

2. **Data Protection and Privacy:** The IT Act addresses the protection of personal and sensitive information and imposes obligations on organizations that collect, store, and process such data. It is crucial for Product Managers to ensure that customer data is handled securely, with proper consent and adherence to data protection principles.

3. **Cybercrimes and Offenses:** The Act defines various cybercrimes such as unauthorized access, hacking, identity theft, cyberbullying, and distribution of obscene content. Product Managers should consider implementing robust security measures to protect customer data from unauthorized access and ensure compliance with the Act.

4. **Liability of Intermediaries:** The IT Act provides certain protections to intermediaries (such as internet service providers, social media platforms, and e-commerce platforms) for content posted by their users. However, these intermediaries must comply with certain due diligence requirements to qualify for such protections.

5. **Digital Signatures and Certificates:** The Act recognizes digital signatures and certificates as legally valid alternatives to physical

signatures. Product Managers should consider integrating digital signature functionality into their products if it involves electronic transactions or document signing.

Representative features a Product Manager may consider addressing the compliance:

1. **Robust Data Protection Measures:** Implement strong encryption, access controls, and data anonymization techniques to protect customer data. Regularly assess and update security protocols to meet evolving threats.

2. **Privacy Settings and Consent Management:** Provide users with granular privacy settings and consent management options to give them control over their personal information.

3. **Secure Authentication Mechanisms:** Implement multi-factor authentication, biometric authentication, or other secure login methods to prevent unauthorized access to user accounts.

4. **Transparent Data Usage Policies:** Clearly communicate to users how their data will be collected, stored, and used. Obtain explicit consent and provide easy-to-understand privacy policies.

5. **Incident Response and Reporting:** Establish an incident response plan to handle data breaches or cyber incidents promptly. Have a mechanism in place to report such incidents to the appropriate authorities as required by the IT Act.

6. **Compliance Audits and Documentation:** Conduct periodic audits to ensure compliance with the IT Act. Maintain comprehensive documentation of data protection and security practices.

It is important to consult legal experts who specialize in IT Act to ensure that your product meets all the regulatory requirements.

4.2 Digital Personal Data Protection Bill, 2023 (DPDP)

The Digital Personal Data Protection Bill, 2023[A] aims to regulate the processing of digital personal data while recognizing individuals' rights to protect their data and the need for lawful data processing. It includes provisions for financial penalties for breaches. The Bill intends to introduce data protection laws with minimal disruption, enhance the Ease of Living and the Ease of Doing Business, and promote India's digital economy and innovation ecosystem.

Scope & Application

The Bill applies to the processing of digital personal data, which includes collection, storage, or any other operation on personal data. It covers Data Fiduciaries, which include persons, companies, and government entities processing data. The Bill also addresses the rights and duties of Data Principals, who are the individuals to whom the data relates.

Key Principles

1. **Consented, Lawful, and Transparent Use:** Personal data should be processed with consent, legally, and transparently.

2. **Purpose Limitation:** Personal data should only be used for the purpose specified at the time of obtaining consent.

3. **Data Minimisation:** Only the necessary amount of personal data should be collected.

4. **Data Accuracy:** Data should be correct and updated.

5. **Storage Limitation:** Data should only be stored for as long as needed.

6. **Reasonable Security Safeguards:** Measures should be in place to protect personal data.

7. **Accountability:** Breaches of the Bill should be adjudicated, and penalties should be imposed for breaches.

8. **Protection of Children's Data:** The Bill requires parental consent for processing children's data and prohibits processing that is detrimental to children's well-being or involves tracking, monitoring, or targeted advertising.

It is important to consult legal experts who specialize in DPDP Bill to ensure that your product meets all the regulatory requirements.

4.3 General Data Protection Regulation (GDPR)

The General Data Protection Regulation (GDPR)[2] is a comprehensive data protection regulation that was implemented by the European Union (EU) to safeguard the privacy and personal data of individuals within the region.

Here is a brief overview of GDPR and some features that can help address its requirements:

1. **Scope and Application:** GDPR applies to organizations that process the personal data of individuals within the EU, regardless of the organization's location. It sets out specific rights for individuals and imposes obligations on organizations handling personal data.

2. **Lawful Basis for Processing:** GDPR requires that organizations have a lawful basis for processing personal data. Product Managers should ensure that they have obtained valid consent from individuals, or that they have another legal basis (such as contractual necessity or legitimate interests) to process personal data.

3. **Individual Rights:** GDPR grants individuals various rights, including the right to access their personal data, request its erasure, rectification, or restriction of processing, and the right to data portability. Product Managers should consider implementing features that enable individuals to exercise these rights easily, such as providing self-service options in the product interface.

4. **Data Minimization and Purpose Limitation:** GDPR emphasizes collecting only the necessary personal data for a specific purpose. Product Managers should ensure that data collection practices are aligned with GDPR principles and that data is not used beyond the defined purposes without obtaining additional consent.

5. **Security and Accountability:** GDPR requires organizations to implement appropriate technical and organizational measures to ensure the security of personal data. Product Managers should

prioritize features that enhance data security, such as encryption, access controls, and regular security audits.

6. **Data Breach Notification:** GDPR mandates that organizations promptly notify the supervisory authority and affected individuals in the event of a data breach that poses a risk to individuals' rights and freedoms. Implementing features that facilitate timely identification and reporting of data breaches is crucial.

Representative features a Product Manager may consider addressing GDPR compliance:

1. **Consent Management:** Develop features that enable explicit consent collection, including the ability for individuals to provide and withdraw consent easily, and mechanisms to record and document consent.

2. **Privacy Settings and Preferences:** Incorporate granular privacy settings within the product, allowing individuals to control the types of data collected, the purposes for which data is used, and the visibility of their information.

3. **Data Access and Portability:** Enable individuals to access and export their personal data stored in the product, allowing them to obtain a copy of their information and facilitate data portability.

4. **Data Retention and Deletion:** Provide features that allow individuals to request the deletion or anonymization of their personal data, ensuring compliance with GDPR's data minimization and retention principles.

5. **Security Measures:** Implement robust security features, such as encryption, access controls, and secure data storage, to protect personal data from unauthorized access or breaches.

6. **Data Protection Impact Assessment (DPIA):** Integrate features that help conduct DPIAs, which assess the potential risks and impact of data processing activities on individuals' privacy, ensuring compliance with GDPR's accountability requirements.

It is important to consult legal experts who specialize in GDPR to ensure that your product meets all the regulatory requirements.

4.4 California Consumer Privacy Act (CCPA)

The California Consumer Privacy Act (CCPA)[3] is a comprehensive privacy law enacted in the state of California, United States. It was designed to enhance consumer privacy rights and provide greater control over personal information for California residents. CCPA grants consumers the right to know what personal information is collected about them by businesses, the right to opt out of the sale of their personal information, and the right to request the deletion of their personal data.

Here is a brief overview of CCPA and some features that can help address its requirements:

1. **Consumer Rights:** CCPA grants consumers the right to access their personal information collected by businesses and the right to know how it is being used. Consumers can also request that their personal information be deleted.

2. **Notice and Transparency:** Businesses are required to inform consumers about the categories of personal information they collect and the purposes for which the information is used. This information must be disclosed in a privacy policy or through other means.

3. **Opt-Out of Sale:** Consumers have the right to opt out of the sale of their personal information to third parties. Businesses must provide a clear and conspicuous link on their website homepage titled "Do Not Sell My Personal Information" to facilitate this opt-out process.

4. **Data Security:** Businesses are required to implement reasonable security measures to protect the personal information they collect from unauthorized access, disclosure, or destruction.

5. **Non-Discrimination:** Businesses cannot discriminate against consumers who exercise their CCPA rights. This means that businesses cannot deny goods or services, charge different prices, or provide a different level of service based on a consumer's exercise of their privacy rights.

Representative features a Product Manager may consider addressing CCPA compliance:

1. **Consent Management:** Implement a robust consent management system to obtain explicit consent from consumers for collecting and using their personal information. This system should allow users to easily provide or withdraw consent and manage their preferences.

2. **Data Access and Deletion:** Provide mechanisms for consumers to access and download their personal data, as well as request deletion of their information. This feature should include an authentication process to verify the identity of the consumer making the request.

3. **Opt-Out Mechanism:** Incorporate an opt-out mechanism that allows consumers to easily and clearly express their preference to not have their personal information sold to third parties. This can be in the form of a dedicated "Do Not Sell My Personal Information" link on the product's website or app.

4. **Privacy Policy Updates:** Ensure that the product's privacy policy is updated to comply with CCPA requirements. It should clearly explain the types of personal information collected, the purposes for which it is used, and how consumers can exercise their privacy rights.

5. **Enhanced Data Security:** Strengthen data security measures to protect consumer information. This includes implementing encryption, access controls, regular data backups, and employee training on privacy and security best practices.

It is important to consult legal experts who specialize in CCPA to ensure that your product meets all the regulatory requirements.

4.5 Payment Card Industry Data Security Standard (PCI-DSS)

The Payment Card Industry Data Security Standard (PCI-DSS)[4] is a set of security standards established by major credit card companies to ensure the secure handling of customer credit card data. It applies to any organization that accepts, processes, stores, or transmits credit card information. Compliance with PCI-DSS is essential for businesses that handle payment card data to protect both their customers and their own reputation.

PCI-DSS provides a comprehensive framework that includes a set of requirements for building and maintaining a secure payment card environment. The standard covers various aspects of data security, including network architecture, data encryption, access controls, vulnerability management, and regular testing. Its primary objectives are to prevent data breaches, protect cardholder information, and ensure the integrity of the payment card system.

Representative features a Product Manager may consider addressing PCI-DSS compliance:

1. **Secure Data Transmission:** Implement secure encryption protocols (such as TLS) to protect the transmission of credit card data between your product and external systems. Use secure channels and protocols to prevent unauthorized interception.

2. **Data Storage Protection:** Employ strong encryption methods to safeguard any stored credit card data. This includes encrypting data at rest, such as in databases or storage systems. Limit access to encrypted data to only authorized personnel.

3. **Access Controls:** Implement robust access controls to ensure that only authorized individuals can access customer credit card data. This includes role-based access control, strong authentication mechanisms (e.g., multi-factor authentication), and monitoring of user activities.

4. **Regular Security Audits and Testing:** Conduct periodic security audits and vulnerability assessments to identify and address potential weaknesses in your product's security infrastructure. Perform penetration testing to simulate real-world attacks and assess your product's resilience.

5. **Compliance Reporting:** Develop reporting capabilities that assist in demonstrating compliance with PCI-DSS requirements. This

may involve generating audit logs, tracking and documenting security incidents, and maintaining records of security measures implemented.

It is important to consult legal experts who specialize in PCI-DSS to ensure that your product meets all the regulatory requirements.

4.6 Health Insurance Portability and Accountability Act (HIPAA)

The Health Insurance Portability and Accountability Act (HIPAA)[5] is a U.S. federal law enacted in 1996 to protect the privacy and security of individuals' health information. HIPAA establishes standards and regulations for the use, disclosure, and safeguarding of Protected Health Information (PHI) by healthcare providers, health plans, and other entities that handle sensitive health data.

HIPAA comprises two main components: the Privacy Rule and the Security Rule.

1. **Privacy Rule:** The Privacy Rule sets forth regulations governing the use and disclosure of PHI. It grants individuals certain rights over their health information and imposes obligations on covered entities to protect that information. It also outlines requirements for obtaining patient consent, providing notice of privacy practices, and ensuring that data is handled securely.

2. **Security Rule:** The Security Rule complements the Privacy Rule by establishing specific safeguards to protect electronic PHI (ePHI). It outlines technical, physical, and administrative measures that covered entities must implement to ensure the confidentiality, integrity, and availability of ePHI. This includes measures such as access controls, encryption, audit controls, and employee training.

Representative features a Product Manager may consider addressing HIPAA compliance for a product relying on customer health data:

1. **Data Encryption:** Implement robust encryption mechanisms to protect the confidentiality of stored and transmitted health data. This includes both data at rest and data in transit.

2. **Access Controls:** Implement strong user authentication and authorization mechanisms to ensure that only authorized individuals can access sensitive health information. Role-based access control and two-factor authentication are recommended.

3. **Audit Trails and Logging:** Implement comprehensive logging and auditing capabilities to track and monitor access to health data. This helps in identifying any unauthorized access attempts or security breaches.

4. **Secure Data Storage and Transmission:** Ensure that customer health data is stored securely on servers that meet HIPAA-compliance standards. Similarly, transmission of data between systems should occur through secure channels (e.g., encrypted connections).

5. **Business Associate Agreements (BAA):** If your product involves sharing health data with third-party service providers, such as cloud storage or analytics platforms, establish Business Associate Agreements that outline their responsibilities to maintain HIPAA compliance.

6. **Privacy Policies and Notices:** Clearly communicate your product's privacy policies and procedures to users, ensuring they are informed about how their health data is handled, used, and disclosed. Provide a notice of privacy practices that complies with HIPAA requirements.

7. **Data Retention and Disposal:** Establish policies and procedures for retaining and securely disposing of health data in accordance with HIPAA guidelines. Ensure that data is properly destroyed or de-identified when it is no longer needed.

It is important to consult legal experts who specialize in HIPPA to ensure that your product meets all the regulatory requirements.

4.7 Children's Online Privacy Protection Act (COPPA)

The Children's Online Privacy Protection Act (COPPA)[6] is a federal law in the United States that aims to protect the privacy and personal information of children under the age of 13. COPPA was enacted in 1998 by the Federal Trade Commission (FTC) and imposes certain requirements on operators of websites, online services, and mobile apps that are directed toward children or knowingly collect personal information from children.

Under COPPA, operators are required to provide notice and obtain verifiable parental consent before collecting, using, or disclosing personal information from children. Personal information includes details like full name, home address, email address, phone number, geolocation data, and persistent identifiers such as cookies or device identifiers. The law also mandates operators to take reasonable measures to ensure the security of the collected information.

Representative features a Product Manager may consider addressing COPPA:

1. **Age verification:** Implement a robust age verification mechanism to ensure that users are above the age of 13 before collecting any personal information. This can include asking for the user's birthdate during the signup process or using third-party age verification services.

2. **Parental consent:** Develop a process for obtaining verifiable parental consent before collecting personal information from children. This could involve sending a consent form to the parent via email or through a postal mail-based process.

3. **Privacy policy:** Create a comprehensive and easily accessible privacy policy that clearly explains how you collect, use, and disclose personal information, particularly regarding children. Make sure it is written in clear and simple language that parents and children can understand.

4. **Parental control tools:** Provide parents with tools and features that allow them to review, edit, or delete their child's personal information. This may include a parent dashboard where they can manage their child's account and permissions.

5. **Secure data storage:** Implement robust security measures to protect the personal information collected from children. This involves encrypting the data, regularly auditing security practices, and ensuring that only authorized personnel have access to the information.

It is important to consult legal experts who specialize in COPPA to ensure that your product meets all the regulatory requirements.

4.8 Common Activities

Whatever the applicable regulations be, there are few activities the Product Manager should initiate to ensure the product meets the regulatory requirements.

1. **Vendor Management:** Evaluate and manage relationships with third-party vendors who process consumer data on behalf of the product. Work with legal teams to put in place contractual agreements to ensure vendors comply with relevant regulatory requirements.

2. **Staff Training & Awareness:** In collaboration with the subject matter experts, educate Product Management teams, Product Design teams, Product Development teams, and Product Operations teams about the requirements, and best practices, and ensure they understand their role in maintaining compliance.

3. **Seek Proper Opinions:** It is important to consult regulations and legal experts who specialize in relevant regulations and laws to ensure that the product meets all the regulatory requirements.

9

Hypothesis, Experiment & MVP

Hypothesis, Experiment, and Minimum Viable Product (MVP) play pivotal roles in the product development lifecycle, especially for Product Managers seeking to create successful products.

Hypotheses turn an idea or opportunity into a clear direction by articulating assumptions about user needs, market dynamics, or product features. They serve as the foundation for experiments, guiding the design of tests to validate or invalidate these assumptions.

MVPs are a manifestation of this hypothesis-experiment cycle, representing the smallest version of a product that can be built to validate the value the hypothesis indicates. They enable Product Managers to test key assumptions with minimal resources, gather early feedback from users on the value the product delivers, and iterate based on real-world usage data.

1. Hypothesis-Driven Product Development

Hypothesis-driven product development is an approach that stems from the scientific method. It emphasizes the creation and validation (or invalidation) of hypotheses in the context of a product idea. By continually testing and refining based on real-world feedback, Product Managers can ensure they're building products that truly resonate with users, ultimately enhancing their chances of success in the market.

1. **Hypothesis Formulation**: Before any feature is built or change is made, a clear hypothesis is formulated. This hypothesis typically takes the form of: "If we [make this change/introduce this feature], then [specific observable outcome] will happen because [reason]."

2. **Minimum Viable Product Definition**: Rather than building a full-featured product from the start, an MVP is developed. This is the simplest subset of the product that allows the team to test

the hypothesis with real users in the real market to confirm that it delivers the promised value.

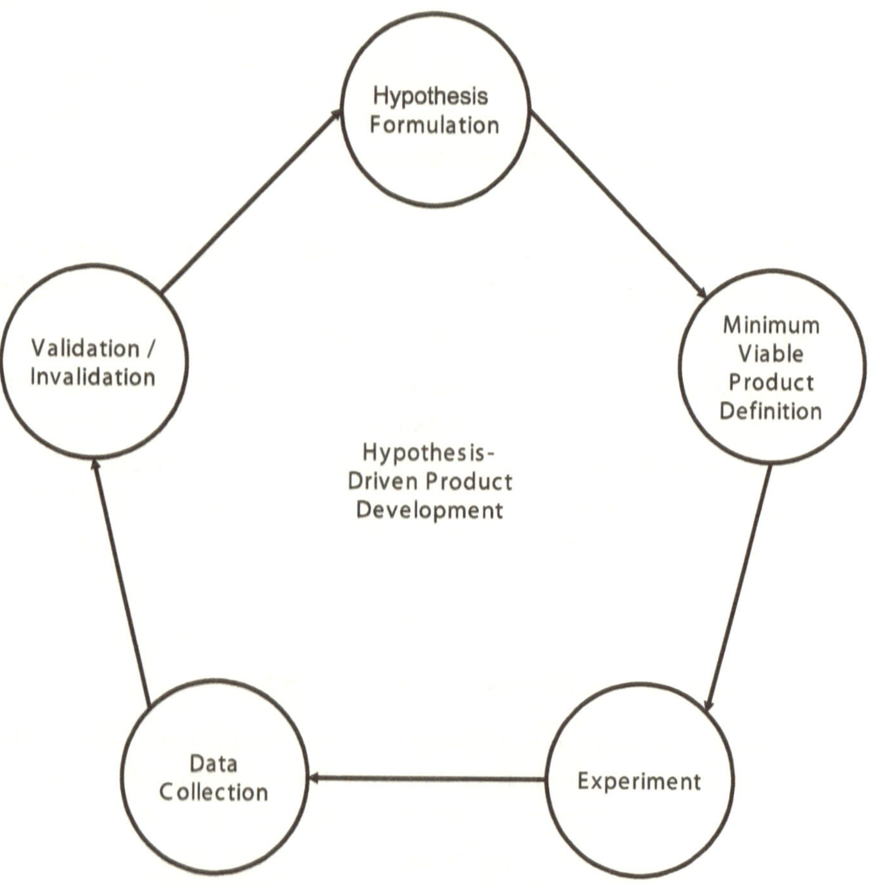

Fig 11: Hypothesis-Driven Product Development

3. **Experimentation**: Once the MVP or a new feature is released, it's observed in a controlled environment or with a segment of users. This could involve A/B testing where one group sees the new feature and another does not, allowing for a comparison between the two groups.

4. **Data Collection**: After deploying the change or feature, data is collected to see if the expected outcomes are being achieved.

5. **Validation/Invalidation**: The results are then analyzed to validate or invalidate the hypothesis. If the results support the hypothesis, the change may be fully implemented. If not, the team returns to the drawing board, often using the insights gained from the failed experiment to formulate a new hypothesis.

Advantages

1. **Risk Reduction**: By testing hypotheses on a smaller scale, companies can avoid the potentially huge costs of building and launching a product that doesn't meet market needs.

2. **Data-Informed Decisions**: Decisions are based on actual data from user interactions rather than solely on intuition or assumptions.

3. **Flexibility**: Products can pivot based on the lessons from testing, allowing for more adaptive and agile development.

4. **Enhanced User Experience**: With continuous feedback from real users, products can be refined and improved to better cater to user needs and preferences.

By continually hypothesizing, testing, and refining based on real-world feedback, Product Managers can ensure they're building products that truly resonate with users, ultimately enhancing their chances of success in the market.

2. Product Hypothesis

In the context of product development, a hypothesis is a clear, testable statement predicting the outcome of a change or introduction of a feature in a product. It acts as an informed guess based on data, user feedback, market research, or the product team's intuition.

Structure of a Product Hypothesis

A typical product hypothesis has three core components:

Action/Change

This refers to the specific alteration or addition proposed for the product. It can be a new feature, design change, or system optimization.

Example: "Introduce a 'one-click checkout' feature..."

Observable Outcome

This is a quantifiable or qualifiable change that is expected as a result of the action or change. It's crucial for this outcome to be measurable, as it will be the primary metric for validating the hypothesis.

Example: "...then our conversion rate will increase by 10%..."

Reasoning

This offers a rationale or justification for the predicted outcome. It might be based on user feedback, market research, trends, competitive analysis, or insights from data.

Example: "...because users have reported that the current checkout process is too lengthy."

Example Scenario

Scenario 23: A Product Manager wants to explore opportunities at the intersection of GenAI and Messaging. To analyze the opportunity, the leadership has tasked the Product Manager to start with a hypothesis to get started. The Product Manager uses the structure above to formulate one.

Action/Change: "If we introduce the MsgMsg App with AI-powered instant translation..."

Observable Outcome: "...then digitally-savvy individuals will reduce the time taken to communicate across language barriers by at least 50%..."

Reasoning: "...because the app eliminates the need for external translation tools or manual translations, offering seamless and accurate translations in real time, making cross-language conversations effortless and more efficient."

---

3. Experiment Canvas

An idea often stems from research, opportunities, threats, or even serendipitous discoveries. As a Product Manager delves deeper into the concept, securing funding becomes essential. Before fully investing, it's crucial to methodically validate the idea through targeted experiments. This ensures that each assumption is tested and its value is proven.

An experiment is a simplified or lo-fi action, sometimes non-technical and at other times technical, designed to validate a core hypothesis. This approach facilitates gradual investment in an idea, guiding it from inception to a valuable, revenue-generating product.

The Experiment Canvas is a lean innovation tool. It allows you to articulate the hypothesis, the experiment, along with success and failure criteria.

3.1 Using the Canvas

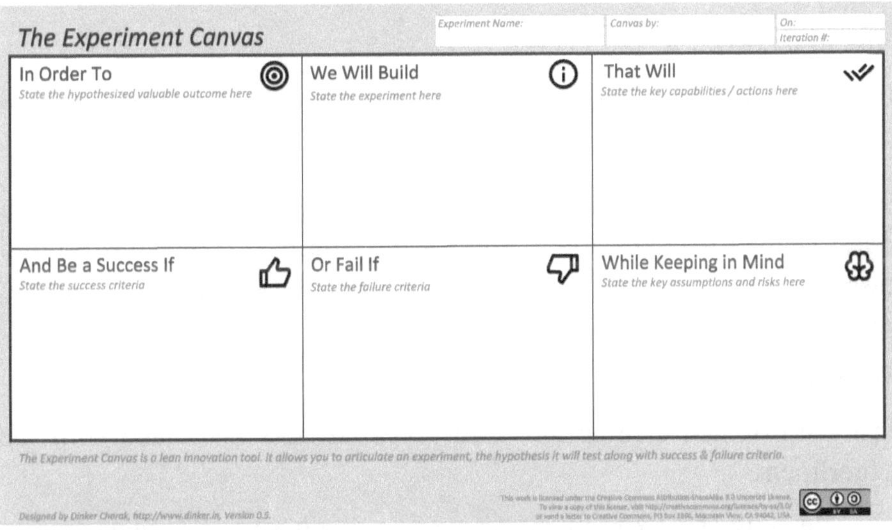

Fig 12: The Experiment Canvas

The various components are:

1. In Order To

2. We Will Build

3. That Will

4. And Be a Success If

5. Or Fail If

3.2 Detailed Overview

Let us look at the various sections of this canvas:

In Order To

State the hypothesized outcome (value) clearly to ensure the hypothesis is well-understood.

We Will Build

Describe the specific experiment to be conducted.

That Will

Outline the key capabilities or actions undertaken as part of the experiment.

And Be a Success If

Define the success criteria to gauge the experiment's effectiveness.

Or Fail If

Specify the failure criteria. Note that not meeting the success criteria doesn't equate to failure. Often, success and failure criteria revolve around distinct metrics. Failing to avoid the failure criteria indicates a need to revisit and re-strategize.

While Keeping in Mind

List the essential assumptions and potential risks associated with the experiment.

Reading the Experiment Canvas as a cohesive statement aids in refinement, so try vocalizing it during the refining process.

3.3 Example Scenario

> **Scenario 24**: A Product Manager is asked to devise an experiment to validate a key capability of the MsgMsg App.
>
> Based on the Elevator Pitch and some research, the Product Manager details an experiment for the MsgMsg App using the Experiment Canvas.

In Order To determine the effectiveness and accuracy of the instant language translation feature in the MsgMsg App,

We Will Build a beta version of the MsgMsg App emphasizing its language translation capabilities,

That Will allow bilingual users to have conversations within the app while switching between multiple languages,

And Be a Success If

1. Users rate the translation accuracy highly

2. The time taken for translations is less than or comparable to leading translation apps

3. MsgMsg App's translation feature shows comparable, if not better, performance against other popular translation platforms

Or Fail If

1. Users consistently rate the translation accuracy as low or mediocre

2. Translation speed is significantly slower than leading competitors

3. The AI translation feature is not the most valued feature

While Keeping in Mind

1. Bilingual users' prior experiences and biases with other translation tools

2. Possible network delays or technical glitches affecting translation speed

3. Subjectivity in users' perception of "accuracy" in translations

Download Experiment Canvas

https://bit.ly/plcu-experiment-canvas

4. Elevator Pitch Canvas

Imagine this scenario: An individual encounters a top-tier executive or perhaps a venture capitalist while sharing an elevator ride to the latter's office. In the brief minute or two, the individual has the chance to articulate an innovative idea, justify its potential, and pique the interest of this influential figure enough to secure funding. Is the individual prepared?

This encapsulates the essence of the elevator pitch: the ability to convey both vision and value within the fleeting duration of an elevator journey.

Yet, the true merit of an elevator pitch isn't just in such serendipitous encounters, which are, after all, quite rare. The genuine value lies in the clarity it brings to founders and their core teams. Crafting an elevator pitch mandates a structured, lucid thought process about the product or service.

4.1 Using the Canvas

For many founders, distilling vast amounts of knowledge, insights, opportunities, and overarching visions into a concise presentation can be daunting. This is where the elevator pitch proves invaluable, serving as a tool to crystallize and communicate the essence of their venture.

The Elevator Pitch Canvas is a lean innovation tool. It allows you to create a brief and easy-to-memorize description of your product and its purpose.

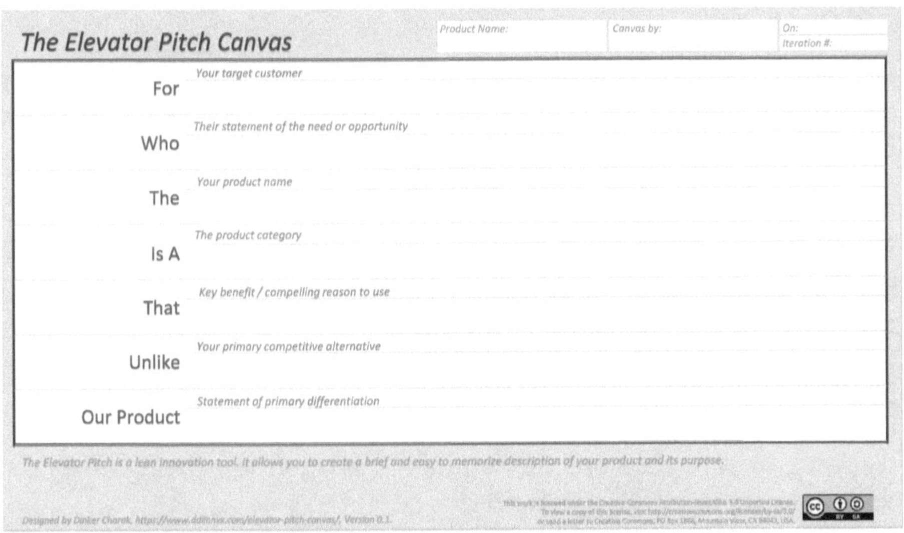

Fig 13: The Elevator Pitch Canvas

4.2 Detailed Overview

The Elevator Pitch Canvas offers a structured approach to distill the essence of a product into a brief, impactful message. Here's a detailed breakdown of its sections:

For (Target Customer)

Identify the primary audience or demographic for the product. This section should specify a distinct and focused customer segment, ensuring that the message resonates most effectively with its intended recipients.

Who (Need or Opportunity)

Articulate the primary need, pain point, or opportunity that the product addresses for the specified target customer. This sets the context by highlighting the problem or gap in the market.

The (Product Name)

Simply state the name of the product, ensuring recognition and recall.

Is A (Product Category)

Define the category to which the product belongs. This provides clarity about the nature or genre of the offering, placing it within a recognizable framework for the listener.

That (Key Benefit)

Emphasize the main capabilities of the product. Instead of an exhaustive list, this section should focus on a singular, standout benefit that aligns with the need or opportunity identified earlier.

Unlike (Primary Competitive Alternative)

List the main competitors or alternative solutions available in the market. By doing so, one positions the product in relation to existing offerings, setting the stage for differentiation.

Our Product (Primary Differentiation)

Elaborate on what sets the product apart from the competition. This is where the primary USP is highlighted, reinforcing the product's unique value proposition and establishing its edge in the market.

By following this canvas, creators can ensure that their elevator pitch is comprehensive, coherent, and compelling, maximizing its impact within a brief interaction.

Ultimately, the Elevator Pitch should sound like a coherent sentence. Reading it aloud while refining helps. Practice, practice, practice, refine your pitch, and deliver it confidently.

4.3 Example Scenario

> **Scenario 25**: Imagine what the Elevator pitch for Google Search would have been?
>
> **For** those with access to the WorldWideWeb **Who** seek specific information on the web, **The** Google Search **Is A** search engine **That** crawls the web and indexes information in a unique way **Unlike** Altavista, Infoseek, Dogpile, Yahoo, Lycos, Looksmart, Excite, Webcrawler, AskJeeves, Inktomi, MSN, Overture and AllTheWeb, **Our Product** uses the number of links to a page (and few other secret tricks) to identify the most relevant result for your search among the first 20 results.

> **Scenario 26**: Given AI-based technology is growing, a founder wants to evaluate an AI-based messaging app. The founder chose to use the Elevator Pitch Canvas to test the idea with a friend.
>
> **For** the digitally-savvy individuals seeking efficient and intelligent communication tools, **Who** value streamlined and predictive messaging, saving time and enhancing clarity in both personal and

> professional interactions, **The** MsgMsg App **Is A** next-generation AI-powered messaging application **That** uses advanced AI algorithms to provide real-time message suggestions, translate languages instantly, and tailor user experiences based on communication patterns **Unlike** traditional messaging apps like Messenger or WhatsApp, **Our Product** harnesses the power of cutting-edge AI, transforming mere message into a predictive, personalized, and productive experience.

5. Hypothetical Press Release

One simple but effective tool for articulating a product's vision, purpose, and success markers is the press release. Often overlooked as a mere announcement, an exercise in creating a well-crafted press release can serve as a beacon, guiding both internal teams and external stakeholders toward a shared understanding of the product's purpose and potential impact.

It is a common practice among many Product Managers to write a hypothetical press release as a vision document as the first step. This approach is considered common among members of Amazon Web Services' team.[1] In fact, this approach of "working backwards" is widely used at Amazon.[2]

We delve deeper into the structure and techniques of writing a press release in the Product Launch chapter.

6. Minimum Viable Product

"Think big, start small" has been a foundational principle of product development, especially after the rise of the Agile movement. The approach emphasizes making deliberate, well-considered incremental steps toward completion. This method promotes continuous learning, enables course corrections based on setbacks, and diminishes the risk of a major failure. Instead, potential mistakes are broken down into smaller, manageable missteps that can be swiftly addressed.

Fig 14: The Squiggle of the Design Process

This journey from an idea to a successful product is never simple and given the small missteps and pivots, the real journey is a complex back-forth-left-right path. This intricate process was astutely depicted by Damien Newman as the "Squiggle of the Design Process."[A]

Identifying the optimal minimum to develop—something that delivers genuine value to the organization, its users, and customers, while also validating the product's utility—is paramount. At this juncture, the concept of the Minimum Viable Product becomes pivotal.

For Product Managers, understanding and effectively implementing the MVP approach can spell the difference between a product's success and its premature decline.

The term "Minimum Viable Product" finds its roots in the lean startup methodology, championed by Eric Ries in his 2011 book The Lean Startup.[2] Ries presented the MVP as a product with just enough features to satisfy early adopters, allowing businesses to gather validated lessons about customers with the least effort. The primary goal of the MVP is not to launch a finalized product but to initiate a feedback loop with users, making it a critical tool in iterative design and product development.

The concept was further refined as "A MVP approach enables you to fail fast and cheaply, while also gathering valuable data from the experiment. As you prove or reject different hypotheses, you build confidence that the problem/solution fit is on the desired path. A Product Manager can then invest more to improve the fidelity of the solution, widen the marketing reach and/or enhancing the solution based on the data gathered — essentially increasing your exposure to risk in a controlled manner."[3]

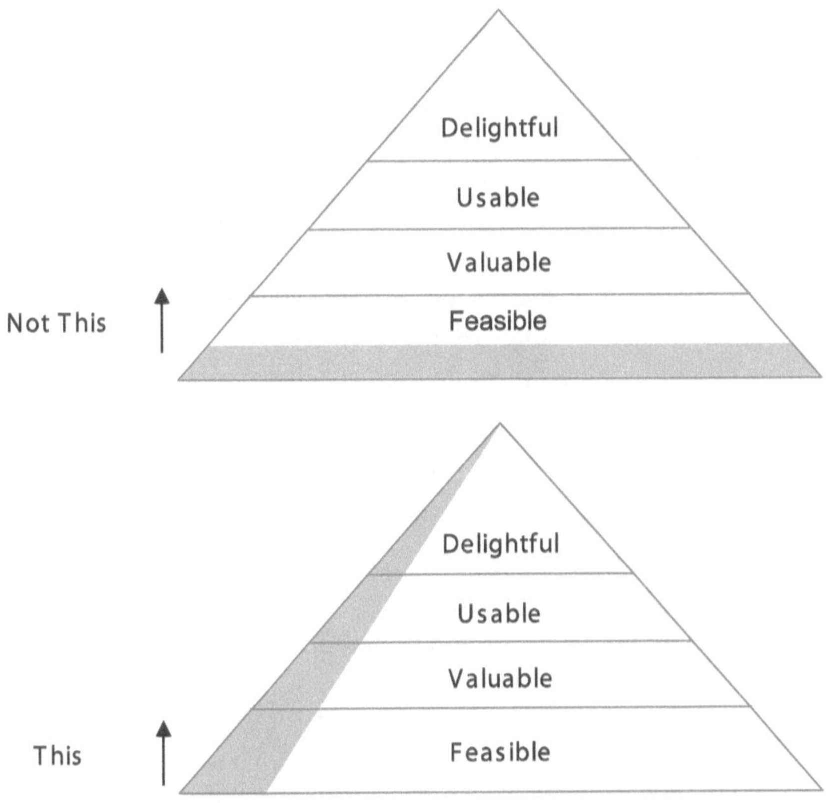

Fig 15: The value MVP should deliver[4]

6.1 Core Principles

1. **Simplicity**: The MVP revolves around the concept of doing more with less. It urges Product Managers to condense their product to its most essential components, shedding any superfluous features that may distract from its core value proposition.

2. **Feedback-Oriented**: By releasing an MVP, Product Managers actively seek feedback from their target audience. This feedback becomes the bedrock for future iterations, guiding the product's direction based on real-world insights rather than assumptions.

3. **Risk Reduction**: Launching an MVP helps in validating hypotheses about the market. By mitigating the risk of investing heavily in a product feature or direction that may not resonate with users, Product Managers can make more informed decisions about where to invest time and resources.

For Product Managers, the MVP approach offers a structured way to navigate the unpredictable waters of product development. It provides a roadmap to:

1. **Prioritize Features**: By focusing on what truly matters for the initial release, Product Managers can ensure they are building a product that meets the core needs of their users.

2. **Accelerate Time-to-Market**: By concentrating on the essential features, teams can release products more quickly, gaining a competitive edge in fast-paced markets.

3. **Build a Customer-Centric Mindset**: MVPs inherently prioritize customer feedback, ensuring that the product evolves in tandem with users' actual needs and preferences.

6.2 Misuse of Term MVP

Minimum Viable Product as a concept is often misunderstood and misused in business circles. It's mistakenly seen as simply the smallest amount of work that can be done, according to a Project Manager's perspective.

The problem with this misunderstanding is that the final product may not actually provide any value to the end user. It might not even be usable at a basic level.

This issue is particularly pronounced in enterprises or famous brands where certain essential features are expected to be included in any product, no matter how minimal, before it's presented to any user, even for a trial.

This situation is aptly captured by the statement: "Everyone loves the concept of MVP, but no one wants to use an MVP."

6.3 MVP For Enterprise Products

When considering enterprise products, the stakes are often much higher due to the necessity for robust InfoSec, stringent compliance standards, minimized failure points, and high reliability. This is in addition to the fact that onboarding cost for an enterprise may remain the same, whether it is an MVP or a full product.

Despite these challenges, Product Managers can adopt several strategies to effectively define an MVP for enterprise scenarios.

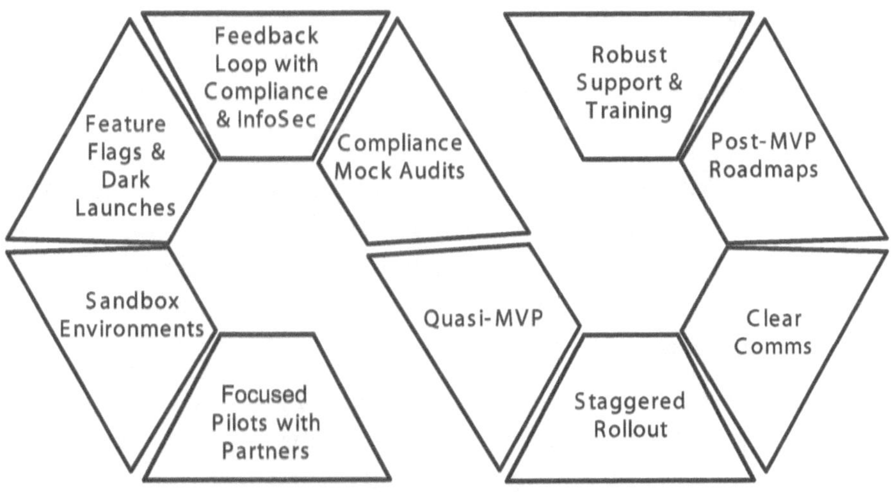

Fig 16: Defining an MVP for Enterprise Scenario

1. **Focused Pilots with Partners**: Engage a select group of trusted enterprise partners in a controlled pilot program. These partners should understand that they're working with an MVP and be willing to provide valuable feedback. Because the environment is controlled and the user group is limited, risks are reduced.

2. **Sandbox Environments**: Create isolated, safe environments where enterprise users can test the MVP without any real-world consequences. This approach keeps the core operational processes of the enterprise unaffected while allowing users to interact with the MVP.

3. **Feature Flags and Dark Launches**: These tools allow specific features or aspects of the MVP to be turned on or off for different users. By providing access to certain features for a select group, Product Managers can gather feedback without disrupting the experience for all users.

4. **Feedback Loops with InfoSec and Compliance Teams**: Involve the enterprise's InfoSec and compliance teams from the outset. Their insights can preemptively address concerns, ensuring that the MVP aligns with the necessary standards.

5. **Compliance Mock Audits**: Before releasing an MVP, conduct a mock compliance audit to identify any potential red flags. While this doesn't replace a full compliance process, it can give a measure of confidence that major requirements are being met.

6. **Quasi-MVPs**: In cases where certain enterprise requirements are non-negotiable (like InfoSec or compliance), develop a quasi-MVP. This MVP would have a fully developed and robust system for the non-negotiable elements, while other features might remain in a more 'minimal' state.

7. **Staggered Rollout**: Begin by introducing the MVP to a small group within the enterprise, allowing for a gradual adjustment period. As feedback is gathered and necessary changes made, the product can be rolled out to larger segments.

8. **Clear Communication**: Ensure that all stakeholders are informed about the nature of the MVP – its objectives, the fact that it's a work in progress, and its expected evolution. Open channels for feedback and create platforms where users can report issues or concerns immediately.

9. **Post-MVP Roadmaps**: Share a clear development roadmap post-MVP launch. Knowing that enhancements and refinements are planned can make stakeholders more receptive to an MVP that might otherwise feel 'incomplete'.

10. **Robust Support and Training**: Given the critical nature of enterprise operations, any MVP should come with comprehensive support and training resources. This not only aids users in navigating potential pain points but also builds trust.

In essence, while the challenges of deploying MVPs in an enterprise setting are real, they're not insurmountable. Through careful planning, transparent communication, and strategic deployment, Product Managers can gather invaluable insights from MVPs without compromising on the enterprise's non-negotiable standards.

6.4 Variations

The concept of the Minimum Viable Product (MVP) has spawned various derivatives to emphasize different aspects of product development and launch. Here are some of them, along with brief descriptions and distinctions:

Minimum Lovable Product (MLP)

MLP emphasizes not just the viability but also the desirability of a product. It's a product version that offers not just the bare minimum to function but also evokes positive emotions from users.

Difference: While MVP aims at minimum functionality to test viability, MLP aims at creating a delightful experience for the users, even in its early stages.

Minimum Marketable Product (MMP)

This is the simplest version of a product that can be sold to customers. It has just enough features to make it marketable and saleable.

Difference: The focus is on what can be sold and marketed effectively rather than just proving viability.

Minimum Feasible Product (MFP)

The MFP focuses on the feasibility of the technological or logistical aspects of a product. It represents the most basic version of a product that proves the feasibility of the core technology or idea.

Difference: While MVP emphasizes testing viability with customers, MFP focuses on internal feasibility (e.g., can this technology work?).

Minimum Usable Product (MUP)

This is a version of a product that has just enough functionality to be usable by users but might not have all the intended features.

Difference: The emphasis here is on usability. An MUP needs to be functional enough for users to achieve their primary goals, even if not all features are present.

Minimum Testable Product (MTP)

An MTP is built specifically for internal testing and might not be ready for external users. It is essentially the earliest version of a product that allows for meaningful testing of its main hypotheses.

Difference: The emphasis is on internal testing rather than customer validation.

Minimum Learnable Product (MLRP)

The MLRP focuses on the product team's learning. It's about creating a version that helps the team gain the most insights and knowledge about users and the market.

Difference: This derivative focuses on maximizing learning for the team rather than primarily addressing market or customer needs.

Minimum Operational Product (MoP):

MoP emphasizes not just the viability for the customers but also the operational efficiency and effectiveness for an enterprise.[5] It starts by understanding various business processes within an enterprise, determining what should be automated, and then applying the MVP approach to those processes. The goal is to create products that deliver value to customers and align with the operational requirements of the business. Key elements include standard operating procedures (SOPs), aligning product milestones with business processes, and facilitating flexibility and responsiveness to evolving business plans.

Difference: While MVP focuses on quickly validating a product concept with minimal functionality from the customer's perspective, MoP adds a layer of enterprise value. MoP seeks to operationalize a product within a business setting, considering both the customer and the enterprise's operational needs.

All of these variations emphasize different purposes of early-stage product development. The appropriate choice often depends on the context, industry, challenges, and goals of the organization. It's also worth noting that while these concepts have distinct focuses, in practice, there can be overlap between them.

6.5 Example Scenario

> **Scenario 27**: The Product Manager has been tasked with formulating an MVP for the MsgMsg App with a Language Translation Feature as a USP.
>
> After due research and applying the MVP thought process, an MVP (Minimum Viable Product) for the MsgMsg App, specifically tailored to validate the language translation feature is proposed.
>
> **Core Functionality**
>
> **Text-based Conversations**: Users should be able to send and receive text messages within the app, similar to any other messaging application.
>
> **Instant Language Translation**: Once a message is received, users should have the option to instantly translate it to their preferred language with a simple tap or button press. Similarly, users should be able to compose messages in their preferred language and then translate them into the recipient's preferred language before sending them.

Language Selection: Users need a simple method to select or change their default language, as well as the language they wish to translate messages into. This could be implemented in user settings or as a quick-access feature within chat windows.

User Interface (UI)

1. Minimalistic, intuitive design focusing on ease of use

2. Clear indication of the original message and translated message for clarity

Visual cues or icons to show successful translations or potential errors

Feedback Mechanism

1. Users should be prompted to rate the accuracy of translations, possibly on a scale from 1-5

2. A quick-access button or link for users to report issues or glitches they encounter

3. An optional short survey or feedback form post-conversation, inquiring about user experience, speed of translations, and areas of improvement

Comparison Tool

For the purpose of the experiment, integrate a feature (perhaps temporary) where users can compare the MsgMsg App translation with another popular translation API (like Google Translate) side-by-side. This will help users evaluate the accuracy and efficiency of MsgMsg App's translation engine relative to established benchmarks.

User Onboarding

1. Quick tutorials or walkthroughs highlighting the translation feature to first-time users

2. Information or tooltips about the experimental nature of the MVP, ensuring users are aware that feedback is vital for improvement

---

Backend & Analytics

1. Real-time monitoring of translation request times to measure speed

2. Tracking of user interactions, especially concerning the translation feature, to collect quantitative data for validation

---

7. Hourglass Model

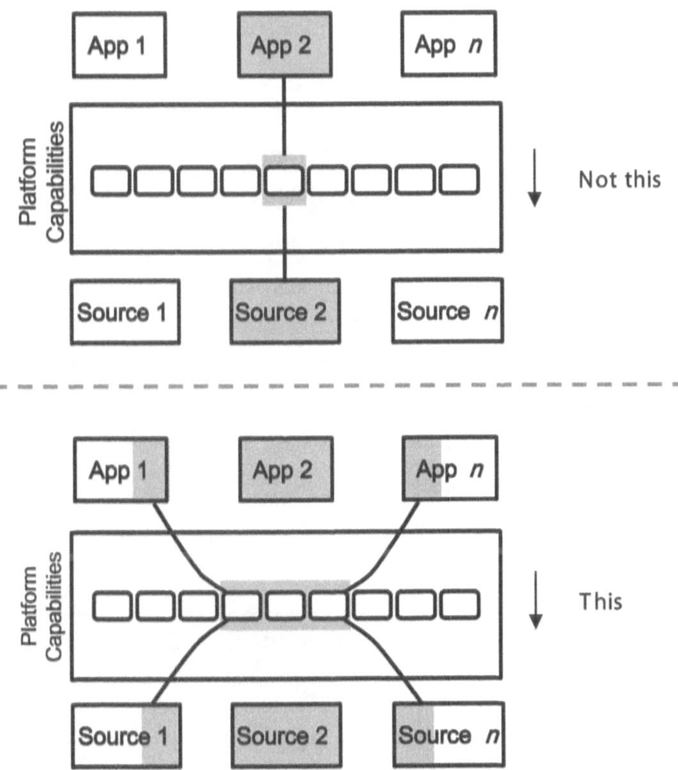

Fig 17: Hourglass Model for Platform MVP [5]

An MVP helps the product team focus on essential business processes to deliver clear, tangible outcomes and value to paying customers. For Platform MVPs, this concept warrants further consideration.

A platform allows data, and control to move across services and systems using channels like desktops, mobile devices, voice interfaces, programmable interfaces, and more while providing processing or value-add.

The Hourglass Model[4] offers a strategic method to define a platform MVP. This entails starting with a broad scope, covering several business processes, then narrowing down to a vital set of capabilities, and finally expanding again to integrate diverse data sources. Just as an hourglass has a broad top, a constricted middle, and a broad base, this approach ensures a comprehensive coverage of business processes, a focused core capability set, and broad data source integration.

When modernizing legacy systems, many opt for the Strangler Approach,[A] emphasizing a thin-vertical slice. However, for platforms, this poses a risk: the new system might mirror the key business process and its data sources too closely, leading to undesirably tight coupling.

For a balanced transition, the Platform Product team should prioritize crafting a minimal set of capabilities. While these should cater to the primary business application, they must also be adaptable enough to be valuable for at least two other business processes. This ensures that stakeholders from these processes engage actively with the platform's Product Manager, allowing the platform's Product Manager to discern and anticipate their evolving needs.

Example Scenario

Scenario 28: A Data Platform is essential, designed to store demographic details of every user.

This platform will cater to the iOS App, Android App, and WebApp, offering functionalities such as user login and the display of their profile picture, nickname, and other personal details. Beyond these applications, the platform will serve other business processes. One such process determines whether a user is a suitable target for cross-selling based on their location and salary. Another process displays to the user their past transactions, presenting opportunities for further purchases. Additionally, the platform facilitates user support.

The primary source for demographic data is the CRM System, where the majority of user details are stored. The comprehensive list of the company's products originates from the Product Master.

Given this context, the Product Manager's objective is to define an MVP for this platform. They decide to use the Hourglass approach.

Step-1: Identification

The Product Manager first identifies the Business Processes and Platform Capabilities and the Data Sources:

1. Business Processes

    a. Login and Display User Profile:

        i. Platforms: iOS App, Android App, WebApp

        ii. Features: Login mechanism, displaying profile picture, nickname, and other user details

    b. Cross-selling Targeting:

        i. Process: Analyze user location and salary to determine cross-selling opportunities

    c. User Product History & Purchasing:

        i. Process: Display products the user has previously bought and offer purchase options for more products

    d. User Support:

        i. Process: Handle user queries, problems, or concerns related to products or their profiles

2. Capabilities for MVP

    a. User Data Management: Ability to store, retrieve, and update user demographic data

    b. Login Mechanism: Secure login integration for the iOS App, Android App, and WebApp

c. Cross-selling Algorithm: Use of location and salary data to identify potential products for cross-selling

d. Product Display: A simple interface to show a user's purchased products and options to buy more

e. Basic Support Ticketing System: A simple mechanism where users can raise queries or issues and get them resolved

3. Data Sources

a. CRM System Integration: Extract user demographic data, including profile pictures, nicknames, location, salary, etc.

b. Product Master Integration: Fetch details of all available products in the company for display and purchasing options

Step-2: Apply Hour-Glass Concept

Applying the concept of the Hour-glass, the Product Manager proposes the following MVP for the Platform:

1. Broader Top (Choose more than one Business Processes)

a. Implement a rudimentary support ticketing system for users to raise concerns or queries

b. Begin with a secure login mechanism integrated across all three platforms (iOS, Android, WebApp) for users to access their data uniformly across all devices

2. Narrow Middle (Minimal Capabilities):

a. Create a basic cross-selling feature using user location and salary. For the MVP, this doesn't need to be highly sophisticated; a simple algorithm can suggest products based on a few criteria

3. Broad Bottom (Decide on needed Data Sources):

    a. Integrate with the CRM system to populate and display essential user profile data (picture, nickname, and other demographics)

    b. Integrate a limited set of products from the Product Master to showcase what users have bought and what they can purchase

10

Business Modeling

Business modeling refers to the process of defining how a product or service will create value for both customers and the organization, and how that value will be captured monetarily. It's the blueprint for how the product fits into the broader business ecosystem and makes financial sense.

1. Product Pricing

Pricing strategies are greatly influenced by the demand for a product or service and are integral to an organization's revenue model. That is why while Product Managers have a great influence on the pricing strategy being adopted, they rarely get to decide on it independently.

The success of any pricing strategy depends on understanding the customer's perception of value, the competitive landscape, and the organization's own cost structure and financial goals. That is why a Product Manager needs to understand cost, margin, and markup.

1. **Cost**: This refers to the expenses incurred from manufacturing, sourcing, or creating the product. It includes materials, labor, supplier fees, and losses, but excludes overhead and operational expenses like marketing and maintenance.

2. **Margin**: Gross margin is the amount your business earns after subtracting manufacturing costs.

3. **Markup**: Markup is the additional amount you charge for your product over the production and manufacturing fees.

1.1 Common Pricing Strategies

1. **Cost-Plus Pricing**: This is the simplest pricing strategy where the selling price is determined by adding a margin (specific amount or percentage) to a product's cost. This ensures that all costs are covered and the business makes a profit. The cost considered tends

to be the operating cost. Operating costs or operating expenses, refer to the costs associated with the day-to-day operations of a business and the cost of development of the product. The aim of this pricing is to recover running costs and have enough margin to invest in growth or research.

Fig 18: Common Pricing Strategies

Illustration 11: Ford Motors and the cheap Model T

In the early 20th century, Ford Motor Company revolutionized the automotive industry by adopting a groundbreaking pricing strategy for its Model T. Instead of basing prices on competitors' rates or market demand, Ford embraced a cost-plus pricing model.

Henry Ford famously said, "I will build a car for the great multitude. It will be large enough for the family, but small enough for the individual to run and care for. It will be constructed of the best materials, by the best men to be hired, after the simplest designs that modern engineering can devise. But it will be so low in price that no man making a good salary will be unable to own one – and enjoy with his family the blessing of hours of pleasure in God's great open spaces."[1]

By prioritizing efficiency and capitalizing on economies of scale, Ford managed to significantly reduce manufacturing costs. This allowed the company to offer the Model T at a price that was within reach of the average American, thus democratizing car ownership and making it accessible to millions of people.

2. **Competitive Pricing**: Pricing is based on the price of competitors' products. This is often used in markets with similar products and can be particularly effective for companies with a clear understanding of their competitors' strategies. The aim of this pricing is to dislodge competition or dominate a market of homogenous products.

3. **Penetration Pricing**: This strategy involves setting a low initial price to attract customers and gain market share quickly. Once a strong customer base is established, prices can be gradually increased. This is very common among startups that often offer their products (or a less capable version) for free.

4. **Skimming Pricing**: Opposite to penetration pricing, skimming involves setting a high initial price to maximize revenue from the early adopters who are less price-sensitive. As the market expands or competition enters, the price can be lowered. Apple is often pointed to as an adopter of this strategy.[2] Another version of this is High-Low pricing where an organization initially sells a product at a high price but lowers that price when the product drops in novelty or relevance.

5. **Value-based Pricing**: This strategy is based on the perceived value of a product or service to the customer rather than the actual cost of production or the market rate. It's often used for unique, innovative products or services with high perceived value. The aim of this pricing is to capitalize on the perceived value and tends to be used when the production cost of the product is not very high. This is not a very common strategy for software products.

6. **Dynamic Pricing**: This strategy involves changing prices based on market demand, time, season, or customer behavior. It's widely used in industries like airline ticketing, hotel room pricing, ride-hailing services, and e-commerce. However, this is not a very common strategy for software products.

7. **Psychological Pricing**: This strategy leverages human psychology to influence purchasing decisions and increase sales. One common technique is known as the "9-digit effect," where prices are set

just below a round number, say at ₹499 instead of ₹500 or $9.99 instead of $10.00. Another tactic is to use pricing strategies that create a sense of urgency or scarcity, such as limited-time offers or "buy one, get one free" deals. These promotions can make customers feel like they are getting a special deal and encourage them to make a purchase.

Illustration 12: Left-digit anchoring

In a Jan 2008 paper authors Manoj Thomas and Vicki Morwitz studied the "psychological mechanisms that underlie consumers' responses to prices."[3]

The judgment and decision-making field identifies three common mental shortcuts, or heuristics, that affect how people make everyday judgments and decisions. These heuristics also play a role in how consumers perceive prices.

1. **Left-digit anchoring effect**: People tend to think the difference between prices like $4.00 and $2.99 is bigger than between $4.01 and $3.00.

2. **Precision effect**: People judge prices based on the number pattern. For example, a price like $391,534 might seem lower than $390,000 because it has more digits, even though it's actually higher.

3. **Ease of computation effect**: People base judgments on how easy or hard it is to calculate. They might think the difference is bigger for easier calculations (like $5.00 - $4.00) than for harder ones (like $4.97 - $3.96).

These heuristics show that price judgments aren't just based on logical thinking but also on instinctive mental shortcuts.

---

8. **Premium Pricing**: This strategy involves setting higher prices for a product than its close competitors. This tactic aims to create the perception among customers that the product is of higher quality and is exclusive, luxurious, or superior in some way. However, it's important to note that premium pricing may not be suitable for every product or market.

Example Scenario

> **Scenario 29:**
>
> **Author's Note** - I employed the concept of value-based pricing for this book. To do this, I distributed a Google Form requesting prospective readers to specify the amount they were comfortable paying for a book on Product Management. No further details were provided at this point.
>
> Subsequently, I presented them with the 'Table of Contents' from this book's draft. In the final stage, I asked them to reconsider the price they would be willing to pay, now with knowledge of the book's contents.
>
> The goal of requesting their willingness to pay for a Product Management book was to establish a base price. This was used for comparison with the price they suggested in the third step. A higher price in the third step would indicate the perceived increased value of the book due to its 'Table of Contents'.
>
> The final pricing strategy incorporates both Value-Based Pricing and Competitive Pricing, creating a blend of customer-perceived value and market considerations.

1.2 Pricing Models

There are several pricing models that are applied to enterprise software products, consumer software products, and mobile apps.

The ideal pricing model depends on the nature of the product, the competitive landscape, and the perceived value by the customer. Here are some common pricing strategies and recommendations for a Product Manager to consider:

Enterprise Software Products

1. **Perpetual Licensing**: This is a traditional model where customers pay a large, upfront fee to use the software indefinitely. This model is best suited for niche software products where customers can extract long-term value. It is effective in a slow-evolving industry where the software is used for years as-is.

2. **Subscription Licensing**: In this model, customers pay a recurring fee to use the software, which includes regular updates and support. This model is useful for businesses that continually update and improve their software. It's beneficial in fostering customer loyalty and providing predictable recurring revenue.

3. **Usage-Based Pricing**: This model ties the pricing to the usage level of the software. It is suitable for software where the value directly correlates with usage, like cloud services, data storage, etc.

4. **Tiered Pricing**: Different pricing tiers are offered, each providing a different level of functionality or usage limits. This model can be effective when serving a diverse customer base with varying needs, budgets and at varying levels of revenue generation.

5. **Bundle Pricing**: Several products or services are packaged together and sold at a lower price than if they were sold separately. This is common for software products.

6. **Price Discrimination**: Different prices are set for different customers or customer segments, based on their willingness to pay, location, purchasing power, etc. This is very rarely used for software products.

Consumer Software Products

1. **Freemium**: This model provides basic features for free, but charges for premium features or services. It's often used in consumer software like productivity apps, music streaming apps, etc. This is a great strategy for gaining user adoption, but it requires a significant percentage of users to convert to the premium version to be profitable.

2. **One-Time Purchase**: This is a model where consumers pay once to download and use the software indefinitely. This model is often used for higher-value apps where consumers are willing to pay upfront, such as professional graphic design tools.

3. **Subscription**: Similar to enterprise software, consumer software can also follow a subscription model. This is increasingly common

for apps that provide ongoing value, like fitness apps, educational platforms, etc.

Mobile Apps

1. **Freemium**: As mentioned, this model offers a free tier and a premium tier. This is particularly effective for gaming apps or productivity apps, where basic usage is free, but additional features or content require payment.

2. **In-App Purchases**: This model provides the app for free but offers additional features, digital goods, or services for purchase within the app. This works well for gaming apps or apps that offer optional enhancements or add-ons.

3. **Subscription**: Subscription models are also used for mobile apps that provide ongoing services or content. Examples include news apps, music streaming apps, or video streaming apps.

4. **Paid Apps**: These are apps where the user pays a one-time fee to download and use the app. This model is less common due to the prevalence of free apps, but can be effective for apps with a strong brand or unique features.

1.3 Pricing Tables

The significance of a well-structured pricing table as a sales and Product Management tool cannot be overstated.

A pricing table is often the point of decision for your customers, determining whether they will invest in a product. It serves as a clear visual representation of a product's various pricing plans and their respective features, helping potential customers compare and contrast them easily.

They can also be viewed as a single-page product pitch. Product Managers wanting to describe a product would consider the following minimal information to describe a product crisply:

1. Key features that make your product useful and valuable

2. Additional features that allow someone to use your product under some special circumstances or at scale

3. How much your product is priced at (based on usage, audience or scale)

4. The easiest way to buy the product

Incidentally, that's also the format of a Pricing Table.

Samples of Product Pricing Tables

Zoom

Fig 19: Screenshot from https://zoom.us/pricing as on Aug 2022

Notice how the product features available are clearly marked as we move to the pricing tiers. There is a clear call out for additional features available across tiers.

JIRA

Fig 20: Screenshot from https://www.atlassian.com/software/jira/pricing as on Aug 2022

Notice how the tiers within product features (Basic, Advanced, etc.) available are clearly marked as we move to the pricing tiers, combining check marks and text.

Ostinato

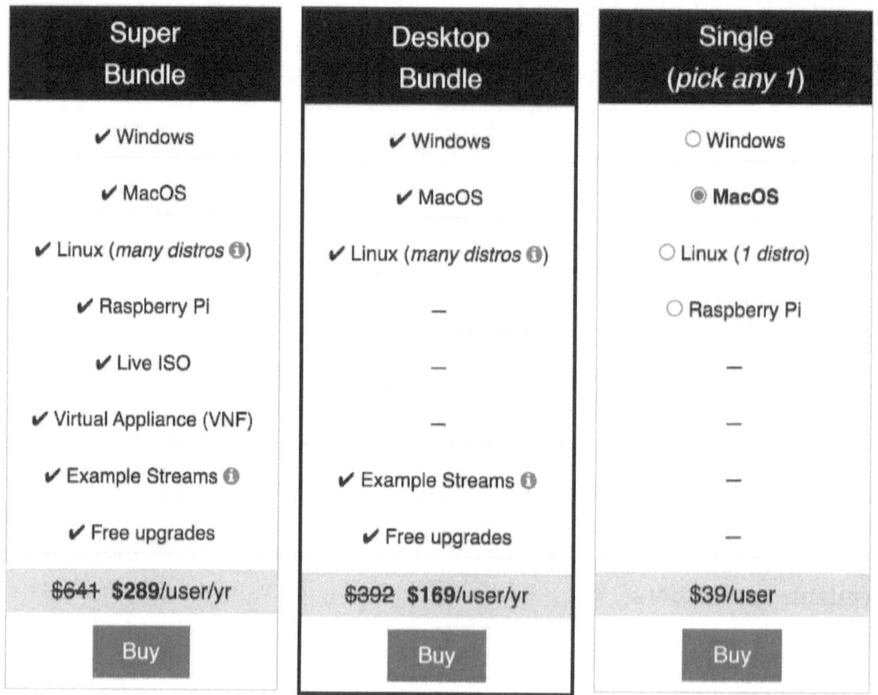

Fig 21: Screenshot from https://ostinato.org/pricing/#tiers as on Aug 2022

Notice how the discount is clearly marked with a slashed out 'before' sitting next to the current pricing.

2. Product Costing

Product Managers play a pivotal role in ensuring that products not only deliver value but also are developed and launched within sustainable budgets. Central to this task is the concept of product costing.

Product costing can be understood as the process of determining the total cost involved in producing or offering a product. This includes not just the direct costs, such as materials and labor, but also overheads and any other indirect costs. In the realm of software, it can encompass everything from the initial ideation phase, development, testing, its maintenance to customer support.

For Product Managers, having an accurate understanding of product costs is essential for several reasons:

1. **Budgeting and Forecasting**: Knowing the costs can help managers set appropriate budgets, prioritize resources, and predict financial outcomes

2. **Pricing Strategy**: The cost of producing a software product influences its selling price, which in turn affects market positioning and competitiveness

3. **Profitability Analysis**: Understanding costs is critical to assessing the profitability of a product, helping managers decide if it's worth continuing, tweaking, or entirely discontinuing

2.1 Common Costing Techniques

Software products present unique challenges for costing, primarily due to their intangible nature and the intricate processes involved. Some of the most common techniques are:

2.1.1 Activity-based Costing

This method allocates costs to specific activities involved in the software development process. For example, costs can be categorized under design, coding, testing, or deployment activities. This approach helps in determining which activities consume the most resources and where efficiencies can be gained.

For instance:

Design Phase: Costs can include tools such as Adobe XD or Figma for UI/UX design, as well as potential expenses if external agencies or services are used for market research or user surveys.

Coding Phase: Direct development costs are considered, but if development tasks are outsourced to a software vendor, their pricing structure becomes significant. They might charge based on:

1. **T&M (Time and Material) Pricing**: Charges depend on the actual hours spent on development and the materials used

2. **Fixed Pricing**: A predetermined amount is charged for a specific development task, regardless of actual hours or materials expended

3. **Cost-Based Pricing**: Costs are based on the vendor's resources and materials with a profit markup

Testing Phase: This includes the salaries of internal testers and any associated costs of external testing tools or platforms. If testing is outsourced, and the vendor operates on a T&M basis, the cost becomes their hourly rate multiplied by the number of hours spent.

Deployment Phase: Costs related to app store listings, server deployment, etc., are considered. If a vendor's platform is utilized for deployment and they charge based on server space or bandwidth usage, it becomes a vital cost to account for.

The Activity-based Costing approach, by categorizing costs under activities like design, coding, testing, and deployment, offers a granular perspective. It aids in discerning which activities are resource-intensive and where potential efficiencies can be realized. Especially when working with external vendors, understanding their pricing models and integrating those into the Activity-Based Costing framework ensures comprehensive budgeting and cost tracking.

2.1.2 Parametric Estimating

Often used in the early stages, this technique uses statistical modeling and historical data to predict costs based on certain parameters or variables.

2.1.3 Feature-Based Costing

As the name suggests, this method breaks down software into individual features or components and assigns costs to each one. It's especially useful when developing modular software or when considering which features to prioritize or omit based on their cost implications.

2.1.4 Expert Judgment

Leveraging the experience and knowledge of experts within or outside the organization can provide insightful cost estimates. Experts use their understanding of similar projects and the specifics of the current project to predict costs.

2.1.5 Analogous Estimating

This approach is based on comparing the current project with past similar projects. Costs are estimated based on historical data and similarities between projects. It's particularly useful when there is a rich database of past projects to reference.

2.2 Challenges in Software Product Costing

While the above techniques work well, exact software product costing is not without its limitations:

1. **Rapid Technological Change**: The swift evolution of technology can lead to cost overruns that were not factored in initially

2. **Unpredictable Issues**: Bugs, security vulnerabilities, and unanticipated user requirements can introduce unforeseen costs

3. **Scalability Needs**: As software grows in user base, there might be additional costs in scaling up infrastructure or support

Product costing, especially for software products, requires a blend of analytical techniques, industry experience, and a bit of foresight.

For Product Managers, understanding these nuances not only ensures that products remain financially viable but also strengthens their position in strategizing, prioritizing, and making informed decisions.

2.3 Example Scenario

Scenario 30: The Product Manager is asked to prepare a costing model for the MsgMsg App using various techniques.

Using Activity-Based Costing:

Here, the Product Manager allocates costs to specific activities involved in developing the MsgMsg App.

1. Design Phase:

    a. UI/UX Design: Costs for tools like Adobe XD or Figma.

    b. Research: Potential costs if external agencies or services are used for market research or user surveys.

2. Coding Phase: Here, if you're outsourcing some development tasks to a software vendor, their pricing model becomes essential:

    a. T&M (Time and Material) Pricing: The vendor charges for the actual time spent on the development and the materials (like software licenses) they use. For MsgMsg App, if AI integration requires 100 hours and the vendor charges $50/hour, that's a direct $5,000 cost. Plus, add any material costs they might charge.

    b. Fixed Pricing: If the vendor agrees to develop the AI messaging feature for a fixed price of $10,000, this becomes the cost for that part of the coding phase, regardless of how much time or what materials they use.

    c. Cost-Based Pricing: The vendor determines the cost of the resources and materials and then adds a markup for profit. If the AI module's actual cost is $7,000 and they add a 30% markup, the charge would be $9,100.

3. Testing Phase: Salaries of internal testers and potential costs if external testing tools or platforms are used. If an external agency (software vendor) is hired for testing and operates on T&M, then their hourly rate multiplied by the hours spent will determine the cost.

4. Deployment Phase: Costs associated with app store listings, cloud deployment, and other such activities. If you're using a vendor's platform for deployment and they charge based on how much server space or bandwidth MsgMsg App uses, this becomes a variable cost to consider.

Parametric Estimating

Based on historical data, if a similar messaging app costs $100,000 for every 10 modules, and MsgMsg App plans to have 30 modules, it might be estimated to cost about $300,000 using parametric estimating.

Feature-Based Costing

1. Break down the app into individual features: AI suggestions, real-time translation, encryption, etc.

2. Assign costs to each feature based on its complexity, development time, and tools required

3. This will help the team decide which features offer the best value for the cost or if any should be postponed for future versions

Expert Judgment

A seasoned developer or a Product Manager with experience in AI-powered apps might be consulted. Based on their expertise, they could provide a rough estimate that developing an advanced AI messaging app like MsgMsg App could cost around $500,000.

Analogous Estimating

If a previous project, say a simpler messaging app without AI, cost $200,000 and took 6 months to develop, and another AI-based project (not a messaging app) cost $300,000 and took 8 months, then the cost of MsgMsg App, an AI-powered messaging app, might be estimated to fall between these two, perhaps closer to the higher end due to the combination of complexities.

3. Business Model Canvas

Business Model Canvas (BMC) is a strategic management and lean startup template for developing new or documenting existing business models. It's a visual chart with elements describing an organization's value proposition, infrastructure, customers, and finances. The canvas is intended to be a simple, accessible way to map out and analyze business models.

The Business Model Canvas was introduced by Alexander Osterwalder, founder of Strategyzer[4]. The Business Model Canvas has since been adopted by countless startups, corporations, and universities as a foundational tool for business strategy and innovation.

3.1 Using the Canvas

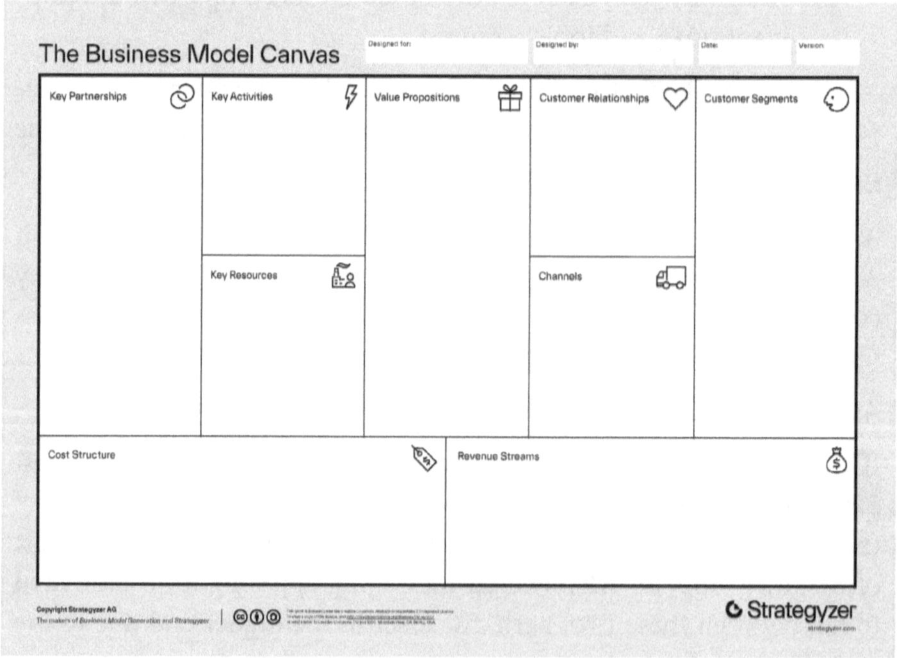

The Business Model Canvas

Designed for: Designed by: Date: Version:

Key Partnerships	Key Activities	Value Propositions	Customer Relationships	Customer Segments
	Key Resources		Channels	

Cost Structure	Revenue Streams

Copyright Strategyzer AG
The makers of *Business Model Generation* and *Strategyzer*

Strategyzer
strategyzer.com

Fig 22: The Business Model Canvas[4]

The suggested sequence is:

1. Value Propositions
2. Customer Segments

3. Channels

4. Customer Relationships

5. Key Partnerships

6. Key Activities

7. Key Resources

8. Cost Structure

9. Revenue Streams

3.2 Detailed Overview

Let us look at the various sections of this canvas:

Value Propositions

What value do we deliver to the customer? Which one of our customer's problems are we helping to solve?

1. **What goes here**: Unique selling propositions, benefits, and reasons why customers would buy/use the product

2. **Product Manager's Input**: Features that make the product stand out, results from user testing, benefits derived from the product, and how it addresses specific pain points or needs of the users

Customer Segments

For whom are we creating value? Who are our most important customers?

1. **What goes here**: Target audience, user personas, and market segments

2. **Product Manager's Input**: Results from market research, understanding of primary and secondary target audiences, and user personas discovered from interviews and data

Channels

Through which channels do our customer segments want to be reached?

1. **What goes here**: The methods and platforms through which the product reaches customers

2. **Product Manager's Input:** Ideal platforms for product distribution, partnerships for distribution, direct vs. indirect sales channels, and online/offline sales methods

Customer Relationships

What type of relationship does each of our customer segments expect us to establish with them?

1. **What goes here**: How does the organization interact with its customers throughout the customer lifecycle

2. **Product Manager's Input**: Post-sale support plans, feedback mechanisms, community engagement strategies, and loyalty program ideas

Revenue Streams

For what value are our customers willing to pay? What do they currently pay? How are they currently paying?

1. **What goes here**: How the business makes money from its customers

2. **Product Manager's Input**: Pricing strategies for the product, potential upsells, subscription models vs. one-time payments, affiliate revenue, and licensing opportunities

Key Resources

What key resources do our value propositions require? Our distribution channels? Customer relationships? Revenue streams?

1. **What goes here**: Assets needed to make the business model work

2. **Product Manager's Input**: Required technologies and platforms, intellectual properties, personnel (like developers or designers), and financial resources for product development and scaling

Key Activities

What key activities do our value propositions require? Our distribution channels? Customer relationships? Revenue streams?

1. **What goes here**: Most important activities needed to execute the organization's value propositions

2. **Product Manager's Input**: Product development roadmap, go-to-market strategies, partnerships to pursue, and user acquisition strategies

Key Partnerships

Who are our key partners? Who are our key suppliers? Which key resources are we acquiring from partners? Which key activities do partners perform?

1. **What goes here**: External organizations, resources, or activities that the organization leverages to achieve its objectives

2. **Product Manager's Input**: Potential collaborators for co-branding, tech partners for integrations, channel partners for distribution, and vendors for essential services

Cost Structure

What are the most important costs inherent to our business model? Which key resources and key activities are the most expensive?

1. **What goes here**: Major costs and expenses related to the business model

2. **Product Manager's Input**: Costs related to product development, maintenance, support, marketing and promotion, user acquisition, and third-party services

For a Product Manager, the Business Model Canvas is a tool to ensure that the product aligns with the business's larger strategy and that there's a clear understanding of how the product fits into the broader business ecosystem. Every decision made in the product's lifecycle should ideally be reflective of, or at least not contradict, the elements laid out in the Business Model Canvas.

3.3 Example Scenario

Scenario 31: Based on an Idea Canvas and an Elevator Pitch Canvas, a Product Manager is tasked to come up with a business model for the MsgMsg App.

Based on the information provided in the Idea Canvas and the Elevator Pitch Canvas, the Product Manager uses the Business Model Canvas to draft a business plan.

Value Propositions

1. AI-powered real-time message suggestions

2. Instant language translation

3. Tailored user experiences based on individual communication patterns

4. Enhances clarity in both personal and professional interactions

5. Transforms standard communication into a predictive, personalized, and productive experience

Customer Segments

1. Digitally-savvy individuals

2. Both personal and professional users who value efficient, intelligent communication tools

3. Individuals who frequently communicate across different languages

Channels

1. App stores (Apple's App Store, Google Play Store)

2. Direct downloads from the MsgMsg App website

3. Partnerships with device manufacturers for pre-installed apps on select smartphones

Customer Relationships

1. Online support and tutorials to make the most of AI-driven features

---

2. Feedback mechanisms within the app to continuously improve the AI algorithms

3. Community engagement through forums and user groups

Revenue Streams

1. Freemium model: Basic features available for free, premium AI-driven features under subscription

2. Licensing the AI technology to other communication tool providers or businesses

3. Ads on the free version with an upgrade to ad-free experience on the premium version

Key Resources

1. Advanced AI algorithms

2. Cloud infrastructure to process and store messages, translations, and personalized suggestions

3. Development and AI research teams

4. Partnerships with language processing and AI development companies

Key Activities

1. Continuous enhancement of AI algorithms

2. User behavior analysis to refine personalization features

3. Marketing campaigns to differentiate from traditional messaging apps

Key Partnerships

1. Smartphone manufacturers for pre-installed applications

2. Cloud providers for scalable infrastructure

3. AI research institutions or companies for cutting-edge algorithm development

4. Language institutions for refining translation capabilities

---

Cost Structure

1. Research & development for AI capabilities

2. Server and cloud storage costs

3. Marketing and promotional activities

4. Support teams and community management

Now that the team has a draft Business Model Canvas, further refinements can be made based on real-world data, feedback, and market dynamics.

---

4. Value Proposition Canvas

Value Proposition Canvas, developed by Dr. Alexander Osterwalder,[5] the co-founder of Strategyzer, is a tool that assists Product Managers in aligning their product with customer needs and expectations.

4.1 Using the Canvas

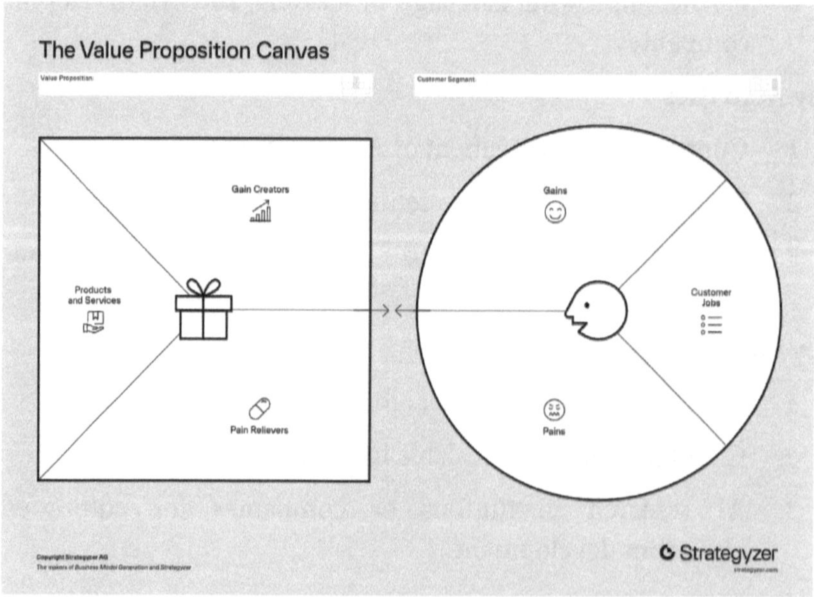

Fig 23: The Value Proposition Canvas[5]

The various components are:

1. Value Proposition:
    a. Products and Services
    b. Pain Relievers
    c. Gain Creators
2. Customer Segment
    a. Jobs
    b. Pains
    c. Gains

4.2 Detailed Overview

The Value Proposition Canvas is divided into two primary sections: the Customer Profile and the Value Map. Each section has distinct components that are critical for understanding the connection between a product's features and the challenges and needs of the target audience.

Value Proposition

1. **Products and Services:** This isn't just about what the product does. It's about ensuring that the product or service aligns with the jobs, pains, and gains identified in the Customer Profile.

2. **Pain Relievers:** This component ensures that the product directly addresses the pains of the customers. For a Product Manager, it's about guaranteeing that every feature or functionality serves a purpose in alleviating identified customer challenges.

3. **Gain Creators:** Innovation lies here. By not just addressing the expected but also creating unexpected delights, Product Managers can set their products apart from competitors.

Customer Segment

1. **Jobs:** As a Product Manager, one needs to deeply understand what customers are trying to achieve. This goes beyond mere tasks. It delves into the emotional undertones, societal pressures, or functional requirements that drive a customer's decisions and

actions. We will delve deeper into this in the Product Design chapter.

2. **Pains:** By identifying customers' pains, Product Managers can tailor their product's features and functionalities to directly address these pain points, offering a more compelling solution.

3. **Gains:** Recognizing potential gains provides an avenue for innovation. It offers Product Managers an opportunity to surpass customer expectations, leading to enhanced satisfaction and loyalty.

Value Proposition Canvas is an indispensable tool for Product Managers. It provides a structured approach to ensure that products are not just functional but are truly tailored to meet the nuanced needs and desires of the target audience.

4.3 Example Scenario

Scenario 32: The Product Manager of the MsgMsg App is collaborating with the Marketing team to create a marketing campaign that speaks directly to the pains the customers are facing. In order to describe the world of the customer and how MsgMsg App addresses it, the Product Manager decided to use the Value Proposition Canvas. Here is the result:

Customer Segment

1. Jobs:

1. Communicate effectively with office mates, neighbors, and others

2. Navigate and integrate into a new multicultural, multilingual metropolitan environment

3. Understand and participate in local cultural nuances, festivities, and traditions

2. Pains:

1. Language barriers, especially when interacting with those who prefer their regional language

2. Feeling left out during interactions due to linguistic challenges

3. Difficulty understanding local announcements/events in regional languages

3. Gains:

1. Effective communication with locals without language hindrances

2. Seamless integration into city life and local communities

3. Enhanced understanding and appreciation of regional traditions and customs

Value Proposition

1. Products & Services:

1. AI-powered real-time message suggestions

2. Instant language translation

3. Tailored user experiences based on individual communication patterns

2. Pain Relievers:

1. Real-time translations allow for instant understanding and response in various Indian languages

2. AI-driven message suggestions that can help in social interactions, ensuring they can engage even when unsure about regional linguistic nuances

3. Personalized experiences ensure that frequent or crucial phrases and translations are readily available

3. Gain Creators:

1. Provides the capability to communicate effectively with diverse groups, fostering stronger relationships

2. Empowers the user to actively participate in local events, traditions, and customs

3. Ensures a smoother transition into a new city and cultural environment, reducing the time to acclimatize

11

Product Definition

Before getting into the intricacies of product definition, let's cover some fundamental concepts.

1. Product Types

Software products encompass a wide range of categories to meet diverse needs. For Product Managers, it's crucial to accurately identify the category their product falls into. This not only ensures clear communication with stakeholders but also promotes the application of relevant development paradigms and patterns.

Here's a comprehensive overview of some common types of software products:

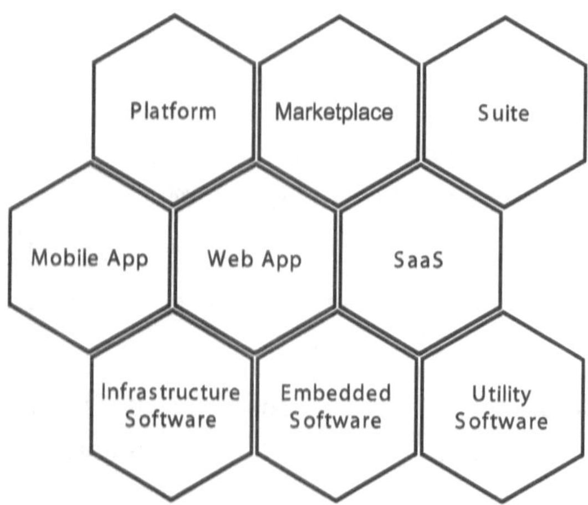

Fig 24: Common Product Types

1. **Platform**: A platform is foundational software that provides a base upon which other applications, processes, or technologies are developed. Examples include operating systems like Windows, MacOS, and Linux, or cloud platforms like Amazon Web Services and Microsoft Azure, or business platforms like Ola or Uber.

Platforms provide developers with tools and services to build and deploy their applications more efficiently.

2. **Marketplace**: A marketplace is a software product that facilitates the buying and selling of goods, services, or information among multiple parties. It typically brings together sellers and buyers in one centralized platform. Examples include Amazon, Etsy, and Upwork. For Product Managers, understanding the needs and motivations of both sides of the marketplace is vital.

3. **Suite**: A software suite is a bundled group of related applications sold together. These applications usually have a common theme or purpose and provide users with a range of functionalities. Microsoft Office, with applications like Word, Excel, and PowerPoint, is a quintessential example of a software suite.

4. **Mobile App**: Mobile applications, often known as apps, are software products designed explicitly for mobile devices such as smartphones and tablets. They can serve a wide range of purposes, from entertainment (like games) to productivity (such as calendar apps or note-taking apps).

5. **Web App**: A web application, or web app, is software that runs in a web browser. Unlike traditional desktop applications, web apps don't require installation on a user's computer. Instead, they are accessed via the browser, typically over the internet. Examples include web-based email clients like Gmail and tools like Google Docs. Web apps are platform-independent, which can be advantageous for broad accessibility.

6. **SaaS (Software as a Service)**: SaaS products are cloud-based services where the software is provided over the internet without the need for installation on individual machines. Users often access the software via their web browser. Subscription models typically monetize SaaS products. In essence, all SaaS applications are web apps, but not all web apps are SaaS. Examples include Slack, Salesforce, and Zoom.

7. **Infrastructure Software**: This software underpins systems and services, facilitating functions such as database management,

network management, and system utilities. Tools like Oracle Database and Cisco's networking tools fall into this category.

8. **Embedded Software**: Embedded software runs on hardware systems (not just computers) and is tailored for specific applications and functions. It can be found in everything from appliances and cars to industrial machines.

9. **Utility Software**: This software is designed to help analyze, configure, optimize, or maintain a computer. Examples include disk tools, antivirus software, and backup utilities.

For Product Managers, understanding these categories and the specific requirements, audiences, and challenges associated with each is critical. Tailoring development, marketing, and support strategies according to the software product type can be the key to success in the market.

2. Customer, User & Client

Understanding the distinctions between a user, a customer, and a client is pivotal for a Product Manager.

Here's a breakdown of these terms:

User

1. **Definition**: An individual who directly interacts with the product

2. **Implication**: Users are those who experience the functionalities of a product firsthand. They might not necessarily be the ones paying for it. However, they are very much concerned about the experience of using the product.

3. **Example**: In a software scenario, an employee using a specific software tool at work is a user, regardless of who made the purchasing decision.

Customer

1. **Definition**: The person or entity that pays for or purchases the product

2. **Implication**: Customers are involved in a transactional relationship and are concerned about the value, cost, and return on investment. They might or might not be the actual users.

3. **Example**: A parent purchasing an educational app for their child. The parent is the customer, while the child (who uses the app) is the user.

Client

1. **Definition**: In a business context, a client is an individual or organization that enters into a professional, often longer-term relationship with a service provider or vendor. This engagement often involves collaboration, trust, and a deeper understanding of needs and objectives.

2. **Implication**: The term "client" usually denotes a deeper, ongoing relationship than "customer." A client might engage in repeated business or work collaboratively with a service provider to achieve specific goals.

3. **Example**: A company that hires a software development agency for multiple projects or an extended period is a client of that agency.

In summary:

- A user interacts with the product
- A customer buys the product
- A client engages in an ongoing relationship with a service provider

It's essential to understand these distinctions, as addressing the needs and expectations of users, customers, and clients requires different approaches and strategies.

3. Lean Canvas

Lean Canvas, a one-page business plan template designed for startups, was created by Ash Maurya[1] in 2010. An adaptation of the Business Model Canvas by Alexander Osterwalder, the Lean Canvas aims to address the needs of entrepreneurs by focusing on problems, solutions, and key metrics.

3.1 Using the Canvas

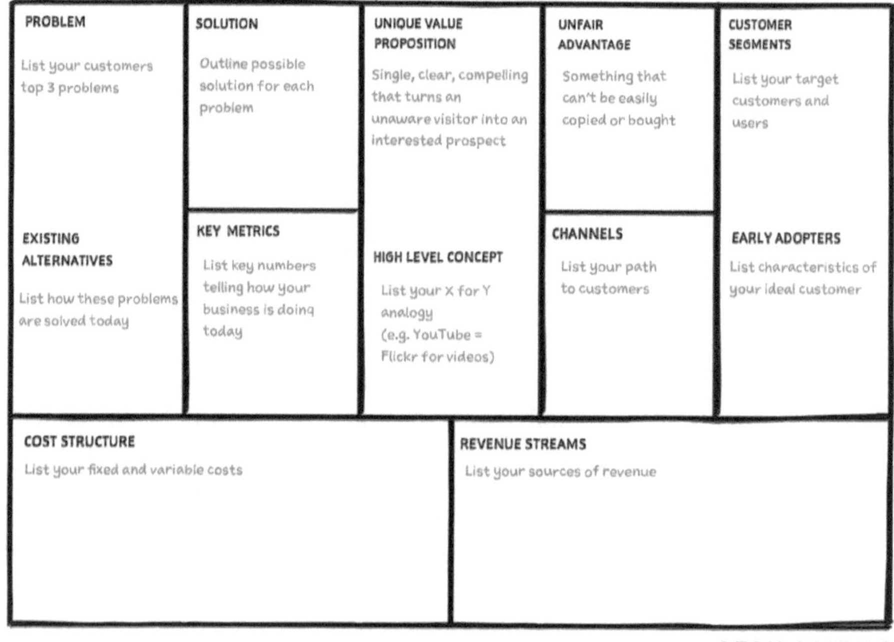

Fig 25: Lean Canvas[1]

The Lean Canvas is divided into nine distinct components, each of which focuses on a vital aspect of a startup. These components are:

1. Problem

2. Solution

3. Key Metrics

4. Unique Value Proposition (UVP)

5. Unfair Advantage

6. Channels

7. Customer Segments

8. Cost Structure

9. Revenue Streams

3.2 Detailed Overview

Problem

In this segment, Product Managers should enumerate the primary 1-3 problems their product aims to resolve. Recognizing these issues is vital, as triumphant startups typically tackle significant challenges that the market might have overlooked or inadequately addressed.

Solution

Within this domain, Product Managers are advised to present potential solutions to the determined problems. Rather than immersing deeply into feature specifics, the preliminary phase should revolve around discerning viable routes to address the challenges.

Key Metrics

Product Managers should ascertain the principal metrics that will stand as indicators of their startup's success. Metrics might range from monthly active users to churn rate or even customer acquisition cost, contingent on the business's nature.

Unique Value Proposition

This should be an articulate and captivating statement that captures the distinctive nature of the product solution. For Product Managers, it can serve as the cornerstone of their product's narrative.

Unfair Advantage

This refers to unique elements that competitors cannot easily replicate or purchase. Such advantages can range from privileged insights, an exemplary team, pioneering market entry, to even an authoritative stature in the industry.

Channels

Product Managers should determine the pathways through which they intend to engage their user base. Channels span a broad spectrum, from brick-and-mortar stores to websites, social media platforms, or even affiliate collaborations.

Customer Segments

Product Managers must pinpoint their core user demographic. Whether the focus is on students, working professionals, parents, or another niche segment, a clear understanding of this audience aids in refining both the product and its marketing strategy.

Cost Structure

This area necessitates a detailed breakdown of the foundational expenses tied to operating the business. It encompasses everything from production expenditures to payroll, promotional budgets, and all other pertinent outlays.

Revenue Streams

In this section, Product Managers should define the revenue modalities for their startup, be it through direct product sales, subscription-based models, affiliate promotions, or any other pertinent revenue channels.

The Lean Canvas is a living document that evolves and can be tweaked as the Product Manager learns more about its customers and the market.

3.3 Example Scenario

Scenario 33: Based on the Idea Canvas and the Elevator Pitch Canvas, the Product Manager of MsgMsg App wants to build a 1-page document about the Product.

The Product Manager uses Lean Canvas and here is the result.

Problem:

Lack of an intelligent messaging platform that enhances both personal and professional interactions

Limitations of existing messaging apps in terms of predictive communication, instant translations, and personalization

Solution:

MsgMsg App, an AI-powered messaging app that offers real-time message suggestions, instant language translation, and tailored user experiences based on communication patterns

Key Metrics:

1. User acquisition and retention rates

2. Frequency of AI feature utilization

3. Conversion of free users to premium

Unique Value Proposition:

1. Transforms standard communication into a predictive, personalized, and productive experience

2. Enhances clarity in both personal and professional interactions

Unfair Advantage:

- Advanced AI algorithms tailored for messaging

- Personalized experiences based on individual communication patterns

Channels:

1. App stores (Apple's App Store, Google Play Store)

2. Direct downloads from the MsgMsg App website

3. Partnerships with device manufacturers for pre-installed apps

Customer Segments:

1. Digitally-savvy individuals

2. Both personal and professional users seeking enhanced, AI-driven communication

3. Global communicators who frequently converse across languages

Cost Structure:

1. Research & development for AI capabilities

2. Server and cloud storage costs

3. Marketing and promotional activities

4. Support teams and community management

Revenue Streams:

1. Freemium model with premium AI-driven features available under subscription

2. Licensing the AI technology to other communication tools or businesses

3. Ad revenue from the free version of the app

4. Product Management Canvas

To effectively communicate across an organization, Product Managers must constantly and consistently articulate the "why," core features, and product adoption journey. The Product Management Canvas serves as a crucial tool to facilitate this communication and arrive at a Product Definition.

The Product Management Canvas aims to address the needs of enterprises by focusing on the key facets of a product, ensuring that these elements are universally understood within the organization.

Unlike other similar canvases, the Product Management Canvas has the Product Team at the heart of it, rather than the product.

Product Managers find that the Canvas prompts them to outline the foundational idea, targeted market, specific customer segment, associated business value, key features, and metrics. Moreover, it highlights essential resources and nudges the Product Manager to address potential risks, all on a single canvas. This compact representation of your product fosters comprehensive communication across the organization, distributing it via email, showcasing it on team walls, or even imprinting it on team apparel.

Once captured on this canvas, the product's 'why,' its core abilities, and adoption journey can be conveyed clearly and effectively.

Historically, the canvas was a checklist for Product Managers to guarantee comprehensive product planning.[2] Its ultimate aim, however, is to portray the dynamic nature of a product. Therefore, the Product Management Canvas should act as a communication bridge among various organizational units, ensuring everyone has a congruent understanding of the product.

4.1 Using the Canvas

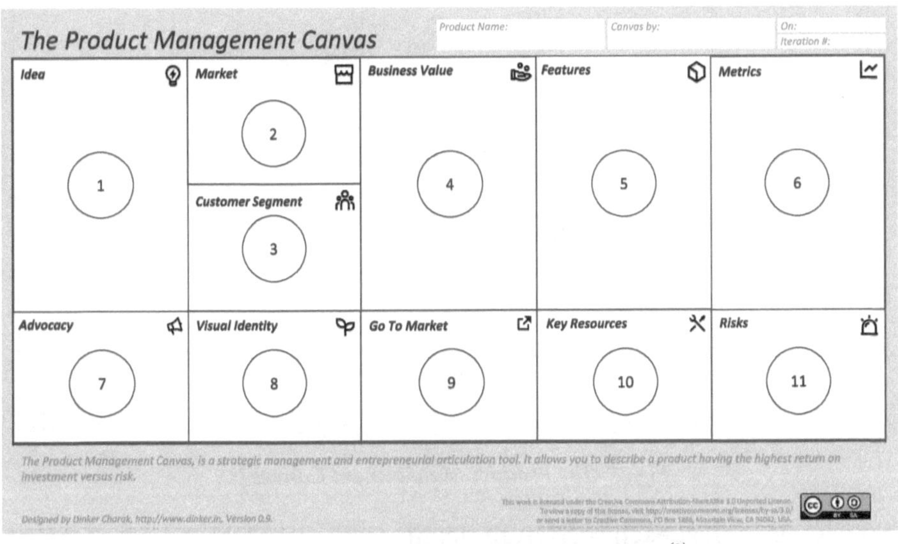

Fig 26: *Product Management Canvas Layout*[2]

The components and their recommended sequence is:

1. Idea

2. Market

3. Customer Segment

4. Business Value

5. Features

6. Metrics

7. Advocacy

8. Visual Identity

9. Go To Market

10. Key Resources

11. Risks

4.2 Detailed Overview

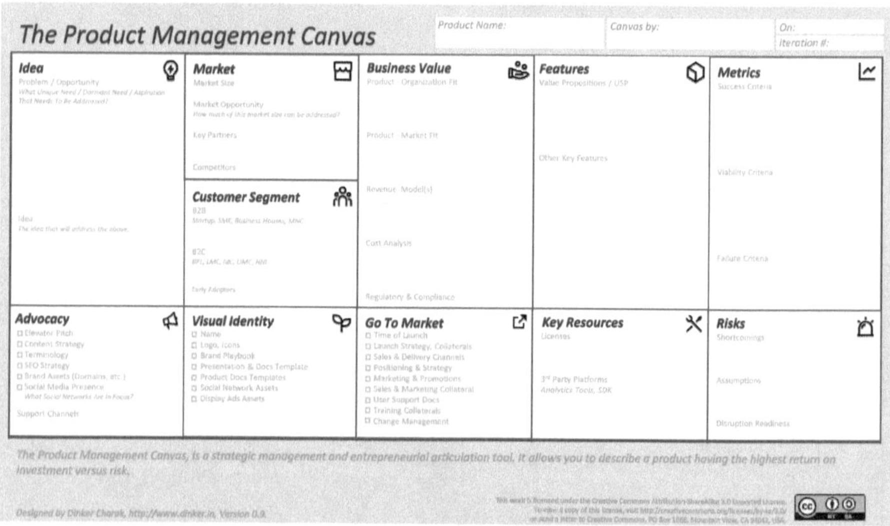

Fig 27: The Product Management Canvas[2]

Now let us look at each section in detail:

Idea

Every product originates from a problem or opportunity. Begin by thoroughly describing the unique or latent needs or the user/customer aspirations your product aims to fulfill. It's essential not just to pinpoint the problem but also to articulate how the product's core concept provides a solution or seizes the opportunity.

Market

Every business operates within a market context. First, quantify the market size, looking at both the total volume and potential. Venture capitalists, for instance, are often keen on substantial market sizes that provide room for competitors and growth. After determining the overall size, zoom in to specify the exact market segment your product seeks to capture. This should give a realistic forecast, balancing ambition with feasibility. Additionally, outline the broader ecosystem – recognize and detail partnerships (data providers, channels, SDKs, etc.) and understand your competition to position your product effectively.

Customer Segment

Every product caters to a specific audience. Identify if your product is primarily B2B (Business to Business) or B2C (Business to Consumer). Dive into granular segmentation: For B2B - Does it cater to Startups, Small and Medium Enterprises, and Large Enterprises? For B2C - Is the focus on segments like Lower Middle Class, Middle Class, or High Networth Individuals? Recognizing these subsets ensures targeted marketing and product features. Furthermore, pinpointing early adopters, influential market players, and innovative consumers provides insights into market penetration strategies.

Business Value

In multifaceted organizations, there's a crucial balance between individual product goals and overarching organizational objectives. Ensure your product aligns with the organization's larger mission, reuses existing tools, integrates seamlessly into established ecosystems, and does not necessitate parallel infrastructure. Clearly articulate the product-market fit, indicating how it meets market needs and stands out. Explore potential revenue models, from subscription-based to freemium. And, while product pricing is crucial, a cursory cost analysis ensures profitability. Lastly, consider regulatory and compliance factors to prevent future roadblocks.

Features

What makes your product stand out? Enumerate the unique selling propositions (USPs) that differentiate it from competitors. Additionally, emphasize other features that enhance user experience, simplify usage, or outperform competitive products.

Metrics

In the age of data-driven strategies, metrics are invaluable. Define clear success metrics to gauge when your product hits its stride. However, also determine the failure metrics, indicators that suggest a need for a pivot or change. For instance, while achieving 1M monthly active users might be a success indicator, if message exchanges don't proportionally increase, it's a red flag. It's essential to understand and track both to ensure the product remains on course.

Advocacy

The power of product advocacy shouldn't be underestimated. This person (product advocate), as Guy Kawasaki aptly said, "sells the dream,"[3] painting a future vision and rallying people towards it. Equip your advocate with the right tools: a compelling elevator pitch, a dynamic content strategy, consistent terminology across departments, a robust SEO plan, the right brand assets, and a targeted social media strategy. It's not about being everywhere, but about being where it matters.

Visual Identity

A product's visual identity goes beyond just aesthetics; it's about brand recognition. Establish a cohesive visual branding strategy, detailing elements like the product name, logo, iconography, branding guidelines, presentation templates, social media assets, and advertising materials.

Go To Market

A product's launch can make or break its trajectory. Ensure the launch strategy is comprehensive, encompassing aspects like product positioning, sales and delivery channels, promotional tactics, stakeholder outreach, sales, marketing, and user support materials. Given that product introductions often necessitate changes in processes, have a change management plan in place.

Key Resources

Every product relies on a myriad of resources. List and monitor essential resources. This can range from tangible assets like licenses (with reminders for renewals) to intangible ones like third-party platforms, analytics tools, and more.

Risks

No product journey is devoid of risks. Proactively list out known limitations, assumptions, and potential pitfalls. Being prepared isn't just about maximizing success but also about foreseeing disruptions. Cultivate a mindset of disruption readiness, evaluating processes and methods regularly to stay agile.

4.3 Example Scenario

Scenario 34: Based on the Idea Canvas and the Elevator Pitch Canvas, the Product Manager fills the Product Management Canvas for MsgMsg App.

Idea:

1. Original Problem or Opportunity: The need for a streamlined and intelligent messaging platform that enhances both personal and professional interactions

2. Product's Solution: An AI-powered messaging app that predicts users' communication needs and offers real-time message suggestions, instant language translation, and a tailored user experience

Market:

1. Market Size: Considering the vast user base of messaging apps, this could be in the billions (exact numbers would require market research)

2. Market Opportunity: A significant portion of the global messaging app user base, especially those seeking enhanced, AI-driven features

3. Ecosystem: Collaboration with AI technology providers, mobile device manufacturers, and potentially other app platforms

4. Competition: WhatsApp, Telegram, and other major messaging apps

Customer Segment:

1. B2C: Targeting digitally-savvy individuals across various socio-economic classes

2. Early Adopters: Tech enthusiasts, professionals reliant on digital communication, and global communicators

3. Influencers: Tech bloggers, digital communication experts, AI enthusiasts

4. Recommenders and Innovators: Leading tech magazines, AI researchers, and digital communication consultants

Business Value:

1. Product-Organization Fit: Fits into the trend of integrating AI into communication platforms, catering to the rising demand for intelligent tools

2. Revenue Models: Freemium (with advanced AI features as premium), partnerships, and possibly ad-based models

3. Cost Analysis: Initial investments in AI and NLP tech, with ongoing costs for technology enhancement and user support. Revenues as expected from premium features and partnerships

4. Regulatory & Compliance: Ensure user data privacy and compliance with international digital communication regulations

Features:

1. Value Propositions/USP: Advanced AI algorithms for predictive messaging, instant language translations, and personalized user experiences

2. Other Key Features: Secure messaging, group chats, multimedia sharing, integration with other apps, and cross-platform compatibility

Metrics:

1. Success Metrics: User acquisition and retention rates, frequency of AI feature utilization, positive user feedback

2. Failure Metrics: High rates of message misinterpretation by AI, privacy breaches, and user drop-offs after initial usage

3. Viability Metrics: Consistent growth in active user base, successful conversion of free users to premium

Advocacy:

1. Elevator Pitch: As provided earlier

2. Content Strategy: Blog posts on AI in communication, video tutorials, webinars, and user stories

3. SEO Strategy: Focus on terms like "AI messaging app," "intelligent communication," and "next-gen messaging"

4. Social Media Presence: Target platforms popular with the digitally-savvy audience, such as Twitter, Instagram, and LinkedIn

Visual Identity:

1. Logo, icons, and product name representing the AI-driven messaging theme

2. Brand Playbook highlighting the intelligent and futuristic essence of the product

3. Social Network Assets: Customized visuals for each platform, promoting the AI-driven uniqueness of MsgMsg App

Go To Market:

1. Launch Strategy: Beta release to gather feedback, followed by a global launch with promotional offers for early adopters

2. Positioning & Promotion Strategy: Highlight the AI advantage of MsgMsg App over competitors

3. Sales & Product Delivery Channels: App Stores (iOS, Android), Direct downloads from the official website

4. User Support Docs & Training Collaterals: Online tutorials, FAQ sections, chat support

Key Resources:

1. Licenses: Required for AI and NLP tech integrations and other third-party platforms

2. Analytics Tools: To measure user engagement, feature utilization, and app performance

Risks:

1. Privacy Concerns: With AI analyzing messages, data privacy is paramount

2. Over-reliance on AI: This may lead to a loss of genuine human connection

3. Misinterpretations by AI: Potential communication errors

Download Product Management Canvas

https://bit.ly/plcu-product-management-canvas

12

Product Branding

Product branding, at its core, is about imbuing a product with a distinct identity, making it recognizable and memorable in the minds of consumers. Product Managers need to understand branding to utilize it effectively and incorporate it into the product.

1. Visual Brand Identity

Visual brand identity plays a crucial role in conveying a software product's essence, promise, and functionality at first glance. It's the visual representation of the brand that forms an integral part of its overall identity. Here are various components of visual brand identity for a software product.

1.1 Logo

Logo is the primary visual element that identifies the software. It should be distinct and easily recognizable, conveying the essence of the software. A logo for a software product requires a blend of creativity, practicality, and versatility. Here are some practical tips to ensure your logo stands out and remains functional across various mediums:

Simplicity

A straightforward and uncluttered design ensures your logo is easily recognizable at any size and in any context. Avoid intricate details that can become muddled when scaled down.

Versatility

Design the logo in a vector format (e.g., using Adobe Illustrator). Vector graphics can be scaled without losing clarity, ensuring the logo looks crisp whether on a business card or a billboard. Test the logo in various sizes to ensure it remains legible and distinctive.

Aspect Ratio

A balanced aspect ratio (close to 1:1 or a slight rectangle) often works best as it allows the logo to fit comfortably in most spaces. Avoid very tall or very wide logos, as they might not fit well in all applications.

Colors

Choose a color palette that resonates with the brand's identity and ensures good visibility on screens and print. Always have a monochromatic version (black on white and white on black) of the logo. It ensures the logo remains effective in situations where color isn't feasible or where it may clash with other colors.

Adaptability

Ensure the logo looks good on both digital screens (computers, smartphones, tablets) and physical mediums (t-shirts, business cards, banners). Consider how the logo will look in grayscale if it'll be used in newspaper advertisements or photocopied documents.

Avoid Trends, Aim for Timelessness

While it's tempting to follow current design trends, the best logos are those that remain relevant and memorable over time. Aim for a design that won't feel outdated in a few years.

Responsiveness

Consider creating responsive logos that can change slightly based on where they're used. For example, you might have a full logo with the brand name and icon for your website but also work as a 32x32 pixel website favicon.

Consider Cultural Implications

If your software product is for a global audience, ensure the logo doesn't have negative connotations or meanings in other cultures.

Distinctiveness

Ensure the logo is distinguishable on devices where a screen is full of many app icons of all colors.

1.2 Color Palette

Colors evoke emotions and associations. The chosen palette should reflect the brand's ethos and be consistent across all brand touchpoints. For software, it's also essential to consider the user interface's color scheme, which is an extension of the brand's palette.

Some practical tips and best practices for selecting a color palette for a software product's visual identity are below.

Less is More

It's generally a good practice to limit the primary palette to 2-3 main colors. You can then have secondary and tertiary colors for specific UI elements or marketing materials. Too many colors can make the design chaotic and less professional.

Ensure Readability and Accessibility

Contrast is crucial. Always test your color choices to ensure there's sufficient contrast, especially for text elements. Use tools like the WebAIM (https://webaim.org/) contrast checker to ensure your color combinations are accessible to individuals with visual impairments.

Consistency Across the Board

Once a color palette is chosen, maintain consistency across all brand touchpoints, whether it's the software UI, marketing materials, or website. This helps in brand recognition and gives a unified brand experience.

Test on Multiple Displays

Colors can appear differently on various screens due to different calibrations and technologies. Always test your color palette on multiple devices and display types.

Global Perspective

If your software is intended for a global audience, be aware of cultural associations with certain colors. What's appealing or neutral in one culture might have negative connotations in another. For example, red commonly symbolizes danger, caution, error, or financial loss in many cultures. However, in China, red signifies financial profit. Meanwhile, in India, red is viewed as auspicious and symbolizes wealth.

Document Your Palette

Once decided, document the specifics of your color palette (including HEX, RGB, CMYK values) in a brand style guide. This ensures consistency in future design decisions and collaborations.

1.3 Typography

Typography is the art and technique of arranging type to make written language legible, readable, and appealing when displayed. It involves selecting typefaces, point sizes, line lengths, line-spacing (leading), and letter-spacing (tracking), and adjusting the space between pairs of letters (kerning). Typography also includes the use of color, layout, and other visual elements to create a cohesive and visually pleasing design.

Some concepts related to typography to keep in mind for a Product Manager are below.

Arial & Inter are Sans Serif fonts

Times New Roman & **Bitter** are Serif fonts

Fig 28: Examples of Serif & Sans Serif Font

Serif Fonts

Serif fonts have small decorative lines or extensions called "serifs" at the ends of their letters. These serifs can vary in design from simple straight-line extensions to more elaborate and curvaceous forms. Times New Roman, Georgia, and Garamond are classic examples of serif fonts.

Serif fonts are often used in print, especially for large blocks of text, such as in books, newspapers, and user manuals. The serifs are believed to help guide the reader's eyes along lines of text, potentially enhancing readability.

Sans-serif Fonts

The term "sans-serif" comes from the French word "sans," which means "without." Thus, sans-serif fonts are typefaces without serifs. They have a more modern and clean appearance due to the absence of those decorative lines. Helvetica, Arial, and Futura are popular sans-serif fonts.

Sans-serif fonts are commonly used in digital design, such as on websites and software interfaces, due to their clear and legible appearance on screen resolutions. They're also frequently chosen for headlines, logos, and other short text elements.

Kerning, Leading, and Tracking

Fig 29: Illustration of Font Kerning, Leading & Tracking

Beyond font selection, consider the space between letters (kerning), lines (leading), and groups of letters (tracking). Proper adjustments here can drastically improve readability and appearance.

Font Pairing

If using more than one font, ensure they complement each other. Various online tools can suggest font pairings based on your primary font choice. It is common to choose a Serif font for headlines and sans-serif for regular text.

2. Social Media Presence

Social media has permeated virtually every aspect of modern life, influencing how people interact, share experiences, and make purchase decisions. As a result, it's not surprising that businesses have turned to social media platforms as key venues for promoting their products and services.

2.1 Components of Social Media Presence

Platform Selection

Each social media platform offers unique attributes, catering to distinct audiences and purposes. Brands must pinpoint platforms where their target demographic predominantly engages and channel their efforts there. A Product Manager is instrumental in discerning the product's market positioning. In collaboration with marketing teams, they should synchronize social media strategies with the product's intrinsic value and audience appeal.

Content Creation

At the heart of Social Media Marketing is compelling content. This encompasses a spectrum from blog posts, videos, and images to infographics and podcasts. Every piece should captivate, inform, and be adeptly tailored to its respective platform. With an intimate understanding of the product's nuances, the Product Manager steers content creators to accentuate product facets that deeply resonate with potential users. In an influencer-centric marketing realm, Product Managers forge connections with influencers whose ethos matches their brand's. This alliance facilitates sharing product narratives, features, and advantages that influencers seamlessly incorporate into their content.

Engagement and Interaction

The essence of Social Media Marketing transcends mere message dissemination; it's about fostering genuine connections. Brands flourish when they actively engage, addressing comments, partaking in dialogue, and valuing feedback. Here, the Product Manager emerges as a feedback sentinel. They meticulously sift through interactions, distilling valuable insights about product enhancements, prospective challenges, and evolving user expectations. Consistency is paramount in a product's portrayal. Whether it's showcasing features or elucidating its USPs, the Product Manager's hands-on involvement ensures a consistent and coherent brand narrative across social platforms.

Analytics and Monitoring

Quantifying the efficacy of Social Media Marketing initiatives is non-negotiable. This metric-driven approach includes monitoring engagement rates, click-throughs, conversions, and other pivotal indicators to ascertain ROI and tweak strategies accordingly. While marketing squads rigorously analyze these metrics, the Product Manager provides a fresh lens, linking product modifications or new features with observable shifts in online engagement. This integrated analysis paints a comprehensive picture of the product's market reception.

13

Product Design

Product design is a pivotal step in bridging the gap between user needs and technological possibilities. At its core, this design process goes beyond mere aesthetics, diving deep into functionality, usability, and user experience. Product Managers navigate the intricate landscape of software development by employing a myriad of methods and frameworks. These tools, ranging from Design Thinking to User Journey mapping to Wireframes, facilitate a comprehensive understanding of user expectations and behaviors.

By harnessing these insights, Product Managers can craft products that not only solve specific problems but also provide intuitive and delightful user experiences.

The synthesis of methodological rigor and innovative thinking ensures that the final design is both optimal and impactful in its real-world application.

1. User-Centered Design

User-Centric Design places the user at the epicenter of product design. In a competitive marketplace, merely functional solutions no longer suffice. Users seek intuitive, personalized, and seamless experiences. User-Centric Design ensures that products are tailored to meet the actual needs, behaviors, and emotions of the end-users, thus fostering better user satisfaction and loyalty. The importance of User-Centric Design is underscored by higher engagement rates, increased market share, and positive word-of-mouth that user-centric products often enjoy.

Various tactics facilitate User-Centric Design, ranging from user surveys to prototype testing. However, Design Thinking stands out as a popular approach. It embraces empathy, iteration, and cross-functional collaboration, ensuring solutions not only solve user problems but also resonate deeply with their aspirations. By prioritizing the user's perspective, Design Thinking and User-Centric Design push the boundaries of what's possible in product design.

1.1 Introduction to Design Thinking

It is paramount to continually evolve the techniques employed to understand and serve the end-user better. Enter Design Thinking—a human-centric approach to problem-solving. This methodology hinges on empathy and iterative design, pushing for solutions that not only meet technical and business requirements but also resonate deeply with users.

At its core, Design Thinking is about adopting a user-centric perspective. This implies looking beyond raw data and understanding the emotions, aspirations, and pain points of the target audience.

1. **Empathy**: At the heart of this process is empathy—the ability to genuinely understand and resonate with user experiences. This drives more informed and user-oriented solutions.

2. **Collaboration**: Design Thinking advocates interdisciplinary collaboration. By bringing diverse teams together—developers, designers, and business stakeholders—the process ensures a multifaceted understanding and approach to problem-solving.

3. **Iterative Design**: The methodology champions an iterative approach. This means continuously refining ideas based on user feedback, ensuring that the final product truly resonates with its audience.

4. **Risk Mitigation**: By focusing on prototyping and testing early in the product development cycle, Design Thinking helps reduce the risk of product-market mismatches.

1.2 Evolution of Design Thinking

Design Thinking, while seemingly modern, has roots that can be traced back to the 1960s. The term was first coined in the context of architecture and urban planning. Herbert Simon's groundbreaking work, "The Sciences of the Artificial," laid the foundational stones for design theory.[1]

Yet, it wasn't until the late 1980s and early 1990s that Design Thinking truly began to take shape as a distinct methodology. At the forefront of this movement was IDEO, a renowned global design firm. Established in 1991 by David Kelley, Bill Moggridge, and Mike Nuttall, IDEO rapidly became emblematic of a human-centric approach to addressing challenges. Their innovative design of products, notably Apple's first mouse,[2] highlighted their distinctive methodology.

Further championing Design Thinking's cause, David Kelley was instrumental in founding Stanford University's d.school. This institution not only built an academic structure around Design Thinking but also amplified its relevance beyond conventional design spheres. The d.school's curriculum centered on the pivotal phases of Design Thinking: Empathize, Define, Ideate, Prototype, and Test, offering a systematic yet adaptable blueprint for innovative problem-solving.

With the proliferation of software applications in every aspect of modern life, the user experience has emerged as a key differentiator.

Product Managers, especially, can find immense value in Design Thinking for a variety of reasons:

1. **User-Centric Products**: As competition intensifies in the software space, products that truly understand and cater to user needs stand out. Design Thinking ensures that user needs are central to product development.

2. **Rapid Prototyping**: The iterative nature of Design Thinking is in line with Agile and DevOps practices popular in the software industry. Rapid prototyping, coupled with swift user feedback, ensures that products are aligned with market needs.

3. **Reduced Development Costs**: By identifying potential flaws or mismatches early in the development process, Design Thinking prevents extensive reworks or modifications at later stages.

4. **Innovation**: The methodology encourages looking at problems from various angles. In the software industry, this can drive innovative solutions, setting products apart from competitors.

1.3 Design Thinking Process

The Design Thinking process, often depicted as a non-linear flow, consists of five main stages:

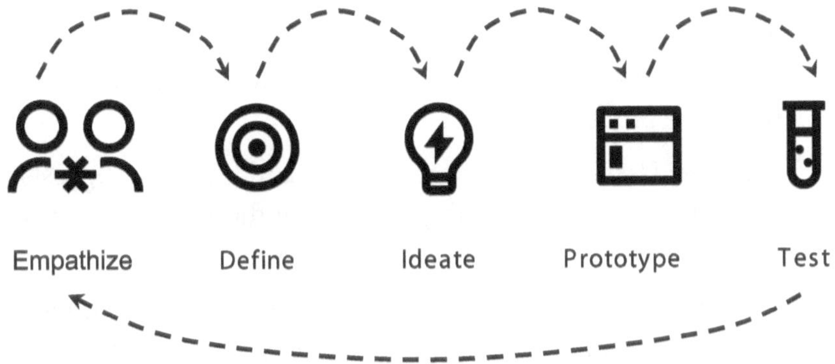

Fig 30: Design Thinking Loop

1. **Empathize**: Understand the users' needs, emotions, and motivations. Conduct interviews, surveys, and observational studies.

    Example: For a B2C meal planning app, the team interviews users to understand the struggles they face while planning meals, their dietary restrictions, and preferences.

2. **Define**: Analyze the gathered information to define the core problems users face.

    Example: The team realizes that users find it difficult to plan varied meals that fit their dietary needs while considering seasonal ingredients.

3. **Ideate**: Brainstorm potential solutions to the defined problems, encouraging creativity and out-of-the-box thinking.

    Example: Solutions could include personalized meal suggestions based on dietary preferences, an integrated shopping list feature, or a community feature where users can share and discover recipes.

4. **Prototype**: Create scaled-down versions or mock-ups of the product to visualize and test the proposed solutions.

    Example: The team designs a prototype of the app interface, showcasing features like the meal suggestion dashboard, shopping list generator, and a user-generated recipe gallery.

5. **Test**: Validate the prototype with users to gather feedback and refine the product.

    Example: Users test the app prototype, and feedback suggests the shopping list feature is highly valued, but the recipe gallery needs improved categorization for easier browsing.

It's worth noting that Design Thinking is iterative. Based on testing results, the process might loop back to previous stages for refinement, ensuring the final product deeply resonates with user needs and expectations.

1.4 Example Scenario

Scenario 35: The Product Manager undertook the Design Thinking process for the MsgMsg App and created the following report for the entire team.

Report: Design Thinking for the MsgMsg App

Empathize: Action Taken:

1. Organized a series of focus group sessions, selecting participants from different backgrounds to represent our diverse target audience.

2. Set up "a day in the life" observations, following individuals to see firsthand their communication challenges in multilingual settings.

3. Collaborated with our UX researchers to disseminate online surveys, capturing wider user sentiments and experiences around messaging and language barriers.

Reflection: It was enlightening to see just how crucial instant translation and context-aware messaging are, especially in multicultural settings. Several participants expressed frustration over existing solutions, indicating a clear market gap.

Define: Action Taken:

1. Analyzed the data collected, collaborating with the data science and UX teams to pinpoint key pain points and user needs

2. Hosted brainstorming sessions with stakeholders to convert raw data into actionable insights

Problem Statement: Our users need a tool that not only bridges language gaps instantly but also understands and predicts their messaging intent in diverse scenarios, making communication seamless and efficient.

Ideate: Action Taken:

1. Organized ideation workshops, involving not just the product team but also engineers, designers, and even some select users

2. Used techniques like mind mapping, sketching, and storyboarding to explore potential solutions

Emerging Ideas:

1. Real-time language translation with slang and dialect recognition

2. AI-driven predictive text that's contextually aware and adjusts based on the conversation's tone and topic

3. Personalized user experience based on observed communication patterns

Prototype: Action Taken:

1. Collaborated closely with the UI/UX teams to create low-fidelity prototypes for our top ideas from the ideation phase

2. Developed a clickable mockup of the MsgMsg App, showcasing key features and user flows

Feedback Loop: Kept an open channel with our engineers and a few trusted users, iterating on the prototype based on their feedback. The constant collaboration ensured a user-centric design approach while staying grounded in technical feasibility.

Test: Action Taken:

1. Rolled out the prototype to a select group of beta testers, ensuring a diverse mix resembling our target audience

2. Collected feedback through in-app surveys, direct interviews, and usage pattern analysis

Findings: While the real-time translation feature was a hit, there were some nuances missed in slang translations. Users appreciated the AI-driven predictive text, but there was feedback to make it more intuitive in certain scenarios.

Next Steps: Iterate on the current prototype, refining features based on the feedback. Plan another round of testing before finalizing the design. The journey has been insightful so far, and I'm optimistic about delivering a product that truly resonates with our users.

End of Report.

2. User Personas

A User Persona is a semi-fictional representation of a target user group based on real data and some educated speculations. Personas help product teams better understand the users they are designing for by giving them a clear picture of who the users are, what they need, and what motivates them.

2.1 Persona Format

A user persona typically includes:

Persona Name

Give your persona a name (e.g., "Digital Dave" or "Homemaker Hannah"). This makes the persona more relatable. Websites like https://www.name-generator.org.uk/ can help you generate a diverse set of names.

Brief Description

A one-liner that captures the essence of the persona (e.g., "Busy working mom juggling career and family" or "Tech-savvy college student on a budget").

Photo/Illustration

To provide a tangible image of the persona, teams often use photographs, which aid in fostering a connection and ensuring easy recall. While some teams might use photos of their members, websites like http://notarealhuman.com/ offer AI-generated deep fake profile pictures. The individuals depicted on these sites are entirely fictional, with features like the face, head, and shoulders crafted by advanced artificial intelligence.

Demographics

Typical demographic attributes are:

1. Age
2. Gender
3. Occupation
4. Education Level
5. Location (e.g., urban, suburban, rural)
6. Marital/Family Status
7. Job Title

Behaviors & Preferences

1. Tech-savviness (e.g., early adopter, laggard)
2. Preferred communication channels (e.g., email, social media, face-to-face)
3. Buying habits (e.g., online shopper, brick-and-mortar loyalist)
4. Hobbies and interests

Motivations

Why they use (or might use) the product, what problems they are trying to solve, and what outcomes they are aiming for.

Goals & Needs

1. Main objectives when using your product/service

2. Broader life or career goals that relate to your product/service

Pain Points & Challenges

1. Issues faced that your product/service aims to solve

2. General challenges related to your product/service domain

Quotes

1-3 short quotes that capture the essence of their feelings, needs, or challenges. This humanizes the persona and makes it memorable.

Brand Affinities (optional)

1. Brands or products they love and why

2. This can give insights into their preferences and aspirations

Journey Map or User Flow (if applicable)

A brief visual representation or list of steps showcasing how the persona might interact with your product/service from start to finish.

Footer (optional)

1. Source Data: Mention the research or sources from which the persona data was derived

2. Date of Creation/Last Update: To ensure that the persona remains updated over time

2.2 Example Scenario

Scenario 36: The Product Manager for the MsgMsg App has studied 3 personas for the app. They want to discuss the personas with the team and decide which one to focus on. For that purpose, the Product Manager uses the format suggested to produce this:

Persona 1: International Irene

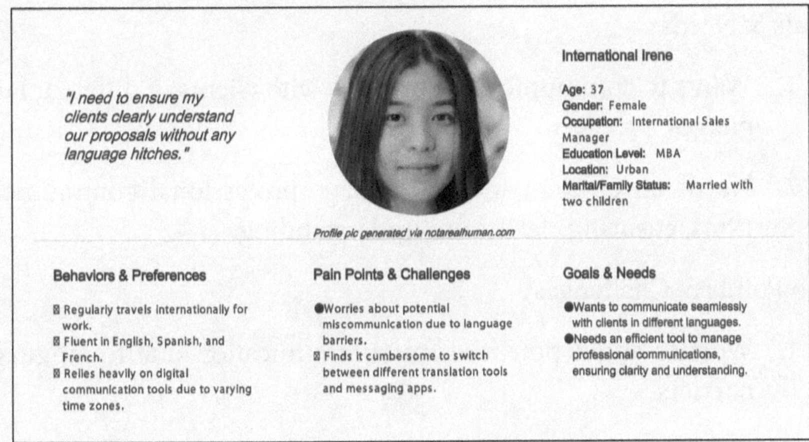

Fig 31: Sample Layout for User Persona

Brief Description

Multilingual business professional who frequently communicates with international clients.

Photo

An image representing a middle-aged professional

Demographics

1. Age: 37

2. Gender: Female

3. Occupation: International Sales Manager

4. Education Level: MBA

5. Location: Urban

6. Marital/Family Status: Married with two children

Behaviors & Preferences

1. Regularly travels internationally for work

2. Fluent in English, Spanish, and French

3. Relies heavily on digital communication tools due to varying time zones

Goals & Needs

1. Wants to communicate seamlessly with clients in different languages

2. Needs an efficient tool to manage professional communications, ensuring clarity and understanding

Pain Points & Challenges

1. Worries about potential miscommunication due to language barriers

2. Finds it cumbersome to switch between different translation tools and messaging apps

Quotes

"I need to ensure my clients clearly understand our proposals without any language hitches."

Persona 2: College-bound Carlos

Brief Description

University student studying abroad, staying in touch with family and friends back home

Photo

Image representing a young male student

Demographics

1. Age: 21

2. Gender: Male

3. Occupation: College Student

4. Education Level: Pursuing Undergraduate Degree

5. Location: Urban campus abroad

6. Marital/Family Status: Single

Behaviors & Preferences

1. Actively uses social media and messaging apps

2. Loves to share experiences from his time abroad

Goals & Needs

1. Wants to keep his family updated about his life without language hiccups

2. Desires to understand academic communications from professors who communicate in the local language

Pain Points & Challenges

1. Sometimes feels disconnected due to the language barrier

2. Struggles with adapting to new academic terms in a foreign language

Quotes

"I wish I could seamlessly chat with my folks without constantly translating."

Persona 3: Metro Mohan

Fig 32: Sample Layout for User Persona

Brief Description

Recent city transplant navigating a culturally diverse metropolitan with multiple Indian languages

Photo

Image representing a young Indian male in his early 30s

Demographics

1. Age: 32

2. Gender: Male

3. Occupation: IT Professional

4. Education Level: Master in Computer Application

5. Location: Bustling Indian Metro City

6. Marital/Family Status: Recently married

Behaviors & Preferences

1. Enjoys exploring the city during weekends

2. Actively interacts with colleagues and neighbors, trying to fit into his new environment

3. Relies on digital tools for navigation, local recommendations, and communication

Goals & Needs

1. Desires to communicate effectively with local office mates and neighbors speaking various Indian languages

2. Wants to build strong relationships and integrate seamlessly into his new city life

3. Aims to understand local cultural nuances, festivities, and traditions

Pain Points & Challenges

1. Struggles with language barriers, especially when interacting with people who prefer their regional language

2. Sometimes feels left out during office banter or neighborhood chats due to linguistic challenges

3. Finds it hard to understand local announcements or events which are often in regional languages

Quotes

"I wish I could understand and respond instantly in any Indian language, making my city life much smoother!"

3. User Proxies

There are instances when a direct line to the actual user is either inaccessible or impractical. High-Net-Worth Individuals (HNIs) might be too preoccupied or disinclined to participate in user studies. Similarly, users in remote areas, or those with certain specialized expertise, might be out-of-reach for direct feedback. Enter the concept of "User Proxies."

3.1 About User Proxies

User proxies are stand-ins or representations of the actual users. These proxies can be internal employees of the organization, Subject Matter Experts (SMEs), or even individuals who have a deep understanding and insight into the customer's mindset, behavior, and preferences. They channel the voice, concerns, and needs of the user, thereby aiding Product Managers in gaining essential insights.

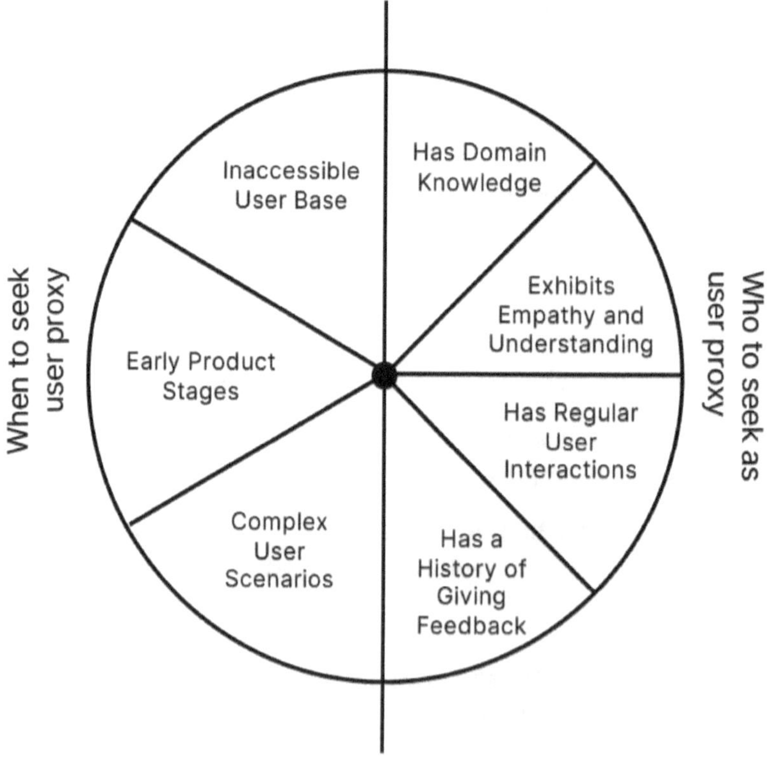

Fig 33: User Proxy

3.2 When User Proxies are Needed

1. **Inaccessible User Base**: As mentioned earlier, HNIs often might not have the time or inclination to be a part of user studies. Similarly, individuals in highly specialized fields or those residing in distant, hard-to-reach areas might be inaccessible.

2. **Early Product Stages**: In the initial stages of a product, when there's a limited user base or the product is in stealth mode, user proxies can help gather initial feedback.

3. **Complex User Scenarios**: For products that cater to niche sectors, such as specific medical equipment or advanced tech tools, everyday users might not possess the depth of knowledge required. Here, an SME, familiar with the intricacies of the domain, can act as a proxy.

3.3 Choosing the Right User Proxy

1. **Domain Knowledge**: One of the foremost qualities to look for in a user proxy is their knowledge of the domain. A sales team member, for instance, can be an effective proxy for a B2B product, as they interact regularly with clients and understand their needs.

2. **Empathy and Understanding**: A user proxy should be adept at understanding and empathizing with the users they represent. They should be able to step into the user's shoes and provide genuine feedback.

3. **Regular Interaction**: Choose someone who interacts regularly with the end user. For instance, customer support personnel can be excellent proxies for certain products, given their regular interactions and understanding of common user issues.

4. **History of Feedback**: Look at historical feedback and insights. Those who have consistently provided valuable and accurate feedback in the past are likely to be good user proxies.

While direct user feedback remains a golden standard in product management, there are situations where this isn't feasible. User proxies emerge as a potent tool in such scenarios, ensuring Product Managers don't lose sight of user needs, preferences, and pain points.

4. Jobs to be Done

"Jobs to be Done" (JTBD) is a framework in Product Management that seeks to understand the underlying motives and objectives behind why consumers choose certain products or services.

It focuses less on the product itself and more on the task or "job" the consumer wants to accomplish. This perspective helps discover products that are more relevant and beneficial to the end user, leading to product adoption and increased loyalty.

The roots of the JTBD theory can be traced back to the late 20th century, but it was in the 2000s that it started gaining significant traction. Notably, it was Professor Clayton Christensen of Harvard Business School who popularized the theory.[3][4]

In his research, Christensen observed that traditional market segmentation and product-focused strategies often missed the mark because they didn't address the core reason people made purchasing decisions. He suggested that consumers essentially "hire" products and services to complete specific jobs. This paradigm shift, moving away from demographic-focused strategies to understanding real-life tasks and challenges faced by users, has since become a cornerstone in modern Product Management and innovation practices.

4.1 JTBD in Action

Consider the drill. Traditionally, one might think people buy drills because they need a drill. However, from a JTBD perspective, people don't necessarily want to drill; they want a hole in the wall. The job to be done here is "create a hole."

Once product developers grasp this concept, they can begin to innovate beyond just drills. What if there was a way to make holes without a drill? Or a drill that requires less effort, makes less mess, or offers precision unlike any other?

One product idea can be adhesive hooks and strips that can hold significant weight. Customers no longer had to drill holes for hanging pictures, frames, or lightweight items. They simply needed to stick the adhesive hook or strip to the wall. It is faster, simpler, less noisy, and does not create a mess behind.

Here, the job – hanging something – remained constant, but the method (or product) used to get the job done evolved.

Example Scenario

Scenario 37: The Product Manager for the MsgMsg App wants to understand a customer. Based on the learning, the following is the analysis using the Jobs to be Done framework:

For "Metro Mohan," the jobs he might be trying to accomplish are:

1. Functional Jobs:

- Communicate Clearly: Mohan wants to convey his thoughts and questions without misunderstandings.

- Language Transition: Mohan needs to quickly switch between languages to understand and respond to conversations.

- Cultural Immersion: Mohan aims to be part of local festivities and traditions. He wants to know the significance and context.

2. Emotional Jobs:

- Feeling Integrated: Being a recent transplant, Mohan desires to feel like he belongs to the metropolitan community and isn't an outsider.

- Building Confidence: Mohan wants the confidence to approach and interact with anyone without the fear of linguistic barriers.

- Feeling Understood: He wishes to be fully understood in his conversations, both in content and sentiment.

3. Social Jobs:

- Establish Relationships: Mohan seeks to make friends, both in his professional circle and among neighbors.

- Professional Credibility: In a work setting, he wants to be perceived as competent and reliable, not hindered by language.

- Being In-the-Know: Mohan doesn't want to miss out on social events or office banter due to language barriers.

4. Supporting Jobs:

- Learning Local Languages: Even if he relies on translation tools, Mohan might have an underlying desire to learn local languages over time.

- Quick Information Retrieval: Whether it's local news, events, or any other local-specific information, Mohan wants to access and understand it quickly.

Using the JTBD framework, we can think about how the MsgMsg App can address these jobs:

- Functional Jobs: Introduce real-time translation, context-specific suggestions, and a cultural guide feature.

- Emotional Jobs: Ensure the app is intuitive and reliable to build confidence. The AI could also provide feedback to Mohan on his language progress, boosting his morale.

- Social Jobs: Perhaps integrate a feature where Mohan can join local chat groups or forums to participate in discussions. These platforms can be moderated by native speakers to help transplants like Mohan integrate.

- Supporting Jobs: Have a language learning or practice mode. Also, integrate a local news or event feed with instant translations.

By understanding these "jobs," the MsgMsg App can be tailored to meet the specific needs of users like Metro Mohan, ensuring a successful product-market fit.

4.2 Jobs to be Done Framework

JTBD focuses on the motives as a way to inform the Product Manager on what the user wants to accomplish and to better serve that. JTBD looks at situations and motivations. This is in contrast to using User Personas, a method that looks at roles and attributes.[5]

To help a Product Manager discover the situation and motives, the JTBD Story format is popularly used.[6]

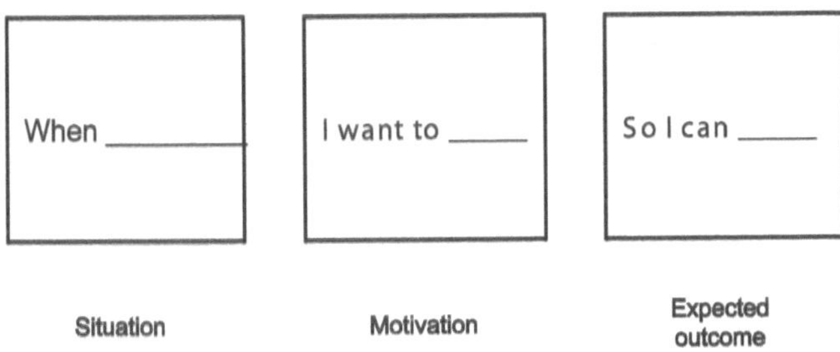

Fig 34: Jobs To Be Done Story Format[7][8]

The 'So I can' helps arrive at the JTBD. This method is often used as an alternative to 'As a _____, I want to _____, So that _____' story format[9] commonly used in Scrum.

These JTBD stories provide actionable insights into the situations a user may be in, the motivations in those situations, and the outcomes the user is aiming for.

Example Scenario

> **Scenario 38**: The Product Manager for MsgMsg App now uses the JTBD Story format to convey what "Metro Mohan" is trying to accomplish.
>
> Here are some stories based on the user persona description for Metro Mohan. This can be a powerful guide for designing features that address his core needs.
>
> **1. Navigating a Multilingual City Environment:**
>
> - When [I meet local colleagues and neighbors who speak various Indian languages] I want to [easily translate their messages in real time] so I can [understand them and respond effectively, building rapport].
>
> **2. Participating in Local Activities:**
>
> - When [I come across local announcements or events that are in regional languages] I want to [instantly translate them] so I can [participate and integrate seamlessly into my new city life].

3. Understanding Cultural Nuances:

- When [I hear about local festivities and traditions which have language-specific contexts] I want to [grasp the linguistic nuances] so I can appreciate the culture and join in celebrations without feeling left out].

4. Digital Integration in Daily Life:

- When [I'm exploring the city during weekends using digital tools] I want [my messaging app to predict and suggest relevant local terms and phrases] so I can [communicate more efficiently with locals and get the best recommendations].

5. Bridging Social Gaps at Work:

- When I [notice I'm missing out on office banter due to language barriers] I want to [quickly understand and join the conversation] so I can [bond with my colleagues and feel more included].

5. Empathy Map Canvas

One tool that has gained prominence in capturing this understanding is the Empathy Map. At its essence, an Empathy Map is a tool that helps product teams delve into users' feelings, thoughts, and needs.

Typically divided into segments like "Says," "Thinks," "Does," and "Feels," it offers a holistic view of user behavior and emotion. This invaluable method traces its origins to Dave Gray, the founder of XPLANE,[10] who devised it as a collaborative approach to attain a deeper understanding of audiences.

5.1 Using the Canvas

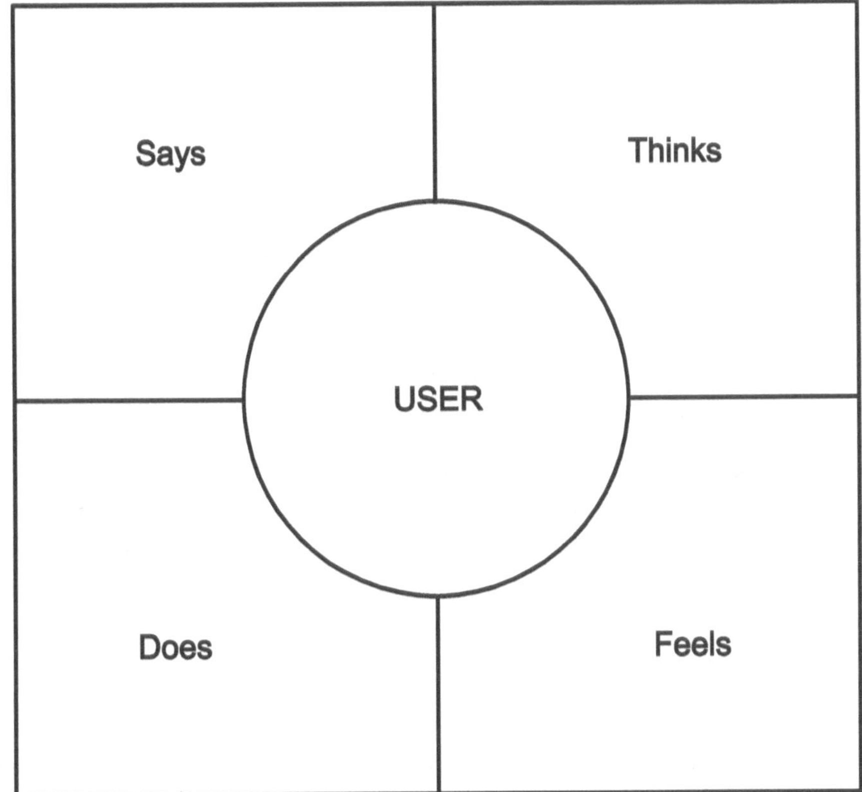

Fig 35: Empathy Map

The various components are:

1. Says

2. Thinks

3. Does

4. Feels

5.2 Detailed Overview

1. **Says**: For a Product Manager, what a user says provides an immediate feedback loop. These are the raw, often unfiltered comments that can highlight pain points, delights, or areas of

confusion. It's essential to note these down accurately without interpreting or paraphrasing.

2. **Thinks**: This component can be a bit challenging as it requires inferential understanding. Product Managers must analyze what's been said, observed, or shared by users and deduce what might be running through their minds. This segment offers an invaluable peek into the user's expectations and preconceived notions.

3. **Does**: By observing user actions, Product Managers can correlate said behaviors with specific features or aspects of the product. Are users skipping a step? Do they repetitively visit a particular workflow? This component offers a treasure trove of actions that can become product capabilities.

4. **Feels**: Emotions can range from frustration and confusion to joy and satisfaction. By empathizing with users' emotions, Product Managers can gain deeper insights into their needs, motivations, and expectations. This understanding enables Product Managers to design products that resonate with users on an emotional level, creating a more engaging and meaningful user experience.

The Empathy Map is a compass that guides Product Managers toward genuine user understanding. It's a testament to the old adage in product management: "Know thy user."

5.3 Example Scenario

Scenario 39: In order to discuss the User Experience Design with the Lead Designer of the MsgMsg App, the Product Manager prepares an Empathy Map to share the details of the persona 'Metro Mohan' collected till now. Here is what the Empathy Map looks like:

Says

1. "I wish I could understand and respond instantly in any Indian language, making my city life much smoother!"
2. "It's hard getting by without understanding regional languages."
3. "I don't want to miss out on the local culture and discussions."

Thinks

1. "Will I ever fit into this new environment?"

2. "Understanding these regional languages might be the key to connecting better."

3. "There must be an easier way to communicate without feeling left out."

Does

1. Actively interacts with colleagues and neighbors

2. Relies on digital tools for navigation, recommendations, and communication

3. Seeks out local events, festivities, and traditions to understand and integrate

Feels

1. Frustration over not understanding or communicating in regional languages

2. Anxiety about feeling left out during office banter or neighborhood chats

3. Eager to integrate and build strong relationships in his new environment

6. Information Architecture

For a Product Manager, it's crucial to help users navigate and understand the information their product provides, especially if users base their decisions on the data the product provides. Recognizing how this information should be methodically organized can play a pivotal role in determining a product's success.

Enter Information Architecture, a discipline that, despite being frequently overlooked, plays a fundamental role in successful software product design. For Product Managers, grasping the concept of Information Architecture, its importance, and its applicability can pave the way for more user-friendly, efficient, and marketable products.

Information Architecture refers to the structuring and organization of information in a manner that makes it user-friendly, intuitive, and accessible. It revolves around the design of a system's structures and the interactions among its components. In essence, it's about designing how information flows.

Imagine walking into a library without a clear categorization of books. If the volumes were haphazardly arranged, finding a specific book would be a daunting task. But libraries have a structured organization – fiction versus non-fiction, genres, authors, and so on. This organization is a physical example of Information Architecture.

In the realm of software products, Information Architecture is analogous to organizing the 'library' of features, functions, and content in an app or website so users can easily navigate and find what they're looking for.

6.1 Importance of Information Architecture

For Product Managers, the importance of Information Architecture can be encapsulated in three points:

1. **Enhanced User Experience**: When information is logically grouped and easy to locate, users can navigate the software seamlessly, leading to a more positive user experience.

2. **Efficient Product Development**: With a clear Information Architecture in place, developers and designers have a roadmap to guide their efforts. This clarity minimizes revisions and the potential for resource-wasting iterations.

3. **Marketability**: A product with a well-thought-out Information Architecture is more user-friendly, which can be a significant selling point. User reviews praising ease of use can improve product reputation and drive further sales.

6.2 Applying Information Architecture in Product Design

Product Managers might wonder, "How can I apply Information Architecture principles to product design?" Here are some of the practical applications of its various aspects.

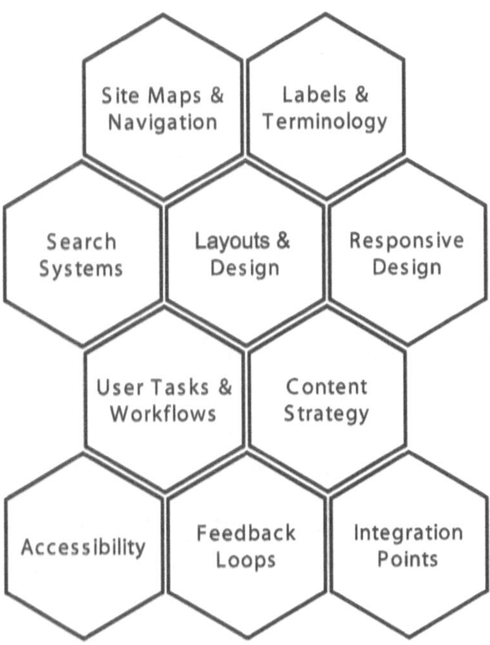

Fig 36: Applications of Information Architecture

1. **Site Maps and Navigation**: Just as a library has an index, a software product should have clear navigation. This involves creating hierarchies that users can easily follow, allowing them to move from one section to another effortlessly.

2. **Labels and Terminology**: The language used in a software product should be consistent and easy to understand. This ensures that users aren't left guessing what certain terms mean, improving usability.

3. **Search Systems**: A robust search mechanism, built on a foundation of good Information Architecture, allows users to find what they're looking for quickly, even if they're unsure where it might be located within the software.

4. **Layouts and Design**: While not strictly about the categorization of information, the way information is presented visually should align with the underlying Information Architecture. A layout

should be intuitive, guiding users through the information in a logical manner.

5. **Responsive Design**: Information Architecture ensures that the information and design are fluid across various screen sizes, providing a consistent experience irrespective of the device. This is accomplished by thoughtfully placing certain information, relaying it or grouping it on specific devices based on usage patterns.

6. **User Tasks and Workflows**: Information Architecture considers the tasks users want to achieve. By understanding and mapping out these workflows, designers can create interfaces that guide users to completion with minimal friction.

7. **Content Strategy**: Information Architecture plays a role in determining what content is displayed and how. This ensures that the most relevant information is prioritized, making it easier for users to digest and understand.

8. **Accessibility**: Good Information Architecture ensures that software products are usable for people with disabilities. This includes providing alternative text for images, ensuring readable font sizes, and maintaining a logical content hierarchy that screen readers can interpret.

9. **Feedback Loops**: Incorporating mechanisms for users to provide feedback, rooted in Information Architecture, can help in continually refining the product. This ensures that the product evolves based on actual user needs and challenges.

10. **Integration Points**: Especially relevant for software with third-party integrations, Information Architecture helps determine how external information or features are incorporated into the product's ecosystem.

For those involved in product design, embedding Information Architecture principles isn't an optional exercise. It's a foundational aspect that, when effectively integrated, can lead to a product that is not only user-friendly but also adaptable, accessible, and aligned with modern user needs. By expanding the applicability of Information Architecture in design, products can achieve a more holistic approach to user experience.

6.3 Example Scenario

Scenario 40: Apply principles of Information Architecture to MsgMsg App website and arrive at key information organizations.

Site Map for MsgMsg App website

1. Homepage
   a. Brief Introduction to MsgMsg App
   b. Key Features Highlight
   c. Download/App Link (if applicable)
   d. Testimonials or User Reviews
   e. Call to Action (e.g., Sign up or Log in)
2. Features
   a. AI-Driven Message Suggestions
      i. How it works
      ii. Benefits
   b. Real-Time Translation
      i. Supported Languages
      ii. User Guide
   c. Communication Pattern Insights
      i. Analytics Overview
      ii. Personalized User Experience
3. How It Works
   a. Getting Started Guide
   b. Tutorials and Walkthroughs
   c. Frequently Asked Questions (FAQs)

4. Pricing
    a. Free Version (if applicable)
    b. Premium Packages
    c. Business Solutions and Plans
    d. Special Offers or Discounts
5. Support & Help Center
    a. User Guides and Manuals
    b. Troubleshooting Tips
    c. Contact Support Form
    d. Community Forum or Discussion Boards
6. About Us
    a. Company History and Mission
    b. Team and Leadership
    c. Press and Media Mentions
    d. Career Opportunities
7. Privacy & Security
    a. Data Handling and Storage
    b. Encryption and Security Measures
    c. User Privacy Rights
    d. Terms of Service
8. Blog & Updates
    a. News about MsgMsg App
    b. Industry Insights
    c. Guest Posts or Collaborations
    d. Product Updates and Changelog
9. Navigation for MsgMsg App

10. Header Navigation:

    a. Home

    b. Features

    c. How It Works

    d. Pricing

    e. Support & Help Center

    f. Blog & Updates

    g. (Sign up/Log in button)

11. Footer Navigation:

    a. About Us

    b. Privacy & Security

    c. Terms of Service

    d. Contact Us

    e. Social Media Icons/Links

    f. Newsletter Signup

Labels and Terminologies used for MsgMsg App

1. Msg IQ: A term that could refer to the AI capabilities within the app, representing the intelligent processing and suggestions made by the system

2. Smart Suggest: The feature that offers real-time message suggestions based on user behavior and context

3. InstaTranslate: A label for the real-time language translation feature, emphasizing its speed and accuracy

4. Pattern Pulse: The analytics or insight section that reveals user communication patterns

5. SafeGuard Encryption: Emphasizing the high level of security and encryption of messages within the platform

6. Talk Trends: An overview or report on the latest trending topics or commonly used phrases within a user's network

7. AI-Assist Mode: A toggle or mode where users can let AI take the front seat in aiding their communication, providing more robust suggestions and automation

8. Unified Inbox: A central place where users can see all their conversations, irrespective of individual or group chats.

9. Global Connect: A feature that allows users to connect with others worldwide, leveraging real-time translations

10. Learning Lounge: A section dedicated to helping users understand and make the most of AI features, with tutorials, tips, and more

11. Privacy First: Settings or features that emphasize user data privacy, allowing them to control AI access and analysis

12. Quick Access Toolbar: A handy toolbar providing shortcuts to AI features or frequently used functions

13. ConvoCloud: Cloud-based backup and storage for conversations, ensuring they're safely stored and easily accessible

14. NLP Insights: Delving deeper into the Natural Language Processing capabilities, showcasing how AI understands and predicts user behaviors

15. Tailored Themes: Personalized chat themes or modes based on user communication patterns or preferences

Integration Points for MsgMsg App

1. Cloud Storage Services:

   a. Purpose: Allow users to send files directly from their cloud storage accounts

   b. Platforms: Google Drive, Dropbox, Microsoft OneDrive, etc.

2. Productivity Tools:

   a. Purpose: Enable users to share tasks, events, or notes directly within chats

b. Platforms: Trello, Asana, Google Calendar, Evernote, Notion, etc.

3. CRM Systems:

   a. Purpose: For professional use, allowing users to quickly share contacts or deal info in chats, or even log communication as CRM notes

   b. Platforms: Salesforce, HubSpot, Zoho CRM, etc.

4. Payment Gateways:

   a. Purpose: Facilitate quick payment transfers or requests within chat windows

   b. Platforms: PayPal, Stripe, Venmo, etc.

5. E-commerce:

   a. Purpose: Enable businesses to communicate with customers, share product details, or even process orders within the chat.

   b. Platforms: Shopify, WooCommerce, Magento, etc.

6. Social Media Platforms:

   a. Purpose: Allow sharing of posts, tweets, or other content directly within chats; also useful for login or signup purposes

   b. Platforms: Facebook, Twitter, Instagram, LinkedIn, etc.

7. Entertainment and Streaming Services:

   a. Purpose: Share songs, videos, or podcasts directly in chats for shared listening or viewing experiences

   b. Platforms: Spotify, YouTube, Netflix, Podcast platforms, etc.

8. Language and Translation Tools:

   a. Purpose: Enhance the app's translation capabilities or integrate specialized language tools

   b. Platforms: Google Translate, Duolingo for language learning prompts, etc.

9. Virtual Assistants:

a. Purpose: Enable command-driven actions within chats, like setting reminders

b. Platforms: Google Assistant, Amazon Alexa, Apple's Siri, etc.

10. Location and Mapping Services:

a. Purpose: Share real-time location or direct users to places using maps

b. Platforms: Google Maps, Waze, Apple Maps, etc.

11. Email Platforms:

a. Purpose: Share emails or specific content from emails directly within chats or receive chat summaries in email

b. Platforms: Gmail, Microsoft Outlook, Yahoo Mail, etc.

12. Collaboration and Video Conferencing Tools:

a. Purpose: Instantly initiate video or audio calls from within the chat environment

b. Platforms: Zoom, Microsoft Teams, Google Meet, Skype, etc.

13. Two-Factor Authentication Services:

a. Purpose: Enhance the security of user accounts

b. Platforms: Authy, Google Authenticator, etc.

14. Feedback and Survey Tools:

a. Purpose: Allow businesses to solicit feedback from chat participants or customers directly within the app

b. Platforms: Typeform, Google Forms, SurveyMonkey, etc.

7. User Journey

For a Product Manager, it's crucial to thoroughly understand users, from their initial interaction with a product to their evolution into loyal advocates. This comprehensive progression is captured in the concept termed "User Journey."

7.1 Defining the User Journey

At its core, the User Journey represents the series of steps or interactions a user undergoes while engaging with a product or service. It maps out the entire experience, beginning with the user's initial awareness of the product, moving through consideration and decision-making stages, leading to the actual usage, and even to post-use reflections and actions. This journey is not just a linear path; it can have its twists, turns, detours, and sometimes even roadblocks.

Here's why mapping the user journey is important for Project Managers.

1. **Insightful Product Development**: Understanding the User Journey can offer Product Managers invaluable insights into what users are seeking, what frustrates them, and where the product might be falling short. These insights can drive innovation, feature prioritization, and improvements.

2. **Enhancing User Experience**: Recognizing the stages of the User Journey and the emotions users might feel at each phase allows for more intentional design. Product Managers can optimize interfaces, features, and flows, ensuring users find value with minimal friction.

3. **Effective Resource Allocation**: By understanding where users might drop off or face challenges, Product Managers can focus resources, be it development time or marketing budget, more efficiently.

4. **Measuring Success**: Key metrics can be associated with different stages of the User Journey. By monitoring these metrics, Product

Managers can gauge product success and identify areas for improvement.

7.2 User Journey Map

While each product might have a unique user journey, the User Journey Map identifies several common stages.

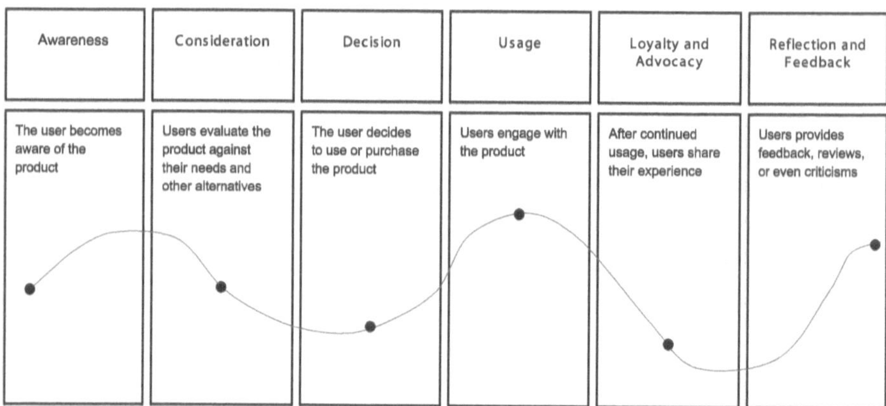

Fig 37: Key Components of User Journey

Awareness

The user becomes aware of the product. What channels are they coming from? What triggers their interest?

Here are example metrics for this stage.

1. **Traffic Source Analysis**: The number and percentage of visitors coming from various channels such as organic search, paid ads, social media, referrals, etc.

2. **Brand Mentions**: How often the product or brand is mentioned on social media, blogs, news sites, etc.

3. **Impressions**: The number of times an advertisement is viewed

Consideration

Users evaluate the product against their needs and other alternatives. What information are they seeking? What doubts might they have?

Here are example metrics for this stage.

1. **Engagement Rate**: Time spent on the product website, pages visited per session, bounce rate, etc.

2. **Content Interaction**: Metrics around how often informational content (like FAQ, testimonials, reviews) is viewed or interacted with

3. **Cart Abandonment Rate**: Percentage of users who add a product to their cart but do not complete the purchase. This indicates doubts or hurdles in the consideration phase.

Decision

The user decides to use or purchase the product. What motivates this choice? Are there any barriers at this stage?

Here are example metrics for this stage.

1. **Conversion Rate**: The percentage of visitors who take a desired action, like signing up for a service or purchasing a product

2. **Average Order Value (AOV)**: Average amount spent when a customer makes an order. A higher AOV suggests users see more value in your offerings.

3. **Checkout Drop-off Rate**: Percentage of users who start but do not finish the checkout process

Usage

Users engage with the product. How intuitive is the interface? What features resonate with them? What challenges do they face?

Here are example metrics for this stage.

1. **Daily/Monthly Active Users (DAU/MAU)**: How often users are engaging with the product

2. **Feature Adoption Rate**: Percentage of users utilizing a specific feature of the product

3. **Customer Support Tickets**: Number and nature of support queries or issues raised, indicating possible challenges faced by users

Loyalty and Advocacy

After continued usage, users share their experiences. Do users become loyal advocates? What encourages them to refer to others?

Here are example metrics for this stage.

1. **Net Promoter Score (NPS)**: Measures user loyalty and their likelihood to recommend the product to others

2. **Customer Retention Rate**: The percentage of customers who continue to use the product over a given period

3. **Referral Rate**: How often current users are referring new users to the product, typically tracked via referral programs

Reflection and Feedback

Users might reflect on their experience, providing feedback, reviews, or even criticisms. How can Product Managers gather and utilize this feedback?

Here are example metrics for this stage:

1. **Customer Feedback Score**: Measures user satisfaction based on feedback forms or surveys

2. **Number of Reviews**: How often users are leaving reviews, both positive and negative

3. **Feature Request Count**: The number of users asking for new features or improvements

For Product Managers, comprehending the User Journey is not a luxury; it's an essential component of creating successful products. It demands empathy, observation, and a commitment to iterative improvement. By fully grasping their users' journeys, Product Managers can not only enhance the usability of their products but also foster deeper, more meaningful connections with their user base.

Example Scenario

Scenario 41: The Product Manager of MsgMsg App tracks the User Journey to understand where the product does not perform as expected.

The Product Manager picks a key metric for each phase. These metrics can indicate the user's experience or engagement. Depending on how the metric is doing, the Product Manager places a dot in the box.

If the metrics are performing well, the Product Manager places the dot high (in proportion to where the current value is against a goal). If the metrics are not performing well, the Product Manager places the dot low (again, in proportion to where the current value is against a goal).

But hand-drawing a smooth curve through all the dots, the Product Manager is able to show visually, how the user's journey is doing as they go from one phase to another.

Based on the analysis the Product Manager decides to focus on features that promote loyalty.

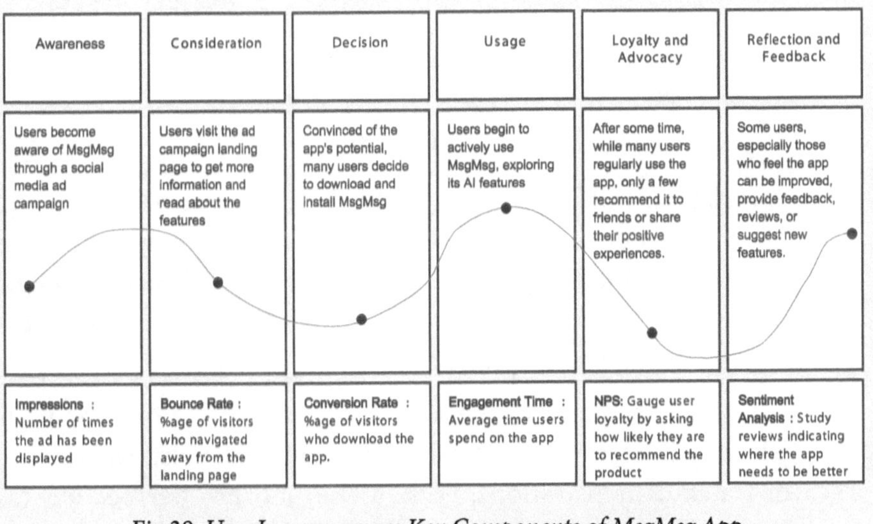

Fig 38: User Journey across Key Components of MsgMsg App

7.3 AIDA Model

The AIDA model, an acronym for Awareness, Interest, Desire, and Action, is a framework used in marketing and advertising to describe the stages a consumer goes through from the first moment they learn about a product to the point of making a purchase decision. Originally conceptualized in the late 19th century, it was credited to E. St. Elmo Lewis, an American businessman, who designed it to describe the process of personal selling and salesmanship.[11]

When viewed in the context of the User Journey, AIDA provides a structured way to understand and design user experiences that align with the psychological stages that users typically traverse.

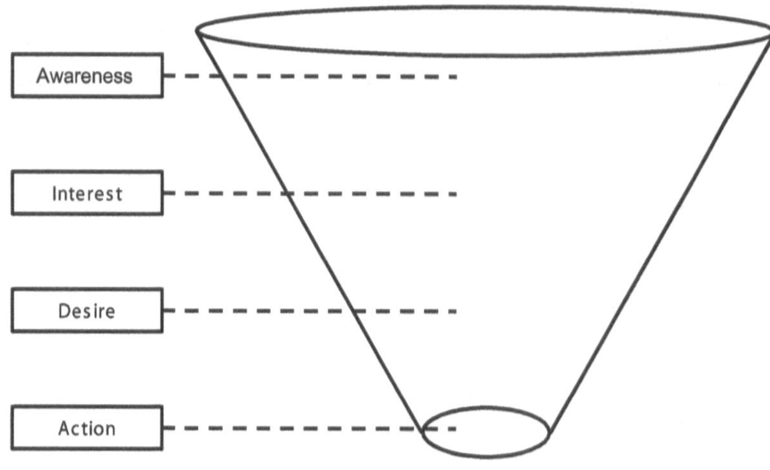

Fig 39: AIDA Funnel

1. **Awareness**: This is the initial stage where the user becomes aware of a product or service, often as a result of marketing campaigns, word of mouth, or organic discovery. In the User Journey context, this is the phase where one needs to grab the user's attention and make a strong first impression.

2. **Interest**: Once aware, the user seeks to learn more about the product. Here, they might delve into product details, read reviews, or watch demonstrations. From a User Journey perspective, this is the phase to provide valuable content, showcase features, and address potential questions, ensuring the user remains engaged.

3. **Desire**: At this stage, the user begins to visualize using the product, developing a personal connection, or seeing its potential benefits in their own lives. In shaping the User Journey, it's crucial to build

emotional engagement, highlight unique selling propositions, and create a sense of need or desire for the product.

4.   **Action**: This is the culmination where the user takes a definitive step, such as purchasing the product, signing up for a service, or downloading an app. For the User Journey, this stage emphasizes reducing friction, offering clear calls-to-action, and ensuring a seamless conversion process.

The AIDA model provides a foundational lens through which to view and design the User Journey. By aligning user experience touchpoints with the stages of AIDA, Product Managers, and designers can craft journeys that resonate with users' psychological progression, leading to more effective user engagement and conversion.

Example Scenario

Scenario 42: The Product Manager of MsgMsg App collaborates with the Marketing team to launch a Google Ad campaign. The ad highlights the benefits of the app. If a user clicks on the ad, the user is taken to a landing page which has more details and a download button. Once the campaign ends, the Product Manager and Marketing Manager build an AIDA Report to share the key stats from the campaign.

Here is the AIDA funnel they use in their report.

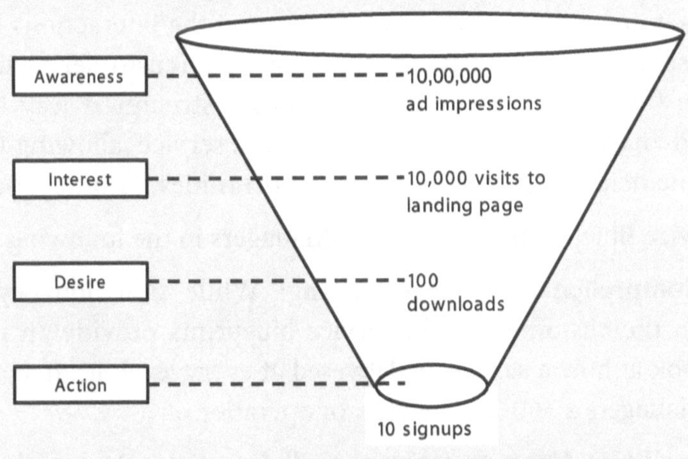

Fig 40: MsgMsg App Camapign's Planned AIDA Funnel

8. Service Blueprint

Product Managers not only oversee the creation and optimization of tangible products but also delve into the design and enhancement of intangible experiences and processes. Herein lies the importance of Service Blueprint. It is a key outcome of Service Design – a discipline that holds significant value, particularly for Product Managers aiming to deliver comprehensive, user-centric solutions.

Service Design refers to the activity of planning and organizing the components of a service, aiming to improve its quality and the interaction between the service provider and its customers. It's an interdisciplinary approach that combines various methods and tools from fields like user experience design, market research, and process modeling, all geared toward creating services that are seamless, efficient, and user-centric.

8.1 Introduction to Service Blueprint

Beyond the visible interactions that users have with a product or service, there's an intricate backstage of processes, tools, and interactions that culminate in the overall user experience. For Product Managers seeking a holistic understanding of this entire ecosystem, the tool of choice is the Service Blueprint.

A Service Blueprint is a detailed visual representation of a service's processes, touchpoints, physical evidence, and the interactions between various service components, both frontstage (customer-facing) and backstage (behind-the-scenes). It provides a structured way to break down and analyze the different elements of a service, allowing teams to identify inefficiencies, bottlenecks, or opportunities for innovation.

Service Blueprints help Product Managers in the following ways.

1. **Comprehensive Understanding**: While user journeys focus on the customer's path, service blueprints provide an in-depth look at how a service is delivered at every level. It offers Product Managers a 360-degree view of operations.

2. **Facilitate Cross-functional Collaboration**: By visualizing the entire service process, service blueprints bridge the gap between

departments, fostering understanding and collaboration between teams that might not typically interact.

3. **Informed Decision-making**: With a clear picture of how each part of the service functions and interrelates, Product Managers can make more informed decisions about where to allocate resources or how to prioritize features.

4. **Spotting Pain Points**: Service Blueprints can highlight where bottlenecks or inefficiencies exist, providing clear targets for optimization.

8.2 Key Concepts

For Product Managers looking to incorporate Service Design principles, it's vital to understand its key concepts.

1. **User Research**: Understanding users' needs, pain points, and preferences is foundational. This can be achieved through methods like interviews, surveys, and observational studies.

2. **Journey Mapping**: This involves charting the user's journey across various touchpoints of service, highlighting areas of friction and opportunities for enhancement.

3. **Service Blueprints**: A more detailed view than journey maps, service blueprints lay out all the processes and touchpoints of a service, often illustrating both the user-facing elements and the behind-the-scenes operations.

4. **Prototyping and Testing**: Before implementing changes, Service Design encourages prototyping new service solutions and testing them with real users to gather feedback and refine the approach.

5. **Stakeholder Alignment**: Ensuring that all stakeholders, from front-line employees to top-tier management, understand and are aligned with the service vision is crucial for consistent delivery.

While we have covered other aspects of Service Design, let us do a deeper dive into Service Blueprint.

8.3 Key Components

1. **Physical Evidence**: Tangible aspects that users can interact with, such as a website interface, a product, or marketing materials

2. **Customer Actions**: Steps or actions that customers take as they engage with the service

3. **Frontstage Activities**: Visible actions of service personnel or technologies that occur directly in view of the customer

4. **Backstage Activities**: Behind-the-scenes actions of service personnel or technologies, hidden from the customer's view

5. **Support Processes**: Additional activities or systems that support frontstage and backstage activities, such as inventory management or data processing

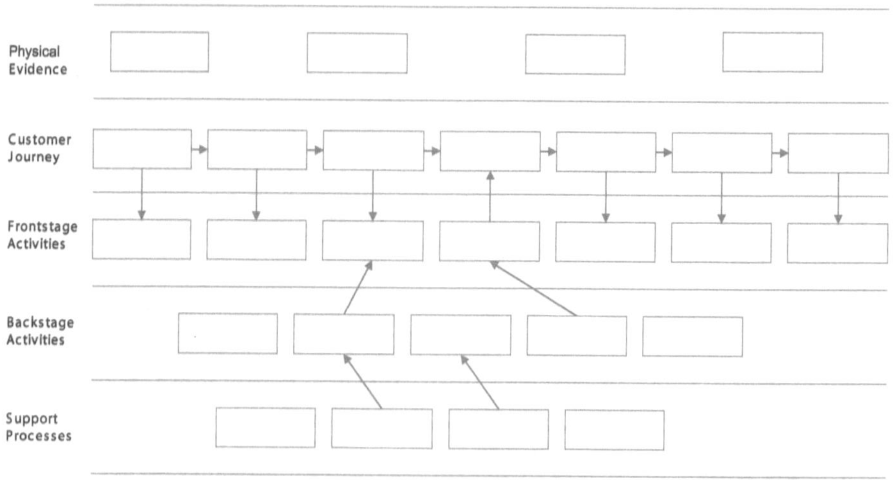

Fig 41: Service Blueprint Layout

8.4 Example Scenario

Scenario 43: An outgoing Product Manager of a Cloud-Based Photo Software wants to onboard a new Product Manager. In order to give the new Product Manager a full view of how the product serves the customer, the outgoing Product Manager lays out a tabular view of the Service Blueprint.

	Awareness	**Interest**
Customer Actions	• The User realizes a need for photo storage and editing capabilities. • Comes across the software on social media, a blog, or via word-of-mouth.	• The User visits the software's website or landing page to gather more information. • Reads about features, checks pricing, and possibly goes through reviews or testimonials. • The User watches promotional or tutorial videos provided by the organization.
Frontstage Activities	• Displaying targeted online advertisements on various platforms. • Sharing informational content and promotional posts on the software's official social media channels. • Encouraging influencers or tech bloggers to review or mention the software.	• Offering an intuitive and informative landing page or website design, complete with features, benefits, and pricing details. • Providing easily accessible and engaging video content or animations highlighting the software's capabilities. • Offering chatbots or live chats to answer user queries in the real time.

	Awareness	**Interest**
Backstage Activities	• Analysis of user behavior and preferences to create targeted ad campaigns. • Collaborations and negotiations with influencers or tech bloggers for promotional activities. • Regularly updating marketing strategies based on market trends and competitor activities.	• Maintenance of the website's server to ensure optimal uptime and performance. • Backend analytics to track user interactions on the website and gather insights on areas of interest. • Integrating and maintaining chatbot or live chat functionalities with the website.
Support Processes	• Market research teams continuously gather data on potential users, market trends, and competitor activities. • IT support ensures that promotional content is appropriately optimized and reaches the target audience. • Partnerships with advertising platforms and agencies to optimize ad delivery.	• Web development teams maintain and update the website's infrastructure, ensuring it's responsive and user-friendly. • SEO specialists optimize content to improve the software's online visibility and organic reach. • Analytics teams review website traffic sources and behavior, providing insights for optimization.

	Consideration	Decision
Customer Actions	• The User compares the software with other alternatives in the market. • Engages with content like FAQs or communicates with customer support to get any questions answered. • Checks for storage capacity, security features, and editing capabilities specific to their needs.	• Decides to give the software a try, possibly opting for a trial version if available. • Sign up, create a new account, and choose a subscription plan.
Frontstage Activities	• Displaying comparison charts or infographics to help users understand how the software stands against competitors. • Making available detailed articles or blogs discussing specific features, benefits, and use cases. • Sending automated follow-up emails or retargeting ads for users who visited the site but didn't sign up.	• Offering a simple and streamlined sign-up process with clear instructions. • Providing attractive offers or discounts for first-time users. • Displaying trust signals such as security badges, testimonials, or user reviews prominently during the sign-up or payment phase.

	Consideration	**Decision**
Backstage Activities	• Data analytics processes to understand user behavior and identify drop-off points or barriers to conversion. • Content management system updates and maintenance to ensure the latest information is displayed. • Automated email systems to trigger follow-up emails for potential leads.	• Secure payment gateways and their continuous monitoring for any potential issues. • Database management to store user sign-up data securely. • Encryption and cybersecurity measures to protect user data during the sign-up and payment processes.
Support Processes	• Customer feedback teams gather and analyze feedback from potential users or those who've abandoned the sign-up process. • Content teams ensure the regular updates and relevance of articles, blogs, and other informational content. • IT support troubleshoots any technical issues users might encounter while exploring the software.	• Finance teams manage pricing strategies, special offers, and monitor transaction processes. • Legal teams ensure compliance with data protection laws, terms of service, and user agreements. • Security teams continuously update and monitor the safety protocols for user data.

	Onboarding / Use	**Engagement**
Customer Actions	• Goes through the onboarding process, which might include tutorials or tooltips. • Begins uploading photos to the platform. • Engages with the editing tools, tries out various features, and customizes settings as per preferences.	• Uses sharing features to share edited photos with friends or on social media. • Engages with community forums or groups associated with the software for tips and tricks. • Receives notifications or emails about new features, updates, or storage use.
Frontstage Activities	• Initiating an engaging onboarding process with tutorials, tooltips, and walkthroughs. • Displaying notifications or pop-ups introducing new features or suggesting popular editing tools. • Sending welcome emails with resources, links to community forums, and tips to get started.	• Incorporating easy-to-use sharing features, integrating with popular social media platforms. • Offering periodic prompts or reminders about unused features or nearing storage limits. • Sending newsletters or emails about new features, software updates, or user stories.

Backstage Activities	• Cloud infrastructure management to facilitate smooth photo uploads and storage. • Continuous updates and maintenance of editing algorithms to ensure optimal performance. • Backend processes to categorize and suggest relevant tutorials or features based on user behavior.	• Integration with social media platforms' APIs to enable seamless sharing functionalities. • Regular backups and data redundancy measures to prevent data loss. • Data analytics tools working behind the scenes to track user behavior and preferences, informing the frontstage prompts and reminders.
Support Processes	• Product training teams provide resources and regular updates for onboarding processes. • IT teams manage server load, especially during high traffic periods, ensuring uninterrupted service. • Research & Development (R&D) teams work on improving software features and introducing innovative tools.	• Integration teams ensure smooth functioning of third-party integrations, like social media sharing. • Quality assurance teams regularly test software functionalities for bugs or issues. • Data analysts work on user data, deriving insights to improve user engagement and satisfaction.

	Retention / Advocacy
Customer Actions	• Renews subscription after finding value in the software's offerings. • Recommends the software to friends or writes positive reviews online. • Engages with the brand on social media or participates in any referral programs if offered.
Frontstage Activities	• Providing seamless subscription renewal processes and offering loyalty discounts or benefits. • Encouraging users to share their experiences through reviews, testimonials, or social media mentions. • Launching referral programs or campaigns, prompting users to invite friends and earn rewards.
Backstage Activities	• Backend systems to manage subscription renewals, send reminders, and process payments. • Database management to store and retrieve user reviews, feedback, and referral data. • Automated systems to manage, track, and reward referral campaigns and user loyalty programs.
Support Processes	• Customer relationship management (CRM) teams work on strategies to retain users and improve loyalty. • Customer support teams undergo regular training on product updates to assist users effectively. • Feedback loops are established with the Product Management team to continually refine and enhance the software based on user reviews and feedback.

Table 15: Service Blueprint Across User's Journey

9. Wireframes

Wireframes are a visual representation or blueprint of a digital product's user interface (UI). They are an essential tool used during the early stages of product development to outline and communicate the layout, structure, and functionality of a software application or website. Wireframes serve several important purposes.

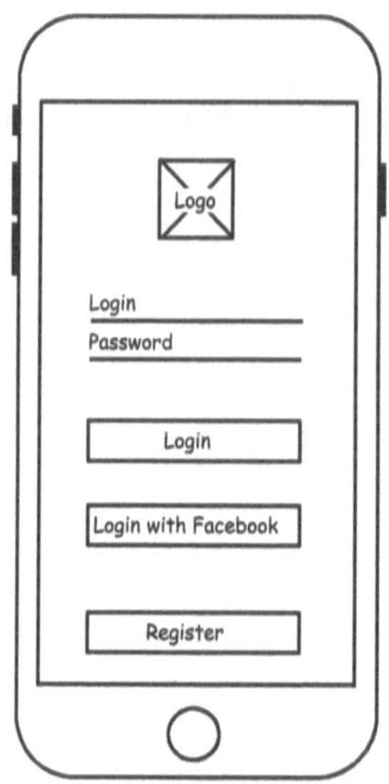

Fig 42: Wireframe for a Login & Register Screen for a Mobile App

1. **Conceptualizing Design**: Wireframes help Product Managers and designers conceptualize the overall design of a product. They provide a basic visual framework that can be used to discuss and refine ideas about how the product will look and function.

2. **Clarifying User Flow**: Wireframes help define the user flow and navigation within the product. They show how users will move from one screen or page to another, ensuring a logical and intuitive user experience.

3. **Identifying Key Elements**: Wireframes highlight the placement of key elements such as buttons, forms, menus, and content areas. This allows stakeholders to focus on the essential components of the interface without getting distracted by aesthetics.

4. **Iterative Design**: As wireframes are a simplified representation, they are easy to modify and iterate upon. This makes it possible to quickly make changes and improvements to the design before moving on to more detailed design stages.

5. **Collaboration**: Wireframes serve as a common visual language that can be shared with cross-functional teams, including designers, developers, and business stakeholders. They facilitate communication and alignment among team members by providing a clear reference point.

6. **Cost-Efficiency**: By working with wireframes early in the product development process, teams can identify potential issues and make adjustments before significant time and resources are invested in detailed design and development.

Wireframes can vary in fidelity, from low-fidelity sketches or digital drawings to high-fidelity wireframes that closely resemble the final product's design. Low-fidelity wireframes are often used in the initial ideation phase to quickly capture and communicate ideas, while high-fidelity wireframes are more detailed and may include elements such as color schemes and typography.

9.1 Creating Wireframes

Here's a step-by-step guide on how a Product Manager can create wireframes.

Understand Requirements

Begin by thoroughly understanding the project's goals, target audience, and user requirements. Gather input from stakeholders, designers, and developers to ensure a clear understanding of what the product needs to achieve.

Define the User Flow

Before creating wireframes, map out the user flow and the key interactions that users will have with the product. Determine the sequence of screens or pages users will encounter.

Choose Wireframing Tools

Select a wireframing tool or method that suits your needs.

Some popular options include:

1. **Pen and Paper**: For low-fidelity sketches and quick ideation

2. **Whiteboard**: Great for collaborative brainstorming sessions with the team

3. **Digital Wireframing Tools**: Software tools like Balsamiq, Sketch, Adobe XD, Figma, or wireframing features in prototyping tools like InVision

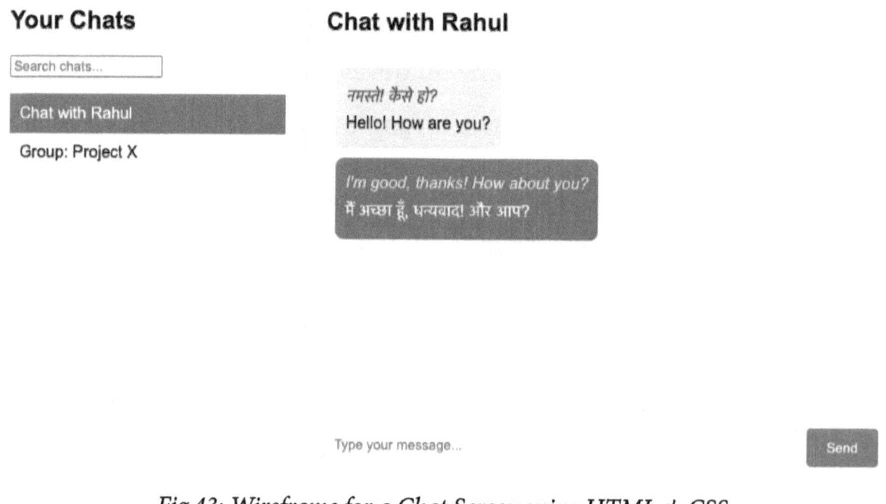

Fig 43: Wireframe for a Chat Screen using HTML & CSS

4. **HTML & CSS**: With the availability of frameworks like Twitter's Bootstrap and ChatGPT producing HTML code, sometimes Product Managers can use HTML pages as wireframes.

Start Creating Wireframes

Begin creating wireframes based on the user flow and requirements. Here are some key principles to keep in mind.

1. **Start with low-fidelity wireframes**: Focus on layout, content placement, and basic functionality rather than aesthetics.

2. **Use stock images**: Simple shapes and placeholders to represent UI elements like buttons, forms, images, and text are commonly available for reuse.

3. **Label**: Label elements and add annotations to explain functionality and interactions.

Iterate and Refine

Share your wireframes with the team, including designers, developers, and stakeholders, to gather feedback and make improvements. Iterate on the wireframes as needed to address any issues or suggestions.

Finalize and Handoff

Once the wireframes are approved and validated, work with designers and developers to transition from wireframes to visual design and development. Ensure that everyone involved understands the wireframes and their intended purpose.

Document and Maintain

Keep a record of the wireframes and any changes made during the design and development process. This documentation can be valuable as a reference for product updates.

9.2 Consider High-Fidelity Wireframes

Depending on the project's stage and requirements, you may choose to create high-fidelity wireframes. These include detailed design elements like colors, fonts, and images, and they can provide a more realistic representation of the final product's look and feel.

9.3 Collaborate and Communicate

Throughout the wireframing process, maintain open communication with your team and stakeholders to ensure alignment and a shared vision of the product's direction.

Creating wireframes is an essential skill for a Product Manager, as it helps bridge the gap between concept and execution, facilitating effective communication and collaboration during the product development process.

10. Accessibility

Accessibility, in the digital world, refers to the design of products, devices, services, or environments to be usable by as many people as possible, including those with disabilities. When we speak of 'accessibility,' we often think of ramps, elevators, or Braille. But in the digital era, accessibility includes ensuring websites, mobile apps, software, and other digital platforms are designed in ways that everyone, including individuals with disabilities, can use and benefit from them.

10.1 Benefits of Accessibility

1. **Inclusion and Equity**: At its core, accessibility ensures that everyone has an equal opportunity to access information, engage with digital services, and contribute to the digital world. By not considering accessibility, we inadvertently exclude a significant portion of the population.

2. **Wider Audience**: There are over a billion people worldwide with some form of disability. Ensuring accessibility broadens your market reach and can have direct economic benefits.

3. **Legal Implications**: Many regions around the world have implemented laws and regulations requiring digital accessibility, and non-compliance can lead to legal ramifications.

4. **Enhanced User Experience**: Accessible design practices often lead to a better user experience for everyone, not just people with disabilities. For instance, clear fonts, intuitive navigation, and meaningful alt-text for images benefit all users.

10.2 Good Practices for Product Managers

1. **Start Early with Accessibility in Mind**: It's easier (and more cost-effective) to build with accessibility from the outset rather than retrofitting.

2. **Use Accessibility Guidelines**: Familiarize yourself with the Web Content Accessibility Guidelines (WCAG), which offers a

wide range of recommendations for making web content more accessible.

3. **Engage Users**: Actively seek feedback from users with accessibility needs. Regular testing with actual users, including those with disabilities, can provide invaluable insights.

4. **Invest in Training**: Ensure that your team is well-informed about accessibility principles and practices. This includes designers, developers, and content creators.

5. **Tooling and Automation**: Utilize tools that check for accessibility compliance automatically. While they don't replace manual testing, they can be a valuable asset in catching common accessibility issues.

6. **Consider All Types of Disabilities**: Accessibility doesn't just mean catering to those with visual impairments. It includes considerations for auditory, cognitive, neurological, physical, speech, and visual disabilities.

10.3 Regulations Related to Accessibility

While accessibility guidelines and standards are present across the globe, here are some of the most prominent regulations:

1. **Americans with Disabilities Act (ADA)**: In the U.S., the ADA prohibits discrimination based on disability. While it doesn't mention websites explicitly, court decisions and the Department of Justice's stance have set the precedence that websites should be accessible.

2. **Web Content Accessibility Guidelines (WCAG)**: Although not a law, WCAG is the most widely adopted standard for web accessibility globally. Many laws and policies reference WCAG as their benchmark.

3. **Section 508**: In the U.S., this amendment to the Rehabilitation Act of 1973 requires federal agencies to make their electronic and information technology accessible.

4. **European Accessibility Act**: In the EU, this act harmonizes accessibility requirements for various products and services, including computers, telephones, banking services, and e-books.

5. **The Rights of Persons with Disabilities Act, 2016**: This is an example from India, where the government encourages accessibility to all citizens.

Accessibility is more than just a 'nice-to-have' feature or a legal requirement. It embodies the principles of inclusivity, ensuring that the digital realm is open and usable for everyone. As Product Managers, weaving accessibility into the fabric of our products makes both ethical and business sense.

14

Product Architecture

Product Architecture refers to the high-level structure of a product, focusing on the way components or modules are organized and integrated to meet user needs. It serves as a blueprint that outlines the features, functionalities, user interface design, and how each element contributes to creating a cohesive user experience. The focus here is more on what the system should do to meet the business and user requirements, rather than how it should do it.

The terms "Product Architecture" and "Technical Architecture" are at times used interchangeably. They both are concerned with different aspects and levels of abstraction of the product.

In order to remove any confusion between the two, a quick look at what Technical Architecture is. **Technical Architecture** is a detailed plan that specifies how a system will be constructed. It describes the technologies to be used, the structure of the data, the interaction between system components, the methods of communication, and other technical details. It is generally created by a solutions architect and serves as a guide for developers and engineers during implementation.

1. Product Architecture Diagram

A Product Architecture Diagram provides a visual representation of the high-level structure of a product, its components, and their interactions. It serves as a blueprint for understanding the key features, functionalities, and user interface design of a product, highlighting how each element contributes to the overall product design.

By visualizing the product architecture, teams can better understand the system's complexity, identify potential bottlenecks or dependencies, and make informed decisions about prioritization and resource allocation.

Illustration 13: Roo Kids App

In 2015, 30 million kids were active online, with 7.5 million of them in the US using Facebook. Instant messaging was a popular trend among these kids, with 10 million using such apps. However, these apps often have weaker privacy policies compared to Facebook, raising concerns for parents, especially regarding their kids interacting with strangers.

Roo Kids, developed by Gungroo (my now-defunct startup) addressed these concerns by offering a safe platform akin to 'WhatsApp for Kids.' It allowed parents to manage their kids' contacts, set curfew hours, and filter out inappropriate language.

Moreover, kids could report abuse, and the app offered various fun features like stickers, themes, doodles, and puzzles, ensuring an enjoyable and secure messaging experience for kids.

Following is a simplified version of Product Architecture I used to share with investors.

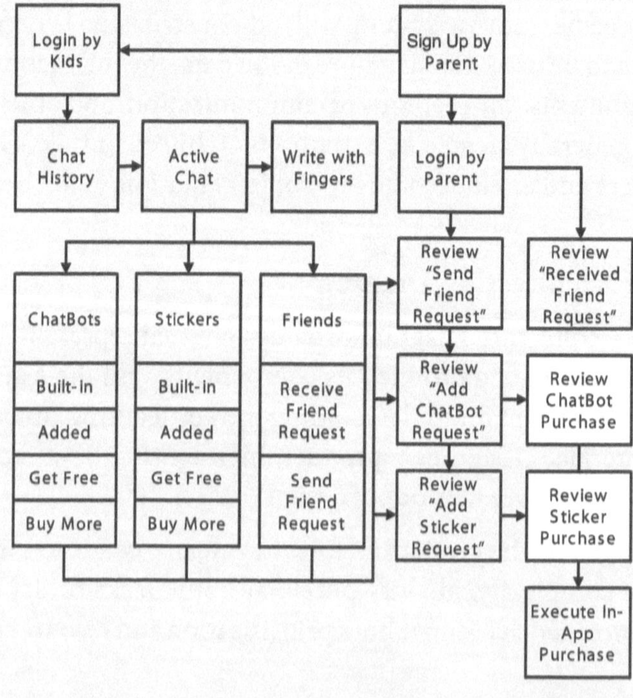

Fig 44: Product Architecture of Now Defunct Roo Kids App

Example Scenario

Scenario 44: Tasked by the CEO with developing a basic e-commerce website to explore the intricacies of its construction, the Product Manager initiates the process by creating a Product Architecture Diagram.

This foundational blueprint outlines the website's various capabilities, providing the development team with a structured roadmap for planning and implementation.

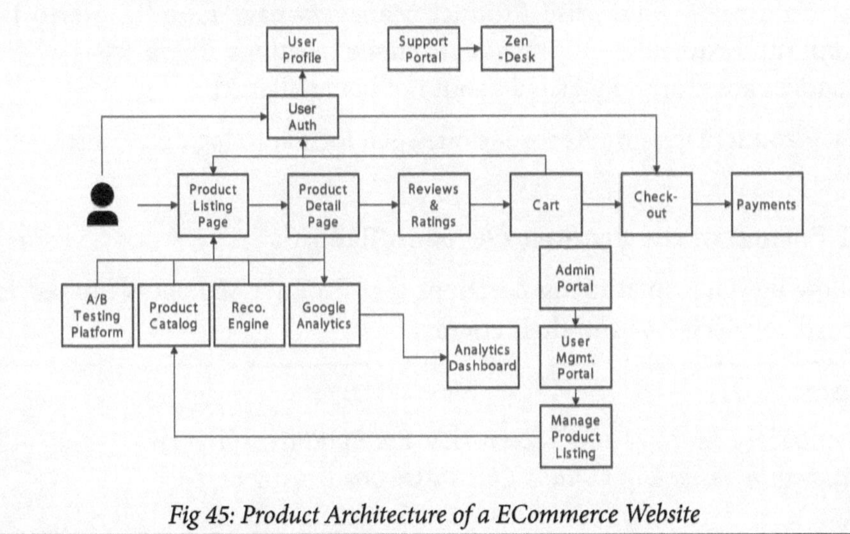

Fig 45: Product Architecture of a ECommerce Website

2. Product Decision Records

Every decision has a context. Many times that context is ephemeral. In an enterprise setting, products last a long time and teams see a lot of churn. Thus, it is important to note the context under which a decision regarding the product was made.

Every decision needs a review. All decisions are made at a moment in time and have a context. Thus, it is important for decisions to be revisited every so often. This is to ensure the decision is still valid.

Every decision has a scope. All decisions affect a part of the product design or a version of the product. So, they have a time/space scope that should be considered during reviews.

Every decision has consequences. All decisions are made to arrive at an intended consequence. It is important to regularly review if the decision is still leading to the intended consequences. And then there are always unintended ones that time reveals (if your product has that life or adoption).

Thus, it is very important to create decision logs for your product. It is an important tool to help teams that work on the products after you understand the decisions and make better calls as the product evolves. These calls may include what to retain, what to change, and what to kill.

And many enterprise Product Managers have found these to be useful (unfortunately) during assign-blame meetings after a crisis where attendees are more concerned about not being blamed.

Product Decision Record is one such format to log decisions.

2.1 Format of the Product Decision Records

Following is a format to log decisions that Product Managers can use to record key decisions and their context:

Name

Typically, a number and a summary. Eg: *PDR001: Have Two Passwords instead of Usually One Password During Login*

Date

Many collaboration tools allow you to enter Date using their component. Try using those tools as they add date as structured content.

Status

Possible values are:

STATUS	DESCRIPTION
Open	Still under discussion. But has been logged to facilitate a formal discussion and approval.
Accepted	Approved. Either in the implementation stage or already implemented.
Rejected	Not to be implemented. While it may have been rejected, it is important to log what was rejected.

Name

Typically, a number and a summary. Eg:

PDR001: Have Two Passwords instead of Usually One Password During Login

Date

Many collaboration tools allow you to enter Date using their component. Try using those tools as they add date as structured content.

Status

Possible values are:

STATUS	DESCRIPTION
Open	Still under discussion. But has been logged to facilitate a formal discussion and approval.
Accepted	Approved. Either in the implementation stage or already implemented.
Rejected	Not to be implemented. While it may have been rejected, it is important to log what was rejected.

Scope

Mention the Product version or the duration as the scope of the decision

Context

Describe the context of the decision.

Decision

The decision itself.

Consequences

Effects of the decision. Both the desired one and any possible undesired side effects.

Review Trigger

Usually, a time period, change in underlying assumption or known breaking point.

Author(s)

Optional.

Download Product Decision Records Sample

https://bit.ly/prd-sample

15

Product Metrics

Product metrics are essential tools for Product Managers to measure and track the performance and success of their products. These metrics provide valuable insights into how users are interacting with the product, what features are resonating with them, and where improvements can be made.

1. The Measure of Success, the Zone of Struggle, and The Measure of Failure

The Measure of Success tends to be customer-centric. Here are some examples.

"Our Customer Retention score is 90%."

"Our Net Promoter Score is 80%."

"Our Churn Rate has never crossed 10%."

"Our Conversation Rate from trial to paying customer is 50%."

"Our Monthly Active Users are growing at a rate of 210% month-on-month."

"Our Monthly Recurring Revenue is growing at a rate of 230% month-on-month."

"Our Customer Lifetime Value is $300 and growing."

Such metrics are very important and should be well crafted. They allow a business to focus on the right behavior expected from a product.

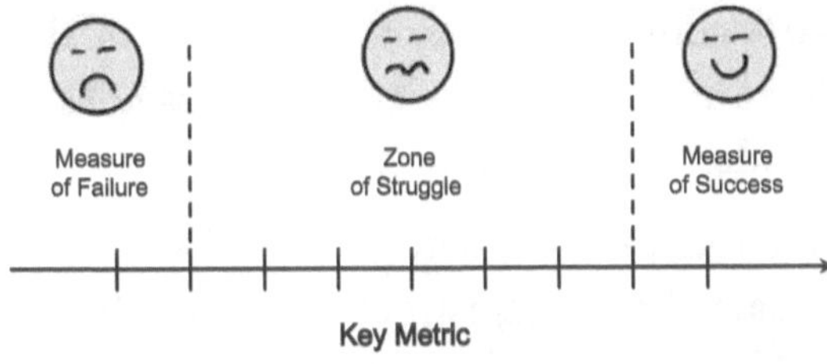

Fig 46: The Measure of Success, the Zone of Struggle, and The Measure of Failure

1.1 Understanding Measure of "Success"

Imagine a scenario in which a Product Manager has identified the conversion rate from trial users to paying customers as the pivotal Key Performance Indicator (KPI). The Product Manager ambitiously sets a target conversion rate of 50% as the benchmark for success.

When metrics reveal a 49% conversion rate, is the product considered a failure? Quite the contrary; it's a near miss that warrants slight adjustments rather than a complete overhaul. The Product Manager would likely continue on the current trajectory, making incremental improvements.

But what happens if the conversion rate dips to 45%? Is this indicative of product failure? Again, the answer is nuanced. It's a sign of lagging performance but not catastrophic failure. A savvy Product Manager would proceed with caution, iterating and refining the existing strategy.

A 40% conversion rate introduces a gray area. Here, the alarm bells might start ringing faintly in the distance. The Product Manager needs to critically assess whether minor setbacks have snowballed into more significant issues that necessitate a strategic pivot.

When the conversion rate plunges to 30%, the alarm bells grow louder. At this point, it's clear that foundational elements might be flawed. Serious consideration is given to reverting to the basics or executing a strategic pivot.

A further decline to 20% triggers a comprehensive review, encompassing user studies, market analyses, consultations, and a re-evaluation of the entire go-to-market strategy. While the product's success is now seriously in question, giving up is not yet the answer. Instead, a radical transformation becomes the focus.

Even at a 10% conversion rate, the question of shutting down the product or performing a hard pivot looms large. At what point is it reasonable to consider the product a sunk cost?

If the conversion rate stagnates below 5% for three consecutive months—despite data-driven adjustments and significant iterations—the

Product Manager would likely face the difficult decision to either shut down the project or implement a substantial pivot.

This understanding of KPIs and metrics is often well-grasped in the startup ecosystem but may be less appreciated within larger enterprises.

1.2 A Case for Measure of "Failure"

The concept of "Failure Metrics" occupies a significant space on the Product Management Canvas. Below is an illustrative example featuring three distinct thresholds for a key metric: the conversion rate of trial users to paying customers.

Threshold	Duration	A Product Manager's Analysis
Conversion Rate > 50%	–	"Success! Our strategy is working. The focus now shifts to continuous learning and incremental improvements."
Conversion Rate <= 50%	–	"Concerning! A suboptimal conversion rate signals a need for reevaluation. Success hasn't eluded us; we merely need to recalibrate and improve our existing strategy."
Conversion Rate <= 5%	Over 3 months	"Critical Situation! At this juncture, it's prudent to question if we are throwing good money at a bad idea. Are we trapped in a sunk-cost fallacy? The compelling case for winding down or making a significant pivot cannot be ignored."

Table 16: Illustration of Threshold of Failure

While these metrics serve as a compass, it's crucial to understand that falling short of the Success Metrics does not necessarily spell doom for the product. Such situations merely place the product in the 'Zone of Struggle,' where the product hasn't yet aligned with the market but hasn't failed either.

So, when does one determine that it's time to move on? This is where the importance of having a well-defined "Measure of Failure" comes into play. By establishing failure metrics and continuously comparing actual performance against them, a Product Manager can make informed decisions about whether to persevere, pivot, or pull the plug.

1.3 Measure of Failure

As illustrated in the above example, differentiating between Metrics of Success and Metrics of Failure is imperative, albeit challenging. While people are naturally inclined to focus on success, a disciplined Product Manager understands the value of clearly defining Metrics of Failure. These aren't just the antithesis of Metrics of Success; they serve as distinct measurements, often incorporating different variables and units.

Characteristics of Metrics of Failure:

1. **Range of Values**: Similar to Metrics of Success, Metrics of Failure are usually defined as a band of values, rather than a single pinpointed figure. This provides room for nuanced interpretation and action.

2. **Time-Sensitivity**: Unlike Metrics of Success, Metrics of Failure often include a temporal element. In the previous example, a conversion rate less than or equal to 5% sustained over three months triggers a failure alert.

3. **Spectrum Placement**: Metrics of Failure could mirror Metrics of Success but occupy an opposite position on the performance spectrum. For example, if high customer engagement is a Success Metric, low engagement over a defined period might constitute a Failure Metric.

4. **Zone of Struggle**: An adept Product Manager ensures that there's an adequate buffer between Metrics of Success and Metrics of

Failure. This intermediary area is known as the Zone of Struggle, where the product hasn't fully succeeded but hasn't failed either.

5. **Distinct Measures**: Metrics of Failure need not always be inversely related to Metrics of Success. They can be entirely different variables that are critical to the product's viability.

This approach not only aids in capturing success but also prepares the team for potential pitfalls, making it easier to navigate the intricate landscape of product development.

A Product Manager may plan how to react when the product is in any of the above zones:

Metrics	Measure Band	Duration	Action
Measure of Success	Conversion Rate > 50%	–	Keep going. Keep learning. Keep improving.
Zone of Struggle	Conversion Rate <= 50%	–	Renewed Product Analysis, User Research, Market Research, Ecosystem Research, and Competition Research to find the root cause of low conversation rates.
Measure of Failure	Conversion Rate <= 5%	Over 3 months	Record learning and wind up or pivot.

Table 17: Action Plan Based on Success & Failure Metrics

2. Understanding Leading and Lagging Indicators

Leading indicators are forward-looking metrics that provide insights into future performance while lagging indicators are retrospective metrics that reflect past performance.

2.1 Leading indicators

Leading Indicators are metrics that provide early insights or predictive measures of future performance. Leading indicators are also like a compass that helps you navigate towards success. They are proactive in nature and are used to anticipate potential trends or changes that may impact the desired outcome. Leading indicators are forward-looking and help stakeholders make informed decisions to optimize strategies, identify opportunities, or address potential issues before they become critical.

Using leading indicators enables a Product Manager to make data-driven decisions, and take proactive actions to optimize performance and achieve success for the business as a whole.

Stakeholder	Explanation Of Leading Indicators	Examples
Business Aspect	Leading indicators are like a compass that provides early insights into potential trends or changes in the business, such as customer engagement levels, qualified leads generated, or revenue growth rates. By monitoring these metrics, a business leader can make informed decisions to optimize business strategies.	• Customer engagement levels • Qualified leads generated • Revenue growth rates

Product Management Aspect	Leading indicators are metrics that provide early insights into how well the product is being received by customers and its potential impact on the market, such as product adoption rates, customer satisfaction scores, or feature usage. A Product Manager can use these insights to make data-driven decisions and take proactive steps to address any potential issues or capitalize on opportunities.	• Product adoption rates • Customer satisfaction scores • Feature usage
Tech Aspect	Leading indicators are metrics that provide early insights into the performance and health of the technology stack or development process, such as system uptime, code quality, or deployment frequency. A tech leader can use these insights to assess the efficiency and effectiveness of technology operations, make data-driven decisions, and proactively address any potential risks or bottlenecks.	• System uptime • Code quality • Deployment frequency

Table 18: Understanding Leading Indicators

2.2 Lagging indicators

Lagging indicators, on the other hand, are metrics that measure the outcomes or results of past actions or decisions. Lagging indicators are also like a rear-view mirror that provides a retrospective view of past performance for businesses, products, and technology initiatives. They are reactive in nature and provide a historical perspective on performance. Lagging indicators are used to assess the success or failure of a completed initiative or goal and help stakeholders understand the consequences of past actions.

By using lagging indicators and appreciating their retrospective nature, Product Managers can better understand how these metrics can provide valuable insights into past performance and guide decision-making based on historical outcomes.

Stakeholder	Explanation Of Lagging Indicators	Examples
Business Leader	Lagging indicators are like a rearview mirror that provides insights into past performance, such as historical sales data, customer retention rates, or profit margins. These metrics help a business leader understand the results of past actions and decisions.	• Historical sales data • Customer retention rates • Profit margins
Product Manager	Lagging indicators are metrics that measure the impact of past product initiatives, such as the revenue generated from new features, customer feedback on a released product, or user retention rates. These metrics help a Product Manager assess the success of past product efforts.	• Revenue generated from new features • Customer feedback on a released product • User retention rates

Tech Leader	Lagging indicators are metrics that measure the outcomes of past technology initiatives, such as system downtime incidents, bug resolution time, or customer support tickets. These metrics help a tech leader understand the results of past technology decisions and actions.	• System downtime incidents • Bug resolution time • Customer support tickets

Table 19: Understanding Lagging Indicators

2.3 Summary

Both leading and lagging indicators are powerful tools that, when used appropriately, can enable a Product Manager to effectively monitor, analyze, and optimize their performance, and ultimately achieve their strategic objectives.

Leading Indicators	Lagging Indicators
Future-oriented, helps anticipate potential changes or trends	Historical performance, assess past outcomes
Actionable, provides insights that can be acted upon	Measure actual results or outcomes
Early warning signals to detect changes or trends before they become critical	Evaluate the success or failure of completed initiatives or goals
Proactive, drive actions, and optimize strategies	Retrospective, provide a benchmark for performance evaluation
Examples: Sales leads, customer engagement, product adoption	Examples: Historical sales data, customer retention rate, product returns

Table 20: Comparison Between Leading & Lagging Indicators

3. OKR

When it comes to achieving goals, it can be challenging to measure progress and identify areas for improvement. That's where Objectives and Key Results (OKR) come into play. OKR is a popular goal-setting framework that has been adopted by many successful companies, including Google, LinkedIn, and erstwhile Twitter. It is a simple, yet effective way to set measurable goals and track progress towards achieving them.

To establish shared objectives, former Intel Andy Grove suggests to ask two questions[1] and established the concept of OKR:

1. **"Where do I want to go?"** The answer to this provides the objective

2. **"How will I pace myself to see if I am getting there?"** The answer to this provides the key results

This was picked by John Doerr while at Intel and brought over to Google where it is practiced even today.[2]

3.1 What are Objectives and Key Results

Objectives and Key Results are two important components of the OKR framework. The objective is the goal you want to achieve, while the key results are the specific, measurable outcomes that will indicate progress towards that goal. Objectives are typically set on a quarterly basis, and they should be ambitious, inspiring, and achievable. Key results, on the other hand, should be specific, measurable, and time-bound. They should also be challenging but attainable.

3.2 How to Implement OKR

Implementing the OKR framework requires commitment and discipline from everyone involved. Here are the basic steps to implementing OKR in your organization:

1. **Set Organization Objectives:** Start by setting organization-wide objectives that are aligned with your overall mission and vision.

These objectives should be challenging but achievable and should inspire everyone to work towards them.

2. **Define Department Objectives:** Each department should define its objectives that align with the organization's objectives. These should be specific, measurable, challenging but achievable.

3. **Create Key Results:** For each objective, define specific key results that will indicate progress towards achieving the objective. These key results should be measurable and time-bound.

4. **Review and Update:** Review progress towards objectives and key results regularly. This will help you identify areas where you need to improve and adjust your strategy accordingly.

3.3 Benefits of OKR

The OKR framework offers several benefits to organizations that use it, such as:

1. **Clarity:** OKR provides clarity on what needs to be achieved and how progress will be measured.

2. **Alignment:** OKR helps align everyone in the organization towards a common goal.

3. **Focus:** OKR helps teams to focus on what's important and avoid distractions.

4. **Accountability:** OKR creates a sense of accountability, as everyone is responsible for achieving their objectives and key results.

3.4 Google's Method

Fergus Henderson, a software engineer at Google, described the process as[3][4]:

Individuals and teams at Google are required to explicitly document their goals and to assess their progress towards these goals.

- Teams set quarterly and annual objectives, with measurable key results that show progress towards these objectives. This is done at every level of the organization, going all the way up to defining goals for the whole organization.

- Goals for individuals and small teams should align with the higher-level goals for the broader teams that they are part of and with the overall organization goals.

- At the end of each quarter, progress towards the measurable key results is recorded and each objective is given a score from 0.0 (no progress) to 1.0 (100% completion).

- OKRs and their scores are normally made visible across Google (with occasional exceptions for especially sensitive information such as highly confidential projects), but they are not used directly as input to an individual's performance appraisal.

3.5 Limitation of OKR

However, like any other framework, OKR has certain limitations that should be taken into consideration.

1. **Lack of Flexibility:** One of the limitations of OKR is its lack of flexibility. The framework is designed to be simple and easy to implement, which is one of its biggest strengths. However, this simplicity can also be a drawback in certain situations. For example, if an organization's goals and objectives change frequently, OKR may not be the best option as it does not allow for quick adjustments. OKR requires a significant amount of planning and coordination, which can be a hindrance in fast-paced environments.

2. **Overemphasis on Short-Term Goals:** Another limitation of OKR is its overemphasis on short-term goals. The framework is designed to be used on a quarterly or yearly basis, which can lead to a focus on short-term objectives rather than long-term goals. This can be problematic for companies that need to focus on long-term growth and sustainability. Additionally, OKR may not be suitable for projects that require a longer timeframe to

complete. In such cases, a more flexible framework that allows for longer-term planning may be more appropriate.

3. **Excessive Focus on Metrics:** The third limitation of OKR is its excessive focus on metrics. OKR is a data-driven framework that relies heavily on metrics to measure progress and success. While metrics are important, they can also be misleading. Focusing solely on metrics can lead to a narrow focus on achieving specific targets rather than the broader picture, as described by Goodhart's Law. [A] This can result in teams prioritizing the achievement of specific metrics over the overall success of the project or organization.

3.6 Example Scenario

> **Scenario 45**: After due consideration, the Product Manager for the MsgMsg App has decided to use OKR to set up goals for the next quarter. The objective is to increase the number of installations to 1 million mobile devices. Based on this, each team is asked to decide the Key Results they will deliver to help achieve this objective. After discussions, the Product Manager and various teams agreed upon the following Key Results:
>
> Key Results (KRs) based on the objective of "increasing the number of installations to 1 million mobile devices."
>
> **Product Marketing Team:**
>
> 1. KR1: Launch 3 new marketing campaigns targeting primary user personas, leading to a 30% increase in app awareness.
>
> 2. KR2: Collaborate with 10 influencers or bloggers to promote the app and achieve at least 100k new installations through influencer recommendations.
>
> 3. KR3: Increase the app's visibility in app stores by optimizing keywords and gaining at least 500 positive reviews.
>
> **Support Team:**
>
> 1. KR1: Maintain a 95%+ customer satisfaction rate on support queries, ensuring that users' issues don't deter them from installing or recommending the app.

2. KR2: Create a series of 5 video tutorials or FAQs that address the most common user questions, potentially reducing barriers to installation.

3. KR3: Implement a system to flag and escalate critical issues that might cause uninstallations, aiming for a resolution time of less than 12 hours for 90% of flagged issues.

Sign-Up Page Team:

- KR1: Optimize the sign-up process to reduce drop-offs, targeting a conversion rate increase of 20%.

- KR2: Implement an A/B testing strategy to identify the most effective sign-up prompts, aiming for a 15% higher success rate in the winning design.

- KR3: Enhance the mobile responsiveness and loading speed of the sign-up page, ensuring that 99% of the page loads happen in under 3 seconds.

Backend Team:

1. KR1: Ensure 99.9% uptime for the app, guaranteeing that technical outages don't deter potential installs.

2. KR2: Optimize the backend for faster response times, with a target average response of under 500ms.

3. KR3: Implement a referral system where existing users can invite friends to install the app, aiming for a 10% conversion rate on referrals.

AI Translation Team:

1. KR1: Increase the accuracy of AI translations by 15%, enhancing the app's value proposition.

2. KR2: Expand the number of supported languages by 5, tapping into new potential user bases.

3. KR3: Introduce a feedback mechanism where users can report translation inaccuracies, aiming to collect and address feedback for at least 5,000 instances.

4. Key Performance Indicators

Key Performance Indicator (KPI) is a measurable value that demonstrates how effectively an organization is achieving key business objectives or goals. Product Managers use KPIs to assess the success and progress of their products or features.

KPIs are essential for Product Managers as they help in:

1. **Performance Measurement**: KPIs allow Product Managers to track and quantify the performance of their products, features, or projects. They provide insights into whether the product is meeting its intended objectives.

2. **Data-Driven Decision Making**: By analyzing KPIs, Product Managers can make informed decisions about future product enhancements, changes, or pivots based on real data rather than subjective opinions.

3. **Goal Alignment**: KPIs align the efforts of the product team with the overall business goals and strategy of the organization. They ensure everyone is working towards common objectives.

4. **Course Correction**: If KPIs indicate that the product is not performing as expected, Product Managers can take corrective actions to improve its performance and achieve the desired outcomes.

5. **Communication and Reporting**: KPIs serve as a basis for reporting progress to stakeholders, such as executives, investors, or cross-functional teams, allowing everyone to stay informed about the product's performance.

The specific KPIs used by Product Managers can vary depending on the nature of the product, the business objectives, and the stage of the product life cycle. Common examples of KPIs in Product Management include user acquisition metrics, retention rates, customer satisfaction scores, conversion rates, and revenue growth, among others.

4.1 KPIs v/s OKRs

The concepts of KPIs (Key Performance Indicators) and OKRs (Objectives and Key Results) are related but different in their focus and approach. Both are widely used in organizations to measure performance and achieve goals, but they serve different purposes and have distinct characteristics. Product Managers should not confuse the purpose of each.

A few key differences:

1. **Focus**: KPIs are primarily concerned with tracking and measuring ongoing performance and operational metrics. OKRs, on the other hand, are focused on setting ambitious goals and tracking progress toward achieving those goals.

2. **Qualitative vs. Quantitative**: OKRs are more qualitative, focusing on setting meaningful and challenging objectives, while KPIs are purely quantitative, measuring specific numeric targets.

3. **Timeframe and Frequency**: KPIs are measured on an ongoing basis, while OKRs are usually set for specific timeframes (e.g. quarterly) and are revised periodically.

4. **Level of the Organization**: KPIs are commonly used at various levels within an organization for different functions, while OKRs are typically used at higher levels to align the entire organization towards common objectives.

4.2 Example Scenario

> **Scenario 46**: Based on the Key Results the Sign-up Page and Backend Team have signed up for, the team set up some KPIs they want to keep an eye on.
>
> **Sign-Up Page Team:**
>
> Optimize the sign-up process:
>
> - KPI1: Weekly sign-up conversion rate

> Implement an A/B testing strategy:
>
> - KPI1: Conversion rate for each design variant
>
> **Backend Team:**
>
> Ensure 99.9% uptime:
>
> 1. KPI1: Number of minutes/hours of downtime per month
>
> 2. KPI2: Number of outages or incidents reported each month

5. DORA's 4 Key Metrics

The practice of DevOps has emerged as a critical part of the product development. While the term 'DevOps' was coined in 2009,[5] the practices and principles associated with it have deep roots in the Agile and Lean methodologies.

The term "DevOps" was first coined by Patrick Debois and Andrew Clay Shafer in 2009 via the hashtag #DevOps. They came up with the term to denote a new movement that emphasizes collaboration and communication between software developers (Dev) and IT operations (Ops) professionals while automating the process of software delivery and infrastructure changes. The aim is to establish a culture and environment where building, testing, and releasing software can happen rapidly, frequently, and reliably. The term was created as a response to the perceived disconnect and tension between the development and operations teams in IT, which can often lead to project delays, inefficiencies, and reduced quality.

DORA (DevOps Research and Assessment) was founded in 2014 by Dr. Nicole Forsgren, Jez Humble, and Gene Kim, three renowned experts in the field of DevOps. They saw the need for a data-driven approach to understanding and measuring DevOps performance. Dr. Forsgren, a leading researcher in the field of DevOps, brought her expertise in tech performance, measuring software delivery, and generating actionable insights. Humble, the author of the Continuous Delivery book, brought his vast experience in software delivery, and Kim, the author of The

Phoenix Project, brought his deep understanding of DevOps and IT operations.

One of DORA's most notable contributions is the identification and validation of four key metrics that help organizations measure their DevOps effectiveness. These were first highlighted in their State of DevOps 2019 report.[6]

1. **Lead Time for Changes**: This measures the amount of time it takes for a commit to get into production. It reflects how quickly a team can deliver code, from development to deployment. Shorter lead times often indicate a higher level of efficiency and process streamlining. For Product Managers, reducing lead time can result in faster feedback loops and quicker iterations.

2. **Deployment Frequency**: This is a measure of how often an organization successfully releases to production. High-performing organizations deploy code more frequently, which allows for quicker user feedback and reduces the risk associated with any single deployment. Product Managers should aim to increase the deployment frequency to deliver value to the customers more regularly and adapt to changes rapidly.

3. **Change Failure Rate**: This measures the percentage of changes that fail, requiring remediation (such as a hotfix, rollback, fix forward, or patch). High change failure rates can indicate problems with certain aspects of development or operations practices. For Product Managers, understanding this rate can help pinpoint areas for improvement and drive strategies to reduce failure rates.

4. **Time to Restore Service**: This measures how long it takes an organization to recover from a failure in production. High-performing teams can restore service quickly, often in less than an hour. This metric highlights the team's ability to quickly respond to issues, a crucial element for maintaining customer trust and satisfaction.

Software delivery performance metric	Low	Medium	High
Lead time for changes For the primary application or service you work on, what is your lead time for changes (i.e., how long does it take to go from code committed to code successfully running in production)?	Between once per month and once every 6 months	Between once per week and once per month	On-demand (multiple deploys per day)
Deployment frequency For the primary application or service you work on, how often does your organization deploy code to production or release it to end users?	Between one month and six months	Between one week and one month	Between one day and one week
Change failure rate For the primary application or service you work on, what percentage of changes to production or released to users result in degraded service (e.g., lead to service impairment or service outage) and subsequently require remediation (e.g., require a hotfix, rollback, fix forward, patch)	Between one week and one month	Between one day and one week	Less than one day
Time to restore service For the primary application or service you work on, how long does it generally take to restore service when a service incident or a defect that impacts users occurs (e.g., unplanned outage or service impairment)?	46%-60%	16%-30%	0%-15%

Table 21: DORA 4 Key Metrics of DevOps from 2022 DORA Accelerate State of DevOps Report

In their 2022 report they added one more:

1. **Reliability**: This metric evaluates both the adherence to reliability engineering practices and the degree to which teams meet their set expectations. It underscores the significance of maintaining a dependable service that aligns with user expectations. High reliability ensures that while delivery speeds might be fast, the end service is stable and meets user needs consistently. Reliability is closely intertwined with the adoption of Site Reliability Engineering (SRE) practices. However, the benefits of SRE on reliability are seen only when a team achieves a certain level of maturity in SRE practices. Initial stages might not showcase a direct relationship between SRE and reliability, but upon reaching a certain threshold, SRE adoption becomes a strong predictor of improved reliability, which in turn positively impacts overall organizational performance. For Product Managers, prioritizing reliability ensures that rapid deliveries do not compromise the service's integrity and user trust.

As Product Managers, understanding these metrics, and ways to influence them, can provide powerful insights to drive decision-making and strategy. It empowers them to navigate the complexities of DevOps, ensuring the efficient and effective delivery of products that meet the ever-evolving needs of customers.

While the report proposes what ranges of values an 'elite' (dropped in 2022 report), 'high', 'medium,' and 'low' performing teams exhibit, it is important to note that these may not be relevant to all types of products. A common example is any application that needs lots of regulatory and compliance checks may not be about to make multiple deployments per day, it may also not be relevant to their use case. So a Product Manager has to be judicious about what level they aim for.

6. SPACE Metrics

SPACE Metrics were introduced in a paper exploring developer productivity as a fresh approach to define, measure, and predict it.[7]

Developer productivity is crucial for software development teams, and understanding it better could lead to higher-quality software and improved efficiency for organizations, managers, and developers.

The acronym SPACE represents key dimensions to assess productivity: Satisfaction, Performance, Activity, Communication, and Efficiency.

Let's break down the key points.

1. **Satisfaction and well-being**: Developers find fulfillment in meaningful work. Reducing workload stress is vital for a healthy team environment. Including this dimension in productivity metrics is essential.

2. **Performance**: Measuring outcomes, rather than just output, is suggested by the SPACE framework. Understanding team performance requires assessing outcomes at a system level.

3. **Activity**: Tracking developer activity during different phases of software development can offer insights into productivity and efficiency, but it's not sufficient on its own.

4. **Communication and collaboration**: This dimension captures how well a team collaborates and communicates. Transparent communication enhances productivity by improving coordination.

5. **Efficiency and flow**: This dimension gauges the team's ability to work without interruptions and smoothly progress through development processes. DORA metrics are effective for capturing flow at the team level.

6.1 Regarding DORA 4KM and SPACE

SPACE is considered an evolution of DORA 4KM for DevOps and complements it; they can be used together.[8]

- DORA 4 Key Metrics offer excellent North Star metrics for measuring productivity in engineering organizations.

- SPACE Metrics expand on DORA, measuring additional factors that impact productivity and provide indications for improvement.

- Relying solely on DORA metrics may not consider factors like developer happiness, potentially harming team productivity and morale.

- DORA can be a starting point for teams new to measurement but should not be the sole metric used.

Using both DORA and SPACE metrics provides a more comprehensive view of developer productivity and helps foster a productive and content team environment.

7. EEBO Metrics

One of the biggest challenges of a Product Manager lies in bridging the gap between technical development and tangible business outcomes. This is where Engineering Excellence to Business Outcomes (EEBO) metrics come into play.

7.1 About EEBO Metrics

EEBO Metrics are fitness metrics that span the entire engineering lifecycle, right from the conception of a software idea to its final deployment in production.[9] For a Product Manager, understanding these metrics can provide invaluable insights into[10]:

1. **Excellence in Software Development**: These metrics delve into the software's quality, encompassing aspects like code quality, test coverage, and technical debt.

2. **Excellence in Deployment to Production**: They reflect the efficiency of the deployment process by using DORA's 4 Key Metrics, measuring deployment frequency, lead time for changes, and mean time to recovery.

3. **Progress Toward Desired Business Outcomes**: These gauge the business's health and include metrics such as user satisfaction, time to market, and revenue growth.

The beauty of EEBO metrics lies in their ability to offer a direct line of sight from engineering practices to business results.

For a Product Manager, this translates into:

1. **Clear Value Articulation**: By understanding the EEBO metrics, Product Managers can effectively communicate the business impact of engineering efforts to stakeholders.

2. **Guidance for Long-Term Projects**: These metrics serve as a beacon, ensuring that the product's engineering quality remains consistent throughout its lifecycle.

3. **Clarity of Contribution**: Team members gain clarity on how their work integrates with larger business objectives, fostering a sense of purpose and direction.

7.2 The Concept of Fully Modeled Metric

Metrics, in their basic form, give us numbers and values. However, for them to be truly valuable to a Product team, they need to encompass more depth.

The concept of a 'Fully Modeled Metric'[11] emerges as a holistic approach to understanding metrics.

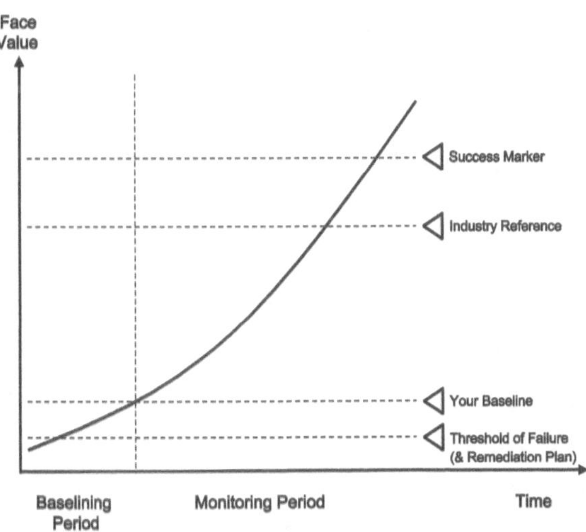

Fig 47: Fully Modeled Metrics[12]

Let's unpack the layers that make up the full model.

1. **Success Marker:** A predefined benchmark that indicates the desired outcome or goal of the metric. It signifies when the metric has achieved its purpose.

2. **Failure Thresholds:** These delineate the limits beyond which the metric's performance is considered unsatisfactory or detrimental. Recognizing these thresholds allows the team to take corrective action promptly.

3. **Industry Reference:** It's crucial to gauge how a metric stands in comparison to industry standards or competitors. This reference provides context and offers a clearer understanding of where the team stands in the broader market landscape.

4. **Team's Current Baseline:** Before any improvement can be made, it's essential to understand the current performance level. This baseline provides a starting point against which progress can be measured.

5. **Baselining Period:** The specific timeframe chosen to measure the baseline. It offers a snapshot of the metric's performance during that period, providing context for future evaluations.

6. **Directionality:** Metrics are diverse. Some might consider a lower value as a success, such as defect rates, while others might see higher values as a sign of progress, like user engagement rates. Understanding the preferred direction of a metric is vital for accurate interpretations.

7. **Remediation Plans:** It's not enough to identify when a metric underperforms. There must be pre-established plans detailing steps to rectify deviations, ensuring timely and effective action.

8. **Ownership Matrix:** Using frameworks like RACI (Responsible, Accountable, Consulted, Informed)[13] ensures there's absolute clarity on who holds which responsibilities regarding a metric. This becomes particularly vital when a metric underperforms, as a clear ownership structure prevents the adverse effects of blame games and knee-jerk reactions.

In essence, a Fully Modeled Metric goes beyond mere numbers. It encapsulates a strategic approach to measurement, allowing for proactive action, clearer accountability, and, ultimately, more meaningful outcomes. Such depth and structure prevent common pitfalls, fostering a constructive environment where metrics drive positive change.

7.3 The Concept of Fitness Metrics

In the book 'Building Evolutionary Architectures', a fitness function is described as "an objective evaluation reflecting specific architectural attributes."[13]

A Fitness Metric is a comprehensively designed metric that gauges the efficiency of an activity in reaching its intended objective. Furthermore, it determines how effectively a team is contributing to the realization of the desired business outcome.

A Fitness Metric should be:

1. **Multivariate**: Derived from multiple data points, making them harder to manipulate

2. **Holistic**: Focusing on the broader effectiveness of processes rather than a narrow subset

3. **Transparent**: Every team member should understand how these metrics correlate with the overarching vision

7.4 Recommended EEBO Metrics

Engineering Excellence to Business Outcomes (EEBO) Metrics play a pivotal role in linking the technical facets of a product to its business outcomes. Each EEBO Metric is a fitness metric and should be fully modeled.

Here's a look at the recommended EEBO metrics:

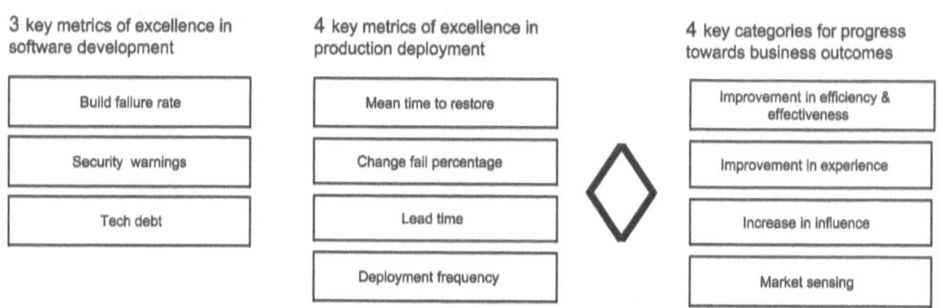

Fig 48: EEBO (Engineering Excellence to Business Outcomes) Metrics

1. **Build Failure Rate**: A measure of how frequently software builds fail. A lower rate indicates a more reliable and robust development process.

2. **Security Warnings**: Number of warnings raised during security assessments. Fewer warnings suggest a safer and more secure product.

3. **Tech Debt**: Amount of work postponed during the software development phase. Managing this metric helps maintain product quality and ensures long-term scalability.

4. **Mean Time To Restore (MTTR)**: Average time taken to restore a system or application after a failure. A shorter MTTR indicates a more resilient system.

5. **Change Fail Percentage**: Percentage of changes that fail. A low percentage ensures stability in product updates.

6. **Lead Time**: The duration between the inception of a task or feature request and its completion. Shorter lead times can signify efficient workflows.

7. **Deployment Frequency**: How often deployments occur. A higher frequency can often suggest an agile and responsive development process.

8. **Improvement in Efficiency & Effectiveness**: Evaluates the enhancements in process smoothness and the results delivered.

9. **Improvement in Experience**: Uplift in user experience, indicating how user-friendly and intuitive a product is.

10. **Increase in Influence**: This metric delves into the broader business impact. It measures how a product bolsters the business's influence across various domains. This can be evaluated through:

    a. Market Share Growth: The increase in the proportion of total market sales

    b. Brand Recognition and Perception: How widely and positively the brand is known

    c. Customer Loyalty or Retention Rates: The consistency with which customers return

    d. Partnerships or Collaborations: Forming alliances with key industry stakeholders

    e. Competitive Positioning: Where the product stands vis-a-vis competitors

    f. Regulatory Compliance: Adherence to industry regulations and standards

1. **Market Sensing**: A strategic category that stresses the product's role in aiding executive foresight. Relevant metrics include:

    a. Market Intelligence Gathering: The product's capability to collect and interpret market data

    b. Identification of Emerging Trends: Spotting and responding to new market inclinations or customer preferences

    c. Adaptation Speed: The rate at which product changes can be made in response to market shifts

    d. Innovation Pipeline: A look into upcoming innovative features or solutions

    e. Proactive Market Challenge Addressing: The product's capability to foresee and mitigate potential market hurdles

In summary, these EEBO Metrics offer a comprehensive lens through which a product's technical proficiency can be harmoniously aligned with its business achievements, ensuring both immediate effectiveness and long-term strategic prowess.

7.5 Using EEBO Metrics

Product Managers can harness EEBO metrics in several strategic ways, such as:

1. **Spotting Derailments:** By keeping an eye on EEBO metrics, Product Managers can swiftly detect misalignments between engineering practices and business outcomes. This proactive approach enables timely corrective action, ensuring products remain on track.

2. **Fostering Communication**: Displaying EEBO metrics openly encourages dialogue among team members, ensuring that everyone remains aligned with the product's objectives and progress.

7.6 Common Pitfalls

As Product Managers venture into the realm of EEBO metrics, they should be wary of potential pitfalls, such as:

1. **Over-Analysis**: While EEBO metrics offer a macro view of engineering excellence, they shouldn't be used for microscopic examinations. Product Managers should lean on specific drill-down metrics for detailed insights and complement them with EEBO metrics for broader perspectives.

2. **Metric Inflation**: There's a tendency to continually expand the list of metrics being monitored. However, more isn't always better. Drawing a parallel with Conway's Law, Product Managers should recognize that the structure of metrics should reflect the organization's true needs and not become unnecessarily bloated.

8. AARRR Pirate Metrics

In the vast sea of metrics and analytics that Product Managers must navigate, there emerges a framework that captures the essence of the user journey with a pirate's flair. Coined by Dave McClure,[15] the AARRR framework, aptly dubbed "Pirate Metrics," is a systematic approach to understanding and optimizing a product's lifecycle.

8.1 Acquisition: Where the Voyage Begins

At the heart of the user journey is the point of 'Acquisition.' This is where users first interact with the product or platform.

For Product Managers, understanding this phase means asking:

1. Where are users coming from?
2. Which channels are most effective in attracting potential users?

Analyzing the Acquisition metric helps in refining marketing strategies and ensuring that resources are spent on channels that yield the highest return.

8.2 Activation: Ensuring a Memorable First Experience

Once users are onboarded, ensuring they have a stellar initial experience is crucial. 'Activation' dives into:

1. Are users completing sign-up processes?
2. Are they engaging with core features?

For Product Managers, a user who successfully passes the Activation phase is more likely to become a regular and valuable user. It's about ensuring that first impressions aren't just good—they're outstanding.

8.3 Retention: Keeping the Crew Loyal

The 'Retention' phase explores the frequency and consistency with which users return to the product.

Here, Product Managers investigate:

1. What percentage of users are returning after their initial experience?

2. Are users staying engaged over time?

Retention is a clear indicator of the product's long-term value to users. Low retention rates signal a need for product or user experience improvements.

8.4 Referral: When Users Turn into Advocates

The 'Referral' stage is a testament to the product's appeal and value. It addresses the extent to which users are:

1. Recommending the product to others

2. Sharing their positive experiences

For Product Managers, optimizing for referrals can drastically reduce customer acquisition costs and magnify the product's reach.

8.5 Revenue: The Treasure Trove of the Product

The culmination of the user journey is the 'Revenue' phase, where usage translates into monetary value.

Product Managers should be keen on:

1. Understanding which features or services users are willing to pay for

2. Identifying upselling or cross-selling opportunities

Revenue is, of course, a primary indicator of a product's success, but it also provides insights into user preferences and potential areas for expansion or improvement.

8.6 Sailing Ahead with Pirate Metrics

The AARRR Pirate Metrics Framework is a comprehensive roadmap for Product Managers to understand, measure, and optimize the entire user journey. By focusing on these five crucial stages, Product Managers can ensure that they're not just acquiring users, but they're also delivering value, fostering loyalty, and realizing tangible growth.

Having a compass as reliable as the AARRR framework can be the difference between sailing smooth waters or being lost at sea. So, hoist the sails, gather your crew of data, and let Pirate Metrics guide your voyage to product success.

16

Product Roadmap

The product roadmap stands out as one of the most crucial and enduring artifacts a Product Manager can create. Before delving into its intricacies and construction, let's first grasp some key concepts.

1. Product Backlog

A Product Backlog is a meticulously prioritized list of all desired features and activities for a given product. Each entry includes a concise description along with a quantified measure of its business value, often accompanied by the source/inspiration for that particular feature or activity.

This is distinct from a Development Backlog, which is a selection of Epics or Stories that the development team can choose to refine and prioritize for an upcoming sprint.

While the Development Backlog is derived from the Product Backlog, they serve different purposes. The Product Backlog focuses on the broader vision and objectives for the product, whereas the Development Backlog zooms in on specific tasks and stories that the development team commits to completing within the next sprint.

The Development Backlog in a way is derived from a Product Backlog.

1.1 Product Feature Card

A Product Feature Card is a structured record that forms the Product Backlog. Here is a format a Product Manager can use for the Card to record features:

Field	Description
ID	A unique identifier for each backlog item to facilitate tracking and discussion.

Field	Description
Theme / Module	The broader category or functional area to which the backlog item belongs.
Action – Expected Result	A user-centric statement, often in Epic format, describing what the feature aims to accomplish and why.
Assumptions	Preconditions or initial states assumed to be in place before the development of the backlog item can commence.
Priority	A designation of the item's urgency, often categorized as High, Medium, or Low.
Value Ranking	A numerical or ordinal ranking that quantifies the business value of the item relative to other items.
Success Metric	A measurable outcome used to gauge whether the implemented item has achieved its intended impact.
Failure Metric	Criteria that indicate when the item is not meeting its objectives, triggering further analysis or revision.
Status	The current stage of development for the backlog item, such as "To be developed," "In Progress," or "Completed."
Source	The origin of the backlog item, such as Customer Feedback, Market Research, UX Team Feedback, or a Social Media post that lead to the creation of this. It is important to refer to that original content which can be referred to as-is in the future in its original form.

Table 22: Product Feature Card Template

1.2 Example Scenario

Scenario 47: Selection of 3 Product Feature Cards written by a Product Manager developing an e-commerce platform.

Id	Card 1 (User Authentication)	Card 2 (Product Search)	Card 3 (Checkout Process)
ID	001	002	003
Theme / Module	User Authentication	Product Search	Checkout Process
Action – Expected Result	"I want to securely sign in so that my account is protected."	"I want to easily search for products so that I can quickly find what I'm looking for."	"I want to complete my purchase with as few clicks as possible so that it's convenient."
Assumptions	Users have already created accounts; basic infrastructure for authentication is in place.	Product database is populated; basic search functionality exists.	Shopping cart functionality is working; payment gateway is integrated.
Priority	High	Medium	High
Value Ranking	9	7	8
Success Metric	99% of logins are successful and secure.	At least 90% of users find what they are looking for within 30 seconds.	95% of users complete the checkout process without abandoning their carts.
Failure Metric	More than 2% of login attempts result in security breaches.	More than 20% of users leave the site due to difficulty in finding products.	Cart abandonment rate exceeds 10%.
Status	To be developed	In Progress	To be developed
Source	Customer Feedback	Market Research	UX Team Feedback

Table 23: Product Feature Cards for MsgMsg App

1.3 Feature Activity Card

A feature entails more than just its development. While the Product Feature Card guides the Development Team, each feature often requires subsequent actions from the Product Manager.

Consider the recommended checklist format to note essential actions and relevant meta-information that should go with each Feature. Feature Activity Card ensures a holistic approach to feature management that goes beyond mere implementation.

Schedule	Is a GTM time identified?	
	If yes, date?	
Collaterals	Does it need marketing collateral?	
	Does it need sales collateral?	
	Does it need support collateral?	
	Does it need user-specific collateral?	
Change Management	Does it need a change in process?	
	Does it need a change in people & behavior?	
	Does it need a change in how users interact?	
	Does it need a change in tech?	

	Does it bring in regulatory & legal aspects?	
Control	Does it bring in unhandled regulatory & legal aspects?	
	Does it need extra/new licenses?	
	Does it get covered by the existing licensing model?	
Security & Safety	Does it need extra security focus?	

Table 24: Feature Activity Card Template

A 'yes' response to any of these checklist items can expand the scope of work, prompting tasks for other departments such as Marketing and Legal. Therefore, it's crucial to consider factors beyond mere functionality during the implementation phase.

2. Introduction to Feature Prioritization

Often terms like "feature," "capability," and "functionality" are used interchangeably. However, they do have distinctions, which can be important depending on the context.

2.1 Feature

A feature is typically a specific functionality that has a corresponding benefit(s) for the user. It's a distinct element of what a product can do and is often a selling point.

Example: In word processing software, "spell check" could be considered a feature.

2.2 Capability

Capability refers to the power or ability of a product to help a user achieve a certain outcome, irrespective of its features. Thus it can be a potential outcome a user can achieve by using the product.

Example: The word processing software's capability might be described as "enabling users to create, edit, and format documents."

2.3 Functionality

Functionality generally describes the range of operations that can be done with a product, or how a product operates. It's about the tasks or operations that a product can perform.

Example: Within the "spell check" feature of the word processing software, the functionality might include checking grammar, offering synonym suggestions, or allowing users to add words to a personal dictionary.

2.4 Prioritization

Feature prioritization is the process of determining which features should be added to a product and in what order, based on a variety of factors including customer needs, business goals, technical constraints, market dynamics, compliance & regulation, and addressing potential risks like a security threat, tech debt or negative user feedback.

Given that every product team has limited resources, be it time, money, or personnel, Prioritization ensures that these resources are allocated to the most impactful features.

There are many prioritization methods used by Product Managers, some of which are discussed in this chapter.

3. Common Prioritization Techniques

3.1 Prioritization Using Buy a Feature

In this method, stakeholders or customers are given a fictional budget and a list of features with their corresponding costs. They "buy" the features they feel are most important. This helps in understanding what features users value the most.

Example Scenario

Scenario 48: You are the lead developer for a mobile game app, Fantasy Fighters by Timingila Media. As you plan for the next big update, there are several potential features and enhancements your team is considering. To ensure your loyal player base gets features they truly desire, you decide to employ the "Buy a Feature" technique.

Method: You create a list of potential features, each with a price tag based on its development cost (time, resources, etc.). You then provide a group of players with a set amount of virtual currency and ask them to "buy" the features they most want to see in the game.

Potential Features:

1. New Characters: Introduce three new fighters with unique abilities. Price: $100

2. Tournament Mode: A mode where players can compete in brackets for big rewards. Price: $80

3. Story Mode Expansion: Expand the game's storyline with new quests and adventures. Price: $90

4. VR Mode: Play in Virtual Reality. Price: $150

5. Customizable Avatars: Customize the appearance of fighters. Price: $60

6. Night Mode: A darker color theme to ease eye strain during nighttime gaming. Price: $40

Outcome: You invite 50 of your most active players to participate in this activity. Each player receives $200 in virtual currency.

After the activity, the results are as follows:

- New Characters: Bought by 40 players
- Tournament Mode: Bought by 30 players
- Story Mode Expansion: Bought by 20 players

- VR Mode: Bought by 10 players

- Customizable Avatars: Bought by 35 players

- Night Mode: Bought by 45 players

Conclusion: Based on the "Buy a Feature" results:

- "Night Mode" and "New Characters" are the most popular choices and should be prioritized, as they cater to the most significant portion of the active player base.

- "Tournament Mode" and "Customizable Avatars" are also valuable and should be considered for development soon after or alongside.

- "Story Mode Expansion" might be scheduled for a later update, while "VR Mode," even though it's a high-tech feature, is not a priority for the majority of your players at the moment.

- This method not only provides a clear view of player preferences but also engages the community, making them feel involved in the game's development process. It's essential to ensure that the prices set for features are a realistic representation of their actual development cost to avoid biasing the results.

3.2 Prioritization Using Dot Voting

Often used in workshops or brainstorming sessions. Participants are given a certain number of dots (or votes) which they can allocate to different features or ideas. The features with the most dots get higher priority.

Example Scenario

Scenario 49: You're a team leader at Timingila Solutions, a startup focused on developing sustainable technology solutions. The team has brainstormed a series of potential project features for the next quarter, and you need a quick and democratic way to prioritize these. You decide to use the Dot Voting technique.

Method: You list all the feature backlog on a whiteboard or sticky notes. Each team member is given a set number of colored dot stickers. They are then asked to place their dots next to the feature they consider most important or appealing. They can distribute their dots however they wish – placing all on one idea, one on each idea, or any other distribution.

Feature Backlog:

1. Solar-Powered Charging Stations: Building stations in public areas for people to charge their devices

2. Eco-Friendly Packaging: Develop a sustainable, biodegradable packaging solution

3. Green Building Consulting: Offer consultancy for businesses wanting to build eco-friendly offices

4. Urban Farming Kits: Compact kits for city dwellers to grow vegetables and herbs at home

5. Waste Management App: An app to educate and help users reduce and manage their waste

Outcome: After the dot voting process, the results look something like this:

1. Solar-Powered Charging Stations: 12 dots

2. Eco-Friendly Packaging: 8 dots

3. Green Building Consulting: 5 dots

4. Urban Farming Kits: 15 dots

5. Waste Management App: 10 dots

Conclusion: Based on the Dot Voting results:

- The team seems most excited about the "Urban Farming Kits," suggesting it might not only be a valuable project but also one the team is passionate about. This should be considered a top priority.

> - "Solar-Powered Charging Stations" and "Waste Management App" also received a significant amount of votes, indicating they're valued features.
>
> - "Eco-Friendly Packaging" and "Green Building Consulting" get fewer votes. They might be revisited later or re-evaluated to see if they can be adjusted to better align with the team's passion and the organization's goals.

Dot Voting is an inclusive method, allowing every team member to have a say in the decision-making process. It's a visual, straightforward method ideal for situations where a group needs to prioritize a list quickly and all stakeholders have similar influence over the product. However, it's essential to remember that while Dot Voting captures the team's immediate preferences, it doesn't take into account the feasibility or broader strategic implications of choices.

3.3 Prioritization Using Kano Model

The Kano Model, developed by Professor Noriaki Kano in the 1980s, is a framework used to prioritize features in products and services based on how they are perceived by customers and their impact on customer satisfaction.

This model classifies features into five categories:

1. **Basic Needs**: Features that are expected. Their absence would cause dissatisfaction, but their presence doesn't particularly delight users because they take them for granted.

2. **Performance Needs**: Features that can lead to satisfaction if they're implemented well (and to dissatisfaction if they aren't).

3. **Exciters/Delighters**: Unexpected features that can be highly satisfactory if present but won't cause dissatisfaction if they're absent.

4. **Indifferent Needs**: Features that don't significantly sway user satisfaction whether they're present or absent.

5. **Reverse Needs**: Features that can satisfy a certain group of users but might dissatisfy another group.

Example Scenario

Scenario 50: The Product Manager for an electronics company aiming to launch a new smart refrigerator. The Product Manager surveyed potential customers and gathered feedback to understand what features they would find valuable. The Product Manager decided to use the Kano Model to categorize these features based on how they might impact customer satisfaction.

Features & Categories:

- Basic Needs:

    - Cooling: It's a refrigerator, so it obviously needs to cool and preserve food.

    - Energy Efficiency: In today's world, consumers expect appliances to be energy-efficient.

    - Reliable Thermostat: Ensuring the set temperature is maintained consistently.

- Performance Needs:

    - Adjustable Shelves: Allows users to modify the fridge's internal layout based on their storage needs.

    - Fast Cooling: Rapidly cools items placed inside.

    - Digital Temperature Display: Clearly shows the current temperature inside the fridge.

- Exciters/Delighters:

    - Internal Camera: Allows users to view the fridge's contents via a smartphone app without opening the door.

    - Automatic Inventory Tracking: The fridge detects items inside and can suggest recipes based on available ingredients.

    - Integration with Voice Assistants: Users can ask voice assistants about fridge contents, and recipes, or order groceries.

> - Indifferent Needs (based on the survey, some users didn't feel strongly about these):
>   - Color-Changing LED Lights: While it might be aesthetically pleasing, it doesn't affect the fridge's core function.
>   - Customizable Door Alarm Tunes: Some users might like it, but many don't care about customizing the alert sound.
> - Reverse Needs:
>   - Social Media Integration: While some tech-savvy users might enjoy posting about their cooking adventures directly, many users felt this was unnecessary and raised privacy concerns.
>
> Conclusion: Using the Kano Model, the electronics company decided to focus on ensuring all basic needs are flawlessly met while dedicating resources to developing high-quality performance features. The exciters can be added as unique selling points that differentiate the smart refrigerator from competitors. Indifferent needs can be considered based on resource availability and reverse needs should be carefully evaluated to avoid potentially alienating a segment of users.

It's essential to understand that the Kano Model isn't static. Over time, what was once a delighter can become a basic or performance need as customer expectations evolve.

3.4 Prioritization Using MoSCoW

The MoSCoW method is a popular prioritization technique used in Product Management to reach a common understanding among stakeholders about the importance of different requirements.

The MoSCoW method originated from the Dynamic Systems Development Method (DSDM),[1] which was one of the earliest Agile methodologies, developed in the early 1990s.

The name "MoSCoW" is an acronym derived from the four prioritization categories: Must have, Should have, Could have, and Won't have.

1. **Must have**: Features that are non-negotiable and essential for the product release

2. **Should have**: Important but not critical; can be released in a later version if necessary

3. **Could have**: Nice-to-have that don't affect the product's overall effectiveness

4. **Won't have**: Features that are recognized but won't be implemented in the next release

Example Scenario

Scenario 51: You're the Product Manager for a bank that aims to launch a new mobile banking app to better serve its tech-savvy customers and compete in the digital space. You've gathered feedback from customers, stakeholders, and team brainstorming sessions and have come up with several potential features for the app. Due to varying degrees of importance and feasibility, you decide to prioritize these features using the MOSCOW method.

MOSCOW Categories:

- M - Must have: These are critical features without which the app would not function or be valuable

- S - Should have: Important features that enhance the user experience but aren't crucial for the app's initial launch

- C - Could have: Nice-to-have features that are beneficial but not necessary. They can be considered for future versions

- W - Won't have this time: Features acknowledged as potential enhancements but not considered for the current release

Features & Categories:

- Must have:

    - Account Balance Check: Allows users to view their current account balance

    - Funds Transfer: Allows users to transfer money between accounts or to other users

    - Bill Payments: Enables users to pay their bills directly through the app

- Should have:

    - Transaction History: Allows users to view their past transactions over a specified period

    - Account Statement Download: Users can download a statement of their account activity

    - Instant Notifications: Alerts users for account activities like large transactions or when their balance goes below a certain threshold

- Could have:

    - ATM Locator: Finds the nearest ATM based on the user's location

    - Savings Goal Setter: Lets users set savings goals and track progress

    - Dark Mode: A darker color theme for the app to reduce eye strain during nighttime use

- Won't have this time:

    - Chatbot Assistant: A virtual assistant to help users navigate the app or answer common questions

    - Investment Advice: Provides users with investment tips and news

    - Currency Converter: Allows users to convert between different currencies

> **Conclusion**: By using the MOSCOW method, the bank can now focus on implementing the "Must have" features first, ensuring that the app's core functionality is ready for launch. Once those are in place, the team can then look into the "Should have" and "Could have" features. The "Won't have this time" features can be revisited in future app updates after the initial launch.

3.5 Prioritization Using RICE

The RICE method is a prioritization framework specifically tailored for Product Management. RICE stands for Reach, Impact, Confidence, and Effort. This framework helps teams objectively score and rank potential features.

Looking at each component:

a. Reach: How many customers will this feature impact within a certain time frame?

b. Impact: When a customer encounters this feature, how much will it impact them? (e.g., will it increase conversion?)

c. Confidence: How confident are you in your estimates for reach and **impact**?

d. Effort: How many "person-months" will this feature take to implement?

The RICE score is then calculated as:

- RICE score=(Reach×Impact×Confidence)/Effort

Example Scenario

> **Scenario 52**: You're the Product Manager for a startup that is launching a new e-commerce platform. After gathering feedback and brainstorming with your team, you've come up with four potential features that you believe will be crucial for the site. However, due to time and resource constraints, you need to prioritize which features to develop first. The features are:

1. One-Click Checkout: Allows users to purchase with a single click, using saved payment information

2. Product Recommendation Engine: Recommends products to users based on their browsing and purchase history

3. Live Chat Support: Provides users with instant customer service via a chat interface

4. VR Product Preview: Allows users to see and try products in virtual reality before purchasing

Prioritization: Let's prioritize these features using the RICE method.

1. Reach (estimated number of users interacting with the feature per month)

2. Impact (scale from 0.25 for low impact to 3 for high impact)

3. Confidence (percentage, from 50% to 100%, indicating how sure you are of your estimates)

4. Effort (number of person-months required to implement)

Feature	Reach	Impact	Confidence	Effort	RICE Score (Calculation)
One-Click Checkout	10,000	3	90%	2	135,000
Product Recommendation	8,000	2.5	80%	3	53,333
Live Chat Support	6,000	2	75%	2	45,000
VR Product Preview	2,500	2.5	70%	4	8,750

Table 25: RICE Based Prioritization for E-Commerce Platform

For One-Click Checkout: (10,000 x 3 x 0.9) / 2 = 135,000 For Product Recommendation: (8,000 x 2.5 x 0.8) / 3 = 53,333 ... and so on.

Conclusion: Based on the RICE scores, the One-Click Checkout feature should be the top priority, followed by the Product Recommendation Engine, then Live Chat Support, and lastly the VR Product Preview.

3.6 Prioritization Using Rubrics or Affinity Scoring

A Rubric is an evaluation tool or set of criteria used to ensure the consistent application of expectations or outcomes to enable some sort of comparison.

The Rubrics-based approach for feature prioritization uses pre-decided criteria to arrive at a score that can enable prioritizing. Sometimes this is also referred to as Affinity Scoring.

In the course of using the rubric, sometimes other aspects are brought to light, or criteria change or even change in the relevance of a given criteria. The Rubrics-based approach permits such changes and updates itself to reflect new priorities.

One key consideration for using rubrics for the prioritization of features is to be clear about what a feature is. The term Product Feature often lends itself to some ambiguity. There might be some confusion on how fine-grained a feature should be to use in a rubric, the only requirement of this method is to keep them at the same but high level of granularity.

Here are the key steps for building a rubric:

Step 1: Decide on the Product Feature Categories

Most Product Features belong to one of the following categories. While adopting this technique a Product Manager may update this list based on the product. These categories are:

1. **Market Differentiating**: These are the set of features that differentiate your product in the market, especially for the users and promoters.

2. **Product Adoption**: These are the set of features that ensure there is the least resistance path to adoption, recommendation, and invitations to other users.

3. **Cost Reduction**: These are the set of features that reduce the cost of building, maintaining, and evolving a product.

4. **Organizational Check-Boxing**: These are the set of features that the organization wants to be part of the products they produce.

Typically, these tend toward cross-promotion of other products, features that ensure smooth interoperability between products that are part of the same suite, etc.

5. **Market Check-Boxing:** These are the set of features that tend not to be very useful and common when selling to enterprises. These are features that do not bring a lot of value to users. These tend to be needed for passing eligible paperwork or to not stand out as having few / missing features as compared to the competition.

6. **Hygiene:** These are the set of features that are the 'cost of running a business.' These will include, say, Sign-up / Sign-in, profile management, delete the account, and other features that are essential, non-differentiating, and present across all other products in the domain.

7. **Pricing Differentiating:** These are the set of features that a customer will pay extra for or make your product cheaper.

Note: There is a subtle difference between market and pricing differentiation. Market differentiation helps your product to stand out so the customer picks your product over other similar ones. However, if you want the customer to pay a little extra, the pricing differentiators kick in.

"Our toothpaste has salt in it," is a market differentiator. "Our toothpaste tube is 100% biodegradable" is a pricing differentiator to slightly expensive products in the eyes of a responsible buyer.

Step 2: Assigning Importance Score to Product Feature Categories

Not all of the above categories may apply to your product at the stage of maturity it is in and that is OK. The rubric will help you incorporate that into the prioritization process.

First, ensure you are aware of the answers to the following questions.

- Do you know the goal of your product? Is market differentiation one of those goals? Is being premium or cheaper than the competition a goal? Is viral spread or fast adoption such a goal?

- Do you know the goal of the organization?

- Do you know the goal of your customers?

- Do you know the goal of your users?

- Based on the above, you should be able to assign a score to the Product Feature Categories. The following set of examples assigns a score from 1-5.

- A startup that is focused on market penetration could assign more weightage to prioritize features that establish Marketing Differentiating rather than say Cost Reduction.

Example:

Marketing Differentiating	5
Pricing Differentiating	2
Product Adoption	5
Cost Reduction	2
Product Org Check-Boxing	1
Market Check-Boxing	1
Hygiene	3

Table 26: Priority Based Score for Feature Rubric for a Startup

An Enterprise Software company focused on market penetration could assign these weightages that ensure they pass all basic checks by Purchase Office to be evaluated:

Marketing Differentiation	3
Pricing Differentiation	4
Product Adoption	5
Cost Reduction	5
Product Org Check-Boxing	1
Market Check-Boxing	4
Hygiene	3

Table 27: Priority Based Score for Feature Rubric for an Enterprise

Note: A Product Manager may also choose to give zero weightage to a category as it may not be of strategic importance to the product at that moment.

Step 3: Assigning Importance Score to Product Feature within the Category

Now that you have assigned importance to the product category, you need to assign importance to a feature over others within that category. Usually, the following works.

Critical	5
High	3
Medium	2
Low	1

Table 28: Adding Weightage to Introduce Time Value of a Feature

Calculating the Rank

The prioritization rank can be a simple multiple of score and weightage.

Rank = Score X Weightage

Once done for all features, we will have a weighted rank for each feature.

Prioritization

Product Manager can consider this simple approach:

Capability (High-level Feature)	Feature Category	Importance	Score (Higher gets done first)
Feature A	Pricing Differentiating	High	12
Feature B	Pricing Differentiating	Medium	8
Feature C	Product Adoption	Medium	10

Table 29: Prioritization Rubric in Action

Feature A, which brings Pricing Differentiation (score 4) and is deemed high (score 3) will have a score of 12.

Feature B, which brings Pricing Differentiation (score 4) and is deemed medium (score 2) will have a score of 8.

Feature C, which brings Product Adoption (score 5) and is deemed medium (score 2) will have a score of 10.

So the prioritization will be:

Feature A, Feature C, and finally Feature B.

Feature Prioritization Rubrics Template

https://bit.ly/plcu-feature-rubric

3.7 Prioritization Using Value vs Cost (or Effort)

The 2x2 matrix is an invaluable tool in the fields of business, strategy, and management. This framework facilitates the categorization and visualization of items, concepts, or projects, dividing them into four clearly defined quadrants. At the heart of this model lies the principle of dual-dimension plotting, where each dimension usually follows a dichotomous scale.

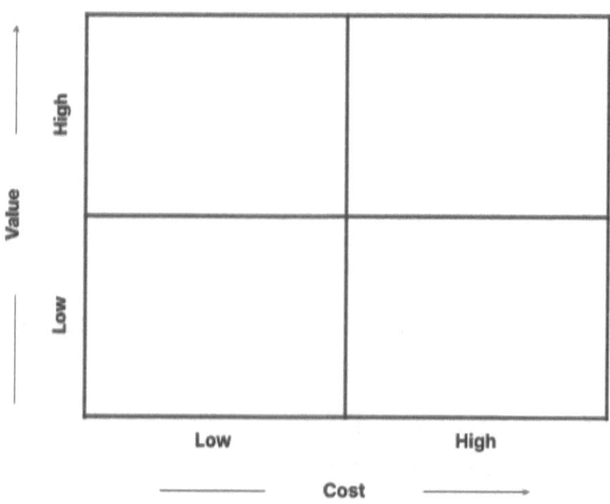

Fig 49: Cost Value Using 2x2 Matrix

Value vs Cost Matrix is a simple 2x2 matrix where features are plotted based on their perceived value and the cost or effort to implement them.

Both axes are bifurcated into 'High' and 'Low' scales. In this specific context, the X-axis represents 'Value' while the Y-axis denotes 'Cost'.

The primary goal for most teams is to achieve maximum value at the least cost. As a result, the 'High Value, Low Cost' quadrant often becomes the focal point for immediate action.

Example Scenario

Scenario 53: You are a Product Manager at Timingila Media, a popular online conspiracy theory debunking video streaming service. After collecting feedback from users and brainstorming internally, the team has shortlisted a few features they believe will enhance the user experience. To decide which features to prioritize for development, you decide to use the Value vs. Cost (or Effort) method.

Method: Plot features on a 2x2 matrix:

- X-axis (Cost or Effort): Represents how much effort, time, or resources are needed to implement the feature.

- Y-axis (Value): Represents the value or benefit the feature brings to users and the business.

Features under consideration:

1. 4K Streaming: Allow users to stream content in 4K resolution.

2. Offline Viewing: Allow users to download and view content without an internet connection.

3. Multi-language Subtitles: Add subtitles in multiple languages for global content.

4. Personalized Playlists: Allow users to create and share personalized playlists of their favorite episodes or movies.

5. Virtual Watch Parties: Users can watch content simultaneously with friends and chat in the real time.

Categorizing Features along Cost-Value Axis:

High Value	• Multi-language Subtitles: Adding subtitles is a relatively low effort since it's mostly content-based, but it provides immense value for a global audience.	• 4K Streaming: This would require significant backend changes and increased bandwidth. However, it would greatly enhance viewing quality and could be a major selling point for cinephiles. • Offline Viewing: While this is technically challenging and may involve licensing considerations, it's highly valuable for users, especially in areas with spotty internet.
Low Value	• Personalized Playlists: This feature is relatively simple to implement but might not be as valuable since not all users may use or need it.	• Virtual Watch Parties: This feature requires real-time synchronization, chat features, and more. While it sounds fun, the overall user base might not find it as valuable compared to other features.
	Low Cost	High Cost

Table 30: Cost Value Analysis for Timingila Media

Conclusion: Using the Value vs. Cost matrix, Timingila Media can focus on rolling out "Multi-language Subtitles" quickly since it provides high value at a low cost. The team can then strategically plan and allocate resources for "4K Streaming" and "Offline Viewing" since they're high-value, high-effort features. "Personalized Playlists" can be developed in between major feature rollouts. "Virtual Watch Parties," given its low value for the high cost, might be put on the backburner or re-evaluated in light of further feedback or technological advancements.

3.8 Prioritization Using Weighted Shortest Job First (WSJF)

Weighted Shortest Job First (WSJF) is a prioritization model used in agile software development and Product Management to help teams determine the sequence or priority of items in a product backlog. WSJF allows teams to make economically sound decisions on what to work on next by considering both the size (or duration) of the job and its relative importance (or weight).

How It Works

WSJF is calculated by dividing the "Cost of Delay" (CoD) by the "Duration" (or job size). The idea is to work on features or jobs that have the highest WSJF score first, as they provide the highest value in the shortest time.

WSJF = Cost of Delay / Duration

Where:

1. **Cost of Delay (CoD)** represents the potential loss of value or the economic impact if a job is delayed. It's a measure of the urgency or importance of the job.

2. **Duration** refers to the estimated time it will take to complete the job.

Example Scenario

Scenario 54: You are a project manager at Timingila Solutions, a software company that develops enterprise applications. Your team has a backlog of features and improvements they can work on for the next release. However, due to resource and time constraints, not all features can be implemented. To determine the optimal order for tackling the features, you decide to use the WSJF technique.

Features:

1. Mobile Integration: Allows users to access the application on mobile devices

2. Data Encryption: Secures user data and ensures compliance with privacy laws

3. User Interface (UI) Redesign: Updates the look and feel of the application for a better user experience

4. Bug Fixes: Addresses various reported issues from customers

Calculating WSJF: Assuming you've estimated the CoD and Job Size for each feature:

Feature	CoD (Value)	Job Size (Effort)	WSJF (CoD/Job Size)
Mobile Integration	8	3	2.67
Data Encryption	10	5	2.0
UI Redesign	6	4	1.5
Bug Fixes	9	6	1.5

Table 31: WSJF Analysis for Timingila Solutions

Outcome: Based on WSJF:

1. Mobile Integration has the highest WSJF value (2.67), suggesting it provides the most significant economic benefit for the effort required. It should be tackled first.

2. Data Encryption comes next with a WSJF of 2.0.

3. UI Redesign and Bug Fixes follow with the same WSJF (1.5).

Conclusion: Timingila Solutions should prioritize the development of the Mobile Integration feature, followed by Data Encryption. UI Redesign and Bug Fixes can be scheduled based on other determining factors or dependencies.

WSJF helps Product Managers prioritize the backlog based on the economic value and effort required, ensuring the team is always working on the most impactful tasks first.

4. Introduction to Building a Roadmap

A product roadmap is (usually) a visual representation that lays the high-level plan for the release of a product over time. It provides a clear overview of when which of the product's features will be available and major milestones. It serves as a guiding document that aligns everyone involved in the product's development and helps prioritize activities and resources.

4.1 Structuring a Roadmap

Creating a roadmap is straightforward. The process involves placing items on a graph where the X-axis represents time and the Y-axis represents different categories of features.

However, the true challenge lies in determining the nature of those categories. Depending on the type of roadmap, they could be stories for a Development Roadmap or a combination of Epics, Features, and Capabilities for a Product Roadmap.

As a Product Manager, it is crucial to maintain clarity regarding the specific nature of each item on the roadmap and ensure consistent usage throughout.

Another aspect of complexity arises when deciding the level of detail on the X-axis, representing time. For a Development Roadmap, the preferred granularity is often measured in Sprints. However, in a Product Roadmap, the timeframe can vary, ranging from sprints to weeks, months, quarters, or even years. In fact, the most effective approach is to have a sliding scale that allows for more granularity at the beginning and longer durations as we move further along the roadmap.

The Y-axis of the roadmap holds the utmost contextual significance. It represents the categories into which the roadmap items are grouped. This categorization ensures that the appropriate focus is given to each category, allowing for a well-balanced product development approach. It's important to note that each category may have different stakeholders, who can track how the product is evolving in relation to their specific requirements.

For instance, in the given example, Product Development is just one of the rows on the Y-axis. There are several other focus areas listed as well, highlighting the diverse aspects that need to be addressed. By organizing the roadmap items into distinct categories, the Product Manager can effectively manage and communicate progress across different stakeholder groups. This promotes transparency and alignment throughout the development process.

	Q4 23	**Q1 24**	**Q2 24**	**Q3 24**	**Q4 24**	**2025**	**2026**
Product Development	*Feature Card*	*Feature Card*	*Feature Card*	*Feature Card*	*Feature Card*	*Feature Card*	*Feature Card*
Experience Design	*Feature Card*	*Feature Card*	*Feature Card*	*Feature Card*	*Feature Card*	*Feature Card*	*Feature Card*
InfoSec	*Feature Card*	*Feature Card*	*Feature Card*	*Feature Card*	*Feature Card*	*Feature Card*	*Feature Card*
Marketing Readiness	*Activity Card*	*Activity Card*	*Activity Card*	*Activity Card*	*Activity Card*	*Activity Card*	*Activity Card*
Sales Readiness	*Activity Card*	*Activity Card*	*Activity Card*	*Activity Card*	*Activity Card*	*Activity Card*	*Activity Card*
Business Model Validation	*Feature Card*	*Feature Card*	*Feature Card*	*Feature Card*	*Feature Card*	*Feature Card*	*Feature Card*
Product Ops Readiness	*Activity Card*	*Activity Card*	*Activity Card*	*Activity Card*	*Activity Card*	*Activity Card*	*Activity Card*
Support Readiness	*Activity Card*	*Activity Card*	*Activity Card*	*Activity Card*	*Activity Card*	*Activity Card*	*Activity Card*
Legal & Compliance	*Activity Card*	*Activity Card*	*Activity Card*	*Activity Card*	*Activity Card*	*Activity Card*	*Activity Card*

Table 32: Sample Format for a Product Roadmap

4.2 Product Calendar

One important aspect of the X-axis is to mark key events that the roadmap should align with. These events serve as significant milestones that the Product Manager aims to target. For instance, if the Product Manager intends to have a major release aligned with the Diwali or Christmas, it allows all stakeholders to understand the required features and their purpose.

These events can encompass a wide range, including internal or external events, as well as events from the roadmap of other dependent systems. By incorporating these events into the roadmap, the Product Manager ensures that the team is aware of the necessary tasks and the reasons behind them. This alignment facilitates a clear understanding of the roadmap's objectives and helps in effective planning and execution.

4.3 Product Release Theme

Product Release Themes are a strategic way of unifying features under a common narrative or goal. They not only add coherence and purpose to product development but also resonate with the user experience, making the product more engaging and meaningful.

For example, a theme around 'Celebration' might involve adding features that enable users to share special occasions, such as festive filters on a photo-sharing app or themed stickers in a messaging app.

Another theme could be 'Empowerment', where a suite of tools is developed to help users accomplish something new or complex, such as a new set of coding tools in a development software or advanced editing features in a design platform.

An 'Efficiency' theme could involve features designed to streamline tasks, such as a bulk upload feature in a cloud storage service or automated responses in a customer support tool.

A theme focused on 'Well-being' might introduce features to monitor and improve users' health and wellness, such as sleep tracking in a fitness app or mindfulness reminders in a mental wellness platform.

The 'Sustainability' theme could drive the development of features that encourage environmentally friendly behaviors, like a carbon footprint tracker in a travel app or energy-saving suggestions in a home automation system. Themes, therefore, provide a focal point for development while aligning product functionality with user needs and societal trends.

4.4 Example Scenario

Scenario 55: The Product Manager responsible for the MsgMsg App has just released the first cut of the Roadmap. The Product Manager knows that the Roadmap will change as the team learns from the market dynamics, user response and usage stats.

	Q4 23	Q1 24	Q2 24	Q3 24	Q4 24	2025	2026
Product Development	Develop core messaging features	Implement AI-driven predictive messaging	Enhance language translation capabilities	Introduce multimedia sharing	Integrate with third-party apps	Continuous feature updates	Explore new messaging trends
Experience Design	User interface redesign	Enhance user onboarding experience	Implement personalized user interactions	Improve accessibility features	Enhance user engagement features	Iterate based on user feedback	Implement cutting-edge design trends
InfoSec	Conduct security audit	Implement end-to-end encryption	Enhance data protection measures	Integrate with security tools	Monitor for vulnerabilities	Regular security audits	Implement advanced security measures
Marketing Readiness	Develop marketing strategy	Launch teaser campaigns	Run beta testing program	Plan official launch events	Execute global marketing campaigns	Measure campaign effectiveness	Plan for long-term marketing strategies
Sales Readiness	Develop sales strategy	Train sales team on product features	Prepare sales materials	Identify target markets	Launch sales campaigns	Monitor sales performance	Develop partnerships for growth
Business Model Validation	Validate revenue streams	Analyze pricing strategies	Conduct market research	Evaluate competition	Adjust business model based on feedback	Monitor market trends	Pivot if necessary based on market dynamics
Product Ops Readiness	Develop product operations plan	Implement agile development practices	Set up product analytics	Establish feedback loops	Optimize product development processes	Continuous improvement of product ops	Scale operations for growth
Support Readiness	Develop customer support strategy	Train support team	Set up support channels	Implement ticketing system	Monitor support metrics	Continuous training and improvement	Scale support operations
Legal & Compliance	Ensure GDPR and other data protection compliance	Review terms of service and privacy policy	Address legal issues related to messaging	Monitor regulatory changes	Update policies as necessary	Conduct regular compliance audits	Stay updated with new regulations

Table 33: Product Roadmap of the MsgMsg App

5. Low-Hanging Fruit Fallacy

In a metaphorical sense, "low-hanging fruit" refers to the easiest tasks, opportunities, or problems to address first, often because they require the least effort or resources compared to other available options.

This term is frequently used in Product Management to describe tasks or objectives that can be quickly accomplished to show progress or gain initial benefits. For example, "Allowing users to choose between different themes or color schemes," can be considered a low-hanging fruit.

While targeting "low-hanging fruit" can be an effective strategy for prioritization in some contexts, especially when immediate results are needed, this approach ends up hurting more in the long term.

This approach should be avoided for the following reasons.

1. **Short-term Focus**: Relying too heavily on easy-to-reach features can lead Product Managers to focus too much on short-term gains and neglect the bigger picture. This results in overlooking longer-term, more strategic features.

2. **Hidden Effort**: While the "low-hanging fruit" might require minimal effort for certain teams like Product Managers or developers, the same might not be true for others. Once the code is committed, InfoSec teams, QA teams, Integration testing teams, and support teams might have to invest substantial time and resources. For these teams, they might end up spending an equal amount of effort on a feature or solution that, from their perspective, offers low value. This can lead to inefficiencies and potential frustrations among affected teams.

3. **Devaluation of Effort**: If a Product Manager constantly prioritizes quick wins, the team might feel that only tasks with immediate results are valued, potentially devaluing deeper, more intensive work.

4. **False Sense of Progress**: Tackling low-hanging fruit can give a false impression of progress. By always choosing the path of least

resistance, it can seem like a lot is being accomplished when, in fact, major challenges remain untouched.

5. **Overemphasis on Quantifiable Results**: Targeting low-hanging fruit often leads to quantifiable and easily measurable outcomes. However, not all valuable results are easily measurable. The approach might neglect qualitative improvements or benefits that are harder to quantify.

To address these issues, it's essential for Product Managers to consider that while there's certainly value in capturing quick wins, it's crucial not to make it a recurring criterion for prioritization.

17

Go-To-Market

"Go-to-market" (GTM) is a strategic action plan that outlines how an organization will sell its products to customers. In product management, the GTM strategy is critical because it addresses the steps needed to move from product development to the market successfully. A robust GTM strategy can significantly influence the product's success in the market, as it determines how the product will reach the end customer and how the product's value will be communicated.

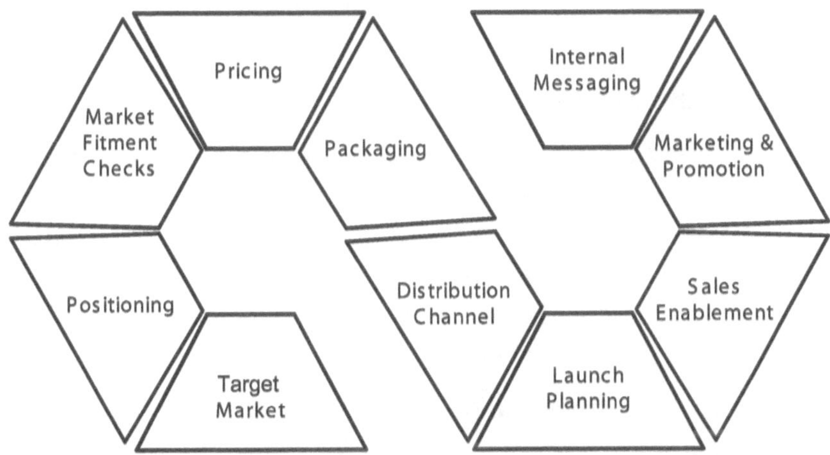

Fig 50: GTM Considerations

1. Target Market

This refers to the process of precisely identifying the market segment or customer group for which a product is being launched. This involves defining the ideal customer profile and gaining a comprehensive understanding of their unique needs, preferences, and challenges.

Effectively catering to diverse customer segments necessitates tailored approaches in terms of positioning, pricing, and messaging. Hence, it is crucial to have a clear comprehension of the characteristics and traits of the target customer segment.

2. Positioning

This process involves analyzing a list of competitors and strategically positioning the product in relation to their strengths and weaknesses. By revisiting the competition analysis, the team gains valuable insights on how to effectively showcase the product's strengths and differentiate it from competitors.

This entails conducting sales training (via, say, Sales Battlecards) highlighting the unique selling propositions and key advantages of the product. By leveraging this information, the marketing and sales teams can strategically position the product to highlight its distinct features and benefits, effectively addressing the needs and preferences of the target market while distinguishing it from competing offerings.

3. Market Fitment Checks

To gauge market fit, key performance indicators and success metrics are identified and tracked. These metrics serve as indicators of the product's acceptance, adoption, and overall performance within the target market. If the measured outcomes continually fall below the predetermined failure threshold, it may be necessary to consider a pivot or even the potential closure of the product.

Regularly evaluating market fit ensures that the product remains aligned with customer demands and market dynamics. By setting clear benchmarks and monitoring performance against them, the team can make informed decisions about necessary adjustments or potential strategic shifts to ensure sustained success in the market.

4. Pricing

This involves critical considerations for a product's success. Price, as a highly sensitive attribute, requires all departments to be well-informed about the pricing policy. While the pricing of a product is determined by various factors, including production costs or the value delivered to customers, the competitive pricing strategies tend to be in focus during GTM strategy building.

When releasing a product, pricing becomes a crucial lever to achieve desired outcomes and effectively cater to the target market. By carefully setting the price and crafting the packaging, an organization can create a strong value proposition that resonates with customers, driving adoption and maximizing revenue potential.

5. Packaging

Packaging encompasses the process of determining the optimal product configurations, bundles, or editions to be offered to customers. This includes aligning the new packaging with the needs and preferences of the target customer segment, ensuring a compelling and appealing presentation.

Similarly, the product can be part of an existing package to either enhance the bundle's value to the customer or push the product to a certain customer segment.

6. Distribution Channels

These are the various ways through which customers can purchase a product. It involves making strategic decisions on how the product will be made available to customers, ensuring accessibility and convenience.

These channels can include direct sales through organization-owned channels, partnerships with distributors or resellers, e-commerce platforms, or a combination of these approaches. The selection of distribution channels is crucial for reaching the target market effectively.

To ensure seamless distribution, it is imperative to maintain reliable and efficient channels with minimal downtime. This entails implementing robust systems and processes that guarantee the uninterrupted availability of products to customers. Additionally, optimizing the purchasing process is essential, aiming to minimize friction and create a hassle-free buying experience.

By carefully selecting and maintaining distribution channels, businesses can enhance their product's reach, enable smooth customer transactions, and ultimately drive higher sales and customer satisfaction.

7. Launch Planning

The Launch Plan encompasses essential activities and timelines related to the product release. This includes determining the release date, scheduling launch-related marketing campaigns, and incorporating introductory offers or promotions to create initial traction.

Creating a comprehensive timeline and detailed plan for the product launch is crucial. This plan outlines the necessary tasks leading up to the launch date as well as post-launch activities aimed at sustaining momentum and maximizing impact.

Having a well-defined launch plan enables development teams to adhere to deadlines, adequately prepare for potential traffic increases, and ensure all departments are aware of key dates to plan their activities around.

It also includes preparing a Frequently Asked Questions (FAQ) document, a list of known issues, helpful hacks or overrides, and identifying key contacts for the Support team within the Product development team. This way, the Support team can proactively address expected questions and have a clear point of contact for handling unexpected inquiries.

By executing a thorough launch plan, businesses can streamline the release process, effectively engage customers, and provide optimal support to ensure a successful and smooth product launch.

8. Sales Enablement

Sales Enablement includes all activities aimed at equipping the sales team with the necessary resources and tools to effectively sell the product. This involves creating sales collateral, such as product presentations, sales scripts, and battlecards, that provide comprehensive information about the product's features, benefits, and competitive advantages. Sales Enablement also includes conducting training programs to ensure the sales team possesses in-depth knowledge of the product and its value proposition.

Additionally, providing ongoing support through regular communication, addressing sales team queries, and sharing market insights enables them to better understand customer needs and successfully position the product. By empowering the sales team with the right knowledge, skills, and resources, Sales Enablement plays a vital role in driving sales success and achieving business objectives.

9. Marketing and Promotion

This involves planning and executing various campaigns across different channels to effectively capture leads and generate traffic. The team needs to be aware of these campaigns, particularly digital ones, to ensure efficient lead capture and traffic acquisition.

Active interactions on social media channels are also crucial. Identifying the social media platforms where the target audience actively participates enables all team members to engage in commenting, resharing, and fostering meaningful interactions.

In addition to scheduling the campaigns, it is important to outline key tasks for each department involved. A well-orchestrated go-to-market strategy requires a well-coordinated launch team, with each department understanding its responsibilities and contributing to the overall success of the launch.

Creating a centralized repository for all product-related information serves as a single source of truth. This eliminates the need for team members to search for information when it is needed, ensuring easy access to all relevant details about the product.

By strategically planning marketing and promotion activities, leveraging appropriate channels for engagement, coordinating tasks across departments, and providing a centralized information hub, the team can maximize the impact of their marketing efforts and drive successful product launches.

10. Internal Messaging

This focuses on establishing a clear understanding of the "Why" behind the product, ensuring all team members are aligned and capable of effectively communicating a uniform message.

As different departments within an organization have their processes and partners, it is crucial to prevent any distortion of the product's purpose. To achieve this, it is essential to cultivate a unified understanding of the product's mission and value proposition across all teams.

By clearly articulating the purpose of the product, team members can grasp the underlying motivation and communicate it consistently. This unified messaging enhances collaboration, fosters a shared sense of purpose, and prevents confusion or mixed signals that may arise from divergent interpretations.

Internal messaging serves as a foundation for effective cross-functional collaboration, enabling teams to work synergistically toward common goals and deliver a cohesive and compelling message to external stakeholders.

By aligning all departments with a singular understanding of the product's purpose, organizations can enhance communication, streamline processes, and maximize their collective impact.

11 Example Scenario

> **Scenario 56**: The planning for the launch of the MsgMsg App is progressing smoothly. An organization-wide meeting has been convened to finalize the Go-To-Market (GTM) strategy, and the Product Manager has been tasked with updating everyone on the GTM Plan.
>
> Based on the various collateral created, including the Product Roadmap and the events calendar, the Product Manager has refreshed the planned GTM and conducted a quick review with the Product team. The Product Manager does not anticipate any surprises, as ongoing meetings and emails have kept everyone well-informed.
>
> However, the Product Manager does anticipate needing to provide further clarifications and receive feedback from other functions based on their capacity, budgets, and how they plan to allocate their responsibilities into various tasks.

Since the meeting is taking place in a large training room, the Product Manager plans to print out the Elevator Pitch, Sales Battlecards, Product Architecture, a few screenshots, and key User Personas on A3 paper and display them on the walls. This way, everyone attending the meeting can easily reference these materials.

The Product Manager has shared the following documents as pre-reading material for the meeting:

Target Market:

1. Digitally-savvy individuals seeking efficient communication tools

2. Professionals and global communicators in culturally diverse metropolitan areas, especially those navigating language barriers

3. Tech enthusiasts and early adopters looking for AI-driven solutions

Positioning:

1. Position MsgMsg App as the next-generation AI-powered messaging app that enhances communication by providing predictive messaging, instant language translation, and personalized user experiences.

2. Highlight its superiority over traditional messaging apps by emphasizing its advanced AI algorithms and tailored user experiences.

Market Fitment Checks:

1. Regularly evaluate user engagement metrics, such as active users, session duration, and feature utilization rates, to ensure the app meets market demands.

2. Conduct surveys and gather feedback to understand user satisfaction and identify areas for improvement.

Pricing:

1. Freemium model: Basic messaging features are free, while advanced AI features (e.g., predictive messaging, advanced translations) are available under a subscription plan.

2. Offer a free trial period for premium features to attract users and demonstrate the app's value.

Packaging:

1. Offer different subscription tiers based on user needs, such as individual, family, and business plans.

2. Bundle premium features with other complementary services or products to enhance value proposition.

Distribution Channels:

1. App Stores (Apple's App Store, Google Play Store): Provide easy access for users to download and install the app.

2. Direct downloads from the MsgMsg App website: Offer alternative download options for users who prefer non-store downloads.

3. Partnerships with mobile device manufacturers: Pre-install the app on devices to increase visibility and accessibility.

Launch Planning:

1. Beta release: Gather feedback from early users to refine the app before the official launch.

2. Teaser campaigns: Generate curiosity and anticipation among potential users.

3. Official launch events: Organize events to create buzz and attract media attention.

Sales Enablement:

1. Provide sales teams with training on the app's features and benefits to effectively communicate with potential customers.

2. Develop sales materials, such as presentations and brochures, highlighting the app's value proposition and key selling points.

Marketing and Promotion:

1. Run targeted marketing campaigns on social media platforms and digital channels to reach the target audience.

2. Collaborate with influencers, tech bloggers, and digital communication experts to promote the app and generate buzz.

3. Offer promotional discounts or incentives to encourage early adoption.

Internal Messaging:

1. Ensure all team members understand the app's positioning, target market, and key features to maintain consistent messaging.

2. Conduct regular internal meetings and updates to keep the team informed about the app's progress and milestones.

This GTM strategy for the MsgMsg App aims to drive user adoption and engagement by effectively targeting the right audience, positioning the app competitively, and executing a well-planned launch and marketing campaign.

18

Product Launch

Introducing a new product to the market can be both thrilling and challenging. Every successful launch has countless hours of meticulous planning and strategizing behind it.

1. Preparing for a Product Launch

This guide highlights 20 critical points that every Product Manager should consider to ensure a seamless and successful product launch.

Soft vs. Full-scale Launch	Distribution Channels		
Optimize the Launch Funnel	Budgeting		
Content Strategy	Segmenting the Audience		
Understand the Buying Journey	Pre-order Options		
Influencer Partnerships	Team Preparation		
Partner Preparation	Setting the Launch Date		
Build Anticipation	Launch Channels	Maximize Online Presence	Leverage Community Platforms
Invest in Paid Campaigns	Capture Leads	Engage Early Adopters	Crisis Management Plan

Fig 51: Product Launch Considerations

1. **Soft vs. Full-scale Launch**: Before everything else, determine the type of launch you're aiming for. A soft launch allows a limited audience to preview the product, helping you gauge initial reactions and make any necessary refinements. Meanwhile, a full-scale launch makes the product fully available to the public, aiming for a significant market splash.

2. **Distribution Channels**: Your distribution channels are crucial. Whether these are affiliates, digital platforms, or physical stores, keep them involved throughout the product launch journey.

3. **Optimize the Launch Funnel**: Consider multiple upsells or bundling with other products. Collaborating with other vendors can also provide cross-promotion opportunities.

4. **Budgeting**: Allocate a budget for all activities surrounding the launch, including marketing campaigns, PR efforts, and potential partnerships.

5. **Content Strategy**: Begin creating content well in advance, from compelling ad copies to informative blog posts. Ensure that content addresses customer pain points, showcases product benefits, and provides other relevant information.

Illustration 14: Airbnb Neighborhoods

When Airbnb was expanding its platform to include more cities and neighborhoods, they wanted to provide travelers with a way to explore and choose accommodations based on the local vibe and attractions.

To achieve this, Airbnb launched "Airbnb Neighborhoods," a content-focused campaign[1] that included detailed guides, photos, and videos highlighting the unique characteristics of each neighborhood. This content was created by local photographers, writers, and Airbnb hosts, giving travelers an authentic and immersive view of each neighborhood.

The "Airbnb Neighborhoods" campaign was a huge success, as it helped differentiate Airbnb from traditional hotel booking platforms and positioned the company as a provider of unique and personalized

---

> travel experiences. The campaign also helped drive user engagement and loyalty, as travelers were more likely to book accommodations through Airbnb after exploring the neighborhood's content.

6. **Segmenting the Audience**: Define your target audience and identify which segment your launch specifically aims to cater to.

7. **Understand the Buying Journey**: Recognize your potential customer's pain points, informational sources, and influencers to tailor your marketing strategies effectively.

8. **Pre-order Options**: Allow eager customers to pre-order, helping to spread out demand and generate early revenue.

9. **Influencer Partnerships**: Engage influencers to help create content and generate buzz, ensuring your product reaches a wider audience.

Illustration 15: Revolve and Aimee Song

The launch of Revolve's new clothing line got a big boost from influencer Aimee Song (@songofstyle).[2]

Revolve partnered with Aimee Song, a popular fashion and lifestyle influencer with a large following on Instagram and other social media platforms. The collaboration involved Aimee curating a collection of clothing pieces from Revolve's new line and promoting them to her audience through sponsored posts and stories.

The partnership was a huge success, with the collection selling out quickly and generating significant buzz on social media. Aimee's endorsement helped to drive traffic to Revolve's website and increase sales, ultimately contributing to the success of the GTM.

---

10. **Team Preparation**: Ensure your team understands the brand voice and is aligned with the launch strategy. Internal communication is key to ensure everyone is on the same page.

11. **Partner Preparation**: Partners like distributors and retailers can help secure better placement and promotion for the product.

12. **Setting the Launch Date**: Establishing a concrete launch date gives you a clear deadline and ensures you maintain the hype around your product. Avoid significant clashing events or seasons that might overshadow your product introduction.

13. **Build Anticipation**: Pre-market your product to stir interest and excitement. Offering early-use incentives and creating dedicated landing pages can boost initial interest.

14. **Launch Channels**: Identify the most effective channels for your business, such as email, SMS, social media, or even in-person events.

15. **Maximize Online Presence**: Promote your product aggressively on social media and other digital publications to reach a broader audience.

Illustration 16: Fyre Festival's Social Media Hype

The Fyre Festival, a music event organized by Fyre Media Inc. founders Billy McFarland and rapper Ja Rule, was set to be a luxurious experience on Great Exuma, a Bahamian island, in April and May 2017. The festival's promotion heavily relied on social media, especially Instagram, targeting affluent millennials and influencers.

As part of their social media strategy, the organizers enlisted supermodels like Kendall Jenner, Bella Hadid, and Emily Ratajkowski to post a plain pink tile as their Instagram profile picture, creating intrigue and buzz among their followers.

Additionally, select models were invited to the Bahamas for a photoshoot to further enhance the festival's online presence. The photos from this shoot were widely shared on social media, contributing to the festival's success in generating interest and ticket sales.

However, despite the strong promotional campaign, the festival faced numerous logistical issues and failed to deliver on its promises. This serves as a cautionary tale about the importance of 360-degree planning and managing expectations in any product launch and business venture.

---

16. **Leverage Community Platforms**: Utilize platforms like Product Hunt to generate interest and gather feedback from a tech-savvy community.

17. **Invest in Paid Campaigns**: Consider paid advertising and coordinated PR efforts to ensure a wide coverage of your product launch.

18. **Capture Leads**: Establish mechanisms to gather and nurture potential customer leads, ensuring a steady flow of interested buyers.

19. **Engage Early Adopters**: Attracting early adopters can generate buzz and provide valuable feedback for any last-minute tweaks.

20. **Crisis Management Plan:** Having a plan in place to address potential crises, such as product recalls or negative publicity, can help mitigate damage to the brand.

While product launches can be daunting, a well-strategized plan ensures you're on the right track. It's not just about the launch but also about sustaining momentum and continually improving based on feedback and market dynamics.

1.1 Example Scenario

Scenario 57: Timingila Solutions is a large multinational corporation with over eight development centers spanning six countries and employing over 320,000 individuals, approximately 30,000 of whom are dedicated to software development. Within the engineering department, the company manages a portfolio of over 300 software products, with at least 150 directly serving customers or partners.

Due to its size, geographical spread, and operational silos, the company faces challenges related to duplicated efforts. To address this issue, the Chief Technology Officer (CTO) has initiated an effort to minimize rework by promoting knowledge sharing through an Internal Development Platform.

The Product Manager responsible for the Customer-360 data platform is preparing to launch the platform as a capability on the new IDP.

To achieve this, the Product Manager has developed a comprehensive 20-point Product launch plan and presented it to the leadership.

The key elements of the plan for launching Customer-360 data platform on the new IDP are:

1. **Soft vs. Full-scale Launch:** Opting for a soft launch to a limited audience

2. **Distribution Channels:** Using the company's new Internal Development Platform for distribution

3. **Optimizing the Launch Funnel:** Offering the Customer-360 data platform as an add-on to products requiring basic customer information for their profile pages

4. **Budgeting:** Allocating resources for 10 developers to support onboarding business applications and potential partnerships.

5. **Content Strategy:** Including blog posts, presentations, and approval for a proposed talk at an industry event by the chief architect on 'how to provide regulated access to Customer Data within the org using IDP'

6. **Segmenting the Audience:** Targeting Managing Directors, Technical Architects, and Program Managers in Business Units supported by the customer- and partner-facing apps.

7. **Understanding the Buying Journey:** Implementing a three-step onboarding journey for Business Processes for the owning Managing Director, calling out the technical support from the allocated developers.

8. **Pre-order Options:** Allowing early access to the sandbox and test environments for eager Tech Architects.

9. **Influencer Partnerships:** Engaging the CTO to generate buzz.

10. **Team Preparation:** Conducting sessions to prepare the team for anticipated questions and strategies for sharing information.

11. **Setting the Launch Date:** Timing the launch in January to align with budget planning for the new year.

12. **Building Anticipation:** Securing slots on the Intranet and IDP homepages.

13. **Time-Conscious Launch:** Ensuring the release coincides with the budget planning cycle in January.

14. **Launch Channels:** Leveraging the IDP and Intranet homepages, CTO's townhall, and email communications to all Engineering staff.

15. **Maximizing Online Presence:** Promoting adoption and success stories in IDP newsletters.

16. **Leveraging Community Platforms:** Focusing on engagement through the Intranet and IDP.

17. **Engaging Early Adopters:** Offering additional integration support to early adopters from the allocated developer pool.

18. **Feedback Collection:** Collecting feedback post-launch to refine the platform and communications based on both converted and unconverted leads.

This detailed plan outlines a strategic approach to launching the Customer-360 data platform, emphasizing engagement, communication, and strategic alignment with the company's objectives.

2. Product Launch Collaterals

For a successful product launch, a Product Manager should consider creating the following types of training materials:

Fig 52: Product Launch Collaterals

1. **Product Overview Guide**: This document provides a comprehensive overview of the product, its features, and its unique selling propositions (USPs). It serves as a quick reference guide for team members and stakeholders.

2. **Sales Training Manuals**: These are in-depth guides specifically designed for the sales team. They include product features, benefits, and common objections, along with tactics for overcoming those objections.

3. **Technical Documentation**: Detailed documents or guides that delve into the technical aspects of the product are essential for training support teams and technical staff.

4. **User Manuals**: These guides are aimed at end-users and should be easy to understand. They often include step-by-step instructions, FAQs, and troubleshooting tips.

5. **Quick Start Guides**: Short, easy-to-read guides that provide essential information to get users up and running as quickly as possible.

6. **Onboarding Presentations**: Slide decks or video presentations can be used during team meetings or webinars to onboard team members and other stakeholders.

7. **Role-specific Training Modules**: Depending on the product, separate training modules can be created for different roles within the organization, such as customer service agents, sales reps, or technical support staff.

8. **Demo Scripts**: These scripts guide sales and marketing teams on how to effectively demonstrate the product to potential customers or clients.

9. **Competitive Analysis Sheets**: One-sheeters like the Competitor Analysis Canvas or Competition Landscape Map offer a quick comparison of the product against competitors can be useful for sales teams.

10. **Compliance Reports**: If the product falls under specific regulations or compliance standards, training material outlining these requirements can be crucial.

11. **Promotional Material**: Though not strictly training material, marketing collateral like press releases, brochures, flyers, and promotional videos can also serve an educational purpose for both internal teams and external partners.

12. **Partner or Reseller Guides**: If the product will be sold through third-party vendors or partners, specialized guides that teach them how to market and sell the product are beneficial.

By preparing these types of training materials, the Product Manager ensures that all involved parties—whether internal team members or external partners—are well-equipped to contribute to the product's successful launch.

Let us look closer at some of these.

3. User Manual

Product Managers frequently author the User Manuals for their respective products. These drafts may lead to the final versions or provide foundational material for technical writers. Below is a template that Product Managers can utilize as a starting point.

3.1 Contents of a User Manual

Preface

Product Managers understand that a product will cater to various user types, each with their own unique user journey. Ideally, separate User Manuals should be created to address the specific needs and use by each user group.

Prologue

Name and introduction of the product. The official name, also known alternate names.

Ever found yourself grappling with the discrepancy between Mac OS X's names (eg: Leopard, Snow Leopard, Lion, Mountain Lion) and actual version numbers (eg: 10.8, 10.7, 10.6, 10.5) while searching for a solution to an issue on Google? A good User Manual will make it clear for the user.

Mini version number, logo, and icon should be included, along with a succinct description tailored to the specific user type or audience for which the product is intended.

Quick Start

Include a streamlined user flow that guides users through the simplest and most direct path to get started, perform a 'hello world' action, and exit the application. This could be termed the "TL;DR" or "For the Impatient" version. Extensive use of labeled and annotated screenshots is recommended for clarity and ease of understanding.

User Flows

For products with multiple user flows, dedicate a chapter to each distinct flow. Begin with a concise introduction that outlines the scope of the flow, what it aims to achieve, and potential pitfalls users might encounter. To enhance clarity and user comprehension, it's highly advisable to include an abundance of labeled and annotated screenshots throughout each chapter.

List of Error Messages

Include a comprehensive list of error messages, accompanied by explanations for why a user might encounter each one and recommended steps for resolving the respective scenarios. This will serve as a valuable troubleshooting guide for users, helping them navigate and resolve issues more efficiently.

Support

Include guidelines on how to get in touch with official support, specifying the range of available channels for assistance. Highlight what information should be prepared in advance to facilitate quicker resolution of support requests. Additionally, direct users to public forums where they can seek supplementary help or advice.

FAQ

Even if you start with just a single question, it's essential to include a Frequently Asked Questions (FAQ) section and continue to expand it over time. Guidelines for crafting an effective FAQ can be found in the following section.

3.2 Other Considerations

- **Uniform Structure and Template**: Maintain a consistent layout, complete with standard margins, colors, and design elements. This uniformity helps users quickly understand the purpose of each page.

- **Informative Headers:** In order to help users quickly locate relevant information, provide the name, topic, or purpose of the chapter in the header.

- **Informative Footers**: Always include useful footers that display the page number, product name, and version to help users navigate the manual more effectively.

- **Meaningful Image Titles**: Use descriptive titles for images to clarify their relevance and help users quickly locate specific content.

- **Image Index**: Include an index that lists all images, allowing users to easily find and refer to visuals throughout the manual.

- **Assume Novice Users**: Always write the manual as if the user is a complete beginner who will adhere to your instructions down to the last detail.

- **Peer Review for Usability**: Pass the drafts to someone unfamiliar with the product and seek their feedback to ensure that the information is clear and useful.

- **Page Orientation**: Opt for a Portrait mode layout (Word document) if users are likely to print the manual, and choose Landscape mode (PowerPoint presentation) if it will primarily be viewed on-screen.

4. FAQs

An efficient FAQ section isn't just an add-on, but a necessary component of helping users. Here are some best practices for Product Managers to consider when curating FAQs.

4.1 Prioritize Relevance Over Volume

It's tempting to cover every conceivable question in an FAQ, but it's more beneficial to prioritize questions that users genuinely ask frequently. Constantly updating this section based on user feedback and frequent inquiries ensures that content remains relevant and streamlined.

4.2 Use Clear and Concise Language

Complex jargon or verbose explanations can muddle the clarity of an FAQ. Responses should be direct, easy to understand, and jargon-free, ensuring that users of all expertise levels can grasp the answers.

4.3 Group Thematically

A long list of questions can be daunting. Grouping FAQs by theme or topic makes navigation easier and more intuitive. Whether it's "Billing," "Technical Issues," or "Account Management," categories can guide users to their desired answers swiftly.

4.4 Link to Detailed Resources

While answers should be concise, providing links to more detailed articles, guides, or tutorials can cater to users who seek an in-depth understanding or solution.

4.5 Update Regularly

A product's features, policies, or user concerns aren't static. Regularly reviewing and updating the FAQ section ensures it remains current, relevant, and aligned with the product's evolution.

4.6 Position Prominently

If users can't find the FAQ section easily, its efficacy is compromised. Ensure that it's prominently positioned, ideally linked in the main navigation or footer and labeled clearly.

A FAQ isn't merely a section but it's a tool for preemptive support. Crafting it with care, ensuring clarity, and regularly updating it can elevate the overall user experience, reduce support tickets, and foster user trust.

5. Product Note

A Product Note is a concise document, generally just two pages long, fitting on the front and back of a single printed sheet. This document highlights the essential features, benefits, and specifications of the product. Designed for informed buyers who are familiar with the industry, it provides critical information to help them know the product's capabilities and prerequisites from a user's perspective. Product Notes are widely utilized in trade shows and specialized marketing campaigns.

Product notes can include:

1. **Quick Start Guide**: A streamlined set of instructions to facilitate immediate use of the product

2. **Features**: Highlighted, standout capabilities that offer distinct advantages

3. **FAQs**: Answers to frequently asked questions, aiding in effortless product understanding

4. **Technical Specifications**: Detailed information on hardware and software prerequisites, as well as machine configurations and network requirements for optimal performance

5. **Customer Testimonials**: Authentic endorsements from satisfied customers, showcasing the product's value and efficacy

6. **Purchase Guidance**: Directions on how to acquire the product, including the relevant website links and information on how to connect with a sales representative for personalized assistance

One of my all-time favorite Product Note is for the VxWorks operating system,[3] developed by Wind River, a company where I was formerly employed. This informative note is systematically divided into the following sections:

- Introduction

- Key features

- Few Customers

- Awards Won

- How to Purchase

- Safety Certifications

- Related Tool

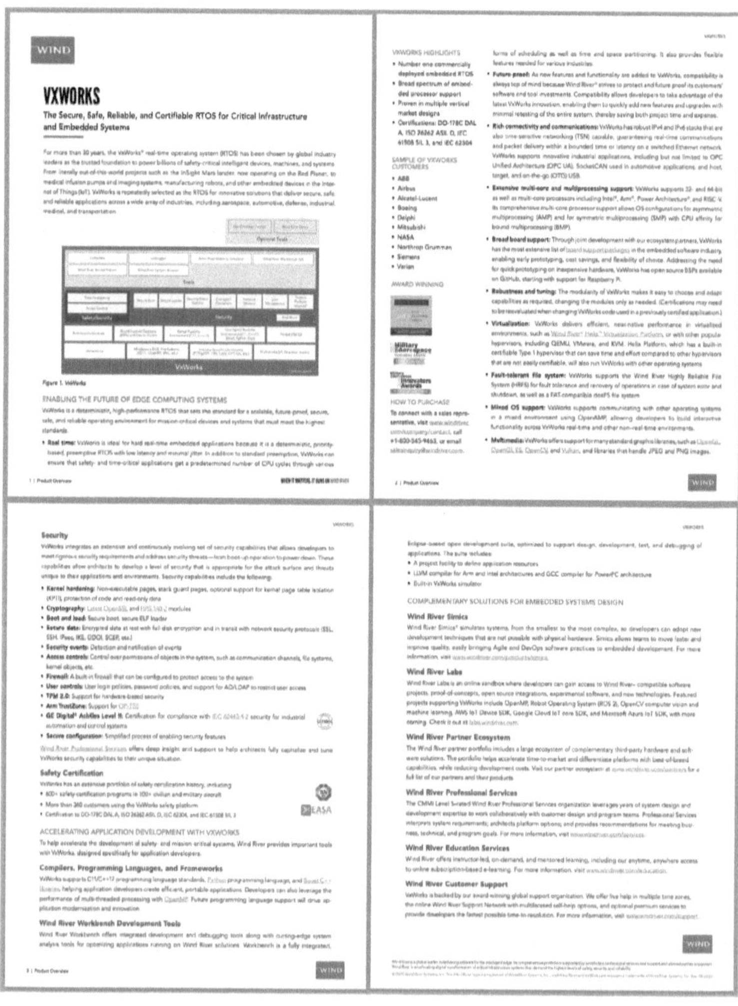

Fig 53: Product Note of Wind River VxWorks[3]

6. Release Note

Release Notes are documents that accompany software updates or new product releases. They serve to inform users, administrators, and other stakeholders about what has changed, including new features, improvements, and bug fixes. These notes provide a high-level overview of the changes, helping the audience understand what to expect and how to best utilize the updated or new software.

6.1 Typical Contents of Release Notes

Common elements found in release notes include:

1. **Version Number and Release Date**: Helps users identify the specific update and when it was released

2. **Introduction/Overview**: A brief description of the release, its importance, and who it is intended for

3. **New Features**: A list or description of new functionalities that have been added

4. **Enhancements**: Upgrades to existing features for better performance, usability, security, and compliance

5. **Bug Fixes**: Details of the issues resolved, often referencing ticket numbers for internal tracking

6. **Deprecations and Removals**: Information about features or functionalities that have been deprecated or removed

7. **Known Issues**: Information about issues that are known but not yet fixed

8. **System Requirements**: Any changes to the hardware or software prerequisites needed to run the product

9. **Installation/Upgrade Steps**: How to install the new version or upgrade from a previous version, if not automated

10. **Acknowledgments**: Credit to contributors, testers, or others involved in the release

11. **Contact Information**: How to reach support, offer feedback, or for general queries

12. **Legal Notice/Copyright**: Any necessary legal information or disclaimers

6.2 Best Practices for Writing Release Notes

- **Audience Awareness**: Know the audience. Technical users may appreciate more detail, while general users might prefer simplified, user-friendly language.

- **Be Clear and Concise**: Avoid jargon and unnecessary complexity. Be straightforward in the descriptions.

- **Use Bullet Points or Lists**: These make the release notes easier to skim and understand quickly.

- **Categorize Changes**: Organize the information under relevant sub-headings like 'New Features,' 'Bug Fixes,' and other pertinent subheadings.

- **Provide Context**: When listing new features or changes, briefly describe why they are important or how they could be used.

- **Include Visuals**: Screenshots and diagrams can offer a quick understanding of significant changes.

- **Hyperlink to More Information**: Provide links to documentation, FAQs, or blog posts for users interested in a deeper dive.

- **Version History**: Keep a running history of all past release notes for easy reference.

- **Review and Revise**: Prior to publishing, have team members review the notes to ensure accuracy and clarity.

- **Promote**: Make your release notes easily accessible. Share them through relevant channels such as emails, blogs, or within the software itself.

- **Keep It Updated**: If a hotfix or minor release follows shortly after, update the release notes to reflect these changes.

By adhering to these best practices, a Product Manager can create release notes that are informative, easy to understand, and helpful to the users.

7. Sales Battlecards

While all the collateral previously mentioned directly supports the sales process, one document stands out as particularly crucial during sales training: the collection of talking points designed to help salespeople close deals. Often labeled with an exciting title of Battlecard, this document serves as an indispensable tool for sales success.

7.1 Structure of a Sales Battlecard

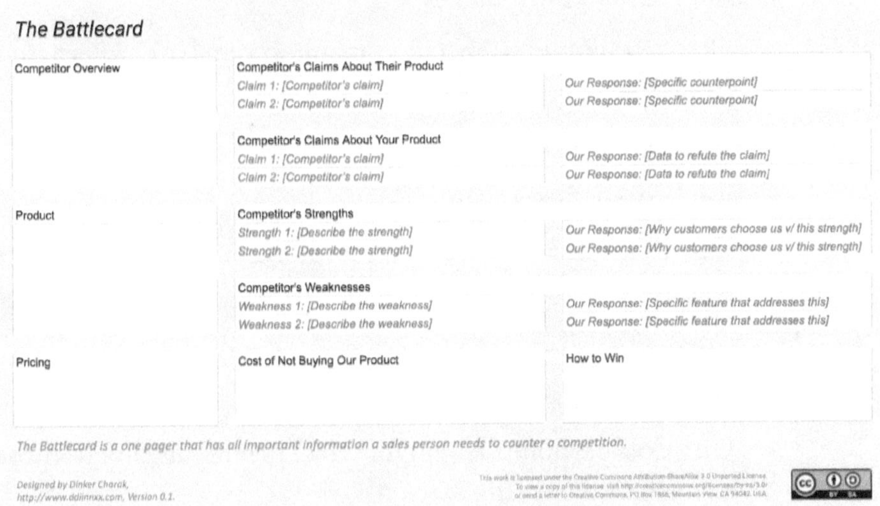

Fig 54: *The Battlecard Template*

7.2 Detailed Overview

Competitor Overview

- **Brief Description**: In less than 50 words, provide a brief description of the competitor, their product, and their target market.

Product

- **Detailed Description**: Go into little more detail about the competitor's product, focusing on its core functionalities.
- **Key Features**: List the key features that make their product stand out in the market.

Pricing

- **Tiers**: Break down the competitor's pricing model, listing what is included in each tier.
- **Special Offerings**: Highlight any free trials, promotions, or unique offerings they provide.

Competitor's Claims About Their Product

- **Claim**: [Competitor's claim]
  - Our Response: [Specific counterpoint or alternative perspective]

Competitor's Claims About Your Product

- **Claim**: [Competitor's claim]
  - Our Response: [Specific counterpoint or data to refute the claim]

Competitor's Strengths

- **Strength**: [Describe the strength]
  - Our Counterpoint: Highlight why current customers chose our solution over this strength.

Competitor's Weaknesses

- **Weakness:** [Describe the weakness]
  - Our Solution: Point out a specific feature or benefit of our product that addresses this weakness.

Cost of Not Buying Our Product

- Data Point: [Statistical or financial argument]

How to Win

- **Key Talking Points:** Summarize the main arguments for choosing our product over the competitor's.

- **Actions to Guide a Meeting:** List steps or strategies that salespeople should employ in meetings to guide the conversation toward a successful close.

7.3 Example Scenario

Scenario 58: The Product Manager of a rival product competing with the MsgMsg App has been tasked to create Sales collaterals.

The Product Manager chose to use a Sales Battlecard and shared the following.

Competitor Overview

MsgMsg App is an AI-powered messaging app that aims to enhance communication with predictive messaging, instant language translation, and personalized user experiences. It targets digitally-savvy individuals seeking efficient communication tools.

Product

MsgMsg App offers real-time message suggestions, instant language translation, and tailored user experiences based on communication patterns.

Key Features: Advanced AI algorithms for predictive messaging, real-time language translation, and personalized user experiences.

Pricing

Tiers: Freemium model with basic features available for free and advanced AI features offered in premium tiers.

Special Offerings: Possibly free trials for premium features and promotional pricing for early adopters.

Competitor's Claims About Their Product

Claim 1: MsgMsg App claims to provide predictive messaging and personalized experiences.

Our Response: While MsgMsg App focuses on AI-driven features, our product emphasizes user privacy and simplicity, ensuring a more intuitive messaging experience.

Competitor's Claims About Our Product

Claim 1: MsgMsg App claims our product lacks advanced AI features for predictive messaging.

Our Response: Our product prioritizes user privacy and protects users from AI "hallucinating" or giving wrong responses, offering a more reliable messaging experience without compromising on key functionalities.

Competitor's Strengths

Strength 1: MsgMsg App's advanced AI algorithms for predictive messaging and personalized experiences.

Our Counterpoint: Our product's simplicity and focus on user privacy differentiate us from MsgMsg App, offering a more intuitive and secure messaging platform.

Competitor's Weaknesses

Weakness 1: MsgMsg App's complexity and potential privacy concerns due to AI-driven features.

Our Solution: Our product prioritizes user privacy and offers a simpler messaging experience, addressing concerns related to complexity and privacy.

Cost of Not Buying Our Product

Data Point 1: Using MsgMsg App may lead to potential privacy breaches and data misuse as it relies on external AI algorithms.

Data Point 2: Our product offers a simpler, more secure messaging experience without compromising on key features, making it a more reliable choice.

> **How to Win**
>
> *Key Talking Points:* Emphasize our product's simplicity, user privacy, and reliability compared to MsgMsg App's potential privacy concerns and complexity.
>
> *Actions to Guide a Meeting:* Focus on demonstrating the ease of use and security features of our product, highlighting the advantages over MsgMsg App in terms of user experience and privacy protection.

Download Sales Battlecard Template

https://bit.ly/plcu-battlecard

8. Press Release

A press release is an official statement issued by an organization to communicate important news or announcements to the media and the public. The goal is to capture attention and convey information in a concise, clear format that journalists can easily use for their reporting. Press releases are often distributed through wire services or directly to journalists, and they may include multimedia elements like images or videos to enhance the message. They serve as a primary tool for public relations and marketing efforts.

8.1 Contents of a Press Release

A press release usually follows a standardized format to make it easy for journalists and readers to quickly understand the main points. Here are the typical contents and structure:

Letterhead or Logo

Include the organization's letterhead or logo at the top of the press release for branding and legitimacy.

Release Timing

Specify when the information can be made public, commonly indicated as "For Immediate Release," "Embargoed Until [Date/Time]," or "For Release on [Date]."

Headline

Craft a compelling and concise headline that captures the essence of the news. It should grab attention and encourage further reading.

Subhead (Optional)

A subhead can be used to provide additional context or details, serving as an extension of the headline.

Dateline

Indicate the city where the press release is originating and the date of the release.

Lead Paragraph

The lead paragraph should summarize the key points — Who, What, When, Where, and Why — to hook the reader.

Body

- Introduction: A few sentences providing background about the subject
- Details: Further elaboration of the news, which should include quotes from key stakeholders, facts, figures, or data
- Additional Information: Any supporting context or background information

Multimedia (Optional)

Include high-quality images, videos, or infographics that are relevant to the news, if applicable.

Boilerplate

A brief "About Us" section giving background information about the issuing organization, along with its mission and key offerings.

Contact Information

Include the name, position, phone number, and email address of the individual(s) available for media inquiries.

End Notation

Commonly, "###" or "---" is used to signify the end of the press release.

By adhering to this standardized structure, you make it easier for journalists to find the information they need and more likely that your news will be covered in the way you intend.

8.2 Why Write a Press Release

Having a Product Manager draft an initial version of a press release before it gets finalized by marketing can offer several advantages.

1. **Clear Understanding of Product Features and Benefits:** Product Managers often have a deep understanding of the product's features, capabilities, and target audience. This ensures that the technical aspects of the product are accurately described and that its benefits are effectively communicated.

2. **Alignment with Product Objectives:** Product Managers are responsible for the strategic direction of the product, so drafting the press release ensures that the messaging aligns with the product's objectives and roadmap. This ensures a cohesive strategy across different departments.

3. **Early Identification of Value Proposition:** Writing a press release draft can be an exercise in crystallizing the product's value proposition. This clarity benefits not just the press release itself, but also other aspects of product marketing and sales strategy.

4. **Faster Turnaround Time:** Drafting a press release can accelerate the entire process of public announcement because the Product Manager provides a detailed, ready-to-refine draft to Marketing. This ensures that all essential aspects are covered, leaving the Marketing team to focus on refining language, tone, and other elements.

5. **Cross-Functional Collaboration**: Collaboration between Product and Marketing can foster a more unified message and can avoid potential discrepancies or miscommunications. It ensures everyone is on the same page concerning how the product is to be presented to the public.

6. **Message Consistency**: A press release drafted by a Product Manager can set the stage for consistent messaging across various channels. Since Product Managers often interact with different departments (Sales, Engineering, Customer Service), their perspective can help maintain consistency in how the product is talked about within the organization and in public.

7. **Reduces Risk of Misinterpretation**: Technical details are often prone to misinterpretation by those not deeply involved in the product development process. Having the Product Manager draft the release reduces the risk of such errors.

8. **Builds Product Narrative**: Product Managers are generally skilled at storytelling around the product — how it came to be, the problem it solves, and its market significance. This storytelling can form the core of a compelling press release.

9. **Ensures Customer-Centric Focus**: Product Managers often have the most interaction with end-users and thus can ensure that the press release addresses their needs and solves their problems, making the release more relatable and compelling to the target audience.

10. **Test Marketing Messages**: Lastly, drafting a press release can serve as a form of early test marketing. If it's challenging to write a compelling press release, that could be a red flag that the product or feature might not be as marketable as thought, prompting a re-evaluation of its positioning or even its development status.

In summary, having a Product Manager draft the press release ensures that the product is accurately and effectively represented, that the message aligns with strategic goals and the whole process is more streamlined. This collaborative approach can yield a more impactful and coherent press release.

Illustration 17: Following is the press release[4] announcing the release of Roo Kids App, the key product of my earlier and now defunct startup Gungroo:

Instant messaging app 'Roo Kids' helps parents envelop their preteens in a safe cocoon

Industry: Family & pets

Highly rated and touted as a safe 'WhatsApp for Kids', Roo Kids is now available for Android and iOS

Bangalore, India (PRUnderground) April 23rd, 2015

The *Roo Kids* instant messaging app, a product of Bangalore's Gungroo Software has announced the full release of its app, making it easier for parents to rest easy about the safety of their kids. Created with a vision to be a safe and easy to use 'WhatsApp for Kids', it has been well received in the USA, UK and Australia, with a substantial number of downloads originating from these countries. The full release of Roo Kids sees it launch on the Android platform and major updates for iPad and iPhone users.

Roo Kids has been conceptualized to address 2 critical concerns of parents when their kids are online – **firstly**, that of the kids talking to strangers and unknowingly making themselves vulnerable, and **secondly**, kids getting constantly distracted and this impacting their studies and health. The makers of Roo Kids claim that these objectives are achieved with minimum yet critical controls, thus making the app attractive to kids and parents alike.

Elaborating on the thought process behind the changes in the new release, Dinker Charak, founder of Gungroo Software said, "In the new release, we have tried to address all the concerns of parents regarding the online safety of their kids. The other thing is, even though we launched Roo Kids after considerable market research, our 'Aha' moment came when we realized that it is the tablet that the family shares. Thus Roo Kids is highly optimized for iPad, and the new release supports iPhones and Android devices as well".

From a safety viewpoint, this app seems to have covered all bases. Designed to broadly comply with the US FTC's Children's Online Privacy Protection Act (COPPA), Roo Kids comes with safety features like SSL, zero ads on the app, and immediate notifications to parents if the kid reports a user as abusive, thus minimizing chances of online bullying.

On the other hand, parents get to own and review the contact list, blocking suspicious persons and strangers. Parents can also set curfew hours to block the app from working, to make sure the kids have a healthy schedule of activities online and offline.

This does not mean the app is all about parents and safety. It's apparent that the creators of Roo Kids understand that only a truly engaging app can keep the kids from trying other, potentially unsafe apps. They have given a lot of attention to making the app and its UI easy to use and attractive for kids, which includes allowing kids to keep their conversations private. All in all, this app seems to be a win-win for everyone involved.

Gungroo Software, the makers of Roo Kids, are now seeking funds to take the initiative to the next level, including a full COPPA compliance & certification for Roo Kids. Learn more here: https://www.rookidsapp.com/coppa/

About Gungroo Software

Gungroo Software builds safe + fun products for kids. Gungroo is a Bangalore based angel-funded company, helmed by Dinker Charak. Dinker brings diverse experience from working in strategically important roles in Komli, Jivox, Wind River and Fermilab. One of his personal career highs is having been able to contribute to LHC at CERN. Gungroo software is currently at a critical growth stage that's ideal for venture funding.

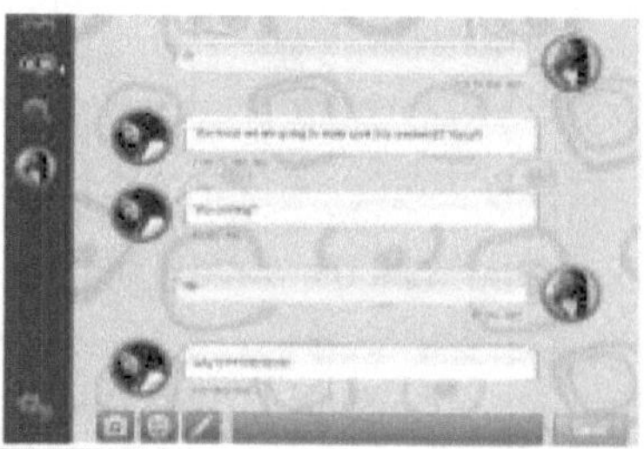

9. Partner or Reseller Guide

Creating a Partner or Reseller Guide is a critical step in building a robust and effective channel launch strategy. This guide serves as a comprehensive roadmap for the partners or the resellers, equipping them with the knowledge, skills, and tools they need to successfully market and sell the product. It also clarifies the benefits and incentives that make the product a profitable opportunity for them.

Typically, these guides share significant content with internal guides but usually omit confidential intellectual property and financial information.

9.1 Training on Product Positioning and Marketing

1. **Understanding the Unique Selling Proposition (USP):** Partners need to understand what sets the product apart from competitors. Clearly outline the USP so that it can be easily communicated to potential customers.

2. **Comparative Advantage Over Competitors**: Product Manager should provide detailed comparisons between the product and key competitors, focusing on features, benefits, and pricing. This helps partners convincingly argue why the product is the better choice.

3. **Handling Objections**: The guide should include a section on common objections that the reseller might encounter and how to effectively counter these. Prepared responses to FAQs can be invaluable here.

4. **Migration Path**: Offer a straightforward, step-by-step process for customers to switch from a competitor's product, covering both technical and non-technical aspects.

Effective training is crucial for empowering your partners to sell more effectively. The better they understand the product and its advantages, the more confident they'll be when positioning it in the market. In turn, this boosts their sales and, by extension, the product's.

9.2 Benefits and Incentives for Partners and Resellers

1. **Profit Margins**: Clearly outline the profit margins that resellers can expect when they sell the product.

2. **Sales Targets and Incentives**: Help to set achievable, yet challenging, sales targets and describe the bonuses or incentives for reaching these milestones.

3. **Marketing Co-op Funds**: If marketing support or co-op funds to help resellers promote the product are provided, explain how they can access and utilize these resources.

4. **Volume Discounts**: Explain if and how resellers can benefit from volume discounts, encouraging them to sell more.

5. **Sales Agreement**: Provide a summary or even a sample sales agreement outlining the terms and conditions, including return policies, payment terms, and other legalities.

This aims to make the business case for why it's profitable and advantageous for partners to work with the product. It is common for a reseller to sell multiple products from multiple organizations. Clearly defined benefits and incentives not only make the product more attractive to sell but also help foster a long-term, mutually beneficial relationship with the partners.

9.3 Good Practices When Creating a Partner & Reseller Guide

1. **Be Clear and Concise**: Use straightforward language, bullet points, and headers to make the guide easy to read and reference.

2. **Use Real-world Scenarios**: Case studies or examples can illustrate how to overcome objections or transition customers from a competitor. Use past scenarios or real customer conversations as the basis of these examples.

3. **Provide Training Modules**: Consider incorporating multimedia like video tutorials, webinars, or interactive quizzes to make the training more engaging.

4. **Secure & Easy Access**: Make sure that the guide is easily accessible, possibly via a secure online portal, so partners can access it whenever they need it.

5. **Feedback Loop**: Encourage partners to provide feedback on the guide so the Product Manager can make continual improvements. Whenever the feedback is incorporated in the product, let the person(s) know. That will build confidence among them that they were heard and the Product Manager has acted on the feedback.

6. **Localization**: If you have international partners, consider translating the guide into different languages and adapting content to suit different cultural nuances in selling and business practices.

7. **Accessibility**: Ensure that the guide is accessible to people with disabilities, possibly by offering it in various formats like PDF, Word, or HTML.

10. Promotional Material

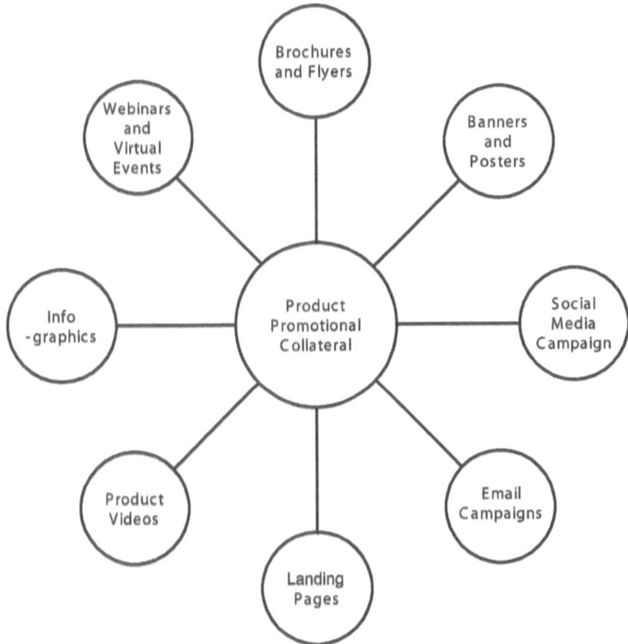

Fig 55: Product Promotional Collateral

Promotional materials play a vital role in the launch and ongoing marketing of a product. They serve to create awareness, generate interest, and ultimately drive sales. They also enable the team, well-wishers, influencers, and beneficiaries to rebroadcast the key messages.

These materials come in various forms, both digital and physical, to reach a broad audience across different platforms and mediums. Here are some common types of Promotional Materials:

1. **Brochures and Flyers**: Printed or digital booklets that provide detailed information about the product, its features, and its benefits. They can be distributed at events, mailed to potential customers, or made available for download on a website.

2. **Banners and Posters**: These can be physical banners displayed at events or retail locations, or digital banners used in online advertising. They offer a visual snapshot of the product and are designed to catch the eye.

3. **Social Media Campaign**: Short, targeted advertisements that appear on platforms like Facebook, Instagram, Twitter, and LinkedIn. They often use compelling images or videos and aim to reach a highly specific audience.

4. **Email Campaigns**: Custom-designed emails sent to a targeted list of subscribers, providing information, offers, or invitations related to the product.

5. **Landing Pages**: Special web pages designed to convert visitors into customers, often used in conjunction with digital advertising campaigns.

6. **Product Videos**: These could be explainer videos, tutorials, or feature highlights that showcase the product in action.

7. **Infographics**: Visually appealing graphics that break down complex information or data related to the product into easily digestible chunks.

8. **Webinars and Virtual Events**: Online events designed to educate potential customers about the product, often featuring experts, demos, and Q&A sessions.

11. Compliance Report

Compliance documents are critical components of a product launch that ensure the new offering meets the regulatory, legal, safety, or quality standards applicable to its domain. These documents serve as proof that the product has been developed, tested, and is being sold in accordance with relevant laws and industry guidelines. The absence of compliance documents can result in legal repercussions, including fines, bans, or even the withdrawal of the product from the market. The Product Manager should work with Legal and Compliance teams to put these together and ensure the Product matches the claims.

11.1 Types of Compliance Documents

1. **Regulatory Approvals**: Official documentation from government or independent agencies that certify the product has met specific industry standards. For example, in the pharmaceutical industry,

this could include Food and Drug Administration (FDA) approvals.

2. **Certificates of Conformity**: These certify that a product meets minimum safety, quality, or performance requirements. For instance, electronic products often need to comply with CE (European Conformity) or FCC (Federal Communications Commission) standards.

3. **License and Permits**: Documents granting permission to manufacture, distribute, or sell a product, particularly for regulated industries like healthcare, food and beverages, or automotive manufacturing.

4. **Environmental Compliance Documents**: Evidence that a product meets environmental regulations, such as waste disposal and energy consumption standards.

5. **Intellectual Property Rights (IPR) Documents**: Legal documentation proving ownership of or rights to use patents, copyrights, and trademarks associated with the product.

6. **Data Protection and Privacy Agreements**: Especially important for software products and platforms that handle user data, these documents detail how the product complies with data protection laws like the General Data Protection Regulation (GDPR) or the California Consumer Privacy Act (CCPA).

7. **Accessibility Certificates**: Documents proving that the product meets accessibility standards, ensuring it can be used by people with disabilities.

8. **Quality Assurance Documents**: Records of quality control tests, inspections, and any associated certifications like ISO 9001.

9. **Ethical Compliance Certificates**: For products that claim ethical sourcing or fair trade practices, documentation is required to support those claims.

10. **Import and Export Documents**: Necessary for products sold internationally, these papers certify that the product meets the import/export regulations and standards of all involved countries.

11. **Labeling and Packaging Regulations**: Proof that the product packaging meets regulations, such as nutritional information on food products or safety warnings on chemicals.

12. **Supplier and Vendor Compliance Forms**: Documentation that ensures any third-party suppliers or vendors also adhere to necessary compliance norms.

11.2 Importance of Compliance Documents

1. **Legal Protection**: Non-compliance can result in severe legal consequences, including fines and bans.

2. **Customer Trust**: Compliance with recognized standards is often viewed as a mark of quality and reliability, thereby attracting more customers.

3. **Market Access**: Certain markets are off-limits unless specific compliance standards are met.

4. **Reduced Liability**: Compliance documents can act as evidence of due diligence in case of lawsuits or other disputes.

11.3 Best Practices for Managing Compliance Documents

1. **Early Planning**: Integrate compliance requirements into the product development process from the get-go.

2. **Expert Consultation**: Involve legal advisors or compliance experts to ensure you understand all the requirements specific to your industry and product.

3. **Regular Updates**: Compliance requirements can change, so it's crucial to keep these documents up-to-date.

4. **Internal Audits**: Conduct regular internal checks to ensure ongoing compliance.

5. **Document Storage**: Keep all compliance documents safely stored, well-organized, and easily accessible for audits or inspections.

6. **Transparency**: Where relevant and possible, make compliance information accessible to customers, partners, and stakeholders to build trust.

By ensuring thorough and accurate compliance documentation, Product Managers can mitigate risks, build consumer trust, and pave the way for a successful product launch.

19

Digital Advertising

1. Introduction to Digital Ads

Digital advertising is a fast-paced and evolving domain, and as Product Managers, it's crucial to keep up with the latest trends and best practices to ensure effective product strategies. Here's a breakdown of some essential aspects of digital advertising you need to know.

1.1 Ad Types

- **Display Ads**: These are the visual ads that appear on websites, often in the form of banners. They can include both text and images.

- **Video Ads**: They are typically found on video platforms like YouTube or within streaming services.

- **Search Ads**: These appear in search engine results when specific keywords are queried.

- **Native Ads**: These are integrated into the content of a website or app and are designed to match the platform's look and feel.

- **Interstitial Ads**: These full-screen ads cover the interface of their host application.

- **Rich Media Ads**: These are interactive ads that can include multiple elements such as video, audio, or other interactive components.

1.2 Click Through URL

The Click Through URL (CTURL) is the hyperlink where the digital marketer wants the user to land after clicking on the ad.

A well-structured CTURL contains:

- **Base URL:** The main landing page.

- **Parameters:** These are tags added to the Base URL after inserting a '?'. These parameters allow analytics tools to track the source, medium, campaign, and other specifics of the incoming traffic. This allows for the right attribution of traffic to a specific campaign and optimization of campaigns.

Scenario 59: How many users will access the link I will use as an example here?

To track that, I created a campaign URL that I am sharing here. Since I use Google Analytics, this CTURL uses related parameters.

The Base URL is the full website URL. I chose 'https://www.dinker.in/plcu'.

Campaign ID allows for the grouping of campaigns when a Product Manager or Digital Marketer is running many campaigns. I chose '001'.

Campaign source can be used to specify the referrer (e.g. google, newsletter). Since the CTURL is in the book, I chose 'book'.

Campaign medium specifies the medium on which the link was presented (e.g. banner, email). Since the CTURL is in the book, I chose 'offline'.

Campaign names are human-centric names as compared to analytics-friendly campaign IDs. These can be the product name, seasonal (diwali_dhamaka), promo code, or slogan (e.g. spring_sale). Since the CTURL is in the book, I chose 'offline2online'.

There are a few more that I did not end up using. This is the CTURL that Google Analytics will be able to ingest:

https://www.dinker.in/plcu?utm_source=book&utm_
medium=link&utm_campaign=offline2online&utm_id=001

Please visit the above URL so I can get the answer to the question, 'How many users will access the link I will use as an example here?'

1.3 Landing Page

This is the page where users are taken when they click on the CTURL.

A landing page should be optimized for fast page loads, and responsive so it can show the key content on a desktop, notepad, or a phone. It is common for landing pages to focus on a key action, whether that means making a purchase, signing up, or any other desired action.

1.4 Tracking Pixels

A tracking pixel is a tiny, 1x1 transparent image placed on a webpage. When a user's browser loads the webpage, it also loads the tracking pixel, which then sends information back to an analytics tool. This allows the tool to track the user's activity on that page, such as whether they made a purchase, signed up for a service, or completed a form.

These pixels are commonly placed on 'Thank you' pages that appear after a user completes an action, like making a purchase or signing up. When the tracking pixel is loaded, it signals to the analytics platform that the desired action has been completed successfully.

By using tracking pixels, advertisers can gather valuable data on user behavior, including page views, conversions, and other events. This data helps them understand the effectiveness of their campaigns and make informed decisions to optimize their advertising strategies.

1.5 Reporting

Performance metrics are compiled into reports. Common metrics include Click-Through Rate (CTR), Conversion Rate, Impressions, and Cost Per Action (CPA). Platforms like Google Ads or Facebook Ads Manager provide detailed reports for advertisers.

1.6 Pricing Models

- CPM (Cost Per Milli): The cost for every 1000 impressions of the ad

- CPC (Cost Per Click): Advertisers pay for each click on their ads

- CPL (Cost Per Lead): Cost associated with acquiring a new lead or sign-up

- CPA (Cost Per Action): Cost when a specific action, like a sale, is completed

1.7 Audience & Ad Targeting

When launching an ad campaign, it's pivotal to define your target audience. Consider factors like demographics, interests, behaviors, and more. Platforms offer various targeting methods, such as:

- Retargeting: Targeting users who have previously interacted with your brand

- Lookalike/Similar Audiences: Targeting new users who resemble your existing audience

2. Display Ads

The ubiquitous nature of display ads, from banners on websites to dynamic content on social media, is a testament to their effectiveness and reach. For Product Managers diving into the realm of digital marketing, a deep comprehension of display ads is crucial.

2.1 The Anatomy of Display Ads

A typical display ad consists of:

- **Headline**: A concise, catchy phrase that grabs attention
- **Image or Graphics**: A visually appealing component designed to resonate with the target audience
- **Body Text**: Additional information about the product or service, usually limited to keep the ad uncluttered
- **Call-to-Action (CTA)**: A directive urging the viewer to engage, such as "Learn More" or "Shop Now"

Display ads stand out as both an art and a science. They combine creativity with data-driven strategies to connect brands with their audiences. For Product Managers, understanding the nuances of display advertising is essential, providing a robust tool in the arsenal to drive brand awareness, engagement, and ultimately, conversions.

2.2 IAB Standard for Display Ads

The Interactive Advertising Bureau (IAB) is a trade association that champions the media and marketing industries, empowering them to excel in the digital economy. With a membership exceeding 700, the IAB includes top media companies, brands, agencies, and technology firms responsible for selling, delivering, and optimizing digital advertising campaigns. The IAB's core activities include setting industry standards and conducting valuable research to drive innovation and growth in digital advertising.

The Interactive Advertising Bureau (IAB) provides standard ad sizes.[1] Few common display ad sizes include:

- Medium Rectangle (300px by 250px)
- Leaderboard (728px by 90px)

- Square (250px by 250px)

- Skyscraper (120px by 600px)

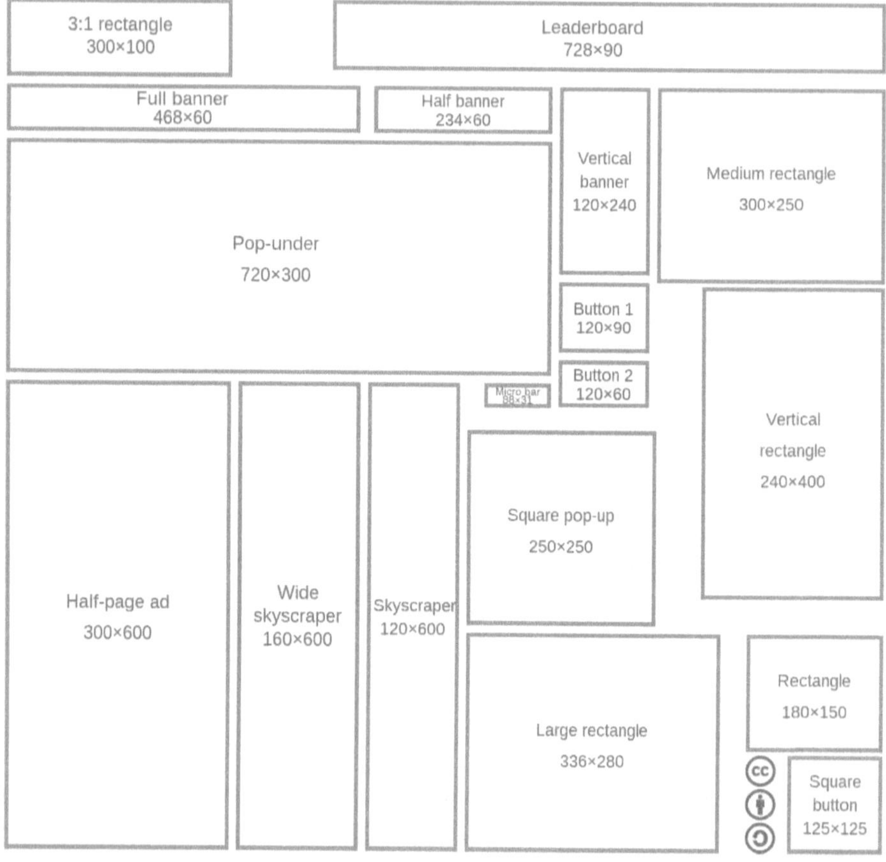

Fig 56: IAB Standard Display Ad Sizes[2]

It's essential to design ads in these sizes to ensure compatibility across multiple platforms.

3. Video Ads

In the digital-first streaming-centric entertainment market, the video format is a potent tool for brands seeking to captivate audiences and tell their stories. For Product Managers, understanding video ads' intricacies is essential to harness their full potential.

3.1 The Anatomy of Video Ads

A typical video ad consists of:

- **Video Content:** The main video footage that conveys the ad's message. This can include live-action footage, reformatted TV ads, animations, or a combination of the above.

- **Audio:** Background music, voiceover, or sound effects enhance the video's impact and help deliver the message.

- **Text Overlay:** Text displayed on the video screen provides additional information, such as the ad's slogan, product features, or a call to action.

- **Call to Action (CTA):** A prompt to encourage viewers to take a specific action, such as visiting a website, making a purchase, or signing up for a service.

- **Video Player:** A chromeless video player focuses solely on displaying the video content without any additional visual elements that could obstruct the ad or take up valuable space.

- **End Card:** A static or interactive screen at the end of the video, often containing additional information or a final CTA.

- **Adaptive Bitrate Streaming:** For online video ads, the use of adaptive bitrate streaming ensures that the video quality adjusts based on the viewer's internet connection speed, providing a smooth viewing experience.

- **Default Settings:** Parameters that can be passed to the video player to specify its default behavior, such as whether the ad should auto-start, be muted by default, play in a loop, or end with an end card. These settings help optimize the viewing experience and engagement with the ad.

3.2 Defining a Video View

The definition of a video view varies by platform and can have implications on advertising cost and pricing. A commonly agreed upon definition is:

- A view is counted when the video plays for a specific duration (often a few seconds).

- Actions like clicks or interactions can also count as views on some platforms. Always consult individual platform guidelines to understand their view-counting criteria.

3.3 Standard Formats for Video Ads

Some of the commonly recognized formats are:

- **Linear Video Ads**: Play before, in-between, or after video content. They are often sized to match the video content's dimensions, commonly 16:9 or 4:3.

- **Companion Ads**: These accompany linear video ads, typically as display banners that remain on-screen during or after the video.

3.4 Pricing Models

- **CPV (Cost Per View)**: This model charges advertisers for each video view. It's essential to understand how a 'view' is defined on each platform. On YouTube, for instance, a 'view' is counted when a user watches 30 seconds of the video or its entirety if it's shorter than 30 seconds.

3.5 Types of Video Ads

- **Pre-roll**: These are videos that play before the main content starts. They are one of the most common video ad types, offering brands a captive audience but can be skipped by viewers if too lengthy or not engaging.

- **Mid-roll**: As the name suggests, these ads play in the middle of the main video content, much like traditional TV commercial breaks. Their interruption of content can be perceived as disruptive, but they often have higher completion rates as viewers are already invested in the content.

- **Post-roll**: These ads play after the main content concludes. While they have the least disruptive nature, viewers might not stick around to watch them, especially if the primary content doesn't hold their attention till the end.

4. Search Ads

Search ads stand out for their precision, timeliness, and relevance. For Product Managers charting the digital marketing strategies of their products, understanding the intricacies of search ads is invaluable. Here's a deep dive into the realm of search ads.

4.1 The Concept of Search Term

A search term is the exact word or set of words a user types into a search engine. It's the query, the burning question, the need that users seek to satisfy. For advertisers, understanding search terms is crucial as they provide insights into the consumer's intent.

4.2 Google AdSense

Google AdSense is credited with making search term advertising mainstream and a big business. It allows publishers in the Google Network of content sites to serve automatic text, image, video, or interactive media advertisements that are targeted to site content and audience. These ads are managed, sorted, and maintained by Google, and they can generate revenue on either a per-click or per-impression basis.

4.3 Choosing the Right Keyword to Bid On

Deciding on the right keyword is a combination of art, science, and strategy. Here's a structured approach:

- **Understand User Intent**: Keywords should align with what your target audience might search for when considering your product or service.

- **Keyword Research Tools**: Platforms like Google's Keyword Planner or SEMrush provide insights into search volumes, competition levels, and even cost estimates for specific keywords.

- **Long-tail Keywords**: These are longer and more specific keyword phrases. While they often have lower search volumes, they typically signify higher intent and can lead to better conversion rates.

- **Competitor Analysis**: Understand what keywords your competitors are targeting. This can provide insights into market trends and highlight potential keyword opportunities or areas of oversaturation.

- **Keyword Relevance**: Ensure that the keywords you bid on are highly relevant to your ad's content and the landing page it leads to. This not only improves click-through rates but also affects the Quality Score, which can impact ad positioning and costs.

- **Constant Optimization**: The world of search is dynamic. Regularly review and refine your keyword strategy based on performance data, changing market conditions, or shifts in your product strategy.

5. Text Ads

Text ads often form the bedrock of many campaigns. These ads, while devoid of flashy visuals or interactive elements, carry the essence of a brand's message in words. For Product Managers, understanding how to effectively leverage text ads is vital to ensure successful campaigns.

5.1 The Anatomy of a Text Ad

A typical text ad can be dissected into several components:

- Heading or Title: This is often the first thing users notice. It's generally bold and stands out. Most platforms, like Google Ads, allow for multiple headline parts, separated by a pipe (|) or a dash (-).

- Description: This is where advertisers provide more information about their product, service, or offer. A good description complements the headline and encourages the user to take action.

- **Display URL**: While it gives users an idea of where they'll go upon clicking, it doesn't have to be the exact landing page URL. It's a cleaner, more readable version.

- **Call to Action (CTA)**: While not a separate component, a CTA is crucial. Whether implicit or explicit, the CTA in a text ad prompts users to take a desired action – be it 'Learn More', 'Shop Now', or 'Sign Up'.

6. Native Ads

Native advertising has emerged as a subtle yet effective way for brands to engage audiences. For Product Managers at the helm of digital strategies, understanding native ads and their distinctive traits is indispensable.

Native ads are promotional messages designed to blend seamlessly with the platform or content in which they appear. Unlike traditional display or banner ads that stand out as external advertisements, native ads mimic the design, style, and voice of the content surrounding them.

6.1 Key Characteristics of Native Ads

- **Integrated, Not Interruptive**: Native ads fit organically within the content, making them less obtrusive and more engaging.

- **Contextually Relevant**: They align with the content they accompany, ensuring relevance and added value for the audience.

- **Transparent**: While they blend in, native ads maintain transparency through labels like "sponsored" or "promoted" to indicate their commercial nature.

6.2 The Appeal of Native Ads

Native advertising capitalizes on a less intrusive approach, which has multiple benefits.

- **Enhanced User Experience**: By not disrupting the natural flow of content consumption, they improve user engagement and perception.

- **Higher Engagement Rates**: As native ads align with the content and context, users are more likely to interact with them.

- **Bypassing Ad Blockers**: Native ads are less likely to be flagged by ad blockers since they're part of the content, not separate from it.

6.3 Types of Native Ads

- **In-feed Ads**: These appear within content streams, like articles on a news website or posts in a social media feed.

- **Search & Promoted Listings**: Ads appearing at the top of search results or as highlighted products in online stores fit naturally within the listing environment.

- **Content Recommendations**: Often found at the end of articles, these suggest related sponsored content to the reader.

6.4 Why Native Ads Differ

While the distinction might seem nuanced, native ads differ fundamentally from other ad formats:

- **Design & Presentation**: Unlike banner ads that stand apart, native ads merge with the platform's design and layout.

- **User Interaction**: Traditional ads seek immediate attention, while native ads engage users subtly, often leading to more profound interactions.

- **Purpose & Intent**: Native ads, while promotional, often prioritize value addition — be it through informative content, entertainment, or relevant suggestions.

- By discerning their unique ability to not obstruct the product experience, Product Managers can harness native ads as a potent tool, driving engagement in an era where the traditional and the intrusive are increasingly sidelined.

7. In-App Ads

Users spend a significant chunk of their digital time within apps. This shift has led to the rise of in-app advertising, offering brands a new avenue to reach consumers. For Product Managers, understanding the dynamics of in-app ads is crucial to harness their potential.

- In-app ads are advertisements displayed within mobile applications. Unlike mobile web ads, which are shown on websites accessed through mobile browsers, in-app ads are integrated into the app experience, tailored to fit organically without detracting from the user's journey.

7.1 Popular In-App Ad Formats

Standard Banner Ads

These are horizontal or vertical rectangles that appear at the top, bottom, or sides of an app's interface. Though common, their small size may limit engagement.

Standard banner ads typically come in two sizes: 320 × 50 or 300 x 250 pixels, and can be static or animated. These ads are commonly found at the top or bottom of a screen and are designed to grab the user's attention without being too intrusive.

The benefits of standard banner ads are their universal compatibility across all screens, their ability to be executed in large volumes due to long-tail inventory, their quick deployment time, and their ease of integration into various platforms. Despite their simplicity, standard banner ads remain a popular choice for advertisers due to their effectiveness in reaching a wide audience with minimal effort and cost.

Interstitial Ads

Full-screen ads that pop up between activity transitions in an app. Many experts recommend placing interstitial ads within games and levels, where they can capture users' attention during natural breaks in gameplay, maximizing their impact.

Interstitial banner ads are larger than standard banners, typically at 320 x 480 pixels.

They offer a broader canvas for messaging, providing greater exposure and recall for advertisers. These ads are visually compelling, making them highly effective for achieving high impressions and conversions. Additionally, interstitial banners can feature animated and interactive rich media content, further enhancing user engagement.

Video Ads

These can be interstitial or placed within content. They automatically play, often offering rewards (in gaming apps) for viewing.

When creating video ads, it's important to adhere to certain specifications. These include a minimum frame rate of 24 frames per second (fps), a maximum length of 15 seconds for animation, and a maximum length of 30 seconds for video, with unlimited user-initiated playback. Additionally, host-initiated video playback can include an additional file size of up to 2.2 MB, also with unlimited user-initiated playback.

The benefits of using video ads are numerous. They provide short, informative content that enhances user experiences. Video ads are particularly effective in conveying brand stories, surpassing other formats in storytelling impact. Moreover, video serves as an excellent format for both informing and educating viewers, making it a versatile and valuable tool in advertising and communication strategies.

Rewarded Ads

Rewarded video ads provide users with a value exchange, offering a free in-app reward in exchange for watching a video ad.

These ads are ideal for achieving high engagement levels, as well as high completion rates. Additionally, rewarded video ads tend to result in high viewer satisfaction, as users receive prizes or rewards after watching the video, enhancing their overall app experience.

Expandable Ads

Expandable ads are a type of rich media ad that starts as a standard 320 × 50 banner and expands in size, typically to 320 x 480, after a user taps on it.

These ads offer more information opportunities through the expansion unit, allowing for the inclusion of videos and interactive elements. They are particularly useful for obtaining valuable traction, as the action-driven expansion allows advertisers to measure the number of times users view the ad content.

Native Ads

Native ads are versatile in size and are often integrated into the content of an app. They are specifically designed to match the app's interface, providing a non-intrusive experience that seamlessly blends with the app's content. Native ads are most effective in environments where users highly value their experience and the advertised product contributes positively to that experience.

7.2 Adapting Across Devices & Screen Sizes

Designing for mobile devices requires careful consideration of various factors, including screen sizes, aspect ratios, resolutions, and user configurations. Accessibility needs further complicate matters, as users may adjust font sizes, colors, and contrast levels.

Product Managers should ensure that their ads are responsive and adaptable across a range of devices and configurations. This approach not only improves the user experience but also maximizes the effectiveness of the advertising campaign. They must keep the following aspects in mind when designing in-app advertising or advertising for their products.

- **Responsive Design**: In-app ads must adapt to various screen sizes and resolutions, ensuring that they look good on both a 5-inch smartphone and a 12-inch tablet. Responsive design techniques allow ads to adjust dynamically based on the screen's dimensions.

- **Device Detection**: Implementing device detection allows advertisers to serve the most appropriate ad format tailored to the specific device's capabilities.

- **Aspect Ratios**: Different devices have different aspect ratios. Designing for the most common ratios and then using scaling techniques ensures ads render appropriately across devices.

- **Consider Platform Differences**: iOS and Android have unique design philosophies. While the ad's core message remains consistent, tweaking design elements to align with platform guidelines can enhance user experience.

- **Test Extensively**: Emulators can simulate how ads appear across various devices. However, real-world testing on multiple devices is indispensable to iron out inconsistencies.

7.3 Challenges & Considerations

- **User Experience**: The balance between monetization through ads and ensuring a positive user experience is delicate. Overloading with ads or using overly intrusive formats can lead to app uninstalls.

- **Load Times**: Heavy ads can slow down app performance. It's essential to optimize ad files to ensure they don't affect app load times.

- **Data Consumption**: Video ads or high-resolution images can consume significant user data. Being mindful of this, especially in regions with expensive data, is crucial.

In-app advertising opens a plethora of opportunities for brands and Product Managers. By understanding the formats and intricacies of designing for various devices, Product Managers can craft strategies that resonate with users, driving engagement without compromising on experience.

8. Ad Serving

The mechanics of ad serving remains a vital cog in the wheel. For Product Managers navigating the digital advertising domain, understanding the intricacies of how ads are served can offer invaluable insights for decision-making and strategy development.

8.1 Introduction to Ad Serving

At its core, ad serving describes the technology and service that places advertisements on websites, apps, and other digital platforms. Ad servers are responsible for making instantaneous decisions about what ads to show to which users and then deliver them accordingly.

8.2 How Ad Placement Works

- **Ad Request**: When a user visits a webpage or opens an app with ad spaces, an ad request is sent to the ad server.

- **User Data Collection**: The ad request contains crucial information, such as the user's location, device type, browsing behavior, and more.

- **Decision Making**: The ad server then decides which ad to display. This decision is based on various factors like the advertiser's targeting preferences, the user's profile, and bidding amounts (in real-time bidding scenarios).

- **Ad Retrieval**: Once the decision is made, the ad server fetches the appropriate ad from its database.

- **Ad Display**: The chosen ad is then displayed to the user in the designated ad space.

- **Tracking & Analytics**: Ad servers also track the user's interaction with the ad—whether they viewed it, clicked on it, etc. This data is crucial for advertisers to measure campaign performance.

8.3 Capabilities of an Ad Server

- **Targeting**: One of the primary strengths of an ad server is its ability to target ads based on multiple criteria: geolocation, device type, user behavior, demographics, and more.

- **Frequency Capping**: This capability limits the number of times a specific user sees the same ad, ensuring overexposure doesn't lead to ad fatigue.

- **Sequencing (or Storyboarding)**: Ad servers can sequence ads in a particular order, allowing brands to tell a story or guide users down a funnel.

- **Retargeting**: Based on user behavior, ad servers can 'retarget' users with ads for products or services they've shown interest in but haven't yet purchased or engaged with.

- **Real-time Reporting**: Ad servers provide real-time data on how ads are performing, offering insights into views, clicks, conversions, and more.

- **A/B Testing**: This allows advertisers to test different versions of ads to determine which one resonates more with the audience.

- **Integration with DSPs and SSPs**: Ad servers can integrate with Demand Side Platforms (DSPs) and Supply Side Platforms (SSPs) for real-time bidding, expanding reach and optimizing ad spend.

- **Inventory Forecasting**: Advanced ad servers can predict available inventory, helping advertisers plan their campaigns more effectively.

Ad serving isn't just about displaying ads—it's about enhancing user experiences, maximizing ROI (return on investment) for advertisers, and ensuring the digital ecosystem thrives. For Product Managers, diving deep into the world of ad serving offers a treasure trove of insights, strategies, and opportunities that can propel digital products to new heights.

9. Ad Publishing

For Product Managers keen on optimizing ad revenue or integrating advertising within their digital products, understanding the mechanics of ad publishing is paramount.

9.1 Ad Integration

When a website wants to display ads, it begins by integrating specific "ad codes" or "tags" onto its pages. These tags serve as placeholders where ads will be loaded.

- **Direct Ad Code**: Sometimes, websites might have a direct partnership with an advertiser and will directly place the specific ad's code onto their page. This means the same ad will always be displayed in that spot.

- **Ad Server Tag**: More often, websites use tags from ad servers. These tags don't contain the content of a specific ad. Instead, they call upon an ad server each time the page is loaded, and the server decides which ad to show based on various factors like user behavior, ad targeting settings, and advertiser bids.

- **Ad Network Code**: Alternatively, websites might incorporate a code from an ad network. Ad networks aggregate ad inventory from various publishers and offer a range of ads. When their code is used, any of the ads from the network's collection could be displayed, based on relevance, bidding, and other factors.

9.2 Pricing Models

The monetization of ad spaces varies based on several models, each with its advantages and considerations.

- **Fixed Spot**: A straightforward model where advertisers pay a fixed amount to occupy a particular ad spot for a specified duration. Rates are often determined by the website's traffic and the prominence of the ad spot.

- **Cost Per Mille (CPM)**: Also known as Cost Per Thousand Impressions, in this model, advertisers pay for every 1000 times their ad is displayed. It's important to note that this is about displays, not clicks or conversions.

- **Cost Per Click (CPC)**: Here, advertisers pay only when a user clicks on their ad. It's favored by many advertisers as they're essentially paying for potential leads.

- **Cost Per Action (CPA)**: This is a results-oriented model where advertisers pay only when users take a specific action after clicking an ad, like making a purchase or signing up for a newsletter.

- **Revenue Share**: In some partnerships, especially with ad networks, publishers might agree to a revenue-sharing model where they receive a percentage of the revenue generated from ads displayed on their site.

Ad publishing is a blend of technology, strategy, and economics. For Product Managers, understanding its nuances is essential, whether the goal is monetizing a digital platform or integrating ads for user engagement.

10. Ad Networks

Ad Networks stand out as one of the pivotal players, streamlining the complex dance between advertisers and publishers. For Product Managers in the realm of digital platforms and services, a robust understanding of how ad networks function can significantly influence strategy and revenue.

10.1 What are Ad Networks

At its core, an ad network is a platform that acts as an intermediary, connecting advertisers looking to place their ads with publishers willing to offer their website or app space for these ads. They aggregate ad inventory from publishers and match it with advertiser demand, ensuring that both parties benefit.

10.2 The Mechanism of Ad Networks

- **Aggregating Inventory**: Ad networks consolidate available ad spaces (inventory) from numerous publishers. This aggregation allows advertisers to reach a broader audience without individually negotiating with each publisher.

- **Matching Ads with Spaces**: Ad networks utilize sophisticated algorithms to ensure that ads are placed on relevant sites, optimizing the chances of user engagement. This matching is often based on content relevancy, user behavior, and demographic information.

- **Dynamic Pricing**: Advanced ad networks might operate on real-time bidding (RTB) models, where advertisers compete in real-time auctions for ad spaces. The highest bidder gets their ad displayed.

10.3 Why Ad Networks are Essential

- **Simplified Process**: Ad networks simplify the process for both advertisers and publishers. Advertisers get access to a wide range of websites without individual negotiations, while publishers can monetize their platforms without seeking out advertisers directly.

- **Optimization and Targeting**: Leveraging user data, ad networks ensure ads are targeted to the most suitable audience, thereby increasing the potential for engagement and conversion.

- **Cost-Effective**: For advertisers, especially smaller ones without vast resources, ad networks can offer a budget-friendly route to reaching wider audiences.

- **Diverse Ad Formats**: Many ad networks support various ad formats like display banners, video ads, native ads, and interstitials, giving advertisers multiple avenues to convey their message.

10.4 Considerations for Product Managers

When offering space on their products to ad networks, Product Managers need to carefully select the right ad format, as discussed earlier. Furthermore, understanding the nuances of ad networks is crucial for choosing the right monetization strategies without compromising the enhancement of user experience. Staying informed about ad network trends and technologies is essential for any forward-thinking Product Manager.

However, besides that, there are a few more things to consider.

- **Revenue Share**: Ad networks typically operate on a revenue-sharing model. Publishers receive a percentage of the revenue generated from ads, while the network retains the rest.

- **Ad Quality Control**: One of the concerns with ad networks can be the quality and relevance of ads. Ensuring a network maintains high standards can enhance user experience and brand safety.

- **User Data and Privacy:** Product Managers should be aware of data privacy laws and ensure that any ad network they collaborate with complies with regulations like GDPR or CCPA.

- **Network Specialization**: Some ad networks specialize in certain niches or industries. Depending on the product, niche networks might offer more relevant ads and better monetization.

11. Programmatic, DSP, and DMP

Programmatic advertising streamlines the buying and selling of ad space in real time using algorithms and data. This approach enables advertisers to precisely target their audience and make informed decisions about which ads to purchase and at what price. It encompasses various ad formats like display, video, native, and social media ads, often leading to improved ad campaign performance and ROI.

In the programmatic ecosystem, Demand Side Platforms (DSPs) and Data Management Platforms (DMPs) play crucial roles. DSPs help advertisers buy ad inventory across multiple exchanges and networks through a single interface, leveraging data to target specific audiences and optimize campaigns. On the other hand, DMPs collect and analyze data to provide audience insights, enabling advertisers to create more targeted and effective campaigns.

Let us understand DSPs and DMPs a bit more.

11.1 Demand Side Platforms (DSPs)

DSPs allow advertisers and agencies to buy ad inventory from multiple ad exchanges and networks through a single interface. They use data and algorithms to help advertisers target specific audiences and optimize their ad campaigns in real time. DSPs are a key component of programmatic advertising, as they enable advertisers to automate the buying process and target audiences more effectively.

11.2 Data Management Platforms (DMPs)

DMPs collect, store, and analyze large sets of data to help advertisers better understand their audiences. DMPs can integrate with DSPs to provide audience insights and targeting capabilities, allowing advertisers to create more targeted and effective ad campaigns. DMPs play a crucial role in programmatic advertising by providing the data needed to target specific audiences and optimize ad campaigns.

12. Digital Enabling Organizations

Digital enabling organizations act as conduits between brands and their audiences.

Digital agencies, in particular, are reshaping the way businesses approach online marketing, branding, and engagement. As Product Managers strive to better position their products in this digital realm, comprehending the operation and influence of these agencies is paramount.

12.1 Digital Agencies

Digital Agencies specialize in crafting online marketing strategies that encompass elements like web design, online advertising, content creation, and more. They assist brands in navigating the digital world, ensuring that their presence is not only felt but also leaves an impact.

How Digital Agencies Operate

- **Client Needs Analysis**: It all begins with understanding a brand's objectives, its audience, and its unique market position.

- **Strategy Formulation**: Agencies devise a digital blueprint—choosing channels, setting budgets, and determining content direction.

- **Content Creation**: From ad design to video production, the agency manages all facets of content generation.

- **Media Planning and Buying**: Using their industry networks, agencies place ads in optimal spots, ensuring maximum visibility and engagement.

- **Performance Evaluation**: Post-campaign, they assess metrics to measure success and refine future strategies.

12.2 Digital Rating Companies

Digital rating companies analyze and provide insights into the performance of online campaigns, website traffic, audience behavior, and more. Their data helps brands and agencies make informed decisions.

How Digital Rating Companies Operate

- **Data Collection**: Using various tools, these companies gather vast amounts of data from websites, social platforms, and other digital touchpoints.

- **Data Analysis**: The raw data is then processed, analyzed, and converted into actionable insights.

- **Report Generation**: Brands receive comprehensive reports detailing campaign performance, audience demographics, engagement metrics, etc.

As the boundaries between the digital and physical worlds blur, the role of digital agencies and rating companies becomes increasingly pivotal.

20

Product Analytics

Product analytics involves analyzing user behavior data to improve the user experience and achieve product goals. A Product Manager should have a deep understanding of product metrics because these metrics allow them to measure the success of a product, make informed decisions, and refine the product strategy.

Below are some key product metrics that a Product Manager should know about.

1. Engagement Metrics

Indicate the depth of user interaction with the product. These metrics provide insights into the depth of user interaction with a product. By understanding how deeply users engage, companies can determine which features are the most valuable or where there may be opportunities to enhance the user experience.

1. **Retention rate**: Percentage of users who continue using the product after a certain period. Example: If 70 out of 100 trial users continue after a month, the retention rate is 70%.

2. **Churn rate**: Percentage of users who stop using the product. Example: If 10 out of 100 monthly subscribers leave, the churn rate is 10%.

3. **Cohort Analysis**: Examines behaviors and metrics of user groups by their acquisition dates. Example: Comparing users who joined in January vs. those who joined in February.

4. **DAU & MAU**: Daily and monthly users. Example: 5,000 users daily, but 80,000 different users in a month.

5. **Session Length**: The time a user is active in one session. Example: On average, users spend 10 minutes per session.

6. **Session Frequency**: User revisit rate. Example: Typical users access the product three times a day.

7. **Time to First Key Action**: Time before a new user finds value. Example: New users make their first post within 2 hours.

8. **Feature adoption**: Usage rate of a specific feature. Example: 40% of users utilize the new editing tool.

2. Satisfaction Metrics

Measure users' contentment with the product. These metrics help in gauging how satisfied users are with the product. Happy users lead to better retention, positive word-of-mouth, and influence over other potential users. It's a way to measure if a product is meeting or exceeding user expectations.

1. **NPS**: Likelihood to recommend the product. Example: A score of 60 means the majority would recommend.

2. **CSAT**: Users rank their contentment. Example: On a scale of 1-5, average satisfaction is 4.

3. **CES**: Ease of product use. Example: Users rate ease as 7 out of 10.

4. **User Ratings**: Ratings given by users. Example: The app has a 4.5-star rating on the App Store.

3. Operational Metrics

The product's efficiency and performance. These figures provide a snapshot of the product's internal performance and efficiency. By monitoring operational metrics, businesses can pinpoint inefficiencies and streamline processes, ensuring that the product runs smoothly and effectively.

1. **Load time**: Feature or product loading speed. Example: The homepage takes 2 seconds to load.

2. **Uptime**: Operational availability duration. Example: The software had 99.9% uptime last month.

3. **Bug rate**: Reported issue frequency. Example: 50 bugs reported this week.

4. **Error Rates**: User-encountered errors. Example: 2% of sessions encounter an error.

4. Growth Metrics

User and market expansion rate. These indicators reflect the product's user growth and expansion in the market. Monitoring growth helps businesses strategize future developments, understand their market positioning, and potentially capitalize on emerging trends.

1. **User growth rate**: User increase percentage over time. Example: 10% more users this month than last month.

2. **Viral coefficient**: New users brought in by a current user. Example: Each user invites 1.5 friends on average.

3. **Referral Rate**: Users who refer others. Example: 20% of users have referred someone.

4. **Referral Acceptance Rate**: Referrals that result in sign-ups. Example: Of all referrals, 50% sign up.

5. Support Metrics

These highlight user concerns and needs. These are essential to comprehend the user's pain points and needs. By analyzing support metrics, businesses can identify common issues users face and can prioritize solutions, leading to an improved user experience.

1. **Ticket volume**: Amount of support tickets raised. Example: 500 support tickets were raised this month.

2. **Resolution time**: Time to address a user's problem. Example: Issues are resolved in 24 hours on average.

3. **Feedback themes**: Recurring feedback topics. Example: "More customization options" appears often in feedback.

6. Quality Metrics

Product's reliability and stability. These indicate the technical stability of a product. In a competitive market, a glitchy or unstable product can lead to decreased user trust and satisfaction. Monitoring and acting on quality metrics ensures that the product maintains a high standard of reliability.

1. **Crash rate**: Product failure frequency. Example: The app crashes in 1% of sessions.

2. **Error rates**: User errors. Example: 3% of actions result in an error.

3. **Technical debt**: Pending improvements and quick fixes. Example: 10 features need rework for optimization.

7. Conversion Metrics

Measures user actions and conversions. Conversion metrics shed light on how effectively the product or feature is driving users towards a desired action, whether it's signing up, making a purchase, or any other user goal. High conversion rates often signify that a product aligns well with user needs and desires.

1. **Conversion rate**: Desired action completion rate. Example: 5% of visitors make a purchase.

2. **Funnel drop-offs**: Abandonment points before conversion. Example: 60% drop off at the payment page.

8. Acquisition Metrics

These metrics focus on how new users discover and start using a product. Focused on how new users discover and start using a product, these metrics provide insights into the effectiveness of marketing strategies and highlight channels bringing in the most users.

1. **CAC**: Cost to acquire a user. Example: Spending $50 on ads to acquire each user.

2. **Sources of User Acquisition**: User source channels. Example: 40% come from social media, 30% from search engines.

9. Monetization Metrics

Financial success indicators. Financial viability is at the core of a product's long-term sustainability. Monetization metrics are paramount for assessing the product's financial success, helping businesses understand if they are achieving a good return on their investments.

1. **ARPU**: Average earnings per user. Example: Each user generates $15 on average.

2. **LTV**: Predicted full-term user profit. Example: A user is expected to bring $500 over their lifetime.

3. **LTV:CAC Ratio**: User value versus acquisition cost. Example: If LTV is $500 and CAC is $50, the ratio is 10:1.

4. **MRR**: Monthly subscription revenue. Example: $20,000 recurring revenue every month.

5. **ARR**: Annual recurring revenue. Example: $240,000 expected yearly from subscriptions.

6. **Churned MRR**: Lost subscription revenue. Example: $2,000 less revenue next month due to churn.

7. **Expansion MRR**: Additional revenue from upsells or cross-sells. Example: Existing users contribute an extra $1,000 through upgrades.

21

Product-Market Fit

Product-market fit refers to the point where a product meets the needs of a specific market segment and begins to see rapid adoption. It's a critical stage for startups and enterprises alike. Achieving a Product-market fit indicates that a product is on the right track and resonates with its intended users.

While the initial hypothesis allows a product to go from 0 to Few, it is the continuous effort to find the Product-market fit that allows the product to go from Few to Many.

1. Fail-Fast Approach

The fail-fast approach, embodied by the mantra "The earlier you fail, the earlier you recover," enables Product Managers to swiftly identify and address potential risks. This methodology is not about courting failure but rather about rapid iteration and risk mitigation.

1.1 About fail-fast

Fail-fast promotes a proactive approach to product development. It urges Product Managers to be keenly aware of potential pitfalls in their product's life cycle, allowing for early identification of risks that might hinder the product from achieving its objectives.

Rather than shying away from these risks, Product Managers are encouraged to formulate strategies to either absorb them or pivot to mitigate their impact. However, the essence of fail-fast lies in its pragmatism. It acknowledges that not all strategies will succeed. In such cases, it's often wiser to view investments as sunk costs or recalibrate the product's core propositions, rather than sinking further into an ineffective trajectory.

It's a methodology that doesn't just champion early failure detection, but also swift recovery, ensuring that products remain viable, competitive, and in tune with market demands. fail-fast propels Product Managers to create adaptable products, making them resilient in the face of unforeseen challenges.

1.2 What fail-fast is Not

Navigating the complexities of product management, one might misconstrue the essence of the fail-fast methodology. It's crucial to delineate what fail-fast isn't to harness its full potential.

1. **It's not a justification for lackluster effort**: fail-fast doesn't suggest giving up prematurely or taking shortcuts. Contrary to the notion that "It's not a cop-out from striving harder," it champions thorough exploration before making informed pivots.

2. **It doesn't advocate for shortsightedness**: Focusing solely on immediate results undermines the broader vision. fail-fast is not about settling for short-term gains; it's about ensuring long-term objectives align with current actions.

3. **It's not a recipe for chaotic decision-making**: While it encourages swift actions, it's far from advocating hasty, uninformed decisions. It's a systematic approach, where every choice is rooted in data and a clear understanding of the implications.

4. **It's not about actively seeking failure**: The aim isn't to fail but to iterate. It's a subtle yet crucial distinction. It pushes teams to refine based on feedback rather than being complacent with initial versions.

5. **It doesn't suggest abandoning endeavors**: While it's true that sometimes products or features need to be dropped, the primary goal isn't to eliminate but to pivot, adjusting the trajectory based on insights.

6. **It's not a deterrent to critical thinking**: fail-fast isn't an invitation to abandon deep analysis. Instead of solely critiquing, it prompts teams to think creatively, looking for innovative solutions to identified problems.

7. **It's not a hallmark of impatience**: Patience remains a virtue in product management. fail-fast is about being decisive but also

recognizing the value of waiting when necessary. It's a delicate balance between action and reflection.

By understanding these nuances, Product Managers can harness the power of fail-fast without falling into potential pitfalls. It's about cultivating resilience, adaptability, and foresight in product development.

1.3 How the Software Industry Has Embraced Fail-fast

The software industry, with its dynamic nature and rapid pace of innovation, has been at the forefront of adopting progressive strategies. Among these, the fail-fast methodology stands out, providing a roadmap for swift iteration and adaptability. Here's how this industry has integrated the fail-fast philosophy into its core.

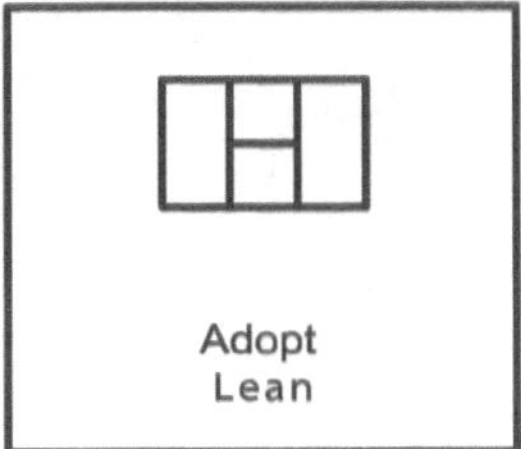

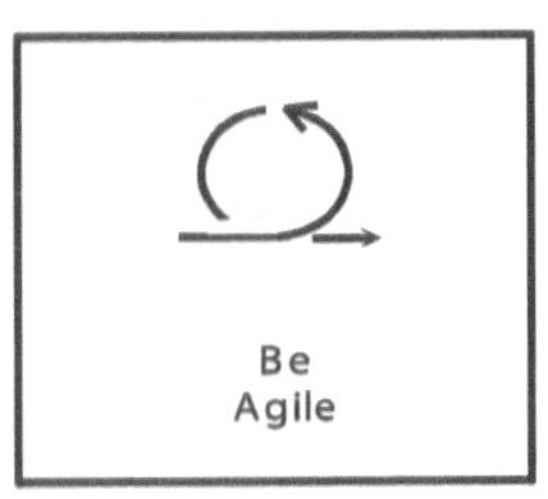

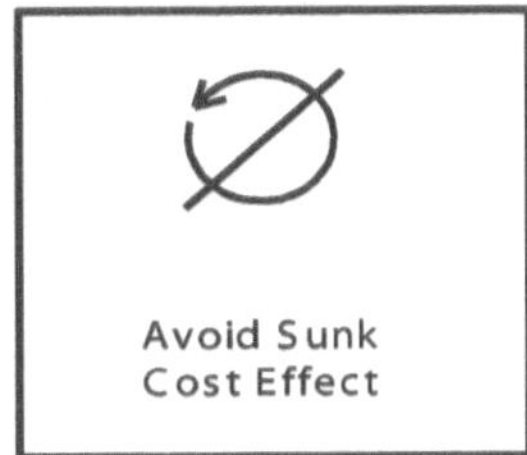

Fig 57: Embracing Fail-fast

Adopting Lean Development

- Lean development isn't just a buzzword; it's a transformational approach to software creation. It propels teams to build products incrementally, continuously refining their strategy based on feedback and market demands.

- By championing experimentation and testing, the lean methodology pushes software teams to investigate and adjust their strategies constantly. It places customer feedback at the center, ensuring that product enhancements are always in line with user expectations and needs.

Embracing Agile Methodologies

- Agile is more than just a development methodology; it's a mindset. Agile methodologies enable software teams to navigate the ever-evolving technological landscape while staying committed to delivering value efficiently.

- The core tenets of Agile, such as prioritizing individuals over processes and valuing customer collaboration, align seamlessly with the fail-fast approach. By promoting transparency, collaboration, and a keen focus on handling uncertainties early, Agile ensures that teams are agile (pun intended) in their response to challenges.

Avoiding the Sunk Cost Fallacy

- Human tendencies often lead us to throw more resources at failing projects, hoping to turn them around. This behavioral bias, known as the sunk cost effect, can be detrimental, especially in the software industry where rapid shifts are commonplace.

- By acknowledging and actively avoiding the sunk cost fallacy, software teams become better equipped to make rational decisions. Instead of persistently investing in untenable projects, they recognize when it's time to pivot or even halt certain initiatives, ensuring resources are allocated optimally.

In embracing the fail-fast methodology, the software industry showcases its commitment to adaptability, innovation, and user-centricity. For Product Managers, understanding how this philosophy is ingrained in the industry's fabric can provide valuable insights into managing products effectively.

1.4 Operationalizing Fail-fast

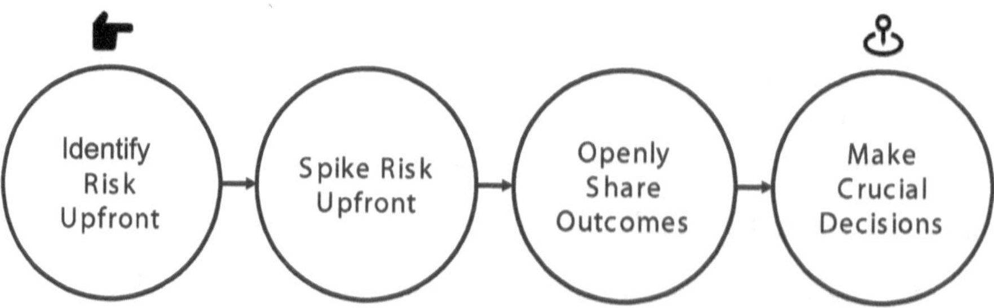

Fig 58: Operationalizing Fail-fast

For a concept as profound as fail-fast to truly make an impact, it must move from being a mere philosophy to a tangible, operational strategy. Here's a deeper dive into how Product Managers can integrate the fail-fast approach into their product development processes.

Identify Risks Upfront

- Recognizing potential pitfalls is the first step towards effective risk management. Product Managers must thoroughly assess all aspects of their products, pinpointing areas like architecture, integration, customer adoption, and scalability that might pose challenges.

- By setting clear metrics for each identified risk area, teams can gauge success objectively, ensuring they're always on the right track.

Spike Risks Immediately

- Taking a proactive stance, Product Managers should immediately devise a spike (a timeboxed task that is created in order to research a question or resolve an unknown) to validate the assumptions tied to each risk. These controlled tests can provide invaluable insights without committing vast resources.

- Armed with clear success and failure metrics for each experiment, teams can rapidly ascertain whether they're headed in the right direction or if adjustments are necessary.

Openly Share Outcomes

- Knowledge-sharing is vital in the fail-fast approach. By broadcasting the specifics of each spike, its outcomes, and the associated pros and cons, teams foster a culture of transparency and collective learning.

- Discussing open items and pending decisions ensures everyone is aligned, facilitating informed decision-making and reinforcing collective ownership.

Make Crucial Decisions

- Equipped with insights from the spikes and team discussions, Product Managers arrive at crucial decision junctures. The choices might involve continuing with the current plan, pivoting based on newfound knowledge, or in some cases, accepting certain investments as sunk costs.

- It's at these junctures that the essence of fail-fast truly comes to life. By making decisive calls rooted in data and collective wisdom, Product Managers ensure products remain relevant, viable, and primed for success.

Operationalizing the fail-fast methodology requires not only a shift in mindset but also a commitment to structured processes and open communication. By weaving these principles into their daily operations, Product Managers can navigate the turbulent waters of product development with agility and confidence.

1.5 Example Scenario

Scenario 60: An enterprise team is about to kickstart a large program to build a Platform. Based on the Ecosystem Mapping, Business Model, and Reference Product Architectures, the Product Manager identified key Risk areas.

Key Risk Area	Key Question to Ask	Next Step
This involves relying on a new 3rd party product	Does the team have confidence that integration / adoption, performance, infosec and expected benefit are fully estimable and obvious	
This involves relying on a new technology / technology paradigm / tool		
This involves a key revenue-generating / value capturing event		If no, then trigger a fail-fast approach
This involves a feature key for user adoption	There is enough evidence of users adopting and paying for the product as designed & planned	
This establishes the basis of UX architecture for the product	There is enough evidence of the scalability, performance, and reliability of the product based on this architecture	

Table 34: Risk Mitigation Plan

Based on the answers the Product Manager designs spikes to address risks early and start on a journey to fail-fast.

1.6 Best Practices for Implementing Fail-fast

When it comes to fully harnessing the potential of the fail-fast methodology, there's more to it than simply understanding its principles. Effective implementation is intertwined with embracing best practices that can bolster its efficacy. Here's how Product Managers can fine-tune their approach:

Centralize Communication

A unified source of truth is invaluable. Maintaining a central document or platform, often termed the 'golden source of info,' ensures stakeholders have consistent, up-to-date knowledge. It minimizes misinformation and keeps everyone aligned on the product's current status and direction.

Promote the Fail-fast Mindset

Constantly referencing the fail-fast approach serves a dual purpose. Firstly, it underscores the commitment to risk mitigation and proactive problem-solving. Secondly, it prevents teams from misconstruing setbacks as outright failures, fostering a constructive attitude towards iteration and learning.

Prepare for Pivots

Change is not just inevitable; it's often desirable. Product Managers should instill an organizational readiness for pivots. Such flexibility ensures teams can rapidly adjust to new insights or market shifts without being paralyzed by previous decisions.

Prioritize Team Alignment

For fail-fast to be genuinely effective, it requires more than just the Product Manager's buy-in. Regular retrospectives, team-building exercises, and open discussions about risks and outcomes ensure everyone is in sync, fostering a collaborative environment where ideas thrive.

Decisiveness is Key

Indecision can be as detrimental as a wrong decision. Even in uncertain scenarios, a relentless pursuit of decision-making is crucial. The mantra here is, "Disagree, but commit." It's better to make a call and iterate based on feedback than to remain stagnant. If a misstep occurs, it's essential to learn, adapt, and sometimes, ask for forgiveness.

By integrating these best practices into the workflow, Product Managers not only elevate the fail-fast approach but also fortify their product's chances of success. It becomes less about risk aversion and more about creating an adaptable, resilient product journey.

2. Fail-Fast Canvas

In Product Management the "fail fast" approach is essential for finding product-market fit. A streamlined template for embracing this methodology encompasses the early identification of potential risks; pinpointing the product stage most susceptible to these threats; immediate actions that the spike team can undertake to forecast and strategize against future risks; and ultimately, after thorough evaluation, the decision to either sidestep the identified pathway or to advance with well-planned risk mitigation. Let us look at a "Fail Fast" canvas that a Product Manager can use to navigate challenges with agility and foresight.

The canvas is a strategic tool designed to aid Product Managers in pinpointing pivotal capabilities during distinct phases of product development. It also underscores the potential risks they might face when transitioning from one phase to the next. This meticulously structured canvas is segmented into various sections, each representing a critical stage in the product lifecycle and the associated considerations.

2.1 Using the Canvas

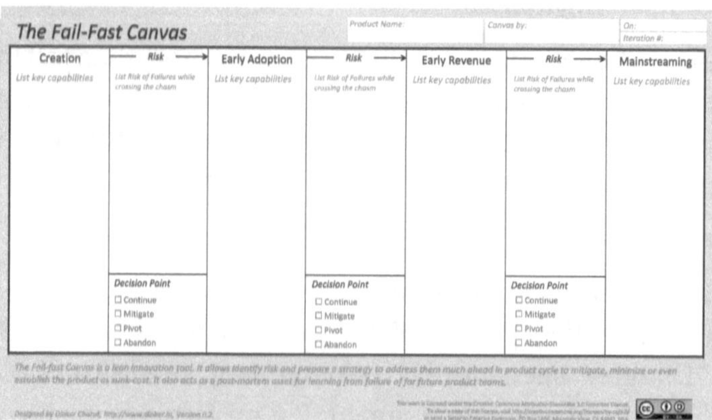

Fig 59: The Fail-Fast Canvas

The canvas helps the Product Manager identify critical capabilities during key phases of product development, and what risks they may encounter when going from one stage to another.

2.2 Detailed Overview

Let us look at the various sections of this canvas:

Creation Phase

Here, Product Managers outline the essential capabilities they intend to focus on during this foundational phase.

1. Risk Assessment: This subsection focuses on potential pitfalls and challenges when bridging the gap between the Creation phase and the Early Adoption phase.

2. Decision Point: After a thorough risk analysis, the team evaluates each capability. They determine whether to persist with the original plan, adjust features to counter the risks, pivot to a different capability, or discard it entirely as they transition to the Early Adoption phase.

Early Adoption Phase

At this juncture, Product Managers enumerate the vital capabilities they aim to integrate during the early market introduction of the product.

1. Risk Assessment: Here, the emphasis is on potential obstacles when transitioning from the Early Adoption phase to the Early Revenue phase.

2. Decision Point: Post risk evaluation, the team decides on the fate of each capability—whether to maintain, alter, pivot, or eliminate—keeping in mind the eventual transition to the Early Revenue phase.

Early Revenue Phase

During this phase, Product Managers lay out the key capabilities meant for inclusion to ensure the product starts generating revenue.

1. Risk Assessment: This section delves into potential hurdles when moving from the Early Revenue phase to the Mainstreaming phase.

2. Decision Point: Once risks are analyzed, the team decides on each capability's trajectory—whether to stick with it, modify, shift focus, or drop it—aiming for a smooth transition into the Mainstreaming phase.

Mainstreaming Phase

In this final stage, Product Managers detail the primary capabilities planned to ensure the product's firm establishment and widespread adoption in the mainstream market.

3. Risk Planning Canvas

The Risk Planning Canvas is a lean innovation tool designed to proactively identify risks. By facilitating early strategizing within the product cycle, the canvas ensures that these risks are addressed and mitigated effectively.

It is a follow-up activity for the Fail-Fast Canvas, providing a comprehensive framework to not only identify and understand risks but also to develop actionable strategies to address them.

3.1 Using the Canvas

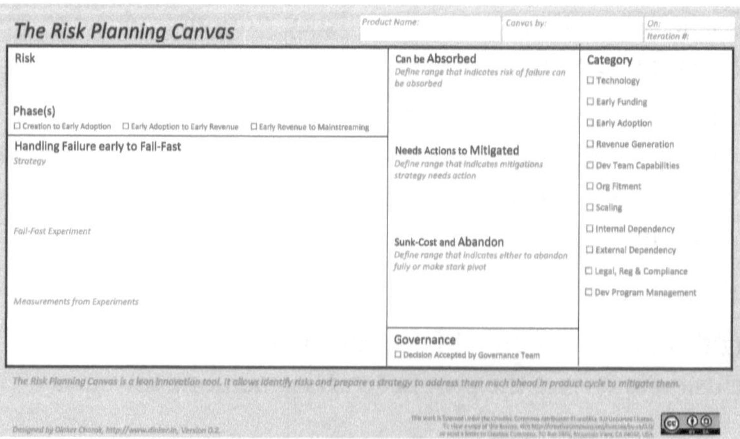

Fig 60: The Risk Planning Canvas

3.2 Detailed Overview

Let us look at the various sections of this canvas.

Risk

Clearly articulate the potential risk or challenge.

Phase(s)

Specify the phase(s) where the risk could manifest.

☐ Creation to Early Adoption

☐ Early Adoption to Early Revenue

☐ Early Revenue to Mainstreaming

Handling Failure Early to Fail-Fast

Describe how the team intends to approach the identified risk.

1. Strategy: Specify the overarching plan or approach to manage or preempt the risk.

2. Spike or Experiment: Detail the experimental steps or pilot tests that will be used to validate or confront the risk.

3. Measurement of Outcomes: Define both the success metric (indicating a favorable outcome of the experiment) and the failure threshold (highlighting the point at which corrective action should be taken).

Can be Absorbed

1. Determine the level of risk that, if encountered, the team can bear or assimilate without drastic adjustments.

Needs Actions to Mitigate

1. Define the level of risk which, if reached, would necessitate immediate interventions or changes in strategy.

Sunk-Cost and Abandon

1. Determine the point at which the risk becomes so significant that the team should consider either fully abandoning the current direction or making a major pivot.

Governance

1. Indicate whether the decision (to absorb, mitigate, or abandon) has received approval or endorsement from the Governance Team.

Category

Categorize the nature of the risk for a more nuanced understanding and strategy development. The Product Manager marks the relevant checkbox:

☐ Technology

☐ Early Funding

☐ Early Adoption

☐ Revenue Generation

☐ Dev Team Capabilities

☐ Org Fitment

☐ Scaling

☐ Internal Dependency

☐ External Dependency

☐ Legal, Regulation and Compliance

☐ Dev Program Management

By leveraging the Risk Planning Canvas, teams can foster a proactive approach to risk management, optimizing their product development journey while being agile in their decision-making processes.

3.3 Example Scenario

> **Scenario 61**: The Product Manager of a Data Platform being built for a global bank wants to fail fast to ensure there are no obvious failures in future due to some oversight.
>
> The Product Manager chooses to use the Fail Fast Canvas to identify the risk and the Risk Planning Canvas to plan for key risks.

The Product Manager first lists out key capabilities:

The Fail-Fast Canvas

Product Name: **Data Platform for a Global Bank** — Canvas by: — On: — Iteration #:

Creation	Risk	Early Adoption	Risk	Early Revenue	Risk	Mainstreaming
List key capabilities	*List Risk of Failures while crossing the chasm*	*List key capabilities*	*List Risk of Failures while crossing the chasm*	*List key capabilities*	*List Risk of Failures while crossing the chasm*	*List key capabilities*
Data Platform that will intake data from legacy system, ensure Data Quality and Governance and make it available to Client onboarding business process for US customers		Support more business processes for 1/ Funds transfer within the bank and 2/ view of client's portfolio and 3/ expand to Latin America		Expand Data Platform to APAC and EMEA and support revenue generating processes that will be identified at later time		Replace the legacy system and move all business processes to new Data Platform

Decision Point (Creation): ☐ Continue ☐ Mitigate ☐ Pivot ☐ Abandon

Decision Point (Early Adoption): ☐ Continue ☐ Mitigate ☐ Pivot ☐ Abandon

Decision Point (Early Revenue): ☐ Continue ☐ Mitigate ☐ Pivot ☐ Abandon

The Fail-fast Canvas is a lean innovation tool. It allows identify risk and prepare a strategy to address them much ahead in product cycle to mitigate, minimize or even establish the product as sunk-cost. It also acts as a post-mortem asset for learning from failure of/for future product teams.

Designed by Dinker Charak, http://www.dinker.in, Version 0.2

Fig 61: The Fail-Fast Canvas

The Product Manager then identifies and lists the risk. While the Product Manager was able to identify the risk for Creation to Early Adoption and for Early Adoption to Early Revenue, the Product Manager was not able to identify risks for the Early Revenue to Mainstreaming phase.

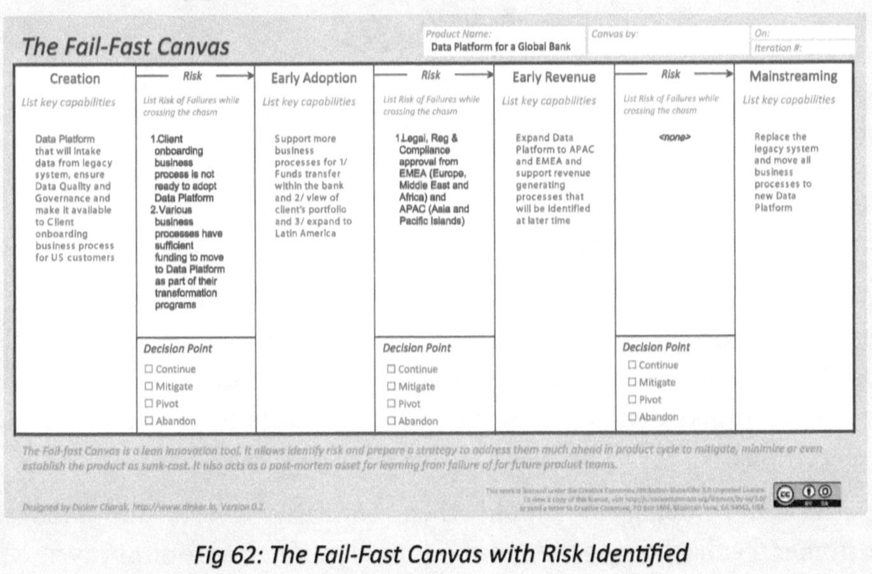

The Fail-Fast Canvas

Product Name: **Data Platform for a Global Bank** — Canvas by: — On: — Iteration #:

Creation	Risk	Early Adoption	Risk	Early Revenue	Risk	Mainstreaming
List key capabilities	*List Risk of Failures while crossing the chasm*	*List key capabilities*	*List Risk of Failures while crossing the chasm*	*List key capabilities*	*List Risk of Failures while crossing the chasm*	*List key capabilities*
Data Platform that will intake data from legacy system, ensure Data Quality and Governance and make it available to Client onboarding business process for US customers	1. Client onboarding business process is not ready to adopt Data Platform 2. Various business processes have sufficient funding to move to Data Platform as part of their transformation programs	Support more business processes for 1/ Funds transfer within the bank and 2/ view of client's portfolio and 3/ expand to Latin America	1. Legal, Reg & Compliance approval from EMEA (Europe, Middle East and Africa) and APAC (Asia and Pacific Islands)	Expand Data Platform to APAC and EMEA and support revenue generating processes that will be identified at later time	<none>	Replace the legacy system and move all business processes to new Data Platform

Decision Point (Creation): ☐ Continue ☐ Mitigate ☐ Pivot ☐ Abandon

Decision Point (Early Adoption): ☐ Continue ☐ Mitigate ☐ Pivot ☐ Abandon

Decision Point (Early Revenue): ☐ Continue ☐ Mitigate ☐ Pivot ☐ Abandon

The Fail-fast Canvas is a lean innovation tool. It allows identify risk and prepare a strategy to address them much ahead in product cycle to mitigate, minimize or even establish the product as sunk-cost. It also acts as a post-mortem asset for learning from failure of/for future product teams.

Designed by Dinker Charak, http://www.dinker.in, Version 0.2

Fig 62: The Fail-Fast Canvas with Risk Identified

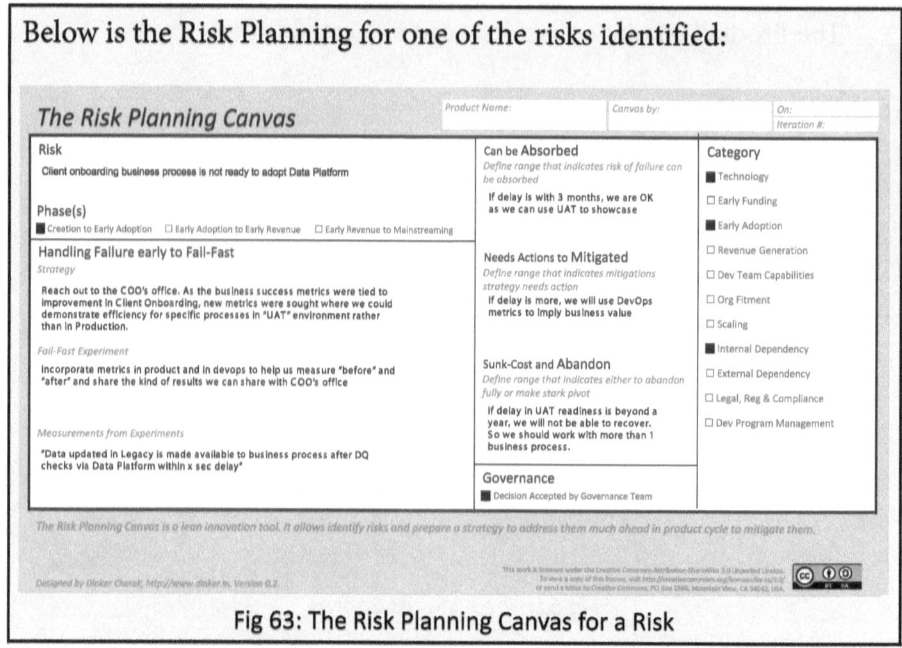

Below is the Risk Planning for one of the risks identified:

The Risk Planning Canvas

Product Name: Canvas by: On: Iteration #:

Risk

Client onboarding business process is not ready to adopt Data Platform

Phase(s)

☑ Creation to Early Adoption   ☐ Early Adoption to Early Revenue   ☐ Early Revenue to Mainstreaming

Handling Failure early to Fail-Fast

Strategy

Reach out to the COO's office. As the business success metrics were tied to improvement in Client Onboarding, new metrics were sought where we could demonstrate efficiency for specific processes in "UAT" environment rather than in Production.

Fail-Fast Experiment

Incorporate metrics in product and in devops to help us measure "before" and "after" and share the kind of results we can share with COO's office

Measurements from Experiments

"Data updated in Legacy is made available to business process after DQ checks via Data Platform within x sec delay"

Can be Absorbed

Define range that indicates risk of failure can be absorbed

If delay is with 3 months, we are OK as we can use UAT to showcase

Needs Actions to Mitigated

Define range that indicates mitigations strategy needs action

If delay is more, we will use DevOps metrics to imply business value

Sunk-Cost and Abandon

Define range that indicates either to abandon fully or make stark pivot

If delay in UAT readiness is beyond a year, we will not be able to recover. So we should work with more than 1 business process.

Governance

☑ Decision Accepted by Governance Team

Category

☑ Technology

☐ Early Funding

☑ Early Adoption

☐ Revenue Generation

☐ Dev Team Capabilities

☐ Org Fitment

☐ Scaling

☑ Internal Dependency

☐ External Dependency

☐ Legal, Reg & Compliance

☐ Dev Program Management

The Risk Planning Canvas is a lean innovation tool. It allows identify risks and prepare a strategy to address them much ahead in product cycle to mitigate them.

Designed by Dinker Charak, http://www.dinker.in, Version 0.2.

Fig 63: The Risk Planning Canvas for a Risk

Download Fail-Fast & Risk Planning Canvas

https://bit.ly/plcu-failfast

4. Market Feedback Metrics

Market feedback metrics can be invaluable tools for Product Managers seeking to find product-market fit. These metrics provide quantifiable insights into customer satisfaction, loyalty, and effort, helping Product Managers understand how well their product meets customer needs and expectations.

Product Managers should then regularly collect and analyze customer feedback using these metrics to identify areas for improvement and validate product decisions.

5. NPS

In the search for a straightforward and effective method to measure this, Fred Reichheld, working for Bain & Company, introduced the Net Promoter Score (NPS). The simplicity of the system, combined with its ability to tap into genuine customer sentiments, saw it quickly gaining traction amongst businesses, from startups to Fortune 500 giants.

5.1 Understanding the Net Promoter Score (NPS)

At its core, NPS seeks to determine the likelihood of a customer promoting an organization's products or services to others. It does so by posing a single simple question:

"On a scale of 0 to 10, how likely are you to recommend our product/service to a friend or colleague?"

Based on the numerical response, customers are then categorized into three groups:

1. **Promoters (9-10)**: These are loyal enthusiasts who will not only keep buying but will also refer others.

2. **Passives (7-8)**: Satisfied customers, but not necessarily loyal. They could easily switch to a competitor.

3. **Detractors (0-6)**: Unhappy customers who could potentially damage the brand through negative word-of-mouth.

The NPS is then calculated by subtracting the percentage of detractors from the percentage of promoters.

5.2 Example Scenario

> **Scenario 62**: Consider a company named Timingila Solutions that offers enterprise software to other businesses. After rolling out a new software update, Timingila Solutions decided to use NPS to gauge its clients' responses.

> **Findings**: Upon surveying its clients with the NPS question, Timingila Solutions' finds the following breakdown:
>
> - 200 respondents give scores between 9-10 (Promoters)
> - 50 respondents give scores between 7-8 (Passives)
> - 25 respondents give scores between 0-6 (Detractors)
>
> Thus, the percentages are:
>
> - Promoters: 75% (200 out of 275)
> - Passives: 18% (50 out of 275)
> - Detractors: 9% (25 out of 275)
>
> NPS = 75% (Promoters) - 9% (Detractors) = 66%
>
> **Outcome**: An NPS of 66 is considered quite strong in most industries, signaling high client satisfaction. Timingila Solutions can then further leverage this data by reaching out to detractors for feedback, nurturing promoter relationships, and working on moving passives up the loyalty ladder.

5.3 Limitations of the Net Promoter Score (NPS)

While NPS has been widely embraced, it is not without its detractors. Here are some of the most commonly cited limitations and criticisms:

1. **Oversimplification**: NPS boils down complex customer feelings and experiences into a single number. This simplification can sometimes overlook nuances and fail to provide actionable feedback.

2. **Focus on Extremes**: Since only the highest scores (9-10) count as promoters, the system might be biased towards extremely positive (or negative) experiences, potentially overlooking the middle ground.

3. **Not Always Predictive**: A high NPS doesn't always translate to increased business growth or vice versa. The score alone might not capture all factors influencing a business's success.

In short, NPS is particularly useful when a business wants a quick, high-level gauge of customer loyalty and overall sentiment. It's an excellent tool for benchmarking and tracking changes in customer sentiment over time.

6. CSAT

CSAT is essentially a measure of a customer's satisfaction with a specific product, service, or transaction.

Businesses typically measure CSAT by asking customers a simple question, such as:

"How satisfied were you with your recent experience/purchase?"

The response options usually range from "Very Unsatisfied" to "Very Satisfied" or a numerical scale, such as 1 to 5, with 1 being "Very Unsatisfied" and 5 being "Very Satisfied".

The CSAT score is then calculated as the average score or the percentage of customers who answer with one of the top two positive response options.

For instance, if using a 5-point scale, an organization might consider scores of 4 and 5 as indicating satisfaction. If 80 out of 100 customers give a score of 4 or 5, the CSAT would be 80%.

6.1 Example Scenario

> **Scenario 63**: WaveRunners is a new line of athletic sneakers released by the footwear brand Timingila Sports. Known for its innovation, Timingila Sports is eager to understand initial consumer reactions to this latest offering. They decide to use the CSAT metric as a primary tool for this feedback and follow these steps:
>
> 1. Identify Touchpoints: Timingila Sports chooses to survey customers shortly after their purchase, ideally after they've had a chance to wear the sneakers a few times.

2. Formulate the Question: They draft a succinct CSAT question: "How satisfied are you with your recent WaveRunners sneaker purchase?"

3. Scale Selection: Timingila Sports goes with a 5-point scale, ranging from "Very Unsatisfied" (1) to "Very Satisfied" (5).

4. Distribution: They include a feedback card in the shoebox and also send an email prompt to those who bought the sneakers online.

5. Collection and Analysis: After a month, they gather the data.

Findings: Out of 5,000 respondents:

- 3,500 rated their experience a 4 or 5 (Satisfied)

- 1,000 rated it a 3 (Neutral)

- 500 rated it 1 or 2 (Unsatisfied)

Outcome: The CSAT score is the percentage of satisfied customers. The score comes out to be (3,500/5,000)*100 = 70%.

In this B2C scenario, employing CSAT gave Timingila Sports immediate insights into how consumers perceived their new product. The simplicity of the CSAT metric provided a quick pulse on customer satisfaction, while the supplementary comments ensured the brand received a fuller picture. This two-pronged approach allowed Timingila Sports not only to understand customer satisfaction but also to gain actionable insights for both product enhancement and marketing strategies.

6.2 Limitations of the Customer Satisfaction Score (CSAT)

While CSAT offers businesses a quick pulse on customer contentment, it's not without its constraints. Some of the more pointed critiques and limitations include:

1. **Momentary Feedback**: CSAT usually captures how customers feel immediately after an interaction, which might not accurately represent their overall sentiment about a product or service.

2. **Lack of Depth**: Similar to NPS, the CSAT's simplicity means it doesn't provide detailed insights into why customers feel a certain way.

3. **Cultural and Subjective Variations**: Satisfaction is a subjective term, and what might be "satisfactory" for one person might not be for another. Similarly, cultural variations can affect how different individuals rate their satisfaction.

4. **Not Always Indicative of Loyalty**: A customer might be satisfied with a single interaction but might not necessarily be a loyal or a repeat customer.

7. CES

In 2010, the Corporate Executive Board Company (CEB), now Gartner, introduced the Customer Effort Score, bringing attention to the idea that reduced customer effort can enhance loyalty.

CES (Customer Effort Score) measures the ease with which customers can get their issues resolved or interact with a product or service.

A typical CES question might read:

"On a scale from 'very difficult' to 'very easy', how was your experience in [specific interaction] with our organization?"

The logic is straightforward. If customers can easily interact with an organization—whether while purchasing a product, seeking support, or navigating a website—they are more likely to remain loyal and make repeat purchases.

Scores are provided on a numerical scale, often from 1 to 7, with higher scores indicating that customers found their experience effortless.

Research on Customer engagement behaviors suggests that when customers believed they exerted less effort, there was a greater likelihood of them spending more, being more loyal, and recommending the service to others.[1] This insight placed CES at the forefront of customer-centric metrics in the modern business landscape.

7.1 Example Scenario

Scenario 64: Timingila Solutions is an organization that provides cybersecurity solutions to other businesses. With the recent launch of a new user dashboard for their clients, Timingila Solutions wishes to ensure that businesses find it easy and intuitive to navigate and use the platform and follow these steps:

1. Identify Touchpoints: Timingila Solutions zeroes in on the first-time setup of the dashboard by its B2B clients as the key interaction point.

2. Formulate the Question: After the initial setup, clients receive a prompt asking: "On a scale from 1 (Very Difficult) to 7 (Very Easy), how easy was it to set up and navigate our new dashboard?"

3. Distribution: An in-app survey is presented to the client after their first login and initial setup.

4. Collection and Analysis: Over a span of two months, feedback from hundreds of businesses is compiled.

Findings: The average score is calculated to be 5.3, suggesting that while many find it relatively easy, there's room for improvement.

Outcome: Timingila Solutions also includes an open-ended question: "What could make your experience smoother?" Feedback indicates some users struggled with integrating third-party tools. Armed with this feedback, Timingila Solutions' development team begins refining the integration process, and within a few months, a more streamlined integration setup is launched.

8. HaTS

One of the tools used to gather feedback is the Happiness Tracking Survey (HaTS).

Happiness Tracking Surveys, colloquially known as HaTS, are short feedback forms that pop up in various Google products, asking users about their experience. These surveys can be seen across a range of Google products from Google Drive and Google Photos to Chrome browser and Android OS.

The goal is to understand how happy users are with a particular product or feature and where improvements can be made. HaTS is best suited for collecting attitudinal data at a large scale directly in the product and over time.[2]

8.1 How to Implement a HaTS

1. **Determine the Survey Frequency**: Decide how often to run the survey. It could be after every major release, quarterly, or any other time frame suitable for the product life cycle.

2. **Choose the Right Platform**: Several tools are available for surveying, such as SurveyMonkey, Google Forms, or in-app survey platforms. Choose one that integrates well with the product ecosystem.

3. **Keep it Concise**: The key to HaTS is brevity. A simple question like, "On a scale of 1-10, how happy are you with [Product/Feature Name]?" is a good start.

4. **Add an Open-ended Follow-up**: To understand the reasons behind the scores, include an optional open-ended question, such as, "What can we improve?"

5. **Segment your Audience**: Not all users are the same. Segmenting users based on factors like usage frequency, subscription tier, or region can provide more nuanced insights. HaTS uses a probability sampling approach[A] to ensure a representative set of a product's segments are randomly selected to be invited to take part in HaTS.

6. **Collect Data**: For HaTS, a best practice is to aim for about 400 - 1000 responses.

7. **Analyze and Act**: Identify trends and act on the feedback. The survey's value is in its actionable insights.

8.2 Potential Challenges

1. **Survey Fatigue**: If run too often, users might get tired of responding, reducing the survey's effectiveness. At Google, the same user will not be invited to HaTS again for another 12 weeks after the previous survey invitation.[2]

2. **Action Paralysis**: While HaTS provides feedback, there might be contradicting opinions. Product Managers need to weigh the feedback against the product vision and strategy.

3. **Expectation Management**: Users might expect immediate changes based on their feedback. Communication is key here.

8.3 Example Scenario

Scenario 65: Introducing a New Food Recommendation Feature on Timingila Delish

Timingila Delish has just rolled out a new feature on its app that provides personalized food recommendations for users based on their past orders, time of the day, and dietary preferences.

1. Survey Initiation:

After a couple of weeks of the feature's rollout, when users open the app after making an order, a Happiness Tracking Survey (akin to HaTS) pops up:

"How satisfied are you with our new food recommendation feature?" Options:

- Very satisfied
- Satisfied
- Neutral
- Unsatisfied
- Very unsatisfied

2. **Gathering Feedback:**

A diverse group of users provides feedback. For instance, vegetarians might note that the recommendations sometimes include non-vegetarian dishes. Another user might comment, "Love the breakfast suggestions, but I wish it would also consider calorie counts!"

3. **Analyzing Data:**

DelishDeliver's team aggregates the survey results. They notice:

- 60% of users are "Very satisfied" or "Satisfied"
- 25% are "Neutral"
- 15% are "Unsatisfied" or "Very unsatisfied"

From the feedback, a common thread emerges: users want more accurate recommendations based on their dietary restrictions.

4. **Iterative Improvement:**

Using the feedback, the Timingila Delish tech team refines the algorithm behind the recommendation feature. They introduce an improved version that provides options to filter recommendations based on dietary preferences like vegetarian, vegan, low-calorie, and so on.

5. **Follow-up Survey:**

A month later, a follow-up survey is sent to users:

"We've improved our food recommendation feature based on your feedback. How do you feel about the changes?" Options:

- Much better
- Slightly better
- No change
- Worse

9. Other Indicators

Monitoring key metrics is essential for understanding product-market fit. Here are some critical metrics, their definitions, and how they may indicate a strong Product-market fit:

Retention Rate

- **Definition**: The percentage of users who continue to use the product over a given period

- **Indication**: A high retention rate suggests that users find consistent value in your product, which is a strong indicator of Product-market fit.

Churn Rate

- **Definition**: The percentage of users who stop using the product over a specific period

- **Indication**: A low churn rate implies that customers are satisfied and are not seeking alternatives, suggesting a good Product-market fit.

Daily/Monthly Active Users (DAU/MAU)

- **Definition**: The number of unique users who engage with the product daily or monthly

- **Indication**: Growing DAU/MAU suggests the product is becoming an essential part of users' routines, indicating Product-market fit.

Customer Acquisition Cost (CAC)

- **Definition**: The average cost to acquire a new customer

- **Indication**: When CAC is low relative to the value derived from customers (LTV), it suggests the product has a favorable market position and Product-market fit.

Lifetime Value (LTV)

- **Definition**: The predicted net profit attributed to the entire future relationship with a customer

- **Indication**: A high LTV compared to CAC implies that customers find long-term value in the product, suggesting a solid Product-market fit.

Usage Frequency

- **Definition**: How often users interact with the product

- **Indication**: High frequency can mean the product is becoming a habit for users, pointing towards Product-market fit.

Feature Adoption Rate

- **Definition**: The percentage of users who adopt and use a new feature

- **Indication**: High adoption rates of new features indicate that the product team is aligned with user needs, a sign of Product-market fit.

Referral Rate

- **Definition**: The rate at which existing users refer new users to the product

- **Indication**: A high referral rate suggests existing users see enough value in the product to recommend it to others, a hallmark of Product-market fit.

Feedback Volume

- **Definition**: The quantity of feedback or suggestions received from users

- **Indication**: While feedback can be both positive and negative, a surge in feedback volume often indicates engagement and investment in the product's future, suggesting Product-market fit.

Time to Value (TTV)

- **Definition**: The time it takes for a user to derive significant value from the product after first use

- **Indication**: A shorter TTV implies that users quickly see the product's value, indicative of Product-market fit.

These metrics, when monitored collectively, give a holistic view of where a product stands in terms of market fit. Adjustments can then be made based on these insights to improve alignment with user needs and market demand.

10. Industry Certifications

For Product Managers looking to distinguish their offerings in a saturated market, understanding the significance and potential of industry certifications is crucial. Sometimes these certifications are crucial to operate in a specific market and are basic to product-market fitment.

These certifications serve as a third-party endorsement, indicating that a product aligns with specified quality, safety, or performance benchmarks.

Thus, a Product Manager must be aware of certifications applicable to their product, grow sufficiently deep knowledge about these, and not only apply the knowledge to guide the product features but also work towards the creation of required documentation.

Certifications are validations from neutral parties that verify a product adheres to a particular set of criteria. Such criteria might address safety measures, environmental considerations, or other industry-relevant standards.

Here's a brief overview of a few such third-party certifications and validations:

1. **CE Marking**: A confirmation that products available in the European Economic Area (EEA) comply with stringent safety, health, and environmental protection criteria.

2. **Energy Star**: Recognizes products adhering to energy efficiency standards outlined by the U.S. Environmental Protection Agency.

3. **UL (Underwriters Laboratories)**: A global entity that evaluates products for safety and reliability.

4. **RoHS (Restriction of Hazardous Substances)**: Sets standardized limits for certain hazardous substances in electronic items.

5. **ISO/IEC 27001**: Details the essentials for creating, executing, upholding, and refining an information security management system.

6. **CMMI (Capability Maturity Model Integration)**: Managed by the CMMI Institute, this assesses the progression of software development processes.

7. **ISO/IEC 25010**: Outlines software product quality tiers and details quality criteria.

8. **OWASP (Open Web Application Security Project)**: Although not a certification per se, OWASP sets the standard in software security, predominantly for web-based applications. Many companies use the OWASP Top Ten as a foundation for their web application security measures.

9. **ISO/IEC 27018**: Concentrates on safeguarding personal data when stored in the cloud.

10. **SSAE 18 (Statement on Standards for Attestation Engagements No. 18)**: Dictates how organizations report on compliance controls.

11. **PCI DSS (Payment Card Industry Data Security Standard)**: Enforces security standards ensuring companies managing credit card details maintain a safe environment. There is a section on this in the Common Regulations chapter.

12. **FCC Certification**: For electronic products in the U.S. that might disrupt radio and TV broadcasts, this certification confirms adherence to the Federal Communications Commission's guidelines.

13. **ISO 9001**: An internationally accepted standard that emphasizes creating, implementing, maintaining, and refining a Quality Management System (QMS) within companies. It revolves around key quality management principles.

14. **ARINC 653**: A specification that pertains to aviation computers and their interfacing. It concentrates on space and time partitioning in avionic computing systems.

15. **DO-178B**: Recognized as a safety-critical standard used in the aerospace industry, it guides the development of airborne systems and equipment software.

By acquainting themselves with these certifications, Product Managers can enhance their product's appeal, trustworthiness, and marketability, especially in sectors where compliance and quality are paramount.

22

Product Re-engagement

To ensure the long-term success and viability of a product in the market, it is important to retain existing users and ensure that they continue to use the product over time. This is where product re-engagement comes into play.

1. Techniques for Increasing Product Re-engagement

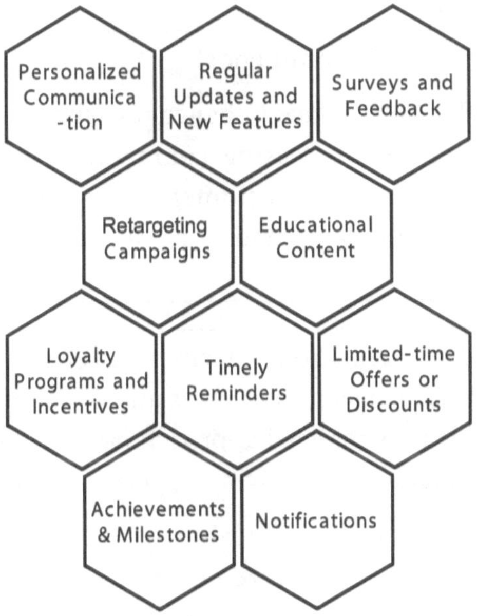

Fig 64: 10 Ways to Re-Engage Users

A high churn rate (rate of users abandoning a product) is a key indicator that work on re-engagement strategies is needed.

Retaining a customer is always a lower cost than acquiring new customers. Retaining existing customers provides a more stable growth trajectory.

Engaged customers are more likely to become advocates for the product, leading to organic growth via word-of-mouth. They are also likely to have a higher lifetime value. They are more familiar with the product, and thus, might be more open to purchasing premium features or recommending the product to others, leading to increased revenues.

1. **Personalized Communication**: Product Managers can use data analytics to understand user behavior. Based on this, they can tailor messages, emails, or in-app notifications to remind users of unused features or updates that might be of interest to them, and offer personalized suggestions or content. For instance, suggesting a new playlist for a music app user or a reading recommendation in a book app.

Illustration 18: Netflix Recommends!

In the early 2000s, Netflix faced challenges with customer retention and engagement due to increasing competition in the DVD rental market. To re-engage with its customers and differentiate itself from competitors, Netflix implemented a personalized recommendation system.

Netflix's recommendation system analyzed customer viewing habits and preferences to suggest movies and TV shows that they were likely to enjoy. This personalized approach helped customers discover new content and made their viewing experience more enjoyable and convenient.

As a result of this personalized communication strategy, Netflix saw a significant increase in customer engagement and retention. The recommendation system became a key feature of Netflix's service.

---

2. **Regular Updates and New Features**: Continuously updating the product and introducing new features can reignite interest among dormant users. Product Managers should ensure that users are made aware of these updates.

3. **Surveys and Feedback**: Engaging users by asking for their feedback or opinions can make them feel valued and heard. It can

also provide insights into why they might have disengaged in the first place.

4. **Retargeting Campaigns**: Using ads to retarget users who have shown decreased engagement can remind them of the product's value, new features, improvements, and offers to bring them back.

5. **Educational Content**: Hosting webinars, tutorials, or creating educational content can help users understand the product better, making them more likely to engage.

6. **Loyalty Programs and Incentives**: Offering rewards, discounts, or exclusive content can motivate users to return and interact with the product.

7. **Timely Reminders**: Notifications can remind users of specific actions they need to take, such as completing a task, checking out a cart, or finishing a course. These nudges can bring users back into the app or service, especially if they have forgotten about a pending activity.

8. **Limited-time Offers or Discounts**: For products that have a monetization model, notifications about limited-time offers, discounts, or special promotions can incentivize users to re-engage.

9. **Achievements and Milestones**: Celebrating user achievements or milestones with congratulatory notifications can boost their morale and encourage further engagement. For instance, acknowledging when a user completes their 100th task or reaches a particular level in a game.

10. **Notifications**: Notifications, when used judiciously, can serve as a powerful tool for Product Managers in re-engaging users. They act as direct touchpoints with the user, providing real-time information, reminders, or prompts that can draw them back into the product.

2. Loyalty Programs

Loyalty programs are critical to increase customer retention and brand loyalty. Loyalty programs come in various shapes and sizes, each tailored to the specific needs and behaviors of the target audience.

For Product Managers, it's essential to understand their audience deeply and align the loyalty program with both the brand's values and the customers' desires.

When implemented effectively, loyalty programs can foster a strong sense of community, increase customer lifetime value, and provide businesses with invaluable data on customer preferences and behaviors.

Here are various ways loyalty programs are implemented across industries, serving as an insightful guide for Product Managers.

2.1 Loyalty Points System

- **How It Works**: Customers earn points for specific actions, typically purchases. These points can later be redeemed for rewards.

- **Example**: Airlines often have frequent flier programs where passengers earn points based on the distance traveled or the ticket price. For instance, Delta Air Lines' SkyMiles allows travelers to accumulate miles, which can later be redeemed for flight discounts or upgrades.

2.2 Punch Card or "Buy X Get Y Free" Model

- **How It Works**: After a set number of purchases or visits, the customer gets a free product or service.

- **Example**: Many coffee shops, like local cafés, will offer punch cards where after purchasing nine coffees, the tenth one is free.

2.3 Badge or Tier Systems

- **How It Works**: This gamified approach offers badges or levels based on specific actions or milestones. Higher tiers typically provide better rewards, encouraging consistent interaction with the product or service.

- **Example**: Foursquare, a local search-and-discovery mobile app, uses badges to reward users for check-ins at various venues. Similarly, hotel chains like Marriott offer tiered loyalty programs (e.g., Silver Elite, Gold Elite) with progressively enhanced benefits.

2.4 Duration-Based Rewards

- **How It Works**: Loyalty is rewarded based on the duration of a customer's association with a brand or service. The longer a customer stays, the better the rewards.

- **Example**: Subscription-based services like software-as-a-service (SaaS) platforms might offer special benefits or discounts to long-term subscribers. Adobe Creative Cloud, for instance, could offer exclusive features or discounts to subscribers who've been with them for over a year.

2.5 Referral Programs

- **How It Works**: Customers are incentivized to refer friends or acquaintances to a service. Both the referrer and the referred person usually receive a reward upon successful referral.

- **Example**: Dropbox famously grew its user base through a referral program, where both the existing user and the new user received extra storage space for successful referrals.

2.6 Exclusive Membership Clubs

- **How It Works**: Customers pay a fee to join an exclusive club that provides them with special benefits, discounts, or early access.

- **Example**: Amazon Prime is a notable example. For an annual fee, members receive benefits like free two-day shipping, exclusive access to movies, TV shows, ad-free music, and more.

2.7 Collaborative Loyalty Programs

- **How It Works**: Brands collaborate to offer shared loyalty benefits, allowing customers to earn and redeem rewards across different businesses.

- **Example**: Credit card companies often partner with a range of brands to offer points that can be redeemed for goods, services, or discounts across multiple industries.

3. Optimizing Power of Notification

While notifications can be a powerful tool, overwhelming users with excessive alerts may result in them muting notifications or, in extreme cases, uninstalling the application. Product Managers need to find a balance and ensure that each notification provides genuine value. Below are prevalent patterns that products utilize to give customers control over the notifications they wish to receive:

Pattern 1

As often seen with airlines when users perform significant actions like booking tickets, they are prompted to select their preferred notification channels. This strategy is particularly effective for crucial alerts that users wouldn't want to overlook, offering a redundancy mechanism. Such an approach is especially suited for the B2C sector.

Pattern 2

Upon receiving a notification, products like Apple or WhatsApp provide users the option to entirely block notifications from the originating source. This method is effective when relaying notifications from various sources outside of the product's control, ensuring customers aren't inundated with alerts. It is a fitting choice for the B2C world.

Pattern 3

Platforms like LinkedIn or Facebook allow users to specify if they wish to block a particular type of notification upon receiving it. This is beneficial when notifications arise from multiple triggers within the product, such as network activities, and there's a need to prevent overwhelming the user. This technique is again well-aligned with B2C platforms.

Pattern 4

Some platforms, especially browsers, upon delivering a notification, offer users the choice to mute either that specific type of notification or alerts from the source for a specified duration. This is particularly useful when notifications serve as alerts for errors or unexpected events, ensuring users aren't bombarded during a sudden surge of such events. This approach is also apt for the B2C realm.

Pattern 5

Platforms similar to Google Groups or AWS prompt users to configure their notification preferences during the initial setup. This comprehensive method accounts for various notification types, modes, and target audiences. It's a strategy typically seen where notifications are selected on behalf of others, making it especially relevant for the B2B environment.

4. Community Building Around a Product

Fig 65: Ways to Build a Community Around the Product

Nurturing a community not only bolsters user engagement but also offers invaluable feedback, strengthens brand loyalty, and amplifies marketing efforts. Following are a few approaches to community building.

Wikis and Knowledge Bases

A well-maintained wiki or knowledge base is an invaluable resource for users, helping them to better understand a product's capabilities and solve issues autonomously.

- **Example**: Software and tech companies like Atlassian and Microsoft have extensive wikis for their products, providing users with documentation, tutorials, and FAQs.

In-Person and Virtual Conferences

Events, whether in person or online, are platforms for users to connect, share experiences, and delve deeper into product intricacies.

- **Example**: Apple's WWDC (Worldwide Developers Conference) and Adobe's MAX are annual events where enthusiasts, developers, and users congregate to explore the latest offerings and updates.

Newsletters

Regular newsletters keep users informed about product updates, new features, and relevant news, ensuring continuous engagement.

- **Example**: Substack, a platform dedicated to newsletters, sees numerous product-focused newsletters that provide updates and deep dives into niche topics.

Messaging Platforms

Real-time messaging platforms like Telegram Groups and Discord Communities offer instant connectivity among users, fostering an environment of rapid feedback and assistance.

- **Example**: Many cryptocurrency projects maintain active Telegram groups or Discord servers, offering immediate support and fostering discussions among community members.

YouTube Channels

Video content offers a dynamic way to showcase product features, tutorials, and user stories, with a potentially vast reach.

- **Example**: GoPro effectively utilizes its YouTube channel to showcase user-generated content, inspiring others to capture similar content using their cameras.

Social Media

Establishing a social media presence allows Product Managers to engage with a broad audience, share updates, and foster discussions.

- **Example**: Coca-Cola and Nike maintain active Facebook and LinkedIn pages, sharing brand stories, product launches, and engaging with their vast user base.

Online Forums and User Groups

A dedicated space for users to share experiences, seek solutions, and discuss product-related topics creates a sense of belonging and aids in problem-solving.

- **Example**: Red Hat has an active user forum where enthusiasts and professionals discuss issues, share solutions, and provide feedback.

Certifications

Offering certifications not only adds credibility to a user's expertise but also instills confidence in potential users about the product's industry relevance.

- **Example**: Cisco's certification programs in networking are globally recognized, ensuring that professionals are well-versed in their products.

5. Certifications for Your Products

A seal of proficiency provided by a certification holds immense value. Product companies run globally recognized certification programs that ensure professionals are adept in handling their products.

For Product Managers considering a similar route for their offerings, the benefits can be manifold, extending beyond mere skill validation. Following are the nuances of creating certification programs and the subsequent advantages they hold.

Structuring the Certification Program

Foundation to Expert Levels

- Start with a foundational certification for beginners or users new to the product.

- Introduce intermediate certifications to challenge and validate more nuanced uses of the product.

- Offer expert-level certifications for the most advanced users. This ensures a hierarchy, providing learners with a clear path of progression.

Blended Learning Approaches

- Use a mix of e-learning modules, instructor-led sessions, and hands-on labs. This caters to various learning preferences and ensures a holistic understanding.

Continuous Evaluation

- Apart from the final certification test, integrate periodic quizzes and challenges. This helps in reinforcing knowledge and keeps the learner engaged.

Recertification

- Technology and products evolve. Ensure that certified individuals update their knowledge by introducing a recertification requirement every couple of years.

Physical and Virtual Issuance

- Certificates are typically issued in two formats: physical and virtual. While the physical certificate is a tangible proof of achievement, the virtual format ensures easy sharing, especially in the digital age.

- Each certificate, irrespective of its format, carries a unique identification number, ensuring its singularity and traceability.

Online Validation System

- Certification providers often set up a dedicated portal on their official website for validation purposes.

- By entering the unique identification number from the certificate, any interested party can pull up basic details about the certification holder. This includes information such as the name of the certificate holder, the date of issuance, the validity period, and the level or type of certification.

- This system not only enables swift verification but also acts as a deterrent against any fraudulent replication or misuse of the certification.

- An emerging trend in the certification world is the inclusion of QR codes on both physical and virtual certificates. Scanning these codes can instantly redirect to the validation page of the certification provider, streamlining the process further.

- While it's vital to provide enough details to validate the authenticity of the certificate, it's equally important to ensure that no sensitive personal information is exposed in the process. Striking this balance safeguards the privacy of certified individuals.

The Multifaceted Advantages of Certification Programs

Credibility and Validation

- Certifications stand as a testament to a user's proficiency. It assures clients, employers, and peers that the certified individual possesses the expertise claimed, building trust in their capabilities.

Expansion of User Base

- A structured learning path often attracts new users. They find it easier to onboard and learn, knowing there's a systematic approach to mastering the product.

Marketing and Branding Benefits

- Certified users often flaunt their achievements, on professional platforms like LinkedIn. This serves as organic marketing for the product.

- The existence of a certification program can be a unique selling point, distinguishing the product in the market and highlighting the organization's commitment to user proficiency.

Revenue Stream

- While many companies offer certifications as a part of their product package, others treat it as a separate entity, generating additional revenue. The perceived value of the certification can justify the investment users make, leading to a win-win situation.

Crafting a robust certification program requires commitment, resources, and an understanding of the end-user's needs. However, the dividends it pays, both in terms of product loyalty and brand recognition, are monumental. As Product Managers, setting up certifications can be a strategic move, positioning the product favorably in the competitive market landscape and fostering a community of proficient and passionate users.

23

Product Optimization

Product optimization ensures that the product continually meets or exceeds evolving customer expectations, achieves business goals, and remains competitive. Here are several techniques that a Product Manager can employ for product optimization

1. Usability Testing

Usability testing is the evaluation of a product by testing it with real users in their environment. It provides valuable insights into how real users interact with a product and where optimizations can be made.

Following are a few common usability testing techniques and their typical applications.

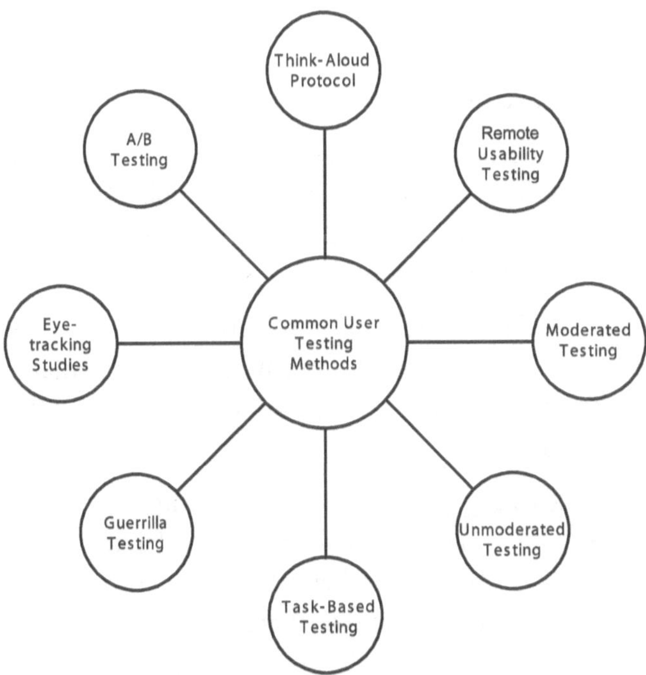

Fig 66: Common User Testing Methods

1.1 Think-Aloud Protocol

When to Use: It's beneficial when seeking to understand the thought processes of users as they interact with a product.

Example: An organization releasing a new photo-editing software might ask users to verbalize their thoughts as they navigate the platform. If a user expresses confusion about a specific tool or button, this signals a potential area for improvement.

1.2 Remote Usability Testing

When to Use: This technique is best when testing users from diverse geographical locations or when logistical challenges make in-person testing difficult.

Example: An e-commerce platform aiming to globalize its services conducts remote usability tests with users from Europe, Asia, and Africa. Through this, they understand region-specific user preferences and pain points.

1.3 Moderated Testing

Moderated testing involves a facilitator guiding users through tasks and scenarios while observing their behavior and collecting feedback. The facilitator can ask questions, provide explanations, and ensure that the testing environment remains controlled.

When to Use: Moderated testing is beneficial when seeking detailed insights into specific aspects of the product. It is particularly useful for complex interfaces or when the team wants to understand the reasoning behind user actions.

Example: An e-learning platform is conducting moderated testing to evaluate a new course navigation feature. The facilitator guides users through the process of finding and enrolling in a course, observing how they interact with the interface, and noting any difficulties they encounter.

1.4 Unmoderated Testing

Unmoderated testing allows users to interact with the product without direct supervision. Users are typically given tasks to complete and asked to provide feedback in the form of surveys or written responses.

When to Use: Unmoderated testing is ideal when a more natural, unguided interaction with the product is desired. It is also useful when testing a larger number of participants or when logistical challenges make in-person testing impractical.

Example: A mobile app development company is conducting unmoderated testing to gather feedback on a new feature. Users are given access to the app and asked to complete a series of tasks, such as setting up a profile or making a purchase, and provide feedback based on their experience.

1.5 Task-Based Testing

When to Use: When the goal is to evaluate the efficiency and effectiveness of specific tasks within the product.

Example: An email service provider might ask users to send an email, attach a file, or set up an out-of-office reply. The ease and success rate of these tasks provide insights into usability.

1.6 Guerrilla Testing

When to Use: When quick, informal feedback is needed on a specific feature or prototype, especially in the early stages of development.

Example: A startup developing a fitness app might take a prototype to a local gym and ask members for immediate feedback on the user interface and features.

1.7 Eye-tracking Studies:

When to Use: When seeking to understand where users naturally look when using a product, identifying hotspots that might be overlooked.

Example: An online retailer might use eye-tracking to assess where users look first on a product page – is it the product image, the price, or the reviews? This can guide design optimization.

2. A/B Testing

A/B Testing (also known as split testing or bucket testing) is a method of comparing two variations of the same thing (webpage, design, content, and other components of a product) against each other to determine which one performs better.

This is a very common testing method in product organizations today. One of the earliest documented and frequently cited cases was shared by the Microsoft Bing team where during A/B Testing a headline variation led to a 12% increase in revenue.[1]

2.1 Why is A/B Testing Essential for Product Managers?

1. **Objective Decision Making**: A/B testing allows Product Managers to base product decisions on actual user behavior rather than intuition or Highest Paid Person's Opinion (HiPPO).

2. **Risk Mitigation**: Before rolling out a feature to all users, A/B testing helps in gauging potential positive or negative impacts, thus reducing business risks.

3. **Continuous Improvement**: A/B tests can be iterative, enabling Product Managers to fine-tune features or designs progressively.

2.2 Tips for Effective A/B Testing

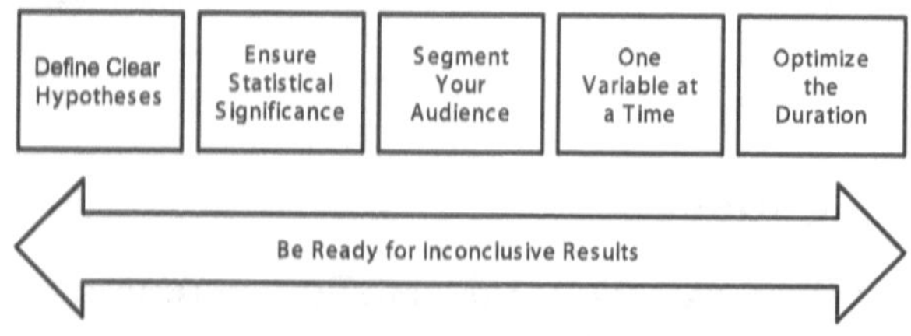

Fig 67: Running Effective A/B Testing

1. **Define Clear Hypothesis / Goal:** Before embarking on any test, be clear on what you aim to learn. For instance, instead of saying "I want to see which button performs better," specify "I hypothesize that the green button will result in a higher click-through rate than the red one." Or, "I want to know between the green button and the red one, which will result in a higher click-through rate."

2. **Ensure Statistical Significance:** A meaningful sample size can lead to inaccurate conclusions. Check the chapter on Sampling to learn more about arriving at an appropriate sample size.

3. **Segment Your Audience:** Not all users behave the same way. Segmenting them based on behavior, demographics, or other criteria can lead to more nuanced insights.

4. **One Variable at a Time:** When testing, change one variable at a time. If multiple elements are changed, it's challenging to pinpoint which one caused the difference.

5. **Optimize the Duration:** Tests should neither be too short (leading to insufficient data) nor too long (causing potential user fatigue).

6. **Be Ready for Inconclusive Results:** Sometimes tests don't provide a clear winner. This, in itself is a valuable insight, suggesting that perhaps the variable being tested isn't as influential as thought.

2.3 Product Capabilities Needed to Conduct A/B Testing

For products to support A/B testing effectively, several capabilities need to be integrated.

1. **User Segmentation:** The system should allow Product Managers to categorize users based on predefined criteria like demographics or location, so different segments can be exposed to different test variations.

2. **Feature Flagging:** This allows Product Managers to turn features on or off for specific user groups, facilitating easy test setups.

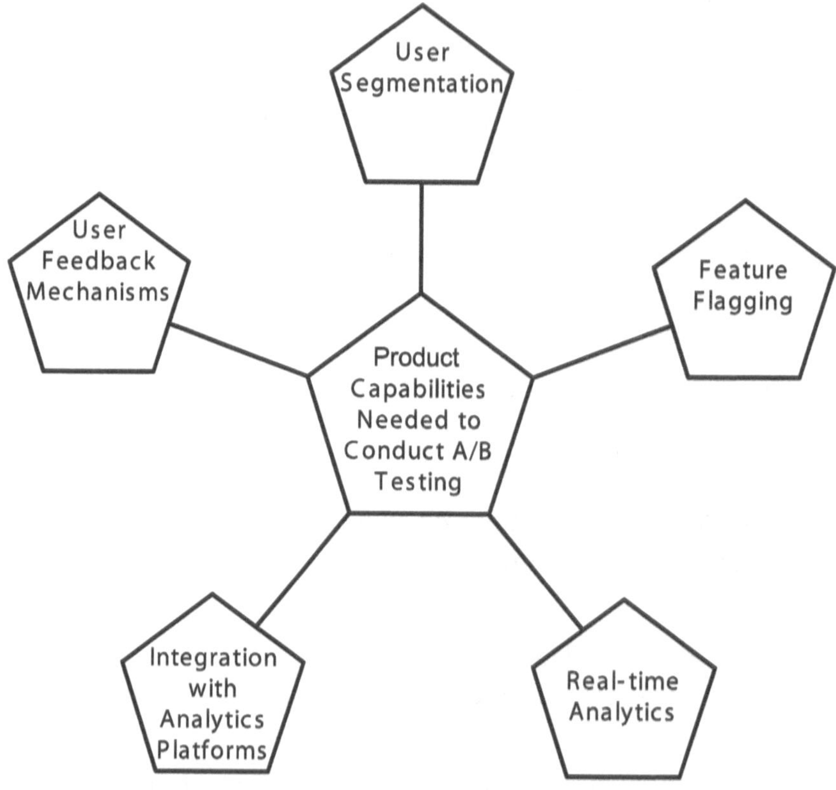

Fig 68: Product Capabilities Needed to Run A/B Testing

3. **Real-time Analytics**: To monitor test results live, products should have the capability to track and present data in real-time.

4. **Integration with Analytics Platforms**: Tools like Google Analytics or Mixpanel offer advanced insights. Ensure that the product can seamlessly integrate with these platforms.

5. **User Feedback Mechanisms**: Beyond quantitative data, qualitative insights from users can add depth to A/B test interpretations. This, however, may not be applicable in the case of large-scale and high-volume A/B Testing.

Thus, Product Managers must invest in equipping their products with the necessary capabilities and follow best practices to harness the full potential of A/B testing.

2.4 Example Scenario

Scenario 66: Sign-up Page for a Subscription Service

- A: The sign-up page displays a large hero image of people using the service with a simple "Sign Up Now" call-to-action (CTA) button.

- B: The sign-up page features a short video testimonial from satisfied customers and a CTA that reads "Join Our Community."

- Goal: Measure which version has a higher sign-up conversion rate.

Scenario 67: Checkout Process for an E-commerce Store

- A: The checkout process is a single, long page requiring users to scroll.

- B: The checkout process is divided into multiple steps with progress indicators.

- Goal: Identify which checkout process has a lower cart abandonment rate.

Scenario 68: Pricing Page for a Software-as-a-Service (SaaS)

- A: The pricing page showcases three tiered plans with monthly pricing.

- B: The pricing page shows the same three plans but emphasizes annual pricing with a discount.

- Goal: Find out which pricing display attracts more customers to the annual payment plan.

Scenario 69: Landing Page for a Workshop Event

- A: The landing page headline reads "Master Your Marketing Skills with Our Workshop."

> - B: The headline reads "90% of Our Attendees Tripled Their Revenue. Join Our Marketing Workshop."
> - Goal: Determine which headline results in more sign-ups for the workshop.

3. Data Analytics

Data analytics in the context of product optimization, with tools like Google Analytics, Mixpanel, and others, help Product Managers obtain actionable insights to drive product decisions.

3.1 The Role of Data Analytics in Product Optimization

1. **Understanding User Behavior**: By examining user interactions with a product, managers can pinpoint areas that engage users the most, as well as sections where users might drop off.

2. **Feature Utilization**: Analytics can reveal which features are most used, which are ignored, and how they are accessed, aiding in prioritizing development resources.

3. **Conversion Analysis**: For products with specific user goals (e.g., e-commerce checkouts or software sign-ups), analytics provides insight into conversion rates and potential obstacles in the conversion funnel.

3.2 Common Applications

- **Audience Segmentation**: Product Analytics tools allow Product Managers to track audience segmented by demographics, location, device type, and more. For instance, if a product is experiencing high bounce rates from mobile users, it could indicate mobile UX issues.

- **Behavior Flow**: This feature visualizes the path users take through a product or site. It can show where users typically enter, the sequence of pages they visit, and where they drop off, offering insights into potential areas of improvement.

- **Goal Setting and Conversion Tracking**: Product Managers can define specific goals (e.g., completing a sign-up or making a purchase) and track conversions to assess performance over time.

- **Event Tracking**: Unlike traditional pageview-based analytics, some tools shine in tracking discrete actions (events) users take. A Product Manager can monitor events like clicking a feature button, playing a video, or sharing content.

- **Funnels**: Create and analyze funnels based on specific events. For instance, for an e-commerce app: viewing a product -> adding to cart -> initiating checkout -> purchase. This allows managers to identify drop-off points and improve conversion rates.

- **Retention Analysis**: Understand how often users return after their initial visit or use. For subscription-based products, can provide insights into user stickiness and the long-term value of different user cohorts.

- **Holistic view**: Product Managers can integrate analytics platforms. For example, linking Google Analytics with Google Optimize allows for A/B testing, with analytics data directly informing which variant performs better in real-world conditions.

Governing User Data

The governance of user data in a product should be a paramount concern for a Product Manager. Trust and Reputation, Regulatory Compliance, Security Risk Avoidance, and finally User Experience are the key reasons to invest time in Data Governance.

This chapter intends to introduce a Product Manager to various concepts around Data Governance and their applicability.

Data governance is a principled approach to managing data during its life cycle, from acquisition to use to disposal.[1]

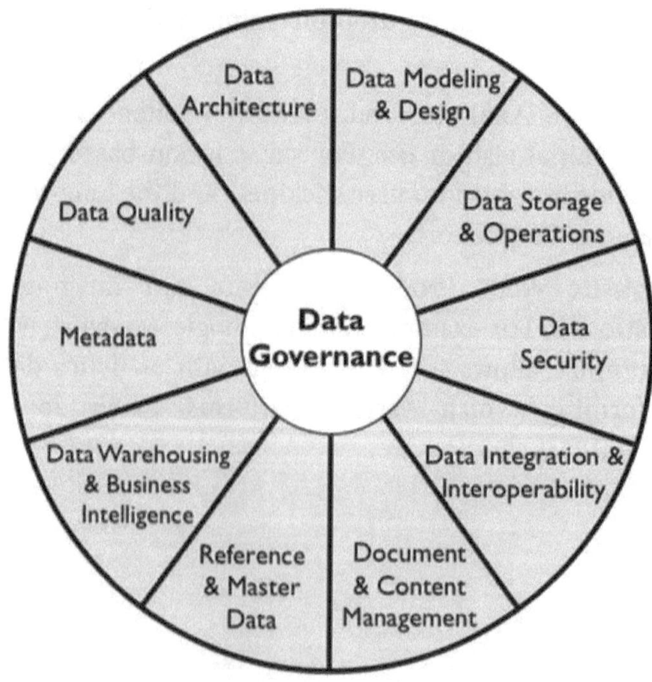

Fig 69: DMBOK v2 Wheel[2]

It encompasses a set of processes, policies, standards, and metrics that ensure the effective and efficient use of information in enabling an organization to achieve its goals. Data governance focuses on improving data quality, ensuring data security and privacy, and meeting regulatory requirements.

DAMA International's Data Management Body of Knowledge, commonly referred to as DMBOK2, presents its framework visually using the "Wheel Diagram."

The wheel represents the functional areas of data management and serves as a comprehensive guide to the disciplines and best practices within the data management domain.

1. Key Components of the DMBOK2 Wheel Diagram

1.1 Central Hub

Data Governance: At the center of the wheel is Data Governance, which reflects its foundational role in the entire data management framework. This central position underscores that governance is integral to all data management activities, providing oversight, policies, standards, and procedures that guide each of the other functions.

1.2 Functional Areas

Surrounding the central hub are the primary functional areas of data management. These represent the distinct but interrelated disciplines within the broader data management domain. Each of these segments has its practices, processes, and methods. Some of the functional areas included are:

Data Architecture: This discipline focuses on the overall structure and blueprint of data across the organization, laying out the foundation for how data will be stored, accessed, and utilized. It encompasses high-level design choices, principles, and policies that dictate how data entities and technologies integrate and align with business strategy and goals.

1. **Product Management Applicability**: Crucial for products that handle, store, or analyze data, whether it's a mobile app, web platform, or SaaS solution.

2. **Product Manager Actions**: Understand the overarching structure of data in the product, ensuring the Architecture made by the Data Architect aligns with business strategy and provides scalability for future growth.

Data Modeling and Design: This area deals with translating business needs into data structures. It involves creating detailed models that outline how data is structured, related, and flows within systems. Data modeling also defines rules, relationships, and constraints for the data.

1. **Product Management Applicability**: Vital when developing databases, APIs, or any system where data structuring and relationships are necessary.

2. **Product Manager Actions**: Collaborate with Data Architects and designers to ensure data models meet product requirements and user needs.

Data Storage and Operations: Managing data storage solutions and databases.

1. **Product Management Applicability**: Important for products that require data storage, like user profiles, transaction records, etc.

2. **Product Manager Actions**: Work with engineering teams to select the right storage solutions, ensuring performance, scalability, and cost-effectiveness.

Data Security: Ensuring that data is protected against breaches, thefts, and unauthorized access.

1. **Product Management Applicability**: Mandatory for any product that collects, processes, or stores user data, especially PII (Personally Identifiable Information).

2. **Product Manager Actions**: Prioritize user data security. Stay updated on security best practices and ensure the product meets or exceeds industry standards.

Data Integration and Interoperability: Combining data from different sources and ensuring seamless data flow across systems.

1. **Product Management Applicability**: Relevant for products that need to interface with other systems, apps, or platforms.

2. **Product Manager Actions**: Ensure seamless data flow and integration capabilities, potentially utilizing APIs, middleware, or integration platforms.

Document and Content Management: Managing unstructured data like documents, images, and other content.

3. **Product Management Applicability**: Useful for products that gather user documents, content-rich platforms, CMS systems, or document management solutions.

4. **Product Manager Actions**: Manage content life cycle, versions, and accessibility, ensuring a good user experience.

Reference and Master Data Management: Ensuring consistency of shared data across the organization. (See following sub-chapters).

5. **Product Management Applicability**: Pertinent for products with shared & standardized data sets across systems or modules.

6. **Product Manager Actions**: Ensure data consistency and accuracy across the product, enhancing user trust.

Data Warehousing and Business Intelligence: Storing and analyzing data to derive insights and support business decisions.

1. **Product Management Applicability**: Important for analytics platforms or products that offer insights and reporting features.

2. **Product Manager Actions**: Focus on storing data in a way that facilitates analysis and provides valuable insights to users.

Metadata Management: Managing information about other data, i.e., data about data.

1. **Product Management Applicability**: Relevant for products that handle vast data sets and need to manage data about data.

2. **Product Manager Actions**: Ensure metadata is accurately captured, aiding in data discovery, analytics, and user understanding.

Data Quality: Ensuring accuracy, consistency, and reliability of data.

1. **Product Management Applicability**: Crucial for all products where data reliability affects user trust or decision-making.

2. **Product Manager Actions**: Regularly validate, clean, and monitor data to maintain high data integrity.

2. Reference Data

Reference data is a type of data used to classify or categorize other data. It typically remains relatively static and is used across an organization to ensure consistency and standardized reporting. Reference data provides context, making transactional data or other types of data comprehensible and usable.

Examples of Reference Data include:

1. **Country Codes**: If an organization operates internationally, it may deal with data from various countries. Using standardized country codes) like IN / IND, US / USA, KE / KEN, DE / DEU or BR / BRA) helps ensure consistency across databases and systems.

2. **Currency Codes**: If you're processing transactions in different currencies, standardized currency codes like INR, USD, EUR, etc., can help you understand and categorize those transactions.

3. **Product Categories**: In a retail setting, products might be categorized under 'Electronics,' 'Apparel,' 'Groceries,' etc. These categories provide context to the type of product being sold or purchased.

4. **Employee Roles or Job Titles**: Standardized titles or roles, such as 'Manager,' 'Analyst,' or 'Director,' help in understanding the hierarchical structure in an organization.

5. **Industry Classification**: Companies might be categorized based on standardized industry classifications like 'Healthcare,' 'Finance,' 'Technology,' and so on.

Importance of Reference Data:

1. **Standardization**: Reference data helps ensure consistency across systems and processes. This is vital for large organizations that rely on multiple databases or systems that need to interact with one another.

2. **Data Integrity**: By providing a set standard of values, reference data helps prevent errors and ensures that the data entered into systems is accurate.

3. **Reporting and Analysis**: For analytics and reporting purposes, having standardized reference data ensures that reports are accurate and consistent, making it easier to derive insights and make informed decisions.

4. **Regulatory Compliance**: In many sectors, regulatory bodies require standardized reporting. Properly managed reference data ensures that these reports meet the necessary standards.

5. **Operational Efficiency**: With standardized categories and classifications, processes can be automated and streamlined, leading to improved operational efficiency.

In essence, while reference data might seem basic or foundational, it plays a critical role in ensuring that systems function correctly, that reporting is accurate, and that operations run smoothly. Proper management of reference data is thus crucial for organizations of all sizes.

3. Master Data

Master Data refers to the consistent and uniform set of identifiers and extended attributes that describe the core entities of an enterprise and is used across multiple systems and business processes. Master data represents the business objects that contain the most valuable, agreed-upon information shared across an organization.

Examples of Master Data:

1. **Customers**: The foundational information about customers, such as their names, addresses, contact details, and transaction histories.

2. **Products**: Details about products an organization sells or produces, including product names, descriptions, classifications, and prices.

3. **Suppliers or Vendors**: Information about the entities from which an organization procures goods or services, including names, contact details, and terms of business.

4. **Employees**: Core information about individuals employed by the organization, including names, job roles, contact information, and employment history.

5. **Assets**: Details about physical or intangible assets owned or managed by the organization, such as machinery, software licenses, or intellectual property.

Importance of Master Data:

1. **Single Source of Truth**: Master data provides a consistent view of core business entities, ensuring that everyone in the organization is working with the same information, thereby reducing discrepancies and errors.

2. **Efficient Business Processes**: With consistent master data, business processes can be streamlined, ensuring that various departments and systems work in harmony.

3. **Improved Decision-Making**: Accurate and consistent master data provides a solid foundation for analytics and insights, leading to more informed decision-making.

4. **Regulatory and Compliance**: In various industries, maintaining accurate master data is not just a matter of efficiency but also a regulatory requirement.

5. **Enhanced Data Quality**: Master data management ensures that data remains accurate, complete, and up-to-date across the organization.

6. **Operational Efficiency**: An accurate master data system can prevent redundant tasks, reduce errors in operations, and improve service delivery.

4. Master Data Management (MDM)

Given the critical importance of master data, many organizations adopt Master Data Management (MDM) strategies and solutions.

MDM is the process of defining, implementing, and managing master data to ensure it is consistent, accurate, and serves the organization's business goals. MDM involves tools, governance, processes, and standards that ensure master data is kept consistent and accurate across the organization.

In essence, while transactional data (like sales or event logs) can be seen as documenting the activities of a business, master data provides the context in which those activities occur. Properly managed master data is essential for maintaining the health and efficiency of the data-driven aspects of an organization.

5. Tokenization

Tokenization refers to the process of substituting sensitive data elements with non-sensitive equivalents, called tokens, which have no intrinsic or exploitable meaning or value.

These tokens can then be used in various systems and databases during development, testing or in production systems without exposing the underlying sensitive data.

Tokenization is particularly important in areas where sensitive data, such as personal identification information, needs to be protected from exposure.

Here's how tokenization typically works.

1. **Input Data:** A piece of sensitive data, like a credit card number, is introduced into a tokenization system.

2. **Token Generation:** The tokenization system generates a random token that corresponds to the sensitive data. This token does not resemble the original data and cannot be easily reversed to derive the original data.

3. **Data Storage:** The original sensitive data is stored securely, often in a highly secure and encrypted vault or database. Only the tokenization system can map tokens back to their original values.

4. **Token Use:** The token, instead of the original sensitive data, can be used in various systems, databases, and applications. If a malicious actor gains access to these tokens, they won't have access to the actual sensitive data.

5. **Detokenization:** When the original data is needed, the token can be submitted to the tokenization system, which then retrieves the real sensitive data from its secure storage.

Tokenization is often contrasted with encryption. While both methods are used to protect sensitive data, they operate differently.

- **Encryption** transforms data into another form or code so that only people with access to a secret key or password can read it. Encrypted data, when decrypted, results in the original data.

- **Tokenization**, as described above, replaces sensitive data with a random and meaningless token.

One of the primary advantages of tokenization over encryption is that even if a token is exposed, it doesn't carry any value or meaning outside the context of the specific tokenization system. This makes tokenization particularly useful for protecting data in environments where there is a high risk of exposure.

5.1 Key Benefits

1. **Data Security:** Even if a hacker manages to breach the online store's database, they won't find actual phone numbers. Instead, they'd

find tokens, which are useless without the specific tokenization system that knows how to detokenize them.

2. **Compliance**: By using tokenization, the online store can reduce its scope for Payment Card Industry Data Security Standard (PCI DSS) compliance, as they aren't directly handling or storing raw credit card data.

3. **Privacy**: Developers and testers in the test environment never see the real names of patients, ensuring data privacy.

4. **Realistic Testing**: While the names are tokenized, the structure remains, allowing developers to test the application in scenarios that mimic the real world without compromising sensitive data.

5.2 Example Scenario

Scenario 70: A healthcare application stores patient records, which include sensitive details like first name, surname, medical history, and more. When creating a test environment, the organization wants developers to work with data that feels real but doesn't expose any actual patient names.

1. **Input Data:**

   a. A patient, named "Jane Smith", interacts with the healthcare system, and her details are entered into the application.

2. **Tokenization Process:**

   a. When moving this data to the test environment, the system sends "Jane" and "Smith" to the tokenization service.

   b. The tokenization service generates random tokens. For "Jane", it produces "LmnO", and for "Smith", it produces "PqrS".

   c. The real names "Jane Smith" are securely stored in the tokenization system's encrypted vault.

3. **Using the Tokenized Data:**

    a. In the test environment, developers now see the patient name as "LmnO PqrS". The structure is the same (two distinct words for the first name and surname), so the data feels real for testing purposes, but it doesn't expose the real name.

    b. When developers test features, like searching for a patient name, they'd use "LmnO" or "PqrS" rather than actual names.

4. **Detokenization (if needed):**

    a. If, for some reason, a conversion back to the original name is needed (typically this isn't required in a test environment), the system can send "LmnO PqrS" to the tokenization service.

    b. The tokenization service looks up its secure mapping and identifies "LmnO" as "Jane" and "PqrS" as "Smith," returning the original name "Jane Smith."

25

Product Support

Offering an outstanding product isn't enough. The experience surrounding that product, especially in moments of trouble, can make or break an organization's reputation and, consequently, its success. Central to this experience is product support. Good support can not only resolve user issues but also be a powerful tool for business growth.

While in larger enterprises, customer support might be a separate department or even outsourced, a Product Manager's oversight and involvement in these aspects can be pivotal.

1. Benefits of Effective Product Support

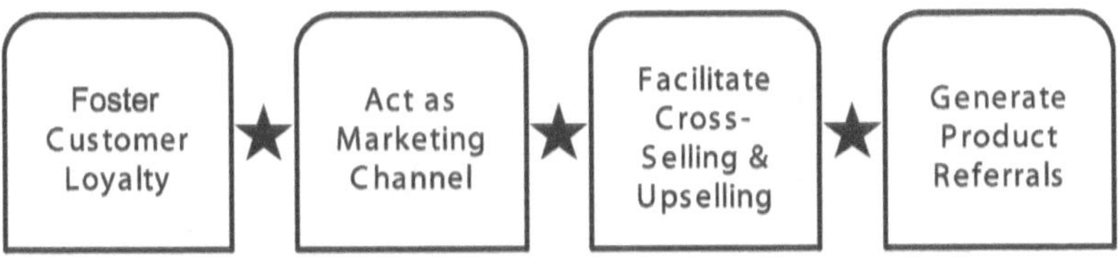

Fig 70: Benefits Effective Product Support Brings

1. **Foster Customer Loyalty**: Loyalty isn't just about making a great product; it's about customers standing by it. When customers know that an organization will promptly and efficiently address their concerns, they're more likely to stick around. This repeat business is invaluable, as it's often more cost-effective to retain existing customers than to acquire new ones.

2. **Act as Marketing Channel**: Word of mouth remains a powerful marketing tool, even in the digital age. A customer who has a positive support experience is more likely to share that experience with others, acting as a brand ambassador. In contrast, negative experiences can quickly become public relations nightmares in the age of social media.

3. **Facilitate Cross-Selling and Upselling**: Effective support teams don't just solve problems; they also identify opportunities. By understanding a customer's needs and challenges, they can recommend other products or services that the customer might find valuable. This isn't pushy salesmanship; it's providing solutions that genuinely benefit the user.

4. **Generate Product Referrals**: Satisfied customers become brand advocates. When they believe in a product and the organization behind it, they're more likely to refer friends, family, and colleagues. These referrals are golden because they come with built-in trust. A recommendation from a trusted source can carry more weight than even the most polished advertisement.

2. Support Channel

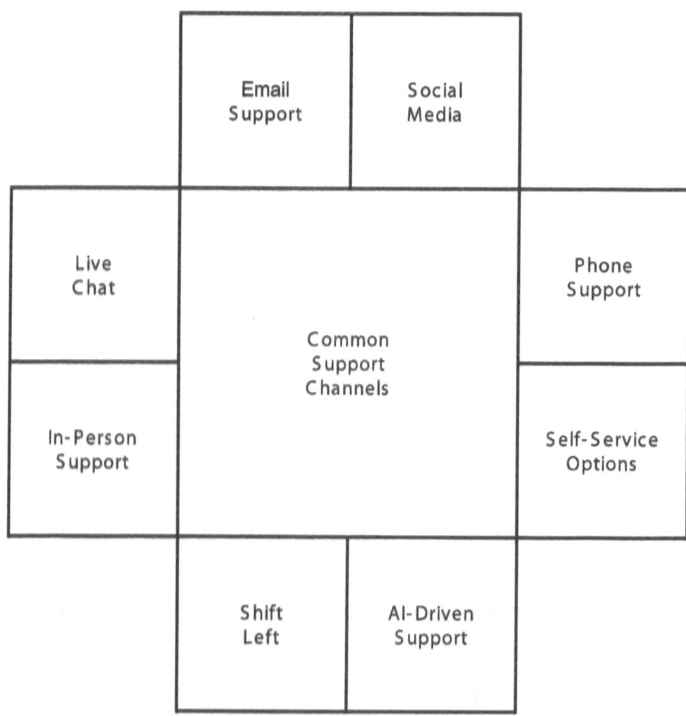

Fig 71: Support Channels

The term Support channel refers to the specific methods through which customers can seek assistance regarding its products. These channels provide a means for users to report issues, ask questions, give feedback, or request additional information. The choice of support channels often depends on the nature of the product, the target audience, and the organization's resources.

The role of a Product Manager is pivotal in aligning these channels with user expectations and optimizing their function.

2.1 Email Support

Predominantly used for non-urgent and detailed queries, email support offers the advantage of comprehensiveness. Users can outline their problems in depth, attaching screenshots or logs if needed.

The Product Manager's responsibility here is to ensure that the response time is optimized, templates are user-friendly, and that there's a robust system to categorize and prioritize incoming emails.

2.2 Social Media

Platforms like Twitter and Facebook have transformed from mere networking sites to pivotal support channels. Users not only seek assistance but also express grievances or appreciation in the public domain.

Product Managers must coordinate with marketing and support teams to ensure timely responses, manage brand reputation, and harness feedback for product improvements.

2.3 Live Chat

When users seek immediate answers, live chat is their go-to channel. It bridges the gap between the impersonality of email and the immediacy of phone calls.

For a Product Manager, it's essential to oversee the integration of efficient chat tools, ensure representatives are well-trained, and monitor the response time to ensure user satisfaction.

2.4 Phone Support

Often reserved for complex or urgent issues, phone support provides a direct line for assistance. The human touch can assuage frustrations and expedite solutions.

A Product Manager should ensure that phone representatives are knowledgeable, that soft skills are continually honed, and that wait times are minimized.

2.5 In-Person Support

In-person support involves sending an expert support person to the user's location to provide assistance or resolve issues.

The Product Manager plays a crucial role in coordinating and optimizing the in-person support process. This includes ensuring that the support person is well-trained and equipped to handle user issues effectively and ensuring access to the necessary tools and resources to resolve issues onsite.

2.6 Self-service Options

Increasingly, users prefer solving problems on their own, making FAQs, knowledge bases, tutorials, and forums indispensable.

The Product Manager's role is to ensure these resources are up-to-date, user-friendly, and address the common pain points, thereby reducing the load on other support channels.

2.7 Shift Left

The "Shift Left" approach emphasizes bringing support activity closer to the end user. By equipping users with tools to trigger automatic fixes or diagnostic processes, dependency on conventional support can be reduced.

Product Managers should focus on integrating user-centric tools, making them intuitive, and educating users on their availability and use.

2.8 AI-Driven Support

With advancements in AI, support processes are becoming smarter and more autonomous. Chatbots, predictive analytics, and ChatGPT-driven troubleshooting are just the tip of the iceberg.

A Product Manager must understand the potential and limitations of AI, ensuring its implementation enhances user experience without compromising the human touch when needed.

2.9 Choosing Right Support Channels

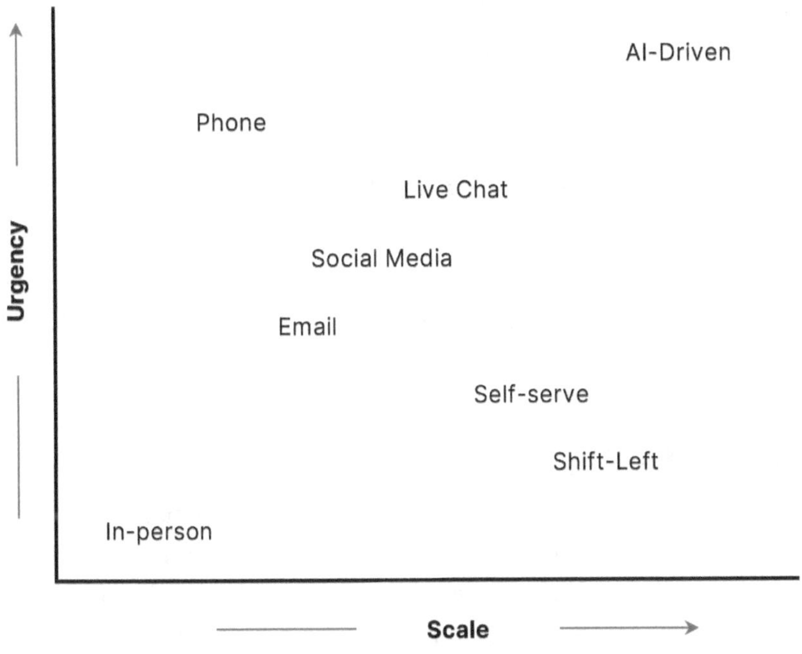

Fig 72: Choosing the Right Support Channels

Here are some principles that can help a Product Manager decide which support channel to use for different kinds of products.

1. **Nature of the Product:** Consider the complexity of the product and the likelihood of users encountering issues. For complex products, channels like live chat or phone support may be more

suitable, while simpler products may require only email or self-service options.

2. **Urgency of Support:** Determine how quickly users need assistance. For urgent issues, phone support or live chat may be necessary, while non-urgent queries can be addressed through email or self-service options.

3. **Scale of Queries:** Consider the potential number of users the product can have. Products with a large user base may require more scalable support solutions, such as chatbots or community forums, to handle a high volume of queries efficiently.

By considering these principles, Product Managers can choose the most appropriate support channels for their products, ensuring that users receive timely and effective assistance.

3. Key Considerations on Product Support

For a Product Manager, understanding the intricacies of customer support is instrumental in enhancing the user experience and ensuring the product's success. Here are some key items for a Product Manager to work on.

3.1 Knowledge Base and Documentation

A Product Manager should facilitate the creation of detailed user manuals and documentation, ensuring they are user-friendly and comprehensive. Regularly updating FAQs based on recurring issues can preemptively address user concerns. Incorporating visuals, whether they're screenshots, videos, or infographics, can often convey solutions more effectively than text alone.

3.2 Response Time and Availability

A Product Manager must ensure that support is responsive and available when users need it. This involves setting and monitoring response time metrics and determining support availability, keeping in mind international users and varying time zones.

3.3 Multilingual Support

For products with a global reach, multilingual support is a necessity. A Product Manager should assess the primary languages of the user base and ensure support materials and representatives cater to these languages.

3.4 Accessibility

Accessibility isn't just about compliance; it's about inclusivity. Ensuring that support channels cater to users with disabilities enriches the user base and extends the product's reach.

3.5 Escalation Procedures

Frontline support can't address all issues. Product Managers should work with support teams to establish clear and efficient escalation paths, ensuring that more complex concerns are addressed promptly by product teams.

3.6 Technology and Tools

From investing in ticketing systems to exploring AI-driven chat interfaces, a Product Manager should be at the forefront of integrating advanced tools that enhance the support experience. Analytical insights from these tools can provide invaluable feedback for future product iterations.

3.7 Continuous Training of Support Personnel

As the product evolves, so should the training of support staff. A Product Manager's role is to ensure that updates, new features, and known issues are communicated to support teams, fostering a synergy between product team and customer support.

3.8 Crisis Management

No product is immune to crises, such as outages or security breaches. Product Managers should collaborate with support and Public Relations teams to draft crisis management procedures, ensuring transparency and promptness in communication.

3.9 Data Privacy and Security

In an era of data breaches, ensuring the privacy and security of user interactions is paramount. Product Managers should work with legal, infrastructure and InfoSec teams to ensure compliance with data protection regulations.

3.10 Learning from Customer Requests

Arguably, one of a Product Managers most crucial roles is to channel feedback from support to product development. By understanding recurring issues, assessing their criticality, and prioritizing them, Product Managers can continuously refine the product, aligning it more closely with user needs.

26

Product Evolution

The evolution of products is a journey that intertwines innovation, market demands, and technological advancements with consumer needs.

At its core, product evolution is the process of a product changing and adapting over time. This can be as simple as improving a product's design for user comfort or as complex as integrating cutting-edge technologies to enhance its functionalities.

1. Key Drivers of Product Evolution

1.1 Technological Advancements

With every leap in technology, products evolve. The transition from landline phones to mobile phones and further to smartphones with touch capabilities exemplifies this shift. As technology becomes more advanced, it provides opportunities for products to offer more to their users.

Illustration 19: The Netflix Pivot

In the early 2000s, Netflix faced a significant challenge as its DVD rental business was threatened by the rise of online streaming services and piracy. The company realized that to survive, it needed to adapt and innovate its business model.

One key strategy Netflix employed was to focus on re-engaging its existing customer base. They introduced a streaming service that allowed subscribers to instantly watch movies and TV shows online, in addition to receiving DVDs by mail. This move not only appealed to existing customers but also attracted a new audience of digital-savvy consumers.

1.2 Changing Consumer Needs

As societies and cultures evolve, so do the needs and desires of consumers. For example, as health consciousness has grown, many food and beverage companies have adapted their products to be healthier or cater to specific dietary needs.

1.3 Market Competition

In a competitive market, brands are always on the lookout for ways to differentiate themselves. This often drives rapid product evolution as companies strive to outdo each other.

1.4 Environmental and Societal Concerns

As global awareness about environmental sustainability grows, products evolve to reduce their carbon footprint or become more eco-friendly. An example is the evolution of cars from gasoline-powered to electric.

2. Evolving In-house Products for Market

Organizations often develop internal products to enhance operational efficiency, streamline processes, or meet specific internal needs. However, there are instances when these internal solutions have the potential to be transformed into marketable products, offering value to external customers and generating additional revenue streams.

> **Illustration 20:** The Slack Story
>
> Originally, Slack started as an internal communication tool[1] for a gaming company called Tiny Speck. However, the company noticed that the tool was more popular and useful than the game itself. They pivoted to focus on Slack as a standalone product, targeting businesses and teams for communication and collaboration. This pivot allowed Slack to capitalize on the growing need for efficient workplace communication tools and became one of the leading platforms in the market.

Let us delve into the process of taking an internal product to market, exploring the reasons why this transition is worth considering, the stages involved, the specific tasks for a Product Manager, and the collaborative efforts required from various teams.

2.1 In-house Products v/s For-market Products

In-house products and for-market products serve distinct purposes within organizations. Understanding the differences between these two types of products is essential for effective Product Management and portfolio management. Let us examine the characteristics and focus areas of In-house and For-market products.

In-house Products

In-house products are developed to address specific internal needs and improve operational efficiencies within an organization. These products are often treated as projects and are tracked as part of a project portfolio. The primary focus of in-house products is to minimize costs and streamline processes, enabling smoother operations and resource optimization.

Since in-house products are designed for internal use, they may not undergo the same level of usability scrutiny and market-driven decision-making as for-market products. Instead, they are driven by the organization's unique requirements and desired outcomes. The success of in-house products is typically measured by their ability to deliver cost savings, improve productivity, and enhance overall operational effectiveness.

Examples of in-house products include customized software solutions for internal teams, process automation tools, and internal communication platforms. These products have a direct impact on internal workflows, employee productivity, and operational efficiencies.

For-market Products:

For-market products, on the other hand, are developed to capture market share and generate revenue for the organization. They are tracked as part of the product portfolio, which focuses on managing a range of products targeted at external customers. The success of for-market products is measured by their ability to attract customers, generate sales, and contribute to the organization's revenue streams.

Unlike in-house products, for-market products undergo market analysis, customer research, and competitive positioning. The emphasis is on understanding market needs, identifying customer pain points, and delivering value that resonates with the target audience. These make for-market products much better than In-house products in most aspects.

2.2 Why Take In-house Products to Market?

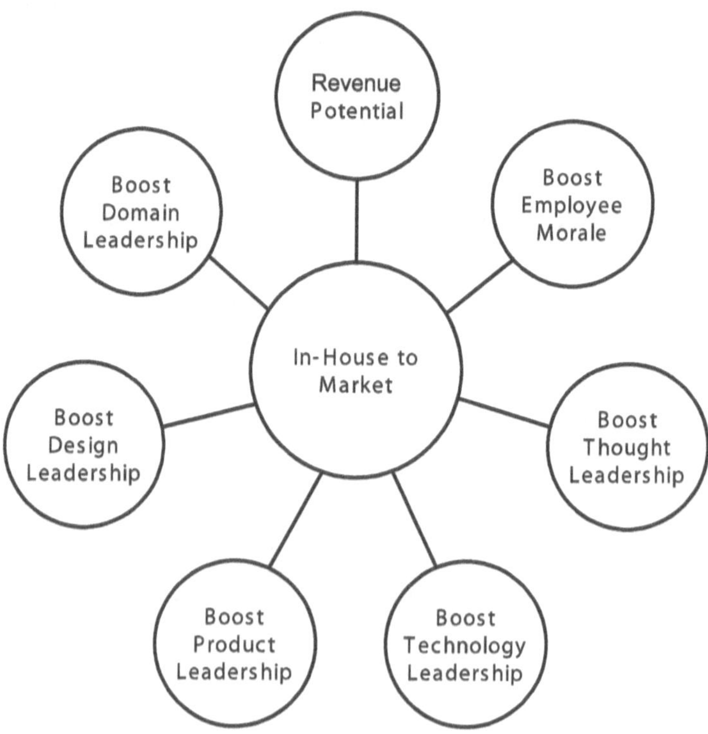

Fig 73: Reason to Take In-house Product to Market

Taking an in-house product to the market offers several benefits for organizations. While the initial development of the product may have been intended for internal use, exploring its potential for external market adoption can yield numerous advantages.

Here are some key benefits of taking an in-house product to market.

1. **Revenue Potential:** By taking an in-house product to the market, organizations have the opportunity to generate additional revenue streams. What was originally developed to address internal needs can now be packaged and sold to external customers, tapping into new markets and revenue potential. This revenue can contribute to the organization's financial growth and sustainability.

2. **Boost Employee Morale:** When employees witness their in-house product being brought to market, it boosts their morale and instills a sense of pride and ownership. It validates their efforts and expertise, showing that their work has value beyond the internal scope. This recognition can enhance employee motivation, engagement, and loyalty.

3. **Boost Thought Leadership:** Taking an in-house product to market can position the organization as a thought leader in its industry. It demonstrates the organization's ability to identify and solve industry challenges, showcasing its innovative thinking and problem-solving capabilities. Thought leadership enhances the organization's reputation and can attract potential customers, partners, and talent.

4. **Boost Technology Leadership:** Bringing an in-house product to the market provides an opportunity to showcase the organization's technological capabilities. It demonstrates proficiency in developing cutting-edge solutions that address market needs. This boosts the organization's technology leadership positioning and can attract attention from industry influencers, investors, and partners.

5. **Boost Product Leadership:** Taking an in-house product to the market allows the organization to showcase its product thinking capabilities. It demonstrates an understanding of market trends,

customer needs, and the ability to develop products that meet those requirements. This leadership in product thinking can differentiate the organization from competitors and attract customers seeking innovative solutions.

6. **Boost Design Leadership:** By bringing an in-house product to the market, organizations can highlight their design leadership. It showcases their commitment to user-centric design, seamless user experiences, and aesthetically pleasing products. Design leadership can enhance the product's market appeal, attract a broader customer base, and differentiate the organization from competitors.

7. **Boost Domain Leadership:** Taking an in-house product to the market allows organizations to establish themselves as leaders in the business domain of the product. It showcases their deep understanding of the specific industry, vertical or domain in which the product operates. This leadership can open doors to collaborations, partnerships, and industry recognition, further enhancing the organization's market position.

2.3 Five Questions to Validate the Market Potential of an In-house Product

To determine the market potential of an in-house product, Product Managers should ask themselves the following key questions:

1. **Who else will buy this?** Product Managers need to identify potential buyers beyond their organization. By naming likely buyers, Product Managers can gain insights into the target market and understand the demand for the product. This exercise helps broaden the perspective and highlights the potential customer base.

2. **What other options will they reject to buy this?** Understanding the existing alternatives and competing products in the market is crucial. Product Managers should identify similar products or solutions already available to potential buyers, including the option for custom-built solutions. This analysis helps determine

the unique selling points (USPs) and differentiators of the in-house product.

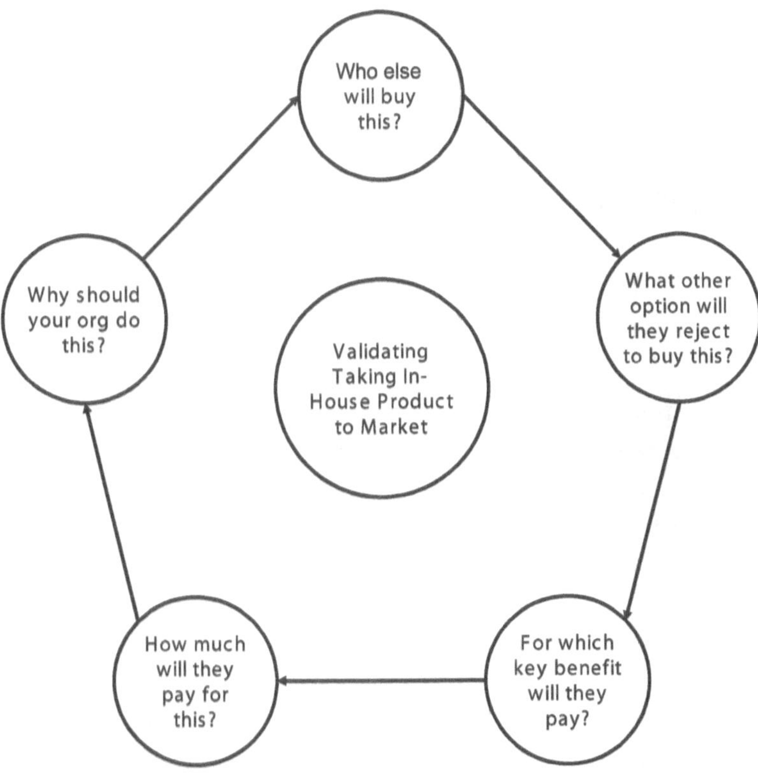

Fig 74: Validating Market Value of In-house Products

3. **For which key benefit will they pay?** Product Managers need to clearly define the key benefit or value proposition that the in-house product offers to potential buyers. This could be a specific problem it solves, a significant improvement it brings, or a unique advantage it provides. Identifying the primary value proposition helps in crafting compelling messaging and positioning for the product.

4. **How much will they pay for this?** Pricing plays a vital role in determining the market potential of a product. Product Managers should conduct market research, analyze competitor pricing, and consider the perceived value of the in-house product

to determine a preliminary pricing strategy. Exploring different pricing models and conducting pricing experiments can help gauge the willingness of customers to pay for the product.

5. **Why should your organization support this effort?** Product Managers need to articulate a strong reason why their organization should support taking the in-house product to the market. This could involve showcasing the revenue potential, growth opportunities, market demand, or strategic alignment with the organization's goals. Analyzing the potential benefits and aligning them with the organization's objectives will help gain support and resources for the product's market validation and subsequent launch.

By addressing these five questions, Product Managers can assess the market potential of their in-house product. The insights gained from this exercise will guide product strategy, market positioning, pricing decisions, and internal advocacy for the product's market validation and successful launch.

2.4 Six Steps of the Evolution

The process of transitioning an in-house product to a for-market product involves several stages, each increasing in complexity. It is important to acknowledge that an external product will be exponentially more complex compared to its in-house version. However, there is also an element of unlearning involved, where certain aspects of what has been built and learned need to be reconsidered. Let's explore the six steps of this evolution.

1. **Unlearn:** It is essential to let go of preconceived notions and approaches that may have worked in the past. Embracing a mindset of experimentation and openness allows for new possibilities to emerge. By unlearning, product teams can approach the market with a fresh perspective and avoid potential pitfalls in future crises.

2. **Re-Analyze:** The next step is to re-analyze the product in the context of the broader market. This involves revisiting the five

questions mentioned earlier and diving deep into the product's purpose, value proposition, and market fit. By taking a holistic view and considering the needs and preferences of the target market, Product Managers can refine their product strategy and align it with market demands.

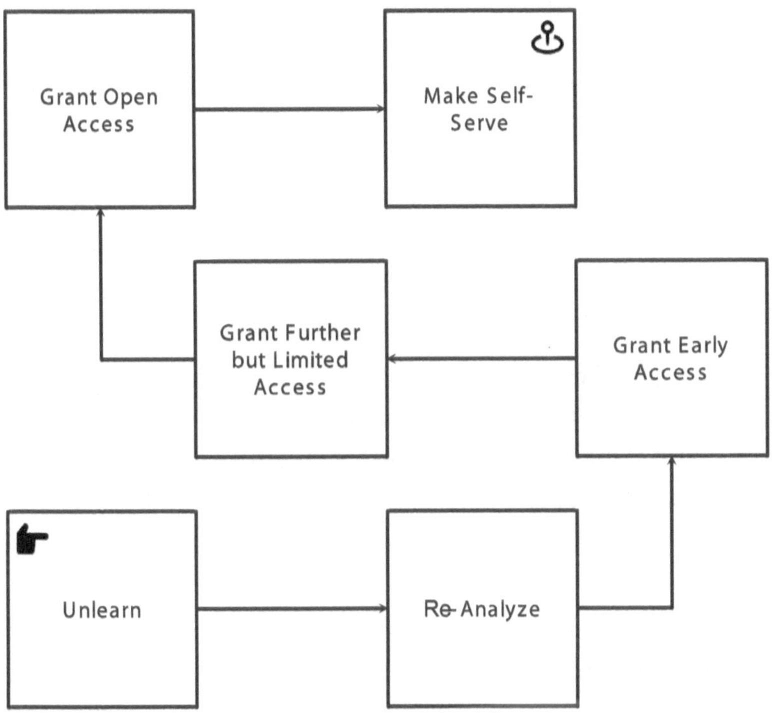

Fig 75: Taking In-house Product to Market in 6 Steps

3. **Grant Early Access:** Once the product has been re-analyzed, test hypotheses and gather feedback by granting early access to key personas within the target customer segment. This allows Product Managers to validate assumptions, understand user needs, and fine-tune the product based on real-world usage. Early access provides an opportunity to refine the product's features, user experience, and value proposition before a wider release.

4. **Grant Further but Limited Access:** Building on the insights gained from early access, the next step is to grant limited access

to a larger audience that represents the key customer segment. This expands the scope of testing and enables Product Managers to gather broader feedback and validate the product's market appeal. It helps in identifying any potential barriers to adoption and understanding the scalability requirements of the product.

5. **Grant Open Access:** The final step is to open access to the product to anyone keen to use it. This stage brings forth a significant increase in complexity compared to the previous steps. The product will now face a diverse range of users, each with unique needs and motivations. Product Managers must be prepared to address a wider set of use cases, support a larger user base, and adapt to unforeseen scenarios. This stage requires robust infrastructure, scalability, and a user-centric approach to accommodate the varying requirements of different users.

6. **Make Self-Serve:** The ultimate goal is to reach a stage where the product can be offered on a self-serve basis, typically through pricing plans. However, it is important not to prematurely estimate or guess this stage. It should be planned for and evaluated based on the product's maturity, market response, and organizational readiness.

By following these six steps, product teams can navigate the evolution from an in-house product to a market-ready product. Each stage brings its own set of challenges and complexities, but with a strategic approach and an openness to unlearn and relearn, the product can successfully transition to the external market, catering to a wider audience and unlocking its full potential.

The following sample roadmap of what needs to be accomplished in each stage can be a good starting point for a Product Manager:

	Unlearn	Re-Analyze	Grant Early Access	Grant Further Access	Grant Open Access	Make Self-Serve
Product	• New Product-Market Fit • New Product Vision • Non-Transferable Components Identification • Competition Analysis • Decoupling Policy	• New Product Management Canvas • Clear Pricing Policy • Tech & Architecture Reassessment	• MVP • Key Analytics • FAQs • Licensing • Bugs and Feedback Mechanism	• Rebuild ecosystem • Piracy & Security • Discounting • E-commerce & Buying • Basic Role Management • Crash Analytics	• Full Role Management • Social Media Support • Incentivise Usage / feedback • Bundling / Unbundling • Usage Analytics & Data	• Revenue Analytics • Fully enabled self-discovery • Automations
Design	• Branding • Design Language	• User Flow • User Experience • New Branding	• User Research based Improvements	• White-labeling	• User Research based Improvements	• User Research based Improvements
Support	• Existing channels Analysis • New Channel Exploration	• Channel prioritization	• Channels • TechNotes, Gotchas	• Build KB based on issues / queries	• Proactive additions to the Knowledge Base	• Social connects • Domain-related additions to Knowledge Base
Marketing	• Decoupling Policy • Decoupling Campaign Planning	• Advocacy • Elevator pitch	• Periodic updates	• Brand value • Competitive differentiation • Power-use updates	• Advertising • Social media engagement • Position papers	• Thought Leadership • RoI-driven marketing and advertising
Commercials	• New P&L model	• Pricing strategy	• Default pricing even if ₹0	• Buy various configs even if discounted	• Variants & packages based pricing	• Easy buy-based access to options
Org	• New Stakeholders	• Rejig Various Team	• Setup Marketing Team	• Setup Support Team	• Setup Sales Team • Setup ProductOps Team	• Setup BizOps Team

able 35: Sample Roadmap of Evolution from In-house to For Market

3. Digital Transformation

Digital transformation is a holistic change process where businesses integrate modern digital technologies into all areas of their operations, fundamentally changing how they operate and deliver value to their customers. It goes beyond mere technology adoption; it's about changing the entire way an organization operates and delivers value.

However, a chasm often emerges between the transformative vision set by CDOs/CIOs and the enduring practices of 'Business As Usual.' Bridging this gap requires a grounded strategy that marries visionary objectives with actionable steps.

One major stumbling block for digital transformation is the disconnect between strategy developers and implementers. All too frequently, these teams operate in silos, lacking collaborative planning. The rush to jump into the technical aspects without proper alignment exacerbates the divide.

1. This disconnect manifests in the following challenges:

2. Misaligned KPIs dictate the perceived value of the developed software and systems.

3. The end product often deviates from the strategic intent.

An erosion of trust emerges between business and technology factions.

3.1 Achieving Digital Fluency

Wherever an organization may be in their digital transformation journey, their success hinges on the adoption of key digital capabilities, described as Digital Fluency Model.[1]

Frictionless Operating Model

Streamline operations to maximize value delivery by leveraging advanced technology strategies, evolutionary organizational ecology, and adaptive leadership styles.

Product Managers can contribute by identifying bottlenecks and inefficiencies in current processes and working with cross-functional teams to streamline operations.

Example: If customer support tickets are taking too long to resolve, the Product Manager might propose implementing a self-service portal or chatbot to automate common inquiries.

Platform Strategy

Ensure your architecture is agile enough to align with your business strategy. This is achieved by exposing core business capabilities as easily consumable services, providing self-service access to data, employing evolutionary architecture patterns, and utilizing advanced delivery infrastructure.

Product Managers can contribute by understanding the organization's strategic goals and ensuring that the platform architecture supports these goals.

Example: If the organization's goal is to expand into new markets, the Product Manager might prioritize the development of a scalable platform that can easily support new regions and languages. Product Managers can use Hour-Glass model to define MVPs for platforms.

Experience Design & Product Capability

Build modern digital products and experiences through a design-led and data-driven approach, iterating through experimentation.

Product Managers can contribute by working closely with designers and developers to create intuitive and user-friendly digital products and experiences.

Example: If the organization is launching a new mobile app, the Product Manager might collaborate with the design team to create a seamless onboarding process for new users.

Intelligence-Driven Decision Making

Establish an organizational infrastructure for leveraging all data assets, including capturing, storing, processing, and self-service exposure of data in a simple, secure, and efficient manner.

Product Managers can contribute by advocating for the use of data analytics and insights to drive decision-making.

Example: The Product Manager might work with the data analytics team to identify patterns in customer behavior that can inform product development and marketing strategies.

Engineering Culture and Delivery Mindset

Execution is key to realizing even the most brilliant business strategies. Technology-driven organizations excel at execution by utilizing modern software development practices.

Product Managers can contribute by promoting a culture of continuous improvement and innovation within the engineering team.

Example: The Product Manager can organize regular hackathons or innovation workshops to encourage engineers to explore new ideas and technologies.

3.2 Four Essential Steps to Achieve Digital Transformation

After defining the desired "to-be" state of key digital capabilities, Product Managers play a pivotal role in transforming legacy business processes and systems. They collaborate with cross-functional teams to modernize existing processes, develop new business processes, and create the necessary systems to support these changes.

For organizations embarking on a robust digital transformation journey, the following steps are imperative:

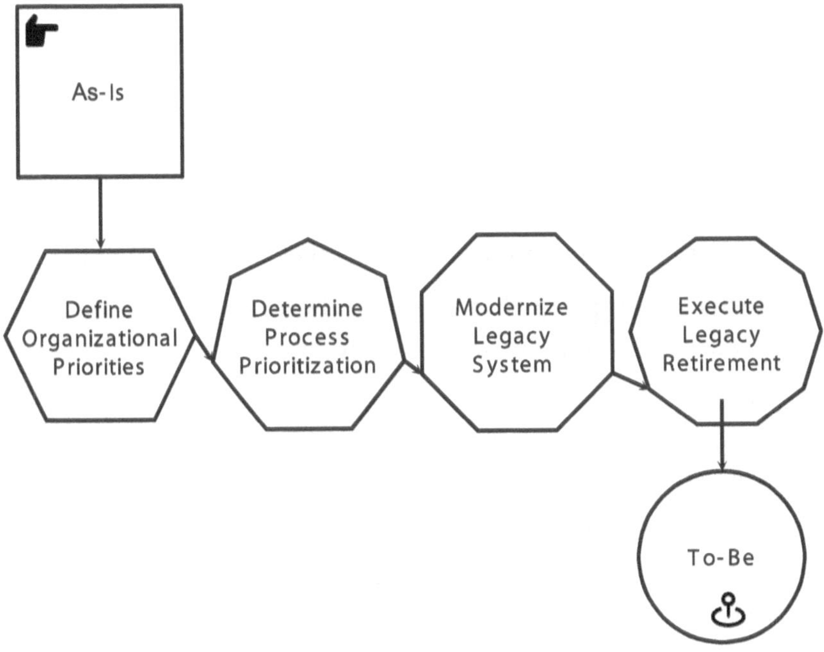

Fig 76: Digital Transformation in 4 Simple Steps

Define Organizational Priorities

1. Product Managers can contribute to the establishment of a clear vision and articulate specific business goals. Their key activities include:

2. **Stakeholder Workshops**: Organize and facilitate sessions with stakeholders to align on the digital transformation vision and objectives. Building Elevator Pitch can help arrive at and communicate the vision.

3. **Requirement Gathering**: Collaborate with different departments to gather requirements and identify the expected outcomes of the transformation.

Market Analysis: Study market trends, user preferences, and competitive analysis to ensure that the organization's digital vision remains relevant and competitive. Product Managers can use tools like Competition Analysis Canvas or do a SWOT analysis.

Determine Process Prioritization

1. Product Managers can contribute to the development of a strategy to sequence the transformation of business processes based on their significance and impact. Their key activities include:

2. **Process Mapping**: Understand and document existing business processes to pinpoint areas needing transformation.

3. **Impact Analysis**: Assess the potential impact of transforming each process on the overall business, both in the short term and long term.

Feedback Loops: Create channels for continuous feedback from users and stakeholders to ensure that prioritization remains aligned with evolving business needs.

Modernize Legacy Systems

1. Product Managers can contribute to the adoption of a systematic approach to update legacy systems, focusing on each business process in turn. Their key activities include:

2. **Technical Evaluation**: Collaborate with the tech team to evaluate the current state of legacy systems and identify challenges and opportunities for modernization.

3. **Integration Planning**: Plan how new systems will integrate with existing systems, platforms, and data architectures.

User Testing: Organize user acceptance testing sessions for modernized processes and systems, ensuring that they meet user needs and expectations.

Retire Legacy Systems

1. Product Managers can contribute to designing a strategy to phase out and decommission outdated systems efficiently. Their key activities include:

2. **Retirement Roadmap**: Create a clear timeline and plan for retiring legacy systems to avoid operational disruptions.

3. **Data Migration Planning**: Collaborate with technical teams to ensure a smooth transition of data from legacy systems to new platforms.

Communication: Continuously update stakeholders on the progress of legacy retirement, addressing concerns and managing expectations.

A Product Manager not only oversees the product's evolution but also ensures that the transformation aligns with business objectives, user needs, and technological capabilities. Their role becomes pivotal in bridging gaps, ensuring alignment, and driving the transformation forward efficiently. They take the plans and convert them into actionable requirements.

3.3 Metrics Driven Approach

Misaligned Key Performance Indicators (KPIs) can lead to a skewed perception of the value of developed software and systems in a digital transformation journey. When KPIs are not aligned with the overarching business goals and outcomes, they may incentivize behaviors that do not necessarily contribute to the desired business impact.

Engineering Excellence to Business Outcomes (EEBO) Metrics offer a more comprehensive and effective approach to guiding digital transformation. Unlike traditional metrics that focus on technical aspects like velocity or cycle time, EEBO metrics bridge the gap between engineering efforts and tangible business outcomes. They provide a clearer picture of how engineering practices impact the overall success of the business.

EEBO Metrics evaluate software development quality, the deployment process, and progress towards desired business outcomes. They help in understanding the value of engineering excellence by measuring its direct impact on business goals such as user satisfaction, time to market, and revenue growth. By adopting EEBO metrics, organizations can ensure that their digital transformation efforts are focused on delivering real business value.

4. Legacy Modernization

Legacy modernization is about updating or replacing outdated systems, while digital transformation is a more profound, organization-wide initiative that leverages digital technologies to drive business value. Thus, Legacy Modernization is a key part of Digital Transformation.

Legacy systems refer to old methods, technologies, or applications that were developed and deployed in the past and are still in use today. They may have once been state-of-the-art, but over time have become outdated compared to newer technologies.

4.1 Characteristics of Legacy Systems

1. **Age**: Typically, these systems have been in use for many years or even decades.

2. **Lack of Vendor Support**: Many legacy systems might no longer be supported by the original vendors.

3. **Limited Interoperability**: Such systems may not easily integrate with newer technologies.

4. **Operational Risk**: Due to outdated technology or unsupported platforms, these systems can pose security and operational risks.

Absence of In-depth Knowledge: Most often, the team that built these systems have either moved to newer roles or other organizations. It is also not uncommon that there is lack of documentation and there is hardly anyone with deep knowledge of the codebase or the architecture.

1. 4.2 Benefits of Legacy Modernization

2. **Operational Efficiency**: Modern systems operate faster and more efficiently than their legacy counterparts.

3. **Risk Reduction**: Updating systems means addressing vulnerabilities, thereby reducing security risks.

4. **Enhanced User Experience**: Modern systems are designed with current user expectations in mind, leading to a better user experience.

Scalability: Modernized systems are built to handle growth and can scale according to business needs.

4.3 Product Manager's Role in Legacy Modernization

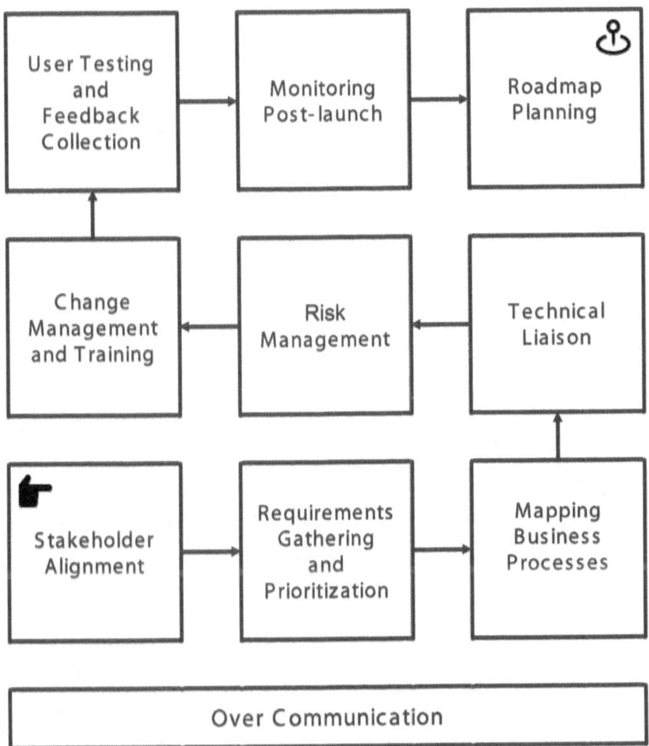

Fig 77: Key Activities of a Product Manager during Legacy Modernization

Legacy modernization projects are complex endeavors that require a multi-faceted approach to ensure that current business needs are met while setting the stage for future growth and technological advancements. Product Managers play a pivotal role in this process due to their unique position at the intersection of business, technology, and user needs.

Following are the key activities of a Product Manager during Legacy Modernization.

1. Stakeholder Alignment

2. **Key Activity**: Conduct workshops and meetings with stakeholders to understand and align on the dependency, objectives, risks, and benefits of the modernization effort.

Key Outcome: Ensures that all parties, from top management to technical teams, share a common vision and purpose.

1. **Requirements Gathering and Prioritization**

2. **Key Activity**: Document existing functionalities of the legacy system and gather new requirements from users and stakeholders. Prioritize these requirements based on business needs, technical feasibility, and user impact.

Key Outcome: Lays the foundation for what features and functionalities the new system should have.

1. **Mapping Business Processes**

2. **Key Activity**: Understand and document how the legacy system fits into current business processes. Use tools like Ecosystem Mapping Canvas to map its ecosystem.

Key Outcome: Helps in ensuring the modernized system integrates seamlessly with the business operations and even streamlines them if possible.

1. **Technical Liaison**

2. **Key Activity**: Work closely with the technical team to ensure that the technical architecture and design of the new system meet the requirements. Be it the Strangler Pattern,[A] Gartner's 5R,[A] or Amazon's 6R[A] approach the CIO or the Technology Leadership opts for, bringing in the perspective of end users, business benefit, and regulatory concerns.

Key Outcome: Bridges the gap between business needs and technical execution.

1. **Risk Management**

2. **Key Activity**: Identify potential risks associated with the migration,

be it data loss, downtime, or system incompatibilities, and work on mitigation strategies.

Key Outcome: Ensures a smoother transition from the legacy system to the modernized platform.

1. **Change Management and Training**

2. **Key Activity**: Facilitate training sessions and provide documentation to help users & operations teams transition from the legacy system to the new system.

Key Outcome: Ensures users feel comfortable and confident using the new system, minimizing disruptions.

1. **User Testing and Feedback Collection**

2. **Key Activity**: Organize user acceptance testing (UAT) sessions, gather feedback, and iterate based on this feedback.

Key Outcome: Confirms that the modernized system meets user needs and expectations.

1. **Monitoring Post-launch**

2. **Key Activity**: After the modernized system is launched, continuously monitor its performance, user feedback, and any potential issues.

Key Outcome: Ensures that any post-launch issues are quickly addressed and the system remains aligned with business goals.

1. **Roadmap Planning**

2. **Key Activity**: Based on feedback, changing business needs, and emerging technologies, plan and prioritize future enhancements and features.

Key Outcome: Positions the modernized system for continuous improvement and adaptation to changing business landscapes.

1. **Over Communication**

2. **Key Activity**: Continuously update stakeholders about the progress, risks, and milestones of the modernization project. Err rather than on the side of over communication than withholding in-

formation assuming the stakeholder might not be interested.

Key Outcome: Keeps everyone informed, maintains trust, and ensures alignment throughout the modernization process.

A Product Manager's role during legacy modernization is multifaceted. They act as the glue between different teams, ensuring that the modernized system not only leverages the latest technology but also aligns with business goals and offers optimal user experience. Their involvement can often make the difference between a successful modernization effort and one that falls short of expectations.

5. Seven Key Interactions During the Evolution

1. The Product Manager's role is pivotal in the evolution of an in-house product to a for-market offering. Throughout this process, the Product Manager will engage with various teams and stakeholders to ensure a successful transition. Here are seven key interactions that the Product Manager will need to focus on besides the software development teams.

2. **Design Team:** Engage with the design team to reassess the user flow and experience of the product. Collaborate on refining the user interface, optimizing the user journey, and enhancing the overall usability of the product. By working closely with the design team, the Product Manager can ensure that the product aligns with market expectations and delivers an exceptional user experience.

3. **Product Team:** Collaborate with the product team to redo the Product Management Canvas. Revisit the product strategy, goals, target market, and value proposition to align them with the market-oriented approach. Work together to refine the product roadmap, prioritize features, and ensure that the product meets the evolving needs of the market.

4. **Quality Team:** Involve the quality team in the process to ensure that the product will function seamlessly when opened up to a wider audience. Collaborate on testing methodologies, quality

assurance processes, and performance optimization. Address any potential scalability or performance issues to ensure a smooth user experience.

5. **Security Team:** Engage the security team to analyze the risks associated with opening up the product to the market. Collaborate on identifying potential vulnerabilities, implementing robust security measures, and ensuring data protection. By working closely with the security team, the Product Manager can mitigate risks and build trust with users.

6. **Marketing Team:** Collaborate with the marketing team on re-branding efforts and developing comprehensive marketing strategies. Work together to create compelling collateral, articles, blogs, advertisements, and other promotional materials that effectively communicate the value proposition of the product. Ensure that the marketing efforts are aligned with the product's positioning and target audience.

7. **Support Team:** Get the support team ready to provide exceptional assistance to users. Collaborate on training support staff, developing knowledge bases, and implementing efficient support channels. It is crucial to ensure that the support team is well-equipped to address user queries, resolve issues promptly, and deliver a positive customer experience.

Sales Team: Collaborate closely with the sales team to enable them to bring in bookings and generate revenues. Provide the necessary product knowledge, sales enablement materials, and ongoing support to empower the sales team to effectively position and sell the product in the market. Align sales strategies with the product's value proposition and competitive advantage.

Evolving products for the market is a complex and intricate process that requires careful planning and collaboration across various teams. By embracing these steps and fostering strong cross-functional partnerships, Product Managers can navigate the complexities and challenges of Product Evolution.

27

"Lights on" Maintenance Mode

After years of market domination, some products may no longer be relevant in a larger context or competitive in the market. However, there are still few paying customers who rely on these products. This is where the concept of maintenance mode comes into play. In maintenance mode, the product team's primary objective is to keep the "lights on" by providing occasional bug fixes and security patches to support the existing customer base.

1. Why Products in Maintenance Mode Matter

1. Products in maintenance mode may not be the primary focus of the organization anymore, but they still hold value. Here are a few reasons why they matter:

2. **Guaranteed Revenue Stream:** Even though the revenue generated by products in maintenance mode might be relatively low, it still provides a guaranteed stream of income until the contracted date. This can contribute to the financial stability of the organization.

Customer Relationships: Customers who continue to use products in maintenance mode have already established a business relationship. By maintaining and supporting these products, the organization can continue to build customer trust and loyalty. This positive experience can also open doors for introducing newer products or value propositions to these customers.

2. How Product Managers Can Make a Difference

Product Managers of a product in maintenance mode have the opportunity to make a meaningful impact. Here are a few ways in which a Product Manager can add value.

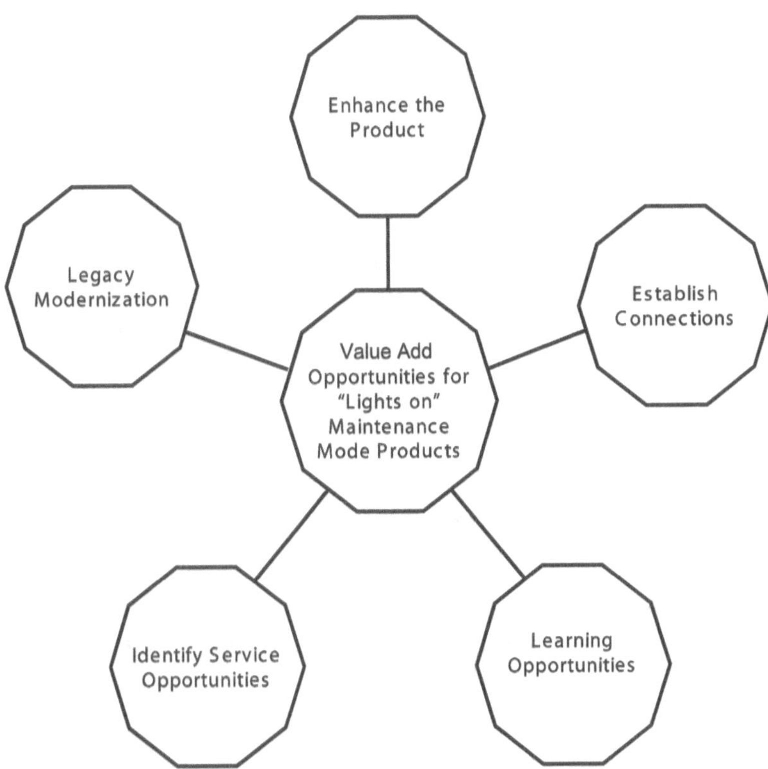

Fig 78: Value Add during "Lights on" Maintenance Mode Phase

1. **Enhance the Product:** While the product may be in maintenance mode, the Product Manager can still introduce performance improvements, security enhancements, and even add new features based on customer feedback. By doing so, the Product Manager ensures that the product does not become abandonware and continues to meet the needs of the customers.

2. **Establish Connections:** Through the team's work with the product in maintenance mode, the Product Manager can establish connections within the customer's organization. Use these connections to open doors for other product sales or collaborations. This not only expands their own network but also helps in promoting other products within the customer's organization.

3. **Learning Opportunities:** Products in maintenance mode often have lower intensity needs, making them an ideal environment for new team members to learn the domain. As a Product Manager, you can facilitate knowledge transfer and provide opportunities for new employees to learn the domain.

4. **Identify Service Opportunities:** Evaluate the existing product and its components to see if any of them can be repurposed and offered as a service to support newer products. This allows for leveraging existing assets and maximizing their value.

Legacy Modernization: Explore if the knowledge and expertise gained from managing the product in maintenance mode can be utilized to offer services like legacy modernization. This can open up new avenues for the organization and cater to customers looking to migrate from older systems.

Product Managers for products in maintenance mode should not feel discouraged or undervalued. Managing such products can offer intellectual challenges and growth opportunities if framed properly. By actively maintaining and improving these products, leveraging customer relationships, and exploring service opportunities, Product Managers can make a significant difference and contribute to the overall success of the organization.

28

Product Retirement

Product Managers should aim to ensure a smooth and respectful retirement process for the software product while minimizing disruption to users and providing support during the transition phase.

1. Here are some common methods that can be followed are:

2. **End of Life (EOL)**: An official End of Life date for the product is decided and announced. After this date, the product will no longer receive updates, patches, or support, making it potentially unsafe and unreliable to continue using.

3. **Lesson Learned or Post-Mortem Blog**: The Product Manager writes a blog or a post-mortem document sharing their experiences, lessons learned, and insights gained during the product's life cycle. This can benefit the community and help others avoid similar pitfalls in their projects. This may be accompanied by documentation and a knowledge base related to the retired product archived or kept accessible for reference by users who might still find it helpful.

Illustration 21: Story on Gungroo Software Pvt Ltd

When I shut down my startup, Gungroo, I wrote a long blog post on the journey, the pivots, many but small successes, decisions to kill products, and finally shut down the shutters.

The blog is now available at my site, dinker.in.

https://bit.ly/failing-since

1. **Open Sourcing**: In some cases, the product may be open-sourced, allowing the community or interested developers to continue maintaining and improving it even after the official support ends.

Illustration 22: Sun Microsystems and OpenOffice

The story of Sun Microsystems and OpenOffice is a prime example of a company open-sourcing a product and breathing new life into it.

In the late 1990s, Sun's StarOffice productivity suite faced dominance from Microsoft Office. While technically superior, StarOffice struggled with market share and profitability.

In 2000, Sun made a bold move: they open-sourced StarOffice, creating OpenOffice. This meant releasing the source code publicly, allowing anyone to freely modify and distribute it.

The decision was met with skepticism, but the results were astounding. OpenOffice quickly gained traction, especially in educational institutions and budget-conscious organizations. Its open nature attracted a global community of developers, leading to constant improvement and localization for various languages.

OpenOffice became a strong competitor to Microsoft Office,[1], capturing significant market share and pushing innovation in the productivity suite space. It also spurred the creation of other open-source office suites like LibreOffice, further solidifying the open-source alternative.

---

1. **Migration or Replacement**: Sometimes, a product is retired because it's being replaced with a newer version or an entirely different product. Users are guided through a migration process to transition to the new offering seamlessly.

2. **Product Discontinuation with No Support**: In some instances, the product may be discontinued with no direct replacement or guidance on alternatives.

3. **Data Export Options**: When retiring a software product that stores user data, they often provide users with an option to export their data before it is permanently removed.

Appendix

5Rs of Application Migration

Gartner's 5Rs of application migration[1] is a framework designed to assist organizations in determining the best strategy for moving applications to the cloud. Each "R" represents a different migration strategy. Here are Gartner's 5Rs:

1. **Rehost**: Also known as "lift-and-shift," this involves moving applications without any modifications. It's basically taking the application as it is and running it in the cloud. This is often the quickest way to migrate, but it may not fully exploit the benefits of the cloud.

2. **Refactor**: With this strategy, you may make some adjustments to the application, such as minor code or configuration changes, to take advantage of cloud-native features. The core architecture remains the same, but the application can utilize some of the cloud platform's capabilities.

3. **Revise**: Here, significant portions of the application are modified before moving them to the cloud. This might involve re-architecting a part of the application or adopting newer frameworks and libraries that are more cloud-friendly.

4. **Rebuild**: This is a more drastic approach where the application is completely redesigned and re-architected using cloud-native capabilities. The application is effectively rebuilt from the ground up, taking full advantage of the cloud's capabilities, but this also requires the most effort.

5. **Replace**: Instead of moving the application, it's decided that it's more feasible to replace it with a commercial Software as a Service (SaaS) application. This means discarding the old application and adopting a new, usually cloud-native, solution that meets the same business needs.

It's essential for businesses to carefully consider which strategy is best for each of their applications based on factors like business requirements, technical feasibility, cost, and expected benefits.

6Rs of Application Migration

Amazon Web Services (AWS) provides a framework for application migration[1] that's often referred to as the "6 R's." These strategies offer guidelines to organizations on how to approach their migration journey to the cloud. Each "R" represents a different migration strategy. Here they are:

1. **Rehost** ("Lift and Shift"): In this strategy, applications are moved to the cloud without making changes. Essentially, it's like picking up the application from your on-premises data center and dropping it in the cloud. This is often the quickest way to migrate.

2. **Replatform** ("Lift, Tinker, and Shift"): This involves making a few cloud optimizations to achieve a tangible benefit, but not changing the core architecture of the application. An example might be moving to a managed database service like Amazon RDS.

3. **Repurchase**: This is about moving to a different product altogether, like shifting from a traditional CRM to a cloud solution such as Salesforce. It's a decision to move to a different product which likely is already cloud-compatible or cloud-native.

4. **Rearchitect**: This is often driven by a strong business need to add features, improve performance, or increase agility that would be difficult to achieve in the application's existing environment. It involves reimagining how the application is architected and developed, often using cloud-native features.

5. **Retire**: During the discovery stage, you might identify IT assets that are no longer useful and can be turned off. This can help save costs both in terms of infrastructure and the operational overhead of maintaining such assets.

6. **Retain**: It might make sense to keep certain applications or workloads in the current environment, either because they're not ready for migration or because they don't have an immediate business justification for migration.

When planning for a migration, organizations will often find that they use a combination of these strategies across their portfolio of applications. The optimal choice often depends on the specific needs and constraints of each application and the overarching business goals.

Active Listening

Active listening is a communication technique that entails fully concentrating on, comprehending, and responding to a speaker, demonstrating a thorough understanding of their message. For Product Managers, who are at the nexus of various teams and stakeholders, mastering active listening is essential to drive product success and build strong, cooperative relationships.

Historically, the concept of active listening can be traced back to Carl Rogers and Richard E. Farson's work in the 1950s in the field of psychology.[1] Their work focused on the power of empathetic listening in human interactions and psychotherapy, highlighting the role of understanding and validating the speaker's feelings. Over the years, the importance of active listening has transcended the realm of therapy and is now considered a critical skill in various fields, including business, education, and conflict resolution.

Active listening is not a passive process; it involves taking an active role in the communication by fully immersing oneself in the speaker's perspective. A listener should not only pay attention to the spoken words but also interpret the speaker's emotions, intentions, and underlying message.

Here are some tips and examples to enhance active listening:

1. **Give Full Attention**: When someone is speaking, give them your undivided attention. Turn off your electronic devices, remove distractions, and focus completely on the speaker.

2. Example: In a team meeting, put your phone away and close your laptop, showing you're fully present and invested in the conversation.

3. **Maintain Eye Contact**: Eye contact signals to the speaker that you are focused on them and their words.

4. Example: In a one-on-one meeting, make a conscious effort to maintain eye contact with the speaker without staring.

5. **Show That You're Listening**: Non-verbal cues such as nodding your head, maintaining a positive facial expression, or leaning in slightly can show the speaker that you're actively engaged.

6. Example: Nod or make appropriate facial expressions when the speaker is making key points, demonstrating that you are tracking their thoughts.

7. **Don't Interrupt**: Wait for the speaker to finish before you respond. Interruptions can derail their train of thought and may make them feel unheard.

8. Example: If you have a question or a point to make, jot it down and bring it up when the speaker has finished their point.

9. **Provide Feedback**: Summarize, paraphrase, and ask questions to ensure you understand the message. This can demonstrate that you've been actively engaged and understand the speaker's point.

10. Example: "If I understand correctly, you're suggesting that we pivot our marketing strategy to focus more on social media?"

11. **Empathize and Validate**: Acknowledge the speaker's feelings and perspectives, even if you don't necessarily agree.

12. Example: "I can see how the delayed timeline might be causing stress for your team."

13. **Avoid Judgment**: Keep an open mind. Listening actively is not about agreeing with the speaker but understanding their perspective.

14. Example: Even if a team member presents an idea that you disagree with, resist the urge to dismiss it outright. Instead, ask more about their rationale and the thought process that led to the idea.

For Product Managers, active listening has become more relevant than ever. As products have grown more complex and multidimensional, so have the team structures and the customer base. Now, Product Managers need to understand the perspectives of different stakeholders, from engineers, designers, and marketers to users from diverse backgrounds. Active listening enables Product Managers to gain a deeper understanding of the needs and wants of these different groups, thereby shaping the product's vision and strategy more effectively.

Digital Personal Data Protection Bill, 2023 (India)

Following is a summary of the Digital Personal Data Protection Bill that was posted on India's government's website.[1]

"The Bill provides for the processing of digital personal data in a manner that recognizes both the rights of the individuals to protect their personal data and the need to process such personal data for lawful purposes and for matters connected therewith or incidental thereto.

1. The Bill protects digital personal data (that is, the data by which a person may be identified) by providing for the following:

    a. The obligations of Data Fiduciaries (that is, persons, companies and government entities who process data) for data processing (that is, collection, storage or any other operation on personal data);

    b. The rights and duties of Data Principals (that is, the person to whom the data relates); and

    c. Financial penalties for breach of rights, duties and obligations.

The Bill also seeks to achieve the following:

    a. Introduce data protection law with minimum disruption while ensuring necessary change in the way Data Fiduciaries process data;

    b. Enhance the Ease of Living and the Ease of Doing Business; and

    c. Enable India's digital economy and its innovation ecosystem.

2. The Bill is based on the following seven principles:

    a. The principle of consented, lawful and transparent use of personal data;

    b. The principle of purpose limitation (use of personal data only for the purpose specified at the time of obtaining consent of the Data Principal);

    c. The principle of data minimisation (collection of only as much personal data as is necessary to serve the specified purpose);

    d. The principle of data accuracy (ensuring data is correct and updated);

    e. The principle of storage limitation (storing data only till it is needed for the specified purpose);

    f. The principle of reasonable security safeguards; and

    g. The principle of accountability (through adjudication of data breaches and breaches of the provisions of the Bill and imposition of penalties for the breaches).

3. The Bill has few other innovative features:

The Bill is concise and SARAL, that is, Simple, Accessible, Rational & Actionable Law as it—

    a. Uses plain language;

    b. Contains illustrations that make the meaning clear;

    c. contains no provisos ("Provided that…"); and

    d. Has minimal cross-referencing.

4. By using the word "she" instead of "he", for the first time it acknowledges women in Parliamentary law-making.

5. The Bill provides for following rights to the individuals:

    a. The right to access information about personal data processed;

    b. The right to correction and erasure of data;

    c. The right to grievance redressal; and

    d. The right to nominate a person to exercise rights in case of death or incapacity.

For enforcing his/her rights, an affected Data Principal may approach the Data Fiduciary in the first instance. In case he/she is not satisfied, he/she can complain against the Data Fiduciary to the Data Protection Board in a hassle-free manner.

6. The Bill provides for following obligations on the data fiduciary:

    a. To have security safeguards to prevent personal data breach;

b. To intimate personal data breaches to the affected Data Principal and the Data Protection Board;

c. To erase personal data when it is no longer needed for the specified purpose;

d. To erase personal data upon withdrawal of consent;

e. To have in place grievance redressal system and an officer to respond to queries from Data Principals; and

f. To fulfill certain additional obligations in respect of Data Fiduciaries notified as Significant Data Fiduciaries, such as appointing a data auditor and conducting periodic Data Protection Impact Assessment to ensure higher degree of data protection.

7. The Bill safeguards the personal data of children also.

a. The Bill allows a Data Fiduciary to process the personal data of children only with parental consent.

b. The Bill does not permit processing which is detrimental to well-being of children or involves their tracking, behavioural monitoring or targeted advertising.

8. The exemptions provided in the Bill are as follows:

a. For notified agencies, in the interest of security, sovereignty, public order, etc.;

b. For research, archiving or statistical purposes;

c. For startups or other notified categories of Data Fiduciaries;

d. To enforce legal rights and claims;

e. To perform judicial or regulatory functions;

f. To prevent, detect, investigate or prosecute offences;

g. To process in India personal data of non-residents under foreign contract;

h. For approved merger, demerger etc.; and

i. To locate defaulters and their financial assets etc.

9. The key functions of the Board are as under:

> a. To give directions for remediating or mitigating data breaches;
>
> b. To inquire into data breaches and complaints and impose financial penalties;
>
> c. To refer complaints for Alternate Dispute Resolution and to accept Voluntary Undertakings from Data Fiduciaries; and

To advise the Government to block the website, app etc. of a Data Fiduciary who is found to repeatedly breach the provisions of the Bill."

Goodhart's Law

Goodhart's Law is a concept introduced by economist Charles Goodhart in the 1970s. It states that "when a measure becomes a target, it ceases to be a good measure."[1] In simpler terms, this means that using a metric as a goal can lead to unintended consequences and distortions in behavior. Chasing the metric becomes the goal rather than achieving the overall outcome.

Why Goodhart's Law Matters

Goodhart's Law is relevant to several areas of life, including business and politics. For example, if an organization sets a sales target for its employees, they may focus solely on achieving that target, even if it means sacrificing quality or customer satisfaction. Similarly, if a government sets a target for reducing crime rates, police officers may be incentivized to focus on low-level offenses instead of tackling more serious crimes.

The Risks of Misusing Metrics

One of the key risks associated with Goodhart's Law is that it can lead to a narrow focus on a specific metric, at the expense of other important factors. This can result in unintended consequences that can be harmful to individuals or organizations. For example, a school that focuses on improving test scores may neglect other aspects of education, such as critical thinking or creativity.

Avoiding the Pitfalls of Metrics

To avoid the pitfalls of Goodhart's Law, it's important to use metrics as a tool for measuring progress, rather than as a target in and of themselves. This means setting goals and targets that are aligned with broader objectives, and using metrics to track progress towards those goals. It also means being mindful of the unintended consequences that can arise from focusing too narrowly on a specific metric.

HEART Framework

The HEART framework is a robust tool in the Product Manager's toolkit. It offers a systematic approach to measure and enhance user experience. By focusing on user-centered metrics, it provides invaluable insights that drive product improvements and align with user needs. As with any framework, its success lies in thoughtful application and regular iteration.

The origins of the HEART framework can be traced back to Google's relentless pursuit of user-centric designs and innovations. Around 2010, Google researchers, including Kerry Rodden, Hilary Hutchinson, and Xin Fu,[1] recognized a gap in the available tools for evaluating user experience. Existing metrics were either too fragmented or didn't holistically represent a product's success from the user's perspective. To address this, they conceptualized the HEART framework. Since its inception, it has been widely adopted within Google and has garnered attention across various industries.

Breaking Down the HEART Framework

The HEART framework categorizes user-centered metrics into five key dimensions:

1. **Happiness**: This measures user attitudes, often gleaned from surveys or feedback mechanisms. It assesses users' satisfaction, perceived ease of use, and net promoter score (NPS). For instance, after interacting with a product feature, how likely are users to recommend it to someone else?

2. **Engagement**: Engagement concerns the depth of user interaction over a certain timeframe. For a social media platform, this might translate to the number of posts shared by users daily. For a digital tool, it could mean the frequency of feature usage.

3. **Adoption**: This refers to the number of new users of a particular product or feature over a specified period. For a Product Manager launching a new feature, tracking adoption can highlight how effectively it's attracting its target users.

4. **Retention**: A direct measure of how many users continue to use the product after their initial experience. It's an indicator of long-term product value. If users aren't returning, it's crucial for Product Managers to identify the reason and iterate accordingly.

5. **Task Success**: This involves metrics like efficiency, effectiveness, and error rate. It evaluates how successfully users can complete specific tasks using the product. For instance, how quickly can a user make a purchase on an e-commerce platform? Or, how often do they encounter errors?

Applying the HEART Framework

For Product Managers, the adoption of the HEART framework requires a systematic approach.

1. **Define Goals**: Begin by establishing clear goals for the product or feature. For example, is the aim to enhance user engagement or increase the adoption rate?

2. **Choose Signals**: Once goals are set, identify signals that indicate whether these goals are being met. If the goal is to boost engagement, a potential signal could be the average time spent by users on the platform.

3. **Determine Metrics**: Based on the signals, select the actual metrics to be tracked. Taking the previous example forward, the metric could be the 'average minutes spent per user per day.'

4. **Iterate**: Like all methodologies, the HEART framework is not a one-size-fits-all solution. Product Managers should regularly revisit and adjust the metrics based on product evolution and feedback.

Likert Scale

The Likert scale is a valuable tool for Product Managers seeking to gather nuanced feedback from users and stakeholders. This scale, developed by psychologist Rensis Likert[1] in 1932, allows respondents to express their opinions or attitudes on a particular topic through a series of statements or questions.

In essence, the Likert scale presents a range of responses, typically from "Strongly Disagree" to "Strongly Agree," enabling participants to indicate the extent to which they agree or disagree with a statement. This format provides a structured way to quantify subjective opinions, making it easier to analyze and interpret the data.

Product Managers can leverage the Likert scale in various ways. For example, when conducting user surveys, they can use Likert-scale questions to assess user satisfaction with specific features or aspects of a product. By analyzing the responses, Product Managers can identify areas for improvement and prioritize product enhancements based on user feedback.

Likert-scale questions can also be used to gauge stakeholder opinions during product development meetings or reviews. By asking stakeholders to rate their agreement with statements about the product roadmap or feature priorities, Product Managers can ensure alignment and address any concerns or misunderstandings early in the process.

Common Scales

Here are some common 5-point scales[2]:

Satisfaction

Very dissatisfied – Dissatisfied – Neither dissatisfied or satisfied – Satisfied – Very satisfied

Likelihood

Very unlikely – Unlikely – Neutral – Likely – Very likely

Level of concern

Very unconcerned – Unconcerned – Neutral – Concerned – Very concerned

Agreement

Strongly disagree – Disagree – Neither agree or disagree – Agree – Strongly agree

Frequency

Never – Rarely – Sometimes – Often – Always

Awareness

Very unaware – Unaware – Neither aware or unaware – Aware – Very aware

Familiarity

Very unfamiliar – Unfamiliar – Somewhat familiar – Familiar – Very familiar

Quality

Very poor – Poor – Acceptable – Good – Very good

Importance

Very unimportant – Unimportant – Neutral – Important – Very important

Example Scenario

> **Scenario 71**: Dear reader, now that you are here, let me use the 'Convenience Sampling' method to seek your feedback using a Likert Scale based survey:
>
> **How satisfied are you with the book as a go-to guide for product life cycle management?**
>
> Very satisfied – Satisfied – Neither dissatisfied or satisfied – Dissatisfied – Very dissatisfied
>
> **This 1-question Survey**
>
> 
>
> https://bit.ly/plcu-likert

Squiggle of Design Process

Damien Newman's "Squiggle" is a visual representation of the design process, illustrating the journey from project initiation to completion. [1] The "Squiggle" captures the messy, non-linear nature of design, particularly in the early stages where uncertainty, exploration, and iterations are common.

Fig 79: Damien Newman's Squiggle[1]

The idea behind the Squiggle is that design doesn't follow a straight and predictable path. Instead, it often starts with a lot of ambiguity. In the beginning, there are many potential solutions and directions the design might take, hence the chaotic squiggling. As the process continues, some of these possibilities are discarded or refined, leading to a clearer direction and eventual solution, represented by the straightening line.

Stages

1. **Beginning**: At the start of a project, the path forward is usually unclear. You might be dealing with an unclear problem statement, limited data, or various challenges that make it difficult to see the way forward. This confusion is shown as a chaotic squiggle.

2. **Research & Synthesis**: As you dive into the project, you begin exploring different avenues, researching, prototyping, and iterating. There's a lot of back-and-forth as you gather information, try out ideas, and adjust based on feedback.

3. **Concept Formation**: As the design process moves forward, some clarity begins to emerge. Decisions are made, certain ideas are favored over others, and the path starts to straighten out.

4. **Completion**: By the end, a clear solution has been reached, and the path forward is straightforward, leading to implementation.

The Squiggle is a helpful reminder that the design process can be chaotic and unpredictable, but that this chaos is a natural part of finding the best solution. It encourages designers to embrace uncertainty and to recognize that clarity often emerges from chaos.

Strangler Pattern

The Strangler Pattern is a design pattern used primarily for software migration. The idea behind this pattern comes from the strangler fig,[1] which is a fig that grows on a host tree, gradually enveloping it and replacing the main tree over time.

When applied to software, the Strangler Pattern is a strategy for migrating from a legacy system to a new system incrementally, rather than trying to rebuild everything from scratch all at once. This can be especially useful when working with large and complex systems that cannot be simply turned off or replaced overnight.

Here's how it works:

1. **Start New alongside Old**: Begin by setting up the new system alongside the existing one.

2. **Redirect Traffic**: As you develop and implement new features or services in the new system, you start to redirect the traffic (or usage) for those particular features from the old system to the new one. This can be done using feature toggles, API gateways, or other mechanisms.

3. **Incremental Migration**: Continue to build out the new system piece by piece, migrating over functionality and redirecting traffic progressively. Over time, more and more of the functionality and traffic will be handled by the new system.

4. **Decommission the Old**: Eventually, the legacy system will have little to no traffic or usage, at which point it can be safely decommissioned and removed.

Benefits of the Strangler Pattern:

1. **Reduces Risk**: By migrating in small increments, you can reduce the risks associated with big bang migrations where everything changes at once.

2. **Immediate Value**: You can release features and improvements in the new system even before the entire system is replaced. This way, users get to see value early and often.

3. **Feedback Loop**: With incremental changes, you can gather feedback more effectively and make necessary adjustments to the new system based on real-world use.

4. **Flexibility**: You are not locked into a long-term migration path. If business needs change or new technology emerges, you can pivot more easily.

In practice, the Strangler Pattern often goes hand in hand with microservices architectures, where individual services can be migrated, replaced, or upgraded independently of others. However, the pattern can also be used in monolithic applications or any other system requiring gradual migration or replacement.

TechRadar

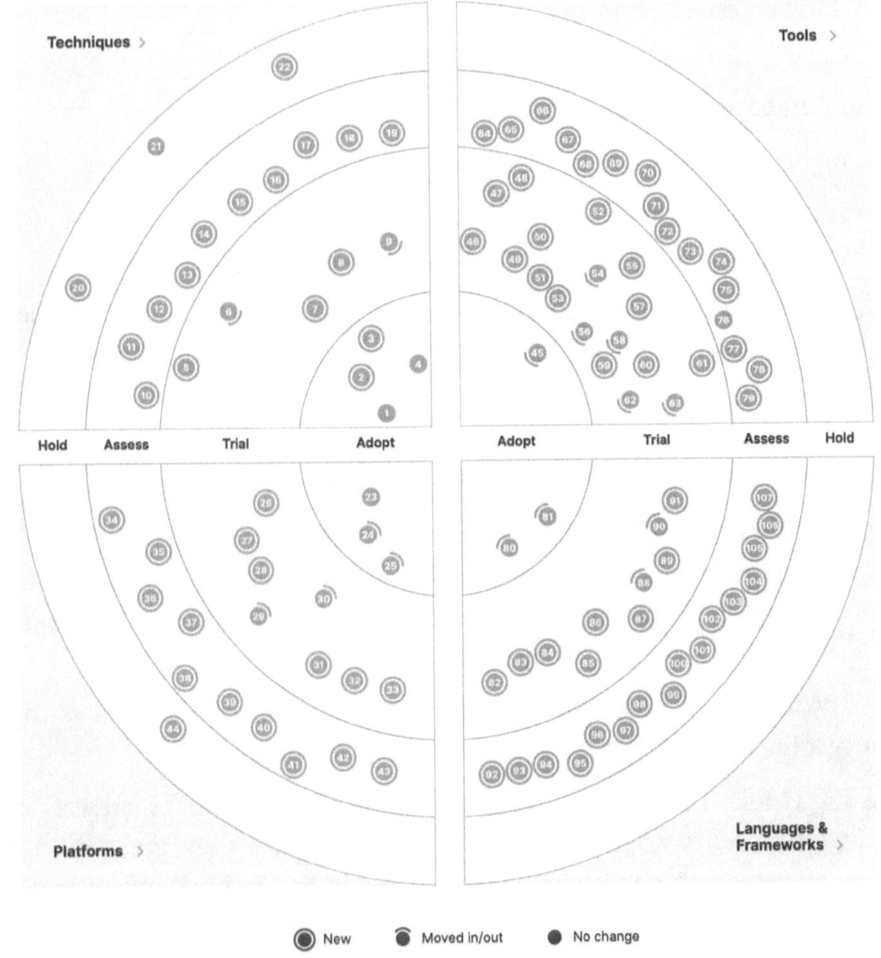

Fig 80: Technology Radar Volume 28

Thoughtworks TechRadar highlights the evolving trends in software development in a succinct and clear format using the analogy of a Radar. Published every six months, it provides an overview of the technologies that Thoughtworks believes are currently relevant in the software industry.

TechRadar aims to help developers and business decision-makers navigate the ever-changing landscape of technology. It provides a snapshot of current technology trends in techniques, platforms, tools, and languages & frameworks.

The Anatomy of the TechRadar

Thoughtworks TechRadar is organized into four main quadrants:

1. **Techniques**: This quadrant focuses on best practices and processes that are being used in software development.

2. **Platforms**: Here, emerging and established platforms that are significant in the current software development scenario are listed.

3. **Tools**: This quadrant showcases various tools that can be utilized by developers to automate processes, test code, or streamline development.

4. **Languages & Frameworks**: This quadrant highlights programming languages and frameworks that are currently trending in the development community.

Within each quadrant, the items are classified into four rings that suggest the level of adoption Thoughtworks recommends:

1. **Hold**: These are technologies that Thoughtworks advises to proceed with caution. It could be because they are currently problematic or are being phased out in favor of better options.

2. **Assess**: These technologies are promising but need further assessment to understand their impact on your organization's context before large-scale adoption.

3. **Trial**: These technologies are worth pursuing and trying out on a project to understand their practical implications and benefits.

4. **Adopt**: These are mature technologies that Thoughtworks recommends for use when appropriate.

The Power of the TechRadar

The primary strength of Thoughtworks TechRadar lies in its ability to communicate complex and rapidly changing information in a simple, easily digestible format. Each edition captures a moment in time, highlighting the shifts in technology trends, thus creating a powerful tool for understanding the technological zeitgeist.

The TechRadar provides an excellent starting point for discussions and decision-making processes about technology adoption. By detailing what is on the horizon, organizations can plan for the future, adopt relevant technologies, and avoid pitfalls.

It is also important to note that TechRadar is the outcome of Thoughtworks' rich experience and collective wisdom. As a globally acclaimed software consultancy company, their recommendations carry significant weight in the industry.

How to Use the TechRadar

Thoughtworks recommends not to use TechRadar as a prescription but as a conversation starter. It's designed to inspire discussions about technology and help organizations make their own decisions based on their unique requirements and contexts. Consider it as a tool for triggering the right conversations, rather than a definitive guide.

References

Identifying Opportunities and Pain-points

(1) https://en.wikipedia.org/wiki/Arthur_Fry. Accessed 21 Feb, 2024.

(2) https://investor.irobot.com/news-releases/news-release-details/irobot-celebrates-two-decades-innovation-robotics. Accessed 25 Feb, 2024.

(3) Chorus, Paul & Bertolini, Luca. (2011). An application of the node-place model to explore the spatial development dynamics of station areas in Tokyo. The Journal of Transport and Land Use. 4. 45-58.

(4) https://mse.utoronto.ca/news/could-a-virtual-slime-mould-design-a-better-subway-system/. Accessed 21 Feb, 2024.

(5) Science Buddies Staff. "Smarter Than Your Average Slime: Maze-solving by an Amoeboid Organism." Science Buddies, 20 Nov, 2020, https://www.sciencebuddies.org/science-fair-projects/project-ideas/Zoo_p060/zoology/slime-mold-solve-maze. Accessed 21 Feb, 2024.

Market Research

(1) https://www.opalco.com/wp-content/uploads/2014/10/Reading-Sample-Size1.pdf. Accessed 30 Mar, 2024.

(2) Ferguson, Philip M. "Clever Hans". Encyclopedia Britannica, 7 Oct, 2019, https://www.britannica.com/topic/Clever-Hans. Accessed 23 Feb, 2024.

(3) Rathjens, Lisa. "Why every company should be doing a Follow Me Home". Intuit Developer, 21 Jan, 2021. https://blogs.intuit.com/2021/01/21/why-every-company-should-be-doing-a-follow-me-home/. Accessed 23 Feb, 2024.

(4) Annual Report 2023. https://www.microsoft.com/investor/reports/ar23/download-center/. Accessed 23 Mar, 2034.

Product Ecosystem Mapping

(1) https://www.dinker.in/ecosystem-mapping-canvas/. Accessed 27 Feb, 2024.

(2) https://en.wikipedia.org/wiki/SIPOC. Accessed 22 Feb, 2024.

Competition Analysis

(1) Puyt, Richard W.; Lie, Finn Birger; De Graaf, Frank Jan; Wilderom, Celeste P. M. (July 2020). "Origins of SWOT analysis". Academy of Management Proceedings. 2020 (1): 17416.

Market Segmentation

(1) https://www.investopedia.com/terms/m/marketsegmentation.asp. Accessed 8 Sep, 2023.

Regulations and Compliance

(1) https://www.indiacode.nic.in/handle/123456789/1999. Accessed 27 Feb, 2024

(2) https://gdpr-info.eu/. Accessed 27 Feb, 2024.

(3) https://oag.ca.gov/privacy/ccpa. Accessed 27 Feb, 2024.

(4) https://listings.pcisecuritystandards.org/documents/PCI_DSS-QRG-v3_2_1.pdf. Accessed 27 Feb, 2024.

(5) https://www.hhs.gov/hipaa/for-professionals/index.html. Accessed 27 Feb, 2024.

(6) https://www.ftc.gov/legal-library/browse/rules/childrens-online-privacy-protection-rule-coppa. Accessed 27 Feb, 2024.

Hypothesis, Experiment & MVP

(1) https://www.linkedin.com/pulse/what-i-learned-from-jeff-bezos-real-power-press-adrian-salamunovic/. Accessed 8 Apr, 2024.

(2) https://www.quora.com/What-is-Amazons-approach-to-product-development-and-product-management. Accessed 8 Apr, 2024.

(3) Ries, Eric. The Lean Startup: How Today's Entrepreneurs Use Continuous Innovation to Create Radically Successful Businesses, United States, Currency, 2017.

(4) https://barryoreilly.com/explore/blog/10-principles-to-transformation/. Accessed 8 Sep, 2023.

(4) https://www.thoughtworks.com/en-au/insights/blog/product-innovation/minimum-operational-product-model. Accessed 8 Sep, 2023.

(6) https://www.ddiinnxx.com/hour-glass-model-platform-mvp/. Accessed 8 Sep, 2023.

Business Modeling

(1) https://www.goodreads.com/quotes/559633-i-will-build-a-car-for-the-great-multitude-it. Accessed 26 Feb, 2024.

(2) https://www.paddle.com/blog/price-skimming. Accessed 26 Feb, 2024.

(3) Thomas, Manoj & Morwitz, Vicki. (2008). Heuristics in Numerical Cognition: Implications for Pricing. Handbook of Pricing Research in Marketing. 10.4337/9781848447448.00015.

(4) https://www.strategyzer.com/library/the-business-model-canvas. Accessed 23 Feb, 2024.

(5) https://www.strategyzer.com/library/the-value-proposition-canvas. Accessed 17 Sep, 2023.

Product Definition

(1) https://www.leancanvas.com/. Accessed 17 Sep, 2023.

(2) https://www.ddiinnxx.com/product-management-canvas/. Accessed 8 Sep, 2023.

(3) https://guykawasaki.com/books/selling-the-dream/. Accessed 6 Oct, 2023.

Product Design

(1) Xinya You & David Hands (2019) A Reflection upon Herbert Simon's Vision of Design in The Sciences of the Artificial, The Design Journal, 22:sup1, 1345-1356, DOI: 10.1080/14606925.2019.1594961 https://www.tandfonline.com/doi/pdf/10.1080/14606925.2019.1594961

(2) https://www.ideo.com/works/creating-the-first-usable-mouse. Accessed 28 Sep, 2023.

(3) https://sloanreview.mit.edu/article/finding-the-right-job-for-your-product/. Accessed 28 Sep, 2023.

(4) https://hbr.org/2016/09/know-your-customers-jobs-to-be-done. Accessed 28 Sep, 2023.

(5) https://medium.com/make-us-proud/jobs-to-be-done-framework-748c761797a8. Accessed 28 Sep, 2023.

(6) https://www.intercom.com/resources/books/intercom-jobs-to-be-done. Accessed 28 Sep, 2023.

(7) Traynor, Des. (2016). Intercom on Jobs-to-be-Done. 978-0-9861392-3-9.

(8) https://www.intercom.com/blog/the-dribbblisation-of-design/. Accessed 28 Sep, 2023.

(9) https://jtbd.info/replacing-the-user-story-with-the-job-story-af7cdee10c27. Accessed 28 Sep, 2023.

(10) https://xplane.com/the-empathy-map-a-human-centered-tool-for-understanding-how-your-audience-thinks/. Accessed 17 Sep, 2023.

(11) https://www.oxfordreference.com/display/10.1093/oi/authority.20110803095432783. Accessed 17 Sep, 2023.

Product Metrics

(1) https://www.amazon.in/-/in/dp/0679762884/. Accessed 8 Sep, 2023.

(2) https://rework.withgoogle.com/guides/set-goals-with-okrs/steps/learn-the-abridged-history-of-OKRs/. Accessed 8 Sep, 2023.

(3) https://arxiv.org/pdf/1702.01715.pdf. Accessed 8 Sep, 2023.

(4) https://github.com/joelparkerhenderson/objectives-and-key-results/blob/main/examples/okrs-by-google/index.md. Accessed 8 Sep, 2023.

(5) https://newrelic.com/blog/nerd-life/devops-name. Accessed 8 Sep, 2023.

(6) https://dora.dev/publications/pdf/state-of-devops-2019.pdf. Accessed 8 Sep, 2023.

(7) https://queue.acm.org/detail.cfm?id=3454124. Accessed 8 Sep, 2023.

(8) https://www.harness.io/blog/space-metrics-get-started. Accessed 8 Sep, 2023.

(9) https://www.eebo.org/. Accessed 8 Sep, 2023.

(10) https://www.thoughtworks.com/insights/blog/engineering-effectiveness/engineering-powering-business-growth. Accessed 8 Sep, 2023.

(11) Engineering Excellence to Business Outcomes Indie Press, 2024.

(12) Engineering Excellence to Business Outcomes Indie Press, 2024. 55-60.

(13) Product Management Untangled: The Art and Science of Product Management, Notion Press, 2024.

(14) Rarsons, Rebecca, et al. Building Evolutionary Architectures: Support Constant Change. O'Reilly, 2017.

(15) https://www.slideshare.net/dmc500hats/startup-metrics-4-pirates-may-2010. Accessed 17 Sep, 2023.

Product Roadmaps

(1) https://www.google.co.in/books/edition/DSDM_Dynamic_Systems_Development_Method/kp656t4p7soC. Accessed 9 Aug, 2023.

(2) https://www.romanpichler.com/tools/the-product-canvas/. Accessed 9 Apr, 2024.

Product Launch

(1) https://contently.com/2014/12/05/how-airbnb-is-using-content-marketing-to-stay-on-top/. Accessed 26 Feb, 2024.

(2) https://www.forbes.com/sites/sboyd/2019/05/13/song-of-style/?sh=1d950e7ac5de. Accessed 26 Feb, 2024.

(3) https://www.windriver.com/themes/Windriver/pdf/vxworks-product-overview.pdf. Accessed 1 Sep, 2023.

(4) https://www.prunderground.com/instant-messaging-app-roo-kids-helps-parents-envelop-their-preteens-in-a-safe-cocoon/0056898/. Accessed 4 Sep, 2023.

Digital Advertising

(1) https://iabtechlab.com/standards/iab-new-ad-portfolio-guidelines/. Accessed 24 Feb, 2024.

(2) https://en.m.wikipedia.org/wiki/File:Standard_web_banner_ad_sizes.svg. Accessed 26 Feb, 2024.

Product Market Fit

(1) https://www.gartner.com/smarterwithgartner/effortless-experience-explained. Accessed 28 Sep, 2023.

(2) Müller, Hendrik, and Aaron Sedley. "HaTS: large-scale in-product measurement of user attitudes & experiences with happiness tracking surveys.". https://research.google.com/pubs/archive/43221.pdf. Accessed 28 Sep, 2023.

Product Optimization

(1) https://hbr.org/2017/09/the-surprising-power-of-online-experiments. Accessed 26 Aug, 2023.

Governing User Data

(1) https://cloud.google.com/learn/what-is-data-governance. Accessed 11 Aug, 2023.

(2) DAMA. Earley, S., & Henderson, D., Sebastian-Coleman, L (Eds.). The DAMA Guide to the Data Management Body of Knowledge (DAMA-DM BOK). Bradley Beach, NJ: Technics Publications, LLC. 2017.

Product Evolution

(1) https://nira.com/slack-history/. Accessed 26 Feb, 2024.

Digital Transformation & Legacy Modernization

(1) https://www.thoughtworks.com/en-in/digital-fluency. Accessed 4 Apr, 2024.

Product Retirement

(1) https://web.archive.org/web/20051223173859/http://searchopensource.techtarget.com/originalContent/0,289142,sid39_gci1011227,00.html. Accessed 25 Feb, 2024.

5Rs of Application Migration

(1) https://www.gartner.com/en/documents/1485116. Accessed 10 Sep, 2023.

6Rs of Application Migration

(1) https://aws.amazon.com/blogs/enterprise-strategy/6-strategies-for-migrating-applications-to-the-cloud/. Accessed 10 Sep, 2023.

Active Listening

(1) https://wholebeinginstitute.com/wp-content/uploads/Rogers_Farson_Active-Listening.pdf. Accessed 5 Aug, 2023.

Digital Personal Data Protection Bill, 2023 (India)

(1) https://pib.gov.in/PressReleseDetail.aspx?PRID=1947264. Accessed 4 Sep, 2023.

Goodhart's Law

(1) Strathern, Marilyn (1997). "'Improving ratings': audit in the British University system". European Review. John Wiley & Sons. 5 (3): 305–321. https://archive.org/details/ImprovingRatingsAuditInTheBritishUniversitySystem

HEART Framework

(1) Rodden, Kerry & Hutchinson, Hilary & Fu, Xin. (2010). Measuring the User Experience on a Large Scale: User-Centered Metrics for Web Applications. 2395-2398. 10.1145/1753326.1753687.

Likert Scale

(1) Jamieson, Susan. "Likert scale". Encyclopedia Britannica, 23 Feb, 2024, https://www.britannica.com/topic/Likert-Scale. Accessed 30 Mar, 2024.

(2) Bhandari, Pritha and Nikolopoulou, Kassiani. Rev. "What Is a Likert Scale? | Guide & Examples". Scribbr.com. 3 Jul, 2020. https://www.scribbr.com/methodology/likert-scale/. Accessed 30 Mar, 2024.

Squiggle of Design Process

(1) The Process of Design Squiggle by Damien Newman. https://thedesignsquiggle.com/download. Accessed 4 Apr, 2024.

Strangler Pattern

(1) https://martinfowler.com/bliki/StranglerFigApplication.html. Accessed 10 Sep, 2023.